COMMUNICATION AND SOCIAL ORDER

An Aldine de Gruyter Series of Texts and Monographs

Series Editor

David R. Maines, *Pennsylvania State University*

Advisory Editors

Bruce Gronbeck • Peter K. Manning • William K. Rawlins

David L. Altheide, **An Ecology of Communication: Cultural Formats of Control**

David L. Altheide and Robert Snow, **Media Worlds in the Era of Postjournalism**

Joseph Bensman and Robert Lilienfeld, **Craft and Consciousness: Occupational Technique and the Development of World Images** (*Second Edition*)

Valerie Malhotra Bentz, **Becoming Mature: Childhood Ghosts and Spirits in Adult Life**

Herbert Blumer, **Industrialization as an Agent of Social Change: A Critical Analysis** (*Edited with an Introduction by* David R. Maines and Thomas J. Morrione)

Dennis Brissett and Charles Edgley (*editors*), **Life as Theater: A Dramaturgical Sourcebook** (*Second Edition*)

Richard Harvey Brown (*editor*), **Writing the Social Text: Poetics and Politics in Social Science Discourse**

Joo-Hyun Cho, **Family Violence in Korea**

Norman K. Denzin, **The Alcoholic Family**

Norman K. Denzin, **Hollywood Shot by Shot: Alcoholism in American Cinema**

Irwin Deutscher, Fred P. Pestello, and Frances G. Pestello, **Sentiments and Acts**

Bruce E. Gronbeck, **Sociocultural Dimensions of Rhetoric and Communication**

Emmanuel Lazega, **Communication and Interaction in Work Groups**

Michael Patrick Madden, A. Susan Owen, and J. T. Hansen (*editors*), **Parallels: The Soldiers' Knowledge and the Oral History of Contemporary Warfare**

David R. Maines (*editor*), **Social Organization and Social Process: Essays in Honor of Anselm Strauss**

David R. Maines, **Time and Social Process: Gender, Life Course, and Social Organization**

Peter K. Manning, **Organizational Communication**

Stjepan G. Městrović, **Durkheim and Postmodernist Culture**

R. S. Perinbanayagam, **Discursive Acts**

William Keith Rawlins, **Friendship Matters: Communication, Dialectics, and the Life Course**

Vladimir Shlapentokh and Dmitry Shlapentokh, **Ideological Trends in Soviet Movies**

Jim Thomas, **Communicating Prison Culture: The Deconstruction of Social Existence**

Jacqueline P. Wiseman, **The Other Half: Wives of Alcoholics**

HOLLYWOOD SHOT BY SHOT
Alcoholism in American Cinema

Norman K. Denzin

ALDINE DE GRUYTER

New York

ABOUT THE AUTHOR

Norman K. Denzin is Professor of Sociology, Communications and Humanities at the University of Illinois, Urbana. He is the author of several books, including *Sociological Methods* (1978), *Children and Their Caretakers* (1973), *The Research Act*, 3rd edition (1989), *Social Psychology*, 7th edition (1991). *The Alcoholic Self* (1987), and *The Recovering Alcoholic* (1987), were nominated for the C. Wright Mills Award in 1988. *The Alcoholic Self* won the Cooley Award from the Society for the Study of Symbolic Interaction in 1988.

Dr. Denzin is the author of over 80 articles in various academic journals. He has been editor of *Studies in Symbolic Interaction* since 1978. He is past-President of the Midwest Sociological Society and has served as Vice President of the Society for the Study of Symbolic Interaction (1976–1977) and secretary of the Social Psychology Section of the American Sociological Association (1978–1980).

ALDINE DE GRUYTER
A Division of Walter de Gruyter, Inc.
200 Saw Mill River Road
Hawthorne, New York 10532

The paper used in this publication meets the minimum requirements of American National Standard for Information Sciences—Permanence of Paper for Printed Library Materials, ANSI Z39.48-1984. ∞

Library of Congress Cataloging-in-Publication Data

Denzin, Norman K.
    Hollywood shot by shot : alcoholism in American cinema / Norman K. Denzin.
        p. cm. — (Communication and social order)
    Includes bibliographical references and index.
    ISBN 0-202-30344-6 (alk. paper). — ISBN 0-202-30345-4 (alk. paper)
    1. Alcoholism in motion pictures.   2. Family in motion pictures.
3. Motion pictures—United States—History.   4. Motion pictures—
Social aspects—United States.   5. United States—Popular culture.
I. Title.   II. Series.
    PN1995.9.A45D46   1991
    791.43′655—dc20   90-24077
                                                                           CIP

Manufactured in the United States of America

10   9   8   7   6   5   4   3   2   1

CONTENTS

ILLUSTRATIONS

ACKNOWLEDGMENTS

The debts that I have incurred in writing this book are many. I would like to thank the following individuals, institutions, and programs for their assistance, support, insights and patience: David R. Maines and Peter K. Manning for their steady presence; Richard Koffler for his enthusiasm, excitement, and willingness to travel to the Museum of Modern Art and help in selecting the stills from the films; Arlene Perazzini, an Aldine old friend, for her careful attention to the manuscript; Mary Corliss and Terry Greskin of MOMA for their assistance in finding the stills and making them available; Richard J. Leskosky and Edwin Jahiel for their help in locating other stills; The Unit for Criticism and Interpretive Theory at the University of Illinois for exposing me to many of the theories that circulate in the pages that follow; Gary Krug, Richard Louisell, Ed Davis, Susan Kray, Wayne Woodward, Jeff Ediger, Pete Ehlke, and Tom Anderson for their assistance in reading the films; Carl J. Couch for fighting with me; Patricia Clough for helping me clarify my purposes; The Research Board of my Graduate College for its financial support; The Institute of Communications Research for making so many outstanding research assistants available to me; The Department of Sociology for making available the initial equipment that permitted the collection of some of these films and their use in the classroom; my classes, which listened to these chapters and watched these films with me; James R. Kluegel and Robert Schoen, my Department Heads, for approving a three-semester leave of absence to work on this project; The Liberal Arts and Science Faculty in a Second Discipline Fellowship fund, which awarded a one-semester leave in Cinema Studies; Bryan Cook for helping me collect these films; Johanna, Rachel, and Nate who listened to me talk about this book for too many years; Katherine Ryan-Denzin, my wife, who patiently sat through many of these films with me, read my drafts, and urged me to finish; and most of all Robert Carringer for his instruction in Cinema Studies, guiding hand throughout, and careful reading of the entire manuscript. I would like to thank Susan Kray for her assistance in proofing.

PREFACE

> "From the earliest-peep-show slapstick of Carry Nation doused in beer through the champagne drenched courtship in *Casablanca* and the drunken cackles of *Arthur* drinking and drunkenness have played significant but often invisible roles in the American cinema."
>
> (Herd and Room, 1982, p. 24)
>
> "We should begin with . . . the way in which the cinema enters our lives."
>
> (Barthes, 1963/1985, p. 11)

This is a book about alcoholics and their places in Hollywood film between the years 1932[1] and 1989. My title, *Hollywood Shot By Shot: Alcoholism In American Cinema* is both playful and serious. For shot by shot, frame by frame, drink by drink, Hollywood has, for over a half century, presented drinking as a normal part of what ordinary and sophisticated people do when they engage in sociable behavior. But for every sober, normal, social drinker, there has been a deviant drinker, be that a sad or laughable "lush," a slightly "giddy, tipsy" imbiber, or an out-and-out drunk.[2] This drinker's decline would be charted, shot by shot, until he or she died, got sober, or was laughed off screen.

Hollywood's treatment of this drinker has vacillated over the years between melodramatic tragedies, melodramas with happy endings, and comedies. This drinker's deviance defined the normal drinker's normality. In the alcoholism film Hollywood would focus on the problem drinker and turn his or her problems with alcohol into occasions for moralistic, didactic discussions of alcoholism and its destructive effects on the person and society. Films such as those analyzed in this work serve as distorted mirrors or fractured reflections of the American concern for its "alcoholism" problem.

Hence while alcoholism films presumably speak to the alcoholic's presence in contemporary American life, they do so by creating a very specific type of discourse. They configure the alcoholic as a "diseased," sick, often insane, violent person who violates the normal standards of everyday life. Films validate these representations by having persons in

xiii

positions of power, usually doctors and psychiatrists, but sometimes members of Alcoholics Anonymous (A.A.) enunciate how and why the alcoholic is a sick person. These tellings are intended to shape what people come to believe and understand about alcoholism and recovery. They have significantly shaped public understandings of alcoholism as a disease and the alcoholic as a sick individual. In the process they alter lives, shape public attitudes, and make money for Hollywood (see Flemming and Manvell, 1985, pp. 138–39; Cook and Lewington, 1979).

In this sense alcoholism films reflect only one version or set of ideas about their subject matter, for example, the A.A. or the medical point of view. They are biased in other ways as well. As social problems films, their messages typically involve ways to treat the alcoholic's situation. They introduce models or pathways for recovery from alcoholism into the social order, including the love of a good woman (or man), A.A., will power, or a spiritual experience (see Room, 1985; Herd, 1986). All but a few (*Barfly*) are antialcoholism. At the same time many of them dress up reality in a way that gives it a sense of naturalness and history that does not correspond to the lived experiences of everyday individuals who are alcoholics. In so doing they may make recovery appear to be easier than it is in actuality, or they may exaggerate, for dramatic purposes, the negative effects of alcoholism on a family situation.

This Work

As a project in cultural and interpretive studies (Williams, 1977; Radway, 1985; Johnson, 1986/87; Carey, 1989; Hall, 1986; Denzin, 1989d, 1990d,e), this work builds on my earlier studies of the American alcoholic (Denzin, 1987a,b,c, 1989b,c,d,e, 1990a,b), which examined, in ethnographic fashion, the lived experiences of active and recovering alcoholics in American society. An unanswered question in these earlier works involved the representations of alcoholics in contemporary cultural texts, especially American film (see Denzin, 1987a, pp. 16–17; 1987b, p. 197; 1989e). While taking the position that lived experiences are shaped by larger meaning-making cultural structures, these earlier studies did not interrogate these broader social and cultural texts in terms of the meanings they convey about the alcoholic and alcoholism. The present work addresses this problem.

I attempt to uncover the recurring symbolic and interactional meanings Hollywood has brought to the alcoholic's experiences. I assume that a project in cultural-interpretive studies must examine how cultural texts, like alcoholism movies, create possibilities of experience that are then lived out in the lives of ordinary interacting individuals in the contemporary postmodern period (see Blumer, 1933 for an earlier example of such work). A fully developed interpretive, cultural sociology of alcoholism (or anything else) would show how the cultural maps the terrains of interactional experience. I intend to offer a methodology and model of interpretation that can be applied not just to film, but to other cultural representations as well (see Denzin, 1990a,e).

By asking how one representational structure, the Hollywood alcoholism film, reflects society back to itself, I intend to speak to the more general problems that are involved in interpreting the relationship between conduct and the cultural representations of that conduct (for reviews of media effects on audiences, including film and television, see Sklar, 1975; Altheide, 1985; Radway, 1984; Jeffre, 1986; Lindlof, 1987; Mukeŕji and Schudson, 1986; Blumer, 1933). My problematics, at one level, are these: "How do cultural representations shape lived experience?" And "How do lived experiences shape their own cultural representations?" That is, how do we join cultural studies with interpretive analyses of the worlds of lived experience?[3]

Alcoholism films typify social experience. They create social types, draw on common stocks of knowledge in the social structure, and distribute that knowledge through their texts, and thereby create structures of interpretation for the movie-goer (see Schutz and Luckmann, 1973). These films draw the viewing self into a structure of experience that can only be subjectively constituted. They are sites for emotional experience. Their meanings lie in the interactions that go on between the viewer and the text. These meanings are emotional, and rooted in the viewer's biography. Indeed the impact of an alcoholism film lies, in part, in its ability to evoke an emotional identification with the film's protagonist(s) and its text. A film works, that is, to the degree that it creates an emotional relationship with the viewer.

Consider the following statements given by viewers of some of the films analyzed in this book. A 40-year-old male is sobering up in a detox center. He has been watching Robert Duvall play Mac Sledge, an alcoholic country-western singer in the film *Tender Mercies.*

> That's me. I beat up the old lady, I used to play the music. Hell, if he can sober up I can too. I got help from these people in here. He didn't have this kinda help. (Denzin, 1989e, p. 53)

Another speaker, a recovering alcoholic, recounts an experience after the made-for-TV movie *My Name is Bill W.* was broadcast:

> I got five phone calls from friends who told me they wondered if they had drinking problems. They knew I was in the Program (A.A.). One fellow from work said that that guy Bill Wilson acted just like he did when he got

drunk and he wondered if maybe he had the same problem. I told to come
to a meeting and see if it felt right. He did and he's coming again
tomorrow. I guess those shows get through to people. (Field interview, 15
April 1989)

A female alcoholic in A.A. describes her relationship with Kirsten in
Days of Wine and Roses:

I can't watch her. The movie was on just the other night. I left the room
when that motel scene came on and she was drunk and Joe came to get
her. That was my mother. My dad sobered up in A.A. but mom never did.
I never forgave her for dying a drunk. When I started having my problems
with booze I remembered how Kirsten left her family and never came
back. I didn't want to lose everything like mom did. (Field interview, 22
March, 1988)

The viewer brings a history to the text of any given film. By constituting
concrete individuals as alcoholics, films create structures of experience
that permit viewer identification. In this process of emotional identification the viewer brings the film into his (or her) life. A problem with
drinking is then intensified. (Members attempt to fit the solutions to the
problem that the film offers to their life experiences.[4])

When a film enters any individual's life it may simply entertain, and
distract, or it may create new interpretations, or it may alter and reinforce, existing understandings (see Goffman, 1974, p. 562). In these
ways it contributes to the member's participation in the structures of
feeling (Williams, 1977, pp. 128–45), and systems of discourse and
meaning that circulate in everyday popular culture (de Certeau, 1984,
pp. 15–28). In certain of the examples above, these films served to move
"alcoholics" from one system of discourse (the everyday) into another
(A.A.).

Alcoholism films are, then, sites for phenomenological-interpretive
study (Merleau-Ponty, 1964, pp. 58–59). They mirror and create, while
they produce images, representations, and stories that simultaneously
derive from, yet challenge the social worlds they attempt to map and
interpret. By studying these films, and our reactions to them, we gain a
greater understanding of how a cultural industry shapes public and
private consciousness. In offering a historical and cultural reading of the
many alcoholics who have appeared center-stage in American film over
the last half-century, I will be treating films as cultural texts, assuming
that they contain meanings and understandings that work their way
through everyday life. An unraveling of these meanings should better
expose the alcoholic's shifting place within American society. In these
films Hollywood forces us to confront alcoholics and alcoholism. In

these pictures some of us find pictures of ourselves. Hence we study ourselves as we view and read about these films.

Ten chapters contain my analysis, which extends from 1932 to 1989. Chapter 1 presents an interpretive framework for reading the "alcoholism film." Chapter 2 examines comedy and the alcoholic. Chapters 3 to 5 take up the "alcoholism films" in the "classic modern period," 1932–1962, and discuss, in turn, the emergence of the alcoholic hero, heroine, and alcoholic family. Chapter 6 focuses on the years 1962–1980, when the "classic paradigm" waned and gave rise to alternative views of the alcoholic. In Chapters 7–9 I examine the contemporary period (1980–1989) and the appearance of the new "diseased" alcoholic family, heroine and hero. Chapter 10 comes full circle and offers a final, but provisional interpretive reading of the alcoholic's places in American film from 1932 to 1989. (The filmography lists all of the films analyzed, giving credit, cast, and production information.) [5]

Notes

1. The starting date of 1932 is not arbitrary. In that year *What Price Hollywood*, the earliest version of *A Star Is Born* cycle (1937, 1954, 1976), was released. With this film Hollywood offered its first major analysis of its own star system and the occupational causes of alcoholism. 1932 also signals the end of the temperance film and the beginning of the modern alcoholism film (see Chapter 1, Table 1).

2. Seven of ten American adults drink alcohol, at least occasionally (Denzin, 1987a, p. 16). Over 90 million Americans regularly use drugs, of one sort or another (Straus, 1982, pp. 140–41). There are over 12 million alcoholics in the United States; nearly one million belong to Alcoholics Anonymous. There are over 30 million adult children of alcoholics in the United States (Black, 1981), and over 4 million alcoholic families.

3. The present work primarily speaks to the cultural side of this problematic. The meanings and experiences that viewers, alcoholic and nonalcoholic, bring to, or have brought to the films I study are, with few exceptions, regrettably absent from my text. This is a major limitation that will be addressed in a subsequent work.

4. It is a common practice in alcoholism treatment centers to show films like the above to clients. One counselor comments, "We want them to see themselves. We want them to see alcoholics. . . . We want them to know they can get better" (Denzin, 1989e, p. 53). There is also another body of film, available on video cassette, that presents the "words of wisdom" of particular experts in the alcoholism field (i.e., Father Martin, Melody Beattie, etc.) and these videos are also shown in treatment centers.

5. Although I have not attempted an inventory of every film that deals with alcoholics and alcoholism, I would appreciate learning about films that I should not have overlooked.

PART I:

INTERPRETIVE STRUCTURES

The motion picture is one product which is never completely consumed for the very good reason that it is never entirely forgotten by those who see it. It leaves behind a residue, or deposit, or imagery and association, and this fact makes it a product unique to our tremendous list of export items.

(Mayer, 1947, p. 34, also quoted by Doane 1987, p. 37)

No cultural product works in isolation, but films are particularly interdependent in their meanings; partly because our reading of them relies on our knowledge and memory of generic conventions, and partly because the star system creates a complex pattern of links which also depends on our filmic memory and expectations. We remember the names of stars in mainstream films long after we have forgotten their fictional names, and meanings produced in one film will be carried over into another by the very presence of a particular actor or actress around which certain connotations have accrued.

(Williamson, 1987, p. 23 in a review of *The Morning After*)

1

Reading the Alcoholism Film

> "Hollywood is in a rut. They don't make
> movies, they remake them."
>
> (Billy Wilder, 1944/1970, p. 88)

This is an interpretive study of a particular category of Hollywood cinema—*the alcoholism film; that movie in which the inebrity, alcoholism, and excessive drinking of one or more of the major characters is presented as a problem which the character, his or her friends, family, and employers, and other members of society self-consciously struggle to resolve* (see Room, 1985, p. 1). Drinking, drunkenness, and alcoholism have played major and minor parts in American cinema since the early 1900s. Between the years 1908 and 1989 Hollywood made at least 600 alcoholism movies.[1] This is an analysis of a selected number of these films (see Table 1), chosen because they are considered to be the best representations of Hollywood's shifting treatment of the alcoholic from the early modern period (1932) to the present (1989).

This investigation differs from earlier studies (Room, 1983a,b, 1985; Herd and Room, 1982; Herd, 1986; Roffman and Purdy, 1981; Cook and Lewington, 1979; McCormack, 1986; Steudler, 1987), which have been guided by purely historical, structural, or semiotic concerns. With few exceptions, this earlier work has not turned back on Hollywood as a meaning-making institution and analyzed in detail the systems of discourse and interpretation that have shaped the creation, definition, and production of alcoholism and the alcoholic subject. Nor have these works followed the evolution and development of the alcoholic subject in American film.

Interpretive Framework

I seek to delineate a complex, multidimensional theme. There is no single agreed on thing called alcoholism, or alcoholic. The meanings of these terms are shaped by social, historical, medical, legal, literary, cultural, ideological, and interactional processes. Americans have always had an ambivalent attitude toward alcohol and the alcoholic, and this has been reflected in the films Hollywood has made about these topics. Americans want to drink and they do not want alcoholics. This has led to the alcoholism alibi. This alibi blames the problem drinker for his or her problems with alcohol. It argues that only a particular class of drinkers become alcoholic (e.g., those from alcoholic homes, or from drinking cultures that abuse alcohol). It offers an interpretive theory stressing moral (will power) and nonmoral (disease) explanations of the alcohol problem (see Beauchamp, 1980, p. 27).

Hollywood, as a meaning-producing, meaning-making social structure, like the social structure that it reflects, has, since its inception, been preoccupied with alcohol, drinking, the drunkard, the problem drinker, and the alcoholic. Since their inception the movies (and now television) have been the "most popular and influential medium of culture in the United States" (Sklar, 1975, p. 1). For nearly a century the alcoholism movies (along with other cultural texts) have defined the alcoholic and alcoholism for American society.

Hollywood's definitions of alcoholism and who an alcoholic is have shifted and changed, as broader, historical, cultural, medical, and ideological meanings changed. For example, films produced during the early silent era 1908–1920 (*The Cure, What Drink Did*) reflected the dry values of the temperance movement. They explained alcoholism as a failure of self will, stressed the evils of drink, punished the sinful drinker (heroes and heroines did not drink), and equated happiness with abstinence (Silverman, 1979, p. 295). Films during prohibition, contrary to the law, were wet, showing drinking in a favorable light (e.g., *Our Dancing Daughters*), although in 1931 two of the greatest figures of the silent film era, Charlie Chaplin and D. W. Griffith, produced antidrinking films in the older temperance tradition (*The Struggle* and *City Lights*).

More specifically, Hollywood's treatment of the alcoholic has been shaped by the following: the temperance movement and its legacies (1800–1919); prohibition (1920–1933), and repeal (1933); the development and elaboration of a film Production Code (1922–1934, 1968, 1972, Cook, 1981, pp. 214–15, 266–67, 426–27, 442–44) restricting what could be shown on screen; the emergence of Alcoholics Anonymous (A.A.) as a national and then international social movement in 1935, coupled with the soon to follow National Council on Problems of Alcoholism in 1937, and the National Council on Alcoholism in 1944; the production of literary works (e.g., *The Lost Weekend, I'll Cry Tomorrow*) and theatre plays (e.g., *The Country Girl, Come Back, Little Sheba*) telling stories about the alcoholic that could be adapted to the screen, and fitted to one or more film genres (e.g., comedy, family melodrama, western, women's film); a shift in national concern about alcoholism as a social problem that required treatment; the emergence of the social realist, social consciousness film within Hollywood (1944–1962, Ray, 1985), coupled with an understanding that successful box office films about alcoholics could be made. A brief discussion of each of these dimensions is required.

In 1922 the Motion Picture Producers and Distributors Association created the Hays Commission, a self-censoring body and a forerunner to the Production Code of 1934, which set in place a series of edicts defining the moral value system represented in Hollywood films. Individuals could not be shown breaking the law. Violence and sexual intimacy could not be presented. The code was quite explicit on drinking. The use of liquor in American life, when not required by the plot, or for purpose of characterization, will not be shown." The Production Code restricted the actual showing of drinking on screen. It was challenged in the late 1940s, and throughout the 1950s (Cook, 1981, pp. 443–44), with the rise of social consciousness, social problems films.

Alcoholics Anonymous was formed in 1935. In 1937 the National Council on Problems of Alcoholism was created. The purpose of this Council, which contained early A.A. leaders, was to "stimulate inquiry into the problems of alcoholism, rather than to inflame moral and emotional passions." In 1944 the National Committee for the Education on Alcoholism, an offshoot of the National Council, emerged and began advocating three simple principles: alcoholism is a disease; the alcoholic is treatable and deserves help; and alcoholism is a public health problem. The National Council immediately began to lobby Hollywood to produce films that embodied these three ideas (Johnson, 1973). In 1945 the first modern alcoholism film, *The Lost Weekend*, was released. It was based on Charles Jackson's novel of the same name, which was an immediate national best seller when it appeared in 1944. Billy Wilder, the director, consulted with A.A. when he made his film version of Jackson's novel. *The Lost Weekend* located alcoholism solidly in the upper-middle classes. Prior to this film (1932–1945) Hollywood had focused its attention primarily on the entertainment industry, and the production of alcoholism films focused on problems of alcoholic stars within the Hollywood System (e.g., *What Price Hollywood?* 1932, *A Star Is Born*, 1937). *The Lost Weekend* was quickly followed by at least 28 films (1945–1962) that took the alcoholic and his or her drinking as their sole, or primary focus (see Room, 1985).

Between the years 1932 and 1945 the above factors came together and produced the conditions necessary for the emergence of the modern, anti-temperance alcoholism movie. Table 1 presents an historical overview of Hollywood's treatment of the alcoholic in the twentieth century. It delineates the key temporal divisions of my study, and lists the films I will be examining.

The five temporal divisions of my study require brief discussion. Because the temperance and Prohibition phases have already been discussed (see also Herd and Room, 1982; Silverman, 1979), only the preclassic, the classic, the interregnum, and the present require discussion. *The preclassic period* references films like *A Star Is Born* (1937) where excessive drunkenness is represented, treatment is offered, but there is

Table 1. *Hollywood's Treatment of the Alcoholic in the Twentieth Century*

Temperance 1909–1920	Prohibition 1921–1934	Preclassic 1935–1945	Classic 1945–1962	Interregnum 1960–1980	Present 1980–
		Representative Films			
The Cure[a]	The Struggle[a]	A Star Is	Lost	Fat City	Tender Mercies
	What Price	Born	Weekend	The Graduate[a]	Shattered
	Hollywood		Come Fill	Woman Under	Spirits
			The Cup	the	Under the
			Harvey	Influence	Influence
			Smash-Up	W.C. Fields	Only When I
			I'll Cry	and Me	Laugh
			Tomorrow	Lady Sings	Arthur
			A Star Is	the Blues	Life of the
			Born	A Star Is	Party
			Come Back	Born	Cracker
			Little		Factory
			Sheba		Betty Ford
			Days of		Story
			Wine and		Morning After
			Roses		Arthur 2
			Country		Ironweed
			Girl		Verdict
			Key Largo		Paris, Texas
					Under the
					Volcano
					Hoosiers
					8 Million
					Ways to Die
					Barfly
					Clean and
					Sober
					My Name Is
					Bill W.
N 10+	151+	40+	28+	400+	36+ = 664

Sources: Krafsur (1976), Munden (1971), Room (1985), and Magill (1986).
[a]Not examined in this study.

no consideration of a disease concept of the condition, nor is the word alcoholism used. In the *classic (modern) period*, the condition is named, alcoholism is presented as a disease, a medical vocabulary describing it is presented, and Alcoholics Anonymous (A.A.) becomes an option for treatment. Males, females, and families get this condition in the classic period, which ends with *Days of Wine and Roses* (1962). *The interregnum* corresponds to the fall in popularity of social realist films, the rise in importance of television as the carrier of cultural messages about alcoholism, and the movie-of-the-week treatment of a variety of social problems, including teenage alcoholism (e.g., *Sarah T.—Portrait of a Teenage Alcoholic*, 1975) incest, sexual violence, and drug addiction (see Gabbard and Gabbard, 1987, pp. 112–14). It extends from 1960 to 1980 and falls into three phases. From 1960 to 1966 an alcoholic drinker is presented, but his or her problems are not connected to alcoholism (e.g., *The Graduate*). Between 1966 and 1976 excessive alcohol and drug use are presented as non problematic recreational activities (e.g., **M*A*S*H)**. The classic illness model reappears in 1976 (e.g., *A Star Is Born)* and continues to 1980. The *present*, or contemporary (postmodern) period continues the themes started at the end of the interregnum, only now alcoholism becomes a clear-cut family disease, which also involves drug abuse (e.g., cocaine addiction).

My investigation charts the transformations of alcoholism and the alcoholic's situation through these five time periods. I give greatest emphasis to the classic and present moments, with equal attention to films that focus, in turn, on the comic alcoholic, or funny drunk, the alcoholic hero, heroine, and the alcoholic family. I use the comic, or funny drunk (e.g., *Harvey, Arthur*) as my initial point of reference, because, as Silverman (1979, p. 288) observes, "Americans through the years have loved to laugh at the boozer." The alcoholism comedies are contrasted to the more serious, and usually melodramatic treatment of the alcoholic's situation. The "happy drunk" comedies keep this safe version of problem drinking alive in the viewing culture.

Film, Everyday Life, and the Cultural Study of Alcoholism

Sociologists have been slow to use film in their studies of alcoholism (see Herd, 1986; Steudler, 1987, p. 46; Room, 1985; McCormack, 1986), yet how a society cinematically represents itself to its members warrants serious sociological study. In the main sociologists have confined their studies of the alcoholic to those methods that generate sociologically defined information on the incidence and correlates of alcoholism, including the following: (1) numbers, tables, graphs, charts and figures, and complex accounts of social trends, and social indicators; (2) data archives and coded categories of the glossed drinking practices of native and primitive peoples; (3) thick descriptions of everyday alcoholic life including ethnographies and life histories; (4) subject quotes from interviews; and (5) attitude reports from surveys (see Cahalan, 1987; Gomberg, 1982; but for exceptions Gusfield, 1963; Herd, 1986; Levine, 1978; room, 1983a).

The Patriarchal Bias

This sociological work has often reflected a patriarchal, male, interpretive bias (Herd, 1986; McCormack, 1986; Steudler 1987; Lerner, 1986; Mitchell, 1984; Richardson, 1981). It has relegated women's perspectives to the margins of the social. In the process it has sustained the traditional belief that "objective" accounts of the social can be given (Barthes, 1957/1972, p. 12), but this belief has equated masculinity with objectivity, and femininity with subjectivity. It has served to obscure the patriarchal bias at the core of the scientific study of alcoholism (Gomberg, 1982, p. 344). Like myth, these documents have reproduced the gender stratification systems of postmodern society. Their depictions and stories of the social, "natural" relations between (alcoholic) men and women have typically been told, seen, and written about through the masculine gaze and voice (see Clough, 1988a,b). My intentions are to reverse these patterns.

Enter Film

Steudler (1987), following Barthes' (1957/1972, pp. 11, 26–28, 56–57, 1981) more general studies of cinema, have challenged those sociologists of everyday life who study alcoholism and deviance to develop a sociology of film. Here I accept this challenge, arguing that the interpretive study of alcoholism must deal with the cultural, filmic representations of intimate, emotional, alcoholic relationships as these social forms are contained within the "alcoholism" film.

Alcoholism films are simultaneously visual records of, and a part of, everyday life (Steudler, 1987, p. 46).[2] These records and representations structure lived experience: they set fashion (going to A.A.), keep tradition and new, emerging cultural understandings alive (e.g., alcoholism is a disease), record tabooed acts (incest, the violent insanity of alcoholics, etc.), and ceremonialize the sacred (recovery). These films are interactional productions. They do not simply assert their truths, "rather we interact with them in order to arrive at conclusions" (Becker, 1986, p. 279). Alcoholism films express particular versions of the social imagination, including the understandings in the 1940s and 1950s that alcoholism was a treatable disease. Such films represent what is "immediately apparent in a given society" (Steudler, 1987, p. 46; e.g., alcoholism is a social problem,). They also allow "the needs, desires and dreams of a period to be projected" into the realms of the social (Steudler, 1987, p. 46; e.g., sobriety for middle-class alcoholics). Films, in this regard, are the perfect site for the Durkheimian analysis of society, culture, drinking, and alcoholism. They encapsulate "the sensitivity, aspirations and dreams of societies in particular historical and sociological situations" (Morin, 1984, p. 402). They have become the repositories of the collective consciousness and subconsciousness of postmodern culture.

Ideology and Film

A basic thesis, already suggested, structures my argument. All representations of cultural experience are ideological and hence must be read for the multiple meanings that are contained within their texts (see Clough, 1988a; Balsamo, 1988, 1989).[3] Alcoholism films do not faithfully reproduce reality. A film "screens" and frames reality to fit particular ideological, or distorted images of "real" social relationships (Steudler, 1987, p. 46). Any film will be a site for the play of multiple ideological versions of reality. Sociological analysis must uncover the ideological distortions that are embedded within any film's text (see below). How a culture-making institution functions can then be analyzed. As a film attempts to build its particular version of reality, in which one set of events is seen as naturally causing another, contradictions and inconsistencies will appear. (For example, in *Days of Wine and Roses*, why does Kirsten, who values family, walk away from her husband and child?) A subversive reading of ideology attempts to uncover these inconsistencies, which lie within the "mythical" structure the film creates (see Barthes, 1957/1972, p. 11).

In representing multiple, contradictory versions of reality, an alcoholism film manages to reflect the very reality it distorts. That is, the contradictions and distortions that are represented are themselves drawn from the contradictions that exist in everyday life. Hence in the 1960s there were women alcoholics like Kirsten who refused to join A.A., and in the 1950s there were housewives like Lola, in *Come Back, Little Sheba*, who were regarded as failures by their neighbors and husbands. There were also women who recovered in A.A., men who walked away from their families and rejected A.A., and housewives who were not like Lola or Kirsten. The distortions that film produces open up corners of everyday life "we had ended up forgetting—that had become, as it were, unfamiliar" (Steudler, 1987, p. 47). In opening up these corners of reality, and by exaggerating particular sets of experiences over others (i.e., the negative as opposed to the positive sides of recovery), films perpetuate stereotypes, fears and anxieties that exist in the culture at large.

However, the visions of real life that the film projects are as valid, or as truthful as any other (Steudler, 1987, p. 47). Truth is always partial, incomplete, and based on a group's or individual's perspective (Becker, 1986, pp. 280–81). The statements that a film makes bear the stamp of the cultural, social, and economic contexts that surround the filmmaker's work. The film is also the product of teamwork, and of political economies of production, distribution, and consumption. Any film, in turn, builds on patterns of meaning and action that exist in the society at large. In so doing it modifies those patterns of meaning, and creates new experiences for viewers. In this way film creates the realities it reproduces on the screen.

A Note on Method

The readings that I will offer involve using narrative as interpretive materials. Although sociologists are accustomed to narrative analyses of interview data (Maines, 1989, 1990) they have less frequently regarded the narrative materials of film or literature as legitimate subject matter. (Indeed, with the exceptions noted above, they have ignored the alcoholism film entirely.) The method that I employ elaborates Hall (1980) who has distinguished three ways to read a cultural text: (1) the hegemonic reading, which takes the reading preferred by the dominant cultural ideology; (2) the negotiated reading, "which attempts to maintain the preferred reading in tandem with the understandings drawn from a class [or gender] position" (Gledhill, 1978; 1978/1985, p. 827); and (3) the oppositional reading, which "transforms the readings offered by the dominant ideology into . . . an oppositional discourse" (Gledhill, 1978/1985, p. 827).

In the present context I will use the term "realist reading" to subsume Hall's hegemonic and negotiated readings, and the term "subversive reading" to reference his oppositional reading. I will argue, after Hall, that ideological meanings are encoded, or built into texts. [(The term decoding refers to how these meanings are read from the text (see Grossberg, 1986, p. 67).] This way of "reading," or interpreting a cultural text differs significantly from what within American sociology has recently been called "cultural sociology" (see Wuthnow, 1987, p. 6; Denzin, 1990d,e).

Strategically, my method involves the following steps. First, obtaining a record of a cultural text (a film, a novel, a scientific article) and subjecting that document to multiple readings (see Denzin, 1987d,

1989e,f for examples). Second, delineating the narrative (story) themes that are present in the text, in particular noting the uses and meanings brought to alcohol, drinking, and the alcoholic. Third, collecting the realist, hegemonic, preferred interpretations of the text (see Denzin, 1989f for an example). In this study these interpretations were based on a reading of the reviews received by each film, as catalogued in Salem (1971, 1982), *Filmfacts,* Magill (1986), *Film Review Annual, The New York Times Film Review Index,* and *Newspaper Abstracts.* The reviews included those printed in the popular press (e.g., *The New York Times, Saturday Review of Literature, Atlantic Monthly, New Republic),* as well as those appearing in more formal, contemporary scholarly film review journals, e.g., *Cineaste, Film Review Quarterly.* Recent sociological (and other) readings of key films from each historical period (e.g., Herd, 1986; Room, 1985; Roffman and Purdy, 1981; Cook and Lewington, 1979) are also analyzed. Fourth, interpreting those readings in terms of their dominant ideological meanings (see Chapter 10 for an intensive, comparative analysis of these reviews). Fifth, developing a subversive, feminist reading of the text, realizing that there will always be multiple subversive and realist interpretations. Sixth, contrasting the subversive, oppositional readings to the "realist" interpretations. Seventh, if possible, securing viewer's and reader's interpretations of the document and connecting these meanings to the experiences of viewers and readers (see Davis, 1989). This method will necessarily work from one case (cultural document) to another as the sociologist builds up interpretations of how particular bodies of cultural work create recurring ideological meanings for viewers and readers.

Selecting the Films

As indicated I am analyzing what I regard as the best exemplars of the alcoholism film. All of these films share one or more of the following characteristics. They (1) are regarded as classics (e.g., *Lost Weekend*), (2) are included on the lists of other researchers, reviewers, and critics (e.g., Room, 1985; Roffman and Purdy, 1981), (3) record the entrance, and then the shifting presence and meaning of A.A. (*Come Fill The Cup,* 1951, *Come Back, Little Sheba,* 1952, *I'll Cry Tomorrow,* 1955, *Days of Wine and Roses,* 1962, *8 Million Ways to Die,* 1986, *My Name Is Bill W.,* 1989), and (4) reflect Hollywood's changing treatment of the alcoholic hero, heroine, and alcoholic family. I also gave primary attention to films that had been nominated for awards (see Filmography), or were current top video rentals, or big moneymakers when they were released, using these criteria as measures of the film's popularity and importance. Each decade since the 1930s has seen the production of at least one major annual

top moneymaking Hollywood alcoholism film. The following films are
the all-time film rental leaders for their decade: *A Star Is Born* for the
1930s, *Lost Weekend* for the 1940s, *Harvey, A Star Is Born, I'll Cry Tomorrow,* and *Country Girl* for the 1950s, *Cat Ballou* and *Who's Afraid of Virginia
Woolf?* for the 1960s, *A Star Is Born* and *The Rose* for the 1970s, *Only When
I Laugh, Arthur, Tender Mercies, The Morning After, Hoosiers, The Verdict,*
and *Sea of Love* for the 1980s (see *Variety,* 1990).[4]

Defining the Genre

A provisional, working definition of the alcoholism film may be given.
(This definition will be reexamined in Chapter 10 once the 36 films in
this study have been fully discussed.) These films appear to be marked
by the following four features. First, a central character, as argued
above, will be characterized as having a problem with alcohol. Second,
the narrative will show the main character drinking, not drinking, trying
to stop drinking, sometimes drinking again, being tested by a crisis
situation, not drinking, and finally establishing a sober, or drunken life-
style. Third, the end of the alcoholism film will position the alcoholic
either back in society, with a family and a job, or outside society, leaving
family and work behind. (This trajectory will vary by the gender of the
alcoholic.) Fourth, sobriety will be accomplished in one of several ways:
(1) the loving care of a woman or man, (2) a spiritual experience, (3) the
intervention of treatment centers and A.A., or (4) will-power (see Herd,
1986). Finally, the alcoholic may be presented in "heroic" dimensions
(see Chapter 3).

The Alcoholism Film as a Social Problems Film

These characteristics define the alcoholism as a genre, or special type
of film.[5] They are ideal-typical formulations, seldom fully present in any
film, although they will reach their fullest expression in the late 1980s
with *Clean and Sober* (1988) and *My Name Is Bill W.* (1989). This genre is a
variant of the social problems film and thus stands in line with films
about mental illness and madness, the juvenile delinquent and the ex-
con, poverty and unemployment, divorce and remarriage, homosexuality, racism, drug addiction, incest, family violence, rape, and pornog-
raphy (see Roffman and Purdy, 1981; Flemming and Manvell, 1985). In
the "Golden era" of Hollywood (1930s to mid 1950s) the social problems
film emerged as a specific genre, or type of film.[6] A product of the
Depression, they receded in wartime; and then accelerated in production near the end of the war.

Like other films made in this era, they were shaped, as noted above,
by the Hollywood formula and the Production Codes of the time (Roff-

man and Purdy, 1981, pp. 1–2). This formula (Roffman and Purdy, 1980, pp. 1–7) conformed to several conventions embodied in the Production Code (Roffman and Purdy, 1980, p. 6; Sklar, 1975, pp. 173–74, 294–96) including producing films that both entertained and educated movie-goers on the central democratic values of American society, i.e., the myths of success, the values of family, home, romantic love, and hard work. These movies, as noted, avoided profanity, and the showing of intimate sexuality, or presenting violence in a positive light. This led to films that borrowed the format of the Victorian melodrama. The narratives are (and were) organized around the poles of good and evil. Heroes and heroines, the good people, are placed in conflict with villians and evil, sexually attractive women and men who tempt them. Heroes and heroines overcome evil and temptation and are rewarded by the love of a "good" woman or man and a place in a respectable, middle-class family. These films, with their happy endings, oedipalized family relations and "situated subjectivity in the system of marriage and kinship . . . and made a subject's succession to power and recognition coterminous with sexually proper self-development" (Clough, 1989, p. 4).

In these films a societal condition, a personal problem, a character flaw, a deviant or violent act, or a stigma is turned into a dramatic device that permits the filmmaker to make moral, political, and ideological comments about the individual, his or her problem, and the larger society that contains, creates, and reacts to that problem. Their distinguishing feature is didacticism; they attempt to teach and inform an audience about a problem and its solution (Roffman and Purdy, 1981, p. viii). They are, with few exceptions *(Barfly)*, antialcoholism.

The alcoholism variant of these films often embodied wish fulfillment, romance, and true love, as they worked out the good–evil, sobriety–alcoholism conflict. In the end of such films evil is destroyed and good is rewarded. These films kept (and keep) fantasies alive. The formula that organized them could be fitted to any social problem. It is this framework that the alcoholism film builds on, typically pitting the alcoholic, not against an institution, but against himself or herself and the disease of alcoholism.

Emotionality in the Alcoholism Film

Alcoholism films are sites for emotional struggle. Four structures of experience shape the intimate relations that create and constrain emotionality in the alcoholism film (Denzin, 1990b). These are the alcoholic drinking act and the euphoric and depressive effects of alcohol on conduct; the absence of alcohol and the negative effects of sobriety on intimacy in the relationship; alcohol drinking desire and sexuality, which is often violent and voyeuristic, and negative emotions connected to the past.

These four structures erode and distort the underlying, positive, intimate foundations of the relationships that are portrayed in a film. They often turn it into a scarred, hollow, empty nightmare of fear and violence. Love may turn to hatred or indifference. Alcohol masks self-feelings, as it creates illusions of intimacy. It feeds destructive lines of interaction that build on past transgressions and violations of trust. Struggles for power and control centered on drinking emerge. Drinking is often a catalyst for the sexual act. Relapses from sobriety may be presented as being caused by the intimate emotions that are associated with sexuality. I will elaborate these emotional features of the alcoholism film in the chapters that follow.

Gender, Alcoholism, and Oedipal Themes

The figure of woman is nearly always present in these texts, typically as the long-suffering wife or girlfriend of the alcoholic. Her presence is doubly significant. Alcoholism is an emotional "dis-ease" of self (Denzin, 1987a, Chapter 6), which affects the alcoholic's emotional, sexual, and intimate relations with others. In the alcoholism film a "technology of gender" (de Lauretis, 1987) operates to reproduce the twisted gendered relations that lie at the heart of the alcoholic relationship. The woman's recurring place in these texts suggests that she is the barometer of alcoholism's effects on family, love, intimacy, self-respect, and work. She defines the alcoholic's place in society. Without her there would be no alcoholism to worry about.

The female, though, is tainted through the use of the "alcoholism alibi." Only a special type of woman would be drawn to such a man. Thus by accounting for alcoholism in society through the use of an argument that says only certain drinkers become alcoholic, Hollywood perpetuates the myth that only certain types of woman are drawn to such types of drinkers. Another alibi is needed, and of course this arises through the suggestion that the alcoholic's other is also a sick person. This interpretation repeatedly occurs from 1932 to 1989, but reaches its fullest expression in the 1980s (see Chapter 7).

To ignore the woman's place in these films would be to ignore how alcoholism films, like all of Hollywood's productions, unltimately tell one story, the story of the gendered human relationship and its universal problems (see Lyman, 1987, 1990 for suggestions in this direction). The alcoholism film is but one variant on this universal story. In it males (and females) with infirmities (alcoholism) live out the universal fear of forming and being contained within a bonded, loving, intimate relationship.

This universal story may be read, as Barthes (1975, p. 10) argued of all narratives, as a "staging of the" Oedipal scenario, involving absent, missing, hidden, and flawed mother and father figures and the consequences of these absences for the normal, moral, and sexual development of males and females who become alcoholic, or mentally ill. The alcoholism film treats this Oedipal myth in very specific ways, often placing the blame for a character's alcoholic condition, in part, on their inability to resolve Oedipal conflicts and develop healthy, normal sexual, emotional relationships with a suitable, morally strong mother or father substitute figure. These films require deconstruction. Often "Oedipal with a vengence" (de Lauretis, 1984, p. 157; also Penley, 1989), they reproduce patriarchal images of the female alcoholic and her relationships with males.

In Conclusion: Anhedonia and the Myth of Wine and Roses

In this sense, alcoholism films are about more than alcoholics and their disease. They are stories about lonely men and women who have not found their place in the social order. These individuals have turned to alcohol as a way of dealing with this situation. Victims of "anhedonia," or an inability to experience pleasure and happiness (Lyman, 1990, p. 3) they use alcohol and drinking as methods of producing a desired inner sense of self. They buy into the culture myth that "wine and roses" bring personal and sexual pleasures with a person of the opposite sex (Barthes 1957/1972, pp. 58–61). They drink in order to be sexually fulfilled, and happily bonded to a member of the opposite sex. In their use of alcohol, the alcoholic often becomes violent and self-destructive. This violence points to the pervasive, irrational, out-of-control side of social life. The alcoholic's violence, loneliness, and despair is everyone's loneliness, and hence these films describe universal features of the human condition. In so doing they speak to a place of irrationality, violence, and the violent emotions in human relationships.

All of the pieces are now in place. Having presented my interpretive framework, defined my subject matter, located it historically, positioned the study of film within a broader cultural studies project, and identified the major themes I will be examining in each film, it remains to turn to the films themselves. In the chapters to follow I will trace the methodological steps outlined above: delineating each film's narrative, isolating the meanings brought to alcohol, drinking, and the alcoholic, examining the film reviews of the text, interpreting these readings in terms of their dominant, ideological meanings, and, where appropriate, developing subversive, feminist interpretations of the film and contrasting these readings with the preferred readings. With the exception of the next chapter, I will move systematically through the preclassic, classic-modern, interregnum, and present historical phases.

Now the films. I start with the "happy alcoholic," positioning the alcoholism comedy in front of the more serious melodramas where the alcoholic's condition leads to death or recovery. In so doing I go some-what out of historical sequence, but justify this departure because the "comic drunk," as Room (1983b, p. 8) observes, is "perhaps the most enduring tradition in the presentation of alcohol on the screen."

Notes

1.   The American Film Institute Catalogue codes, under the categories of alcoholism and/or drunkenness, 151 and 384 films for the 1921–1930 and 1961–1970 years, respectively (see Krafsur, 1976; Munden, 1971). Room (1985, p. 1) lists 28 such films between the years 1945 and 1962. Since 1980 over 40 of these films have been produced.
2.   For example, in such early films as *Come Back, Little Sheba*, Hollywood took Americans inside A.A. meetings. Prior to these filmic versions of the A.A. meetings Americans had to rely either on printed accounts of what A.A. was like (e.g., Alexander, 1941), experience the meetings themselves, or be told about them by those who had.
3.   I am using ideology in the sense intended by Althusser (1971, p. 165). Ideology is "not the system of real relations which govern the existence of individuals, but the imaginary relation of these individuals to the relations in which they 'live' and which govern their existence." For Althusser "all ideology has the function (which defines it) of 'constituting' concrete individuals as subjects" (1971; p. 171). The films that I am reading constitute concrete individu-als (character) as alcoholic subjects who viewers (including alcoholics) can iden-tify with and thus create a sense of subjectivity for themselves. How a text (e.g., a film), and the cultural meanings of the text, ideologically constitute concrete individuals as subjects is one of the basic problems this work addresses.
4.   An additional consideration concerned current availability of the film to the viewing public. All of the films analyzed are readily accessible to any viewer on either video tape for rental, or have appeared on Cable or Public Television within the 1986–1990 time period (see Maltin, 1989; HBO, 1990).
5.   On genre theory see Altman (1987) and Grant (1986). These structural characteristics have similarities to the kind of formal analyses offered by Propp (1958), Todorov (1975), and Altman (1987). I am using them as "sensitizing indicators" (Blumer, 1969, p. 148) that point to certain recurring features of this type of film. As such the "alcoholism" film is my construction. It is a grouping of films. It functions as a guide to the kinds of movies I want to analyze. There are risks with such constructions. They can (1) lead to static analysis that focuses only on structural features of a film's text, producing glosses on the unique features of any given film; (2) canonize the form, where the origins are traced back to a pivotal, or original film, i.e., *Lost Weekend* (see Roffman and Purdy, 1981, p. 257; Herd and Room, 1982, pp. 32–34). Such a move fails to recognize that the original version of the genre is itself a construction and a version of earlier texts, i.e., *The Struggle* or *What Price Hollywood?* In the process, films that depart from the cannon may be ignored, i.e., *Barfly*, as will those that clearly

have an alcoholic in their text *(Key Largo)*, or a person who is suspected of being alcoholic *(Notorious, 1946)*, but do not deal with alcoholism as a main theme; (3) distract the reader from a consideration of how a film as an instance of a genre or type is itself a cultural commodity that is marketed to an audience at a particular moment in time. Alcoholism films, that is, have ready-made audiences, including recovering alcoholics, and adult children of alcoholics.

6. This is Roffman and Purdy's temporal designation. Actually the period 1946–1966 saw a proliferation of films of this type. Made under the banner of "social realism," they began to disappear in the 1960s, to be taken up by television in the 1960s, 1970s, and 1980s and then again by Hollywood in the 1980s, but never with the frequency of this early classic period that followed World War II (see Ray, 1985, p. 273; and the discussion in Chapter 6).

2 The Happy Alcoholic: Elwood and Arthur

> "The screen . . . drunk is a staple figure of fun . . . the drunks in the comedies are not *real* drunks. Members of the same audience when confronted with the genuine article would cross the street . . . summon the police. . . . The last thing they would do is laugh."
>
> (Silverman, 1979, p. 289)
>
> "Comedy drinking is unequivocally good."
>
> (Gilmore, 1987, pp. 12–13)

Consider the following scenes and their dialogue. They are taken from *Harvey* (1950) and *Arthur* (1981). Elwood P. Dowd explains what he and his friend Harvey, an imaginary six foot one and one-half-inch rabbit, do together in the bars. "Harvey and I sit in the bars and we have a drink or two, play the jukebox. Soon the faces of other people turn toward mine and smile. Harvey and I warm ourselves in these golden moments. We have entered as friends and soon we have friends." Veta Louise, Elwood P. Dowd's matronly sister laments, "Not a day goes by without him stepping into a cheap tavern, bringing home a lot of riff raff, people you never heard of before. Definitely Elwood drinks. I want him committed. I can't stand another day with this Harvey."

Arthur Bach, obviously intoxicated, cackling and laughing at his own jokes, shouts out of the window of his Rolls to two stone-faced Times Square prostitutes: "Would the more attractive of you please step for-

19

ward?" One of the women, surly in red hot pants, accompanies him to the Oak Room where they cause a mild scandal. Arthur's loud voice reverberates across the tables, "My God, you're a hooker? I thought I was making out so well!"

Two sad men. Victims of anhedonia. Whimsical Elwood, and loud, brash Arthur take their loneliness into bars, drinking with imaginary friends, or paid hookers. Each man's situation evokes laughter. Arthur mocks and taunts the stuffy high class atmosphere of the Oak Room. Elwood's plight elicits humorous identification. His story, like Arthur's, is told within the framework of a madcap comedy, where serious things happen in funny ways. Lurking in the background of each of their stories is the figure of a woman; angry sister Veta Louise for Elwood; dour Susan, doting grandmother Bach, and vibrant Linda Marolla for Arthur. Their narratives unfold in an Oedipal fashion, with each man finally finding his place with a proper mother and father figure. These screwball comedies, with their romantic plots (Dr. Sanderson and Nurse Kelly, Myrtle Mae and Wilson in *Harvey*, Arthur and Hobson, Arthur and Linda and Susan in *Arthur*), use romantic love as a way of erasing the effects of class differences in the larger society. In these films adults as children enact the parts of lovers (see Schatz, 1981, p. 155). Arthur and Elwood are children who never grow up.

Alcohol and Comedy

In their respective stories, Elwood and Arthur take their places in the culture of the "comic drunk" and the comic Oedipal narratives that have a long and distinguished history within the American entertainment industry, from "the aristocratic screwball comedies of the 30s and 40s, to the Hollywood archetype of the inebriated playboy, to the booze-befuddled movie clowns" (Woodward, 1988, p. 1) of an earlier age (Schatz, 1981, p. 155). This tradition extends from Chaplin's classic (*City Lights*, 1931), which tells the story of Charlie's love for a blind girl and his on and off friendship with a drunken millionaire, through Laurel and Hardy's slapstick comedies, to W. C. Field's drunken escapades as a bank dick, Red Skelton's Freddie the Freeloader and Sheriff Redeye, Jackie Gleason's Bachelor and Joe the Bartender, to Dudley Moore's Arthur in the 1980s (see Room, 1983b, p. 3). Indeed, "the tradition of comic drunkenness continues to the present in popular culture . . . despite the best efforts of the alcoholism movement to convey the message that drunkenness is not funny" (Room, 1983b, p. 8; see also Finn, 1980). It is necessary to examine how these comedies work.

Comedic Structures

Four generic themes structure the relationship between alcohol, drinking, and comedy. Alcohol is solace for the lonely, sorrowful person. Alcohol has the capacity of releasing aggression in the form of satiric comedy and tendentious jokes. It also joins the person with truth and with others. It is a benevolent, socializing spirit. These themes are woven through the "laughable" drunk motif, which is then typically, but not always connected to some version of the Oedipal myth fashioned around a tale of romantic love.

For Elwood P. Dowd, the hero of *Harvey* (1950), played by James Stewart, and for Arthur, the hero of *Arthur* (1981) and *Arthur 2 on the Rocks* (1988), played by Dudley Moore, alcohol serves as an unequivocally good, or benevolent spirit. It does not bring destruction or death to either drinker, although both conditions are metaphorically broached by each film's narrative. These three comedies, separated by a space of nearly 40 years, keep alive the cultural myth that alcohol, drinking, and comedy are somehow intimately connected in a positive way (see Gilmore, 1987, p. 144). They enact the belief that alcohol can produce positive effects for certain drinkers, even when the drinker is defined as an alcoholic, or a chronic drunk.

Harvey and the two *Arthurs* suggest that people are "more human, not less when liberated by drink" (Damrosch, 1982, p. 648), and that in drink, the drinker escapes feelings of loneliness (Gilmore, 1987, p. 145), while achieving a communion and sense of oneness with fellow human beings (Bateson, 1972, p. 329). Each film underscores the belief that drinking allows the individual to "see himself as . . . a *part of the* group" (Bateson, 1972b, p. 329, italics in original). Drinking is presented, in part, "as a quest for human solidarity" (Gilmore, 1987, p. 145). They confirm the argument that alcohol creates cheerful moods.

But even in comedy, alcohol's effects can turn negative. In both *Arthur* films, less so in *Harvey*, drinking, when carried to excess, is shown to be a form of aggression (Gilmore, 1987, p. 145). In building on this theme, the *Arthur* movies elaborate Freud's (1963, pp. 105, 127) contention that the motive for drinking may be satiric comedy, which can be understood to be an act of aggression. Gilmore, following Freud, notes that alcohol apparently facilitates "tendentious jokes . . . [which] are especially favoured as expressions of aggressiveness or criticism . . . against persons in exalted positions . . . the joke . . . represents a rebellion against that authority" (Freud, 1963, p. 127; Gilmore, 1987, p. 146). As I shall show, Arthur's satiric humor, supposedly dependent on his alcohol intake, can be read as an aggressive attack against the authority figures in his life.

Elwood and Arthur, as noted, are sorrowful, lonely men. Elwood longs for friendly companionship and finds it in bars and with his imaginary friend Harvey. Arthur pines for a true love; for a woman who will bring him happiness and release from his dreary, doting, repressive upper-class family. The viewer is led to identify with these lonely men and to cheer for them when the mean, ill-intended people in their worlds are brought to their knees. These people, Elwood's sister and Arthur's father, as if scripted by Aristotle's theory of comedy, behave like villains, while Elwood and Arthur, like characters in a Greek tragedy, act more nobly than those persons who surround and attempt to control them.

Each character is placed in incongruous, problematic situations. The humor and comedy in the films arise, in part, from the resolution of these situations. Elwood is defined as crazy and then as normal. Arthur is called an irresponsible drunk who must marry a highly responsible, controlling woman he dislikes. If he marries this woman he will inherit 750 million dollars. He rejects her and wins acceptance and his inheritance when he marries Linda, the object of his true love. By creating situations in which contradictory definitions of the situation cannot be sustained (Elwood cannot be both crazy and sane) the films establish the conditions for humor to work.

The films are also comedies of manners. Each satirizes the life-style and fashions of the upper, middle, and lower classes. At the same time as comedies, *Harvey* and the two *Arthurs* present themselves as playful departures from the mundane structures of everyday life (see Lynch, 1982, p. 46). In so doing, the films create the spaces for the appearance of the usual array of comedic devices audiences have come to expect from the world of comedy, including ridicule, sarcasm, puns, put-downs, satire, one-liners, and ludicrous, amusing sequences of action that build on themselves, as they gain momentum, change course, suffer disruptions, and fade away into calm, happy resolutions (see Lynch, 1982, pp. 59–60; Flaherty, 1984, pp. 75–77). In the process, the audience feels an emotional flow of identification with each character as he moves through and resolves the problematic situations the "evil" people in his world have created for him. The films have happy endings, as they must, if they are to be perceived as conforming to the canons of comedy.

The Comedy Alibi

The "happy alcoholic" or "happy drunk" is a major type of American hero (see Klapp, 1964, 1969, p. 214 on the hero as a social type) and a character type that many alcoholics aspire to become. The happy alcoholic comes in several varieties. Typically male, he may be the comic, eccentric, playboy drunk who realizes "dreams for people [alcoholics] that they cannot do for themselves" (Klapp, 1969, p. 214).[1] He may be a quiet tippler who is always mellow (i.e., Walter Brennan in *To Have and Have Not*). He may be, like W. C. Fields (see Chapter 6), loud and boisterous, boorish, crude, and vain. He may be charming and absolutely delightful, never far from a drink (i.e., the *Topper*, and *Thin Man* films). Elwood is an eccentric, gentle humored drunk, Arthur a rich, spoiled, pampered playboy. The continued presence of this type of comic drinker in film and television comedy perpetuates the belief that alcohol is an equivocal spirit; its bad effects are primarily produced by irresponsible drinkers, or by sick, alcoholic persons.

This is another version of the alcoholism alibi (Beauchamp, 1980, p. 47) that blames alcoholics for their irresponsible drinking and their alcoholism. It appears now as a dominant, and favorite text within popular culture, wrapped within a genre form, the Hollywood and television drinking comedy (e.g., "Cheers"). By joining alcohol with comedy, the popular (and high) culture displaces alcohol's negative effects into the pleasurable regions of experience historically and traditionally given over to comedy, good times, fun, and nondestructive "drunken comportment" (MacAndrew and Edgerton, 1969). They make being drunk fun. When they join inherited wealth with drunkenness, comedy, and the playboy style of life, they suggest that money buys the freedom to escape, in a funny, eccentric way, the negative effects of excessive drink.

The "happy alcoholic" film supports "the idea that alcohol is normative for modern American culture and that society should help people, especially young people, to adapt to the world of drinking" (Beauchamp, 1980, p. 47). One way to enter this world of drinking is through good humor and good times (e.g., *M*A*S*H*, *National Lampoon's Animal House*, *Cocktail*). The "alcoholism" comedy films shape and define this form of experience. These films clear away "the guilt and ambivalence of a confused past" (Beauchamp, 1980, p. 47) that existed during prohibition. They make drinking an acceptable activity. The alcoholism comedies subvert the social problem's theme of the more traditional "alcoholism" social problems film.

Harvey

The story of *Harvey*[2] may be simply given.[3] One day Elwood P. Dowd brings home an imaginary six foot one and one-half-inch rabbit, a "pooka" named "Harvey." Harvey disrupts the Dowd household, leading Elwood's sister Veta Louise to attempt to have Elwood committed to Chumley's Rest, the local mental hospital. There it is determined, in an in-take interview with the psychiatrist, Dr. Sanderson, that Veta is an alcoholic and suffering from a birth trauma. Veta escapes, returns home, and threatens to sue the hospital. Elwood wanders back home. Dr. Chumley, the owner of Chumley's Rest, meets "Harvey," has several drinks with him at Charlie's bar, and asks Elwood if Harvey can come live with him. Elwood is recaptured and taken back to Chumley's, where he is to be given a shot of formula 977, which shocks people back to reality. Fearing that she will lose the Elwood she loves, Veta intervenes and stops the shot, stating that she wants to live with Elwood and Harvey. Harvey refuses to stay with Dr. Chumley. The film closes with Elwood and Harvey walking together up a hill, into the morning sunrise.

Alcoholism Markers

Harvey is a paradoxical text. It contains few, if any of the markers of the alcoholism film outlined in Chapter 1. Consistent with Hollywood's Production Code, Elwood is never shown actually drinking, although on three occasions in Charlie's Bar he orders drinks for others, or invites people, always strangers, to his home for dinner, or to Charlie's later for drinks. Only Veta is preoccupied with Elwood's drinking, but this is confounded by her problems with the company Elwood keeps, not his actual drinking. No efforts to make him stop drinking are attempted. He is placed in no testing situations. He never attempts to sober up, has no slips, or relapses. Nonetheless the signifiers of alcohol, drinking, alcoholic, and alcoholism are used in four critical places as interpretations of the conduct of Elwood and Veta. Paradoxically Elwood is remembered by audiences and critics as being "a boozer who has a giant invisible rabbit as a pal . . . a benevolent lush" (Crowther, 1950, p. 2478). The film is a comedy about a man who is defined as an alcoholic by critics, but not by himself, or by those in his life.

The first key moment when the markers of drinking figure into the text has already been noted. It involves Veta Louise's description (to Dr. Sanderson) of Elwood's always stopping in cheap taverns before he brings Harvey and a "lot of people you never heard of" home. Here the context of drinking (cheap taverns), and Elwood's drinking friends (riff raff), not his drinking per se, are the reasons for concern over drinking.

The second occasion for the use of the alcoholism, excessive drinker label occurs when Sanderson informs Elwood that his sister "was extremely nervous and plunged right into a tirade on your drinking." Elwood replies, "That was Veta." Sanderson describes her as becoming hysterical, and then comments "Oh, I suppose you take a drink now and then—the same as the rest of us?" Elwood replies, "Yes, I do. As a matter of fact, I would like one right now." Sanderson responds, "Matter of fact, so would I, but your sister's reaction to the whole matter of drinking was entirely too intense. Does your sister drink, Mr. Dowd?" Elwood answers, "Oh, no, Doctor. I don't believe Veta has ever taken a drink." Sanderson counters, noting that it's not alcoholism that's going to be the basis of his diagnosis of her case. He states, "It's more serious than that. It was when she began talking so emotionally about this big white rabbit. . . . I believe she called him Harvey. . . . Her condition stems from trauma. . . . Your sister's condition is serious, but I can help her. She must remain out here temporarily. No one's ever seen a white rabbit six feet high." Here Veta's seeing the rabbit is attributed to her alcoholism, while the intense emotional reaction to Harvey is taken as a measure of a deeper, underlying psychological problem.

The third moment that focuses on drinking occurs when Elwood describes his friendship with Harvey and what they do at bars. This description, also noted above ("Harvey and I sit in the bars"), involves drinking and Elwood's relationship to reality. It counters Veta's description of what he does in bars. Elwood states: "I've wrestled with reality for 35 years and I'm happy to state that I finally won out over it."

Perhaps the most significant interaction involving drinking and alcohol involves Dr. Chumley after he has met Harvey. In a move that aligns the head psychiatrist with the inmates of the asylum, Chumley exclaims: "Flyspecks. I'm spending my life among flyspecks while miracles lean on lamposts at Fairfax and 18th street . . . I'd go to Akron . . . with a pretty young woman . . . a quiet woman . . . I would send out for cold beer. I would talk to her. I would tell her things I have never told anyone . . . I wouldn't let her talk . . . but . . . I would want her to reach out a soft white hand and stroke my head and say, 'Oh, you poor thing!' . . . . Tell me Mr. Dowd, could he—would he do this for me?" With the exception of the above interactions, alcohol figures only indirectly in the story of Elwood and Harvey.

The Critics Read *Harvey* and Find Alcoholism

Film critics read James Stewart's character Elwood, as an "inebriate rabbit fancier" (Hatch, 1951, p. 31), a "rather shiftless person who, as you know, drinks a great deal and spends most of his time with Harvey, a six-foot-plus invisible rabbit" (Hartung, 1950, p. 302), "a boozer who has a giant invisible rabbit as a pal . . . a benevolent lush" (Crowther, 1950, p. 2478), a "perpetually squiffed philosopher . . . who met Harvey one night after one of his elbow-bending soirees at Charlie's place" (*Newsweek*, 25 December 1950, p. 64). The film, according to Merle

Miller, who reviewed it for *The Saturday Review* (1950, p. 26), establishes the point that "it is pretty generally agreed these days that a fellow with a mild buzz on is better than the man who never touches the stuff . . . that's the whole point . . . *Harvey* ought to provide all except WCTU officials a fine hour and a half, even those suffering from holiday hangovers."

Elwood's drinking was seen as the key to his seeing Harvey, hence the phrase "inebriate rabbit fancier." Bosley Crowther (1950, p. 2478) carries this reading one step further and suggests that "Harvey" is a "yarn about a boozer . . . and what happens when the boozer's family, reduced to despair by his behavior, tries to clap him in the looney-bin." *The Garfield Messenger* (1950, p. 23) argued that the "film revolves around the distinction between the blithe spirits who see Harvey . . . and those persons who live in a more realistic world minus white rabbits." McDonald (1950, p. 2021) interprets the film as a "charming excursion into a slightly distorted world where the erratic, irrational behavior of the sane is pitted against the amiability of Elwood P. Dowd and his vividly unseen rabbit." McDonald also sees Elwood's situation as tragic, white Hartung (1950, p. 301) contends that "perhaps everybody has a Harvey; in any case there are worse forms of escape," and Crowther (1950, p. 2478) suggests that Mr. Stewart makes Elwood "a man to be admired."

Only Cook and Lewington (1979, p. 77), summarizing the film in 1979, view the film's message critically. They state (1979, p. 77) "Interesting as one of the few attempts to deal humorously with drinking, *Harvey* is potentially subversive in trying to present non-conforming excessive drinking as a positive escape from a stultifying society." Joseph Wood Krutch, reviewing the Broadway version of *Harvey* (1944, p. 624), went further, proposing that Mary Chase "has given us a sort of Don Quixote in modern dress," while *Newsweek* (1944, p. 83), in its treatment of the play, connected Chase's white rabbit Harvey to Lewis Caroll's white rabbit, which Alice saw. Another reviewer equated Harvey with Mary's little lamb.

Rereading *Harvey*

If the critics valorized the film for its good humor, few took up in detail its underlying negative judgments of psychiatry and its treatment of the alcoholic or mentally ill persons in World War II American society. On the surface about white rabbits and people who see them, underneath *Harvey* is a sustained, humorous criticism of modern psychiatry and its diagnoses of alcoholism, insanity, and sanity. At the same time the film spoofs psychotherapy, chemotherapy, and the traditional psychoanalytic treatment model. The signifiers of drinking, alcohol, alcoholism, and mental illness are central to this message.

Alcoholism, Insanity, and Psychiatry

Alcohol is presented as a social lubricant, and something that persons use when they are in high stress situations (e.g., Sanderson asking Elwood if he wants a drink when they first meet at the hospital). It can be used both by psychiatrists (Drs. Sanderson and Chumley) and by crazy people (Elwood). Alcoholism, on the other hand, is a label, or signifier of insanity that is moved from person to person (Elwood to Veta). It is used as a symptom of an underlying inability to confront reality on a sane, rational basis. It is one of the film's symbols of "insanity" and of a need for treatment. However, what is treated is not alcoholism, but underlying psychological conditions indicative of traumas, and depressions. These underlying conditions are displayed by those persons who see Harvey, which apparently produces traumatic reactions. Excessive drink presumably causes these hallucinations, hence Dr. Sanderson's diagnoses of Veta and Elwood as alcoholics. The film, however, cannot sustain this position, for Veta is obviously neither insane nor alcoholic, nor is Dr. Chumley. So seeing the rabbit cannot be used as a measure of one's sanity.

Yet the film wants to argue that those in the mental health profession, psychiatrists and their attendants, hold prejudicial, stereotyped views of the mentally ill. At various points Elwood is called a cold blooded psychopath, and other terms like neuros, psychos, schizos, and sickies are applied to the residents of Chumleys. In fact the persons who act crazy and violent in the film are not the persons diagnosed as mentally ill. They are the two psychiatrists and Mr. Wilson. The most sane person turns out to be Elwood, the original insane person.

Harvey the Rabbit

The film is about something other than alcoholism and seeing an invisible rabbit. That something else is the human being's fundamental loneliness, anhedonia, and estrangement from self and others (Lyman, 1987, 1990). Along the way the film wants to say that modern psychiatry has no business telling people what is real and what is not real. To clarify this point Dr. Chumley sees Harvey, a point ignored by the critics. Obviously Chumley is neither insane nor an alcoholic. His title makes him the epitome of sanity and rationality, yet he is depicted as a bumbling little figure, who wants to go off to Akron, send out for cold beer, and be stroked with the soft white hand of a strange, pretty, young woman whom he would not let talk. (He also does not want Harvey to leave his life.)

Chumley is reduced to the status of an ordinary, frail human being, not unlike Elwood, who also seeks companionship in white rabbits and drink. But Harvey lends a particular sense of self only to Elwood, and this is given in the fact that he chooses not to stay with Chumley. This special sense of self is given in Elwood's noble, serene acceptance of his life situation, and his genuine acceptance of others for who they are. And this is the film's lesson. The world out there is crazy and insane. One must find one's peace with that world. This peace can be purchased through drink and the companionship drinking creates; with it comes an acceptance of others. In this gesture the film turns back on itself and offers a happy ending. Elwood has Harvey, the bars, and alcohol. Chumley has been enlightened by Harvey. Veta Louise has accepted the rabbit's presence in her life and Myrtle Mae has a suitor (Wilson, the hospital attendant). Seeing Harvey and accepting his presence in one's life now becomes a measure of sanity, rationality, and peace of mind.

Gender and Manners

As a comedy of manners "Harvey" elaborates the above points concerning sanity and reality through its farcical treatment of Myrtle Mae's sexual flirtations with Mr. Wilson, the burly, gruff hospital attendant who Veta called a "white slaver." The romantic byplay between Nurse Kelly and Dr. Sanderson, like the quasi-sexual interactions between Veta and Sanderson and Chumley, is used to poke fun at the psychiatric profession. However, these gender gestures go beyond commentary on psychiatry. They point to an underlying subtext ignored by the critics, which involves gender politics and struggles between patriarchy and matriarchy in the film.

As the family matriarch, Veta is the power figure, and the stand-in for Elwood's mother. It is she who initiates Elwood's hospitalization. Her desire to remove him from the family home was precipitated by his involvement with Harvey, a move that displaced Veta, the mother figure, for an imaginary, sexually neutral gentle other. He stepped outside the Oedipal complex. Hence he had to be punished. But the punishment failed. At this level *Harvey* is an anti-Oedipal film. It exaggerates the position of the domineering female, and then mocks that figure, by forcing her to accept reality on Elwood's, not her grounds.

This anti-Oedipal theme is continued in the films superficially traditional, conventional view of the sexual order. In the end Myrtle Mae has a boyfriend and Sanderson and Kelly are reunited as lovers. But these men are brought to their knees, so to speak, by women. In this way Chase's story attacked the gender stratification system of its day, as it struggled to place women in positions of power and authority over men. Alcoholism and insanity became the bargaining chips in this war between the sexes.

I turn now to the two *Arthur* films, for they pursue, in less profound ways, many of the same themes given in Mary Chase's classic story.

Arthur (1981)

Rich Manhattanite Arthur Bach, a playboy drunk, loves Linda Morolla, an aspiring actress, who works as a waitress. If he marries Susan Johnson, whom he does not love, he will inherit $750 million. If he marries Linda he will lose the money; not wanting to be poor, he breaks off his relationship with Linda. Hobson, his butler, closest friend, and father figure, becomes fatally ill, and during the month of his final illness Arthur sobers up and cares for him. On Hobson's death Arthur returns to drinking, arriving drunk at the church, just hours before his wedding, where he tells Susan he cannot marry her because he is in love with someone else. Susan's father attacks him with a knife and Linda comes to his rescue. Arthur announces that the wedding is off. His wealthy grandmother (Martha) remains seated in the church. Linda proposes, "Do you promise to love me, and obey me and be a good boy?" Arthur replies, "I do. . . . Oh God, things are going to be great. We'll be like the poor people on the subway. . . . I'll get a job. . . . I'll come home from work. We'll eat some cheap disgusting food." Martha interrupts at this point, shouting, "That is out of the question. There has never been such a thing as a working class Bach and there never will be. . . . I've reached a decision. The Bach family must endure, and not on a subway. . . . You have your 750 million dollars." Arthur replies. "I don't know. . . . Money has screwed me up my whole life. I've always been rich and I've never been happy." Linda cuts in, "I've always been poor and I've usually been happy." Martha retorts, "I've always been rich and I've always been happy." Arthur excuses himself from Linda and walks over to Martha's limousine. Linda asks, "What, what happened?" Arthur replies, "Oh, I turned her down. Linda, "Oh." Arthur, "Well she invited us for dinner, and I told her we were having a tuna sandwich. So I turned her down. I took the money, I mean I'm not crazy."

Alcoholism Markers and Finding *Arthur*

With the exception of the scenes when he is caring for Hobson, Arthur is never presented without a drink in his hand, nor is he shown free of the effects of alcohol on his speech and comportment. His high-pitched voice, off-key jokes, slurred speech, and stumbling actions convey the picture of a drunken man barely in control of himself. The reactions of others in his life confirm this interpretation. In various scenes he is called a stinking drunk (by a stranger), a drunk (by his uncle), a millionaire drunken playboy (by his father and Hobson), a weak man (by Hobson), a little shit (by Hobson). Although his drinking is a problem and a challenge for others, including Susan, Hobson, and Linda, on the surface it causes him no problems. Asked not to drink by Susan, he states, "This is what I am. Everyone who drinks is not a poet. Some of us drink because we are not poets." He does not lose a job, for he has none, nor does he lose his inheritance, or the affections of the women who love him.

However, he does lose self-respect. His perpetual drunkenness has reduced him to the status of a self-centered child in the eyes of others, especially Hobson who persists in calling him a spoiled brat. The viewer is also brought to this position. Arthur embodies narcissism. An electric train that runs around his bed. A basketball hoop hangs on one wall. There is a throne he sits on, and the walls are covered with enlarged pictures of him. In a key scene, just before Hobson becomes ill, Arthur laments that no one knows how miserable he is. "The worst part of being me," he states, "is that I could have loved somebody. I'm a failure at everything I do and I'm just in everyone's way." To this Hobson replies, "You spoiled little bastard, you're a man who has everything. But that's not enough. You feel unloved, well welcome to the world Arthur, everyone is unloved. Stop feeling sorry for yourself, and incidentally, I love you. Poor drunks do not find love Arthur. They have few teeth, urinate outdoors, and freeze to death in the summer. I can't bear to think of you that way." To this Arthur replies, "I need Linda." Hobson tells him that "perhaps fate will lend a hand." And so it does, for Arthur ends up getting Linda and all the money.

Arthur's drinking, then, is associated with the three basic problems in his life: his inability to be loved, his loneliness, and his failure to find, until Linda, a woman he loves. These conditions, coupled with his constant drinking, have produced his sense of failure, worthlessness, and being miserable. Yet Arthur does not connect these problems to his drinking, nor do the significant people in his life. He drinks because he is a failure, and because he is alone and lonely, even though he has the constant attention and presence of Hobson, Bidderman, hookers, electric trains, and an endless supply of the very best alcohol. The film connects Arthur's drinking with childish immaturity and irresponsibility. Treated like a child by others, he acts like one. His alcohol-dazed conduct and his flaunting of the authority figures in his life are contained within the immature, playboy framework.

Underscoring this interpretation, the film has him sober up for the month that it takes Hobson to die. In this time period he brings Hobson the very best catered food, showers him with gifts (basketballs, trains, cowboy hats), as if he were reversing their child–adult relationship, and in these material expressions of affection, affirms his love for the man he now calls his father. On Hobson's death he returns to drinking. In this move the film makes it clear that Arthur has not really grown up, turned his life around, and become a sober adult. Rather, whenever he has to confront a conflict, or a stressful situation in his life he must drink. The lessons he learned while caring for Hobson do not hold when he has to deal with the big problem in his life, like marrying a woman he does not love. He ends up an alcoholic who has fallen off the wagon. Saved by fate, he gets the woman he loves as well as the money.

Failing to take a hard look at alcoholism, the film offers the viewer a story with a fairytale ending. Arthur undergoes no transformation of self. The film ends as it started, with Arthur drunk in the limousine, only now he is drunk with a woman he loves. But her love has not sobered him up. The film fails to sustain its earlier promise (and Hobson's hope) that if he got what he wanted, he would grow up, be responsible, happy, and sober.

The Critics Read *Arthur* and Ignore Alcoholism

Movie critics uniformly interpreted Arthur Bach as a throwback to the aristocratic screwball comedies and the fairytale romances of the 1930s and early 1940s (Ansen, 1981a, p. 75; Denby, 1981a, p. 50; Schickel, 1981a, p. 67; Kissel, 1981, p. 36; Rickey, 1981, p. 40), "in the style of Phillip Barry or the Morrie Ryskind of *My Man Godfrey*" (Benson, 1981, p. 1). Locating it within this tradition, they then focused on Arthur's constant intoxication, his dipsomania (Bensen, 1981, p. 1), his true alcoholic wit (Denby, 1981a, p. 50), Moore's "lovable drunk routine" (Auty, 1981, p. 215), his daily amount of alcohol consumption (Gelmis, 1981, p. 7), his perpetually soused state (Ansen, 1981, p. 75), his being a happy alcoholic (Rickey, 1981, p. 40), an alcoholic hero (Ebert, 1981, p. 21), as well as being the "very apotheosis of drunken upper-class obnoxiousness' (Kissel, 1981, p. 36).

Few critically examined the underlying themes of alcoholism in Arthur's character. Canby (1981a, p. 10), however, observed: "Not since Nick and Nora Charles virtually made the dry martini into the national drink . . . has there been quite so much boozing in a movie without hidden consequences. Arthur drinks scotch the way people now drink

Perrier. . . . When he goes giggling around town, sloshed to the eye-balls, he's not seen as a case history but as eccentric."

Ebert (1981, p. 21) goes further, noting that the problems with search-ing for love when you are drunk are many: "(a) no one will want to love you while you are drunk, (b) you are not at your best while you are drunk . . ., (c) you may be too drunk to notice it if someone finally does fall in love with you, and (d) . . . you will wake up hung over and scien-tific studies prove that hangovers dissolve love faster than any leading household detergent." Sterritt (1981, p. 18) said of the film, simply that "The movie *Arthur* and the character Arthur suffer from the same failing: too much drink."

With the above exceptions, the film was interpreted as a comedy that continued a film tradition started in the 1930s. Thus neither the re-viewers, nor the filmmaker, seriously addressed the problems of heavy drinking that would normally be attached to a character, comedic, or otherwise, who drinks the amount that Arthur drinks. For example, never once do Linda or Susan seriously react to Arthur's intoxication. Nor does he ever suffer from a hangover the next morning. The film embodies the comedy form of the alcoholism alibi discussed at the beginning of this chapter.

While *Arthur* was praised in 1981 as a continuation of a comedy form from the 1930s and 1940s, it was reread in the late 1980s as a film typical of the Reagan period of American politics. Richard Corliss wrote of the film, and its sequel: "Seven years ago, at the dawn of the Reagan era, a movie could seem a sweet anachronism, a throwback to giddier times with fewer responsibilities. Today Americans know that there is a price for every excess, fiscal or physical" (Corliss, 1988, p. 76). Perhaps this sense of a price to be paid was in the text, but reviewers in 1981 did not see it. More is involved.

As a film *Arthur* perpetuates, with a twist, the myth of the "happy," rich drunk. Neither alcohol nor money makes Arthur happy. His loneli-ness comes from inside, and in his attempts to run from it he follows the classic alcoholic route of turning to drink. Writer–director Gordon cre-ated a subversive text that critiqued itself from within. He offered a criti-cism of the genre on which he built; earlier comic films like *The Thin Man* or *Topper* failed to explore the deep, inner loneliness of the rich alcoholic. *Arthur* is both a criticism of the manners of the upper class and an explosion of the myth of the happy, playboy drunk. Its use of humor is double-edged; it turns back on Arthur's loneliness, and desire for love, while it exposes the hypocrisy of the monied classes in America. Their males are sexist and do not know what love is, nor do they know how to feel it, or express it, except through ostentatious, material display. Consider now *Arthur 2 on the Rocks*.

Arthur 2 on the Rocks (1988)

Linda and Arthur, four years after their wedding. Arthur is still a drunken playboy. Linda has happily adjusted to life among the rich. Finding that she cannot have children, she initiates efforts to adopt. Arthur's drinking has become problematic. When the woman from the adoption agency makes a home visit she asks about his drinking. Linda reports that he has joined A.A., but it turns out that he has never gone to an A.A. meeting. Enter Burt Johnson, the father of Susan, the spurned woman from the original Arthur, who buys up Arthur's father's firm, with the proviso that the family can still run the corporation, if Arthur is disinherited. He thinks that he can blackmail Arthur into divorcing Linda and marrying Susan. Arthur and Linda are evicted from their mansion, and then from the lower-class apartment that they move into when Johnson buys the building. Just before this happens they are told that there is a baby for them, but Arthur must stop drinking and get a job. Arthur gets a job in a hardware store, which he loses when Johnson buys the store. Linda leaves Arthur. Arthur drunkenly wanders the streets of Manhattan. On Christmas Eve he is visited by Hobson's ghost, who follows him to the shelter where he sleeps. Hobson tells him to stop drinking and stop acting like a spoiled little "shit." Hobson also tells him that he has seen his new son. Arthur pulls himself together, cleans up, stops drinking, and goes to Martha's. She directs him to Noah Curtis, a man who used to be a partner with Burt. Arthur meets Curtis's son, who leads him to a man who was financially destroyed by Burt. Arthur goes to Burt's boat with papers detailing a fraud scheme Burt had executed 10 years earlier. Burt asks Arthur if he wants a drink and Arthur tells him he does not drink. Burt tries to shoot Arthur. Susan tells her father that Arthur does not love her. Burt relents and says Arthur can have his money back. The film ends with a family reunion at the mansion. Linda informs Arthur that she is pregnant. Mrs. Canby from the adoption agency delivers their new child, a daughter, and Arthur moves Fairchild, his new butler, into Hobson's old rooms.

Alcoholism Markers and the Critics

As with Arthur, the markers of excessive drinking in Arthur 2 are multiple. Arthur is seldom not under the influence of alcohol, sobering up only at the end of the film after his interactions with Hobson's ghost. However, in Arthur 2 his drunkenness has caught up with him and become part of his public biography in a way that it was not in Arthur. He has been referred to A.A. The woman from the adoption agency makes his sobriety and holding a job conditions for the adoption of a child. He lives out Hobson's prophecy, and finds himself penniless and drunk on the streets of New York City. He loses Linda as well. But his loss of wealth is not connected to his drinking.

The film, like the original, fails to seriously consider the consequences of heavy drinking for an alcoholic like Arthur. It also does not offer any motivation for his drinking. His periods of sobriety, are, however, connected to his "father–son" relationship with Hobson, suggesting that he can get sober only when Hobson is dying, or speaking to him as a ghost. Both films hinge sobriety on the love of another. In an inversion of the usual good woman–drunk man theme (Herd, 1986), the two *Arthurs* have a father figure producing sobriety.

The attempt to have Arthur grow up and accept adult responsibilities, which is a major theme of *Arthur 2*, was met with uniform rejection by the critics, who also reacted negatively to Arthur's continued drinking and to the rather feeble plot that invokes Hobson as a ghost who sobers up Arthur (Ebert, 1988, p. 19). Playing with the film's title Ebert (1988, p. 19) argued that "sobriety puts humor on rocks in *Arthur 2*." Called by *USA Today* (1988) "funny as a hangover," it was dubbed a disaster by another critic (Kehr, 1988, p. 12), the script was called poverty-stricken by *Newsweek* (1988, p. 68), and for Canby (1988, p. 22): "Seeing *Arthur 2 on the Rocks* is like meeting a once–ebullient witty old friend who has let himself go to pieces. *Arthur* (Dudley Moore) still drinks too much. . . . He looks unhealthy and is no longer funny."

Ebert (1988, p. 19), like other reviewers (Canby, 1988; Kehr, 1988), locates the film's flaw in its attempt to make Arthur a tragic figure (placing him penniless on the streets of New York City). Arthur ceases to be a comic figure when this occurs. He is funny only to the degree that he is not tragic (Ebert, 1988, p. 19). By turning Arthur into a serious figure, the film deprived "his character of its original innocence and charm" (Ebert, 1988, p. 19), which rested in his "plucky determination in the face of utter confusion" (Ebert, 1988, p. 19). In these senses he was a comic, alcoholic hero (see Grant, 1979, pp. 30–36; Ebert, 1981); he always lightheartedly overcame his befuddled dazed, alcoholic situation, and did so in a comic way. In *Arthur 2* he is neither heroic, comic, nor tragically flawed. He is never caught, as the flawed, tragic, alcoholic hero is, between "his drinking and his good intentions" (Grant, 1979, p. 33). Arthur has no tragic flaws. His attempts at humor are crass, cruel, and demeaning. The film fails because it is neither comedy nor melodrama. It does not offer a serious analysis of Arthur's alcoholism. It does not make his drinking funny. Arthur never transcends his alcoholism, nor does he confront it as a moral or personal problem, as the noncomic, alcoholic hero must (Grant, 1979, p. 33). His feeble attempts at heroic action, when he stands up to Bert, are neither heroic nor humorous. These failures are not due to a weakness in character. They are present because *Arthur 2* fails to sustain the Oedipal conflict between Hobson and Arthur that drove the original film. This point was not noticed by the critics, yet it is the key to the failures of *Arthur 2*, for without this father figure to fight with, Arthur is nothing.

Turning back on *Harvey* and *Arthur*

Arthur, like Elwood P. Dowd, is a lonely man. Arthur, unlike Elwood, carries all of the trappings of an active alcoholic. Although Elwood's imaginary doings get him in trouble, Arthur's raucous, irreverent, drunken actions do not lead him to be called insane, a wacko, or psychopathic. His alcoholism has reduced him to the position of a harmless child. Elwood's, in contrast, raises him to the level of a seer of truths, a serene man with insights that others seek.

By framing their commentary within the comedy tradition, these films say that excessive drink, as a way of escaping from society, is both permissible and desirable. In treating their alcoholic protagonists in such different ways, they suggest that alcoholism is a measure of something else, and that something else is the upper class male and his failure to form lasting, meaningful social attachments with others. Money cannot buy happiness.

The three films develop and amplify the relationships between alcohol, drinking, and comedy discussed earlier. They show how the lonely person can find solace in drink. They present alcohol as a benevolent spirit. The films inner comedic structures use Elwood's and Arthur's situations to make aggressive, satiric jokes about society. By never taking up the problem of a "true" problem drinker, the films, as alcoholism comedies, use the label of alcoholic as a means of accomplishing their deeper criticisms of society and its social relationships. *Harvey* makes a "hero," a Don Quixote out of Elwood P. Dowd and celebrates the manners and morals of this kind of man. The two *Arthurs* allow the drunk to poke fun at upper class society. The films create and sustain their own illusions of the "happy alcoholic." They keep alive the idea that there is a proper place in society for certain kinds of eccentric drinkers.

Harvey was conceived by its author as a purely escapist play to entertain audiences during World War II. Like both *Arthurs* it is a triply subversive film. As a comedy of manners, it offers up severe criticisms of psychiatry, and, like *Arthur*, mocks the manners and morals of the monied, educated, upper classes. In making the above comments, these films also speak, in a subversive manner, to the larger issue of men and women in 1950s and 1980s American society. They are lonely, and long for companionship. They seem unable to find someone who cares for them, either in the approved institutions of marriage and family, or in work. They must turn to persons who others say are crazy, or lower class and unmannered, in order to find what they need. These persons, it seems, have found the companionship they seek in establishments like Charlie's bar, or in art deco bedrooms with electric trains and cowboy hats. In such settings they mingle with other lonely people, and share drinks with imaginary friends. In the 1950s and 1980s American society, Chase and Gordon seem to be saying, has no place for its members. In rendering this judgment, the films speak to the universality of the human condition. In a comedic, but tragic manner, they suggest that we are all in need of imaginary help for the loneliness we experience in our daily lives.

Still, in offering these messages, these films argue that unhappiness and anhedonia are conditions that can be cured if people successfully resolve their conflicts with mother and father figures, and find suitable loving companions. Elwood, as noted, rejected Veta for Harvey and found pleasure. Arthur's rejection of Susan, in both films, is a rejection of his father's intentions. Susan signifies the sterile upper class family life Arthur cannot adjust to. Linda represents a form of sexuality and love that is alien to this class system. Stepping outside this family formation, he turns to Martha, Linda, and Hobson as surrogate parents. These benevolent Oedipal figures manage his life for him. Still, Arthur had to confront and live through Hobson's stern warnings and predictions about his life. Linda was unable to replace Hobson as an emotional figure in his life. Hobson had to return from the dead to get Arthur back on course again. This father–son pair constituted a bond that marriage could not break. Oedipal to the core, this buddy relationship sustained Arthur's infantilism. Adult Arthur would never be free of this shadow father figure called Hobson. Arthur's stories show how deeply the popular culture depends on the Oedipal myth (in its missing father figure forms) for its comic treatments of the alcoholic.

Each film-going generation gets, it seems, its "classic" comedy about a "happy drunk," or madcap, eccentric, rich, alcoholic playboy. The chapters that follow turn to Hollywood's version of the "tragic" alcoholic. Just as the comic drunk is a stable part of American popular movie culture, so too is the "tragic" alcoholic who fights to overcome his or her alcoholism. How this all started and then developed in the prohibition, preclassic, and classic–modern periods is the topic of the next three chapters.

Notes

1.   It is significant that the "great" female comediennes," i.e., Mae West, Lucille Ball, Carol Burnett, Mary Tyler Moore, seldom if ever played happy drunks, supporting the conclusion that American culture codes female drunkenness with negative sexual values. (See Herd, 1986, p. 237; McCormack, 1986, p. 43; Harwin and Otto, 1979, p. 37.)

2.   Originally a three-act comedy, which won the Pulitzer Prize for Mary Chase in 1945, and which ran for 1,775 performances on Broadway after its opening in 1944, it had nearly reached the status of international folklore (*Newsweek,* 25 December 1950, p. 64).

3.   There have been numerous revivals of the play: a 1951 Negro Touring Company; 1955 at the Paper Mill, New Jersey with Joe E. Brown; 1967 in New York; 1970 in Phoenix with Stewart and Helen Hayes; 1972 for television on the Hallmark Hall of Fame, also starring Stewart; 1975 in London again with Stewart.

4.   New York critics were divided in their reactions to the Broadway play. Some felt that although it was extremely pleasant it "was not an example of distinguished writing . . . others disapproved of its condoning lunacy and drinking" and others saw it as "a poor mix of fantasy and farce" (*Current Biography,* 1945, p. 100).

PART II

**1932–1962: Defining Alcoholism
for the American Public**

3   A Star Is Born: In Search of the Alcoholic Hero

> "I'm gonna put this whole weekend down, minute by minute . . . I wonder how many others there are like me, poor bedeviled guys on fire with thirst."
>
> (Don Birnam in *The Lost Weekend*)

Hero: A man of distinguished bravery.

Four versions of an alcoholic hero:

What Price Hollywood? (1932): (Julius to Max): "You are slipping all the time with the bottle. All the time you are drunk. You've got to stop."

A Star is Born (1937): (Norman, who has entered a sanitarium to dry out from his perpetual drunkenness, to Oliver): "I'm really cured, but I'm staying another week to get in good shape."

Lost Weekend (1945): (Don to Nat): "Why does he drink and why doesn't he stop? . . . [He's] a booze addict . . . an alcoholic."

Come Fill the Cup (1951): (M.D. to Lew): "You have an incurable disease, alcoholism. . . . You're an alcoholic for the rest of your life. The one drink you don't take is the first one, forever."

These four explanations of problematic drinking—lack of will power, addiction to booze, something you can dry out from, and having the disease of alcoholism—define Hollywood's presentation of the alcoholic in the Prohibition, preclassic, and classic–modern periods. The explanations build on one another. How they do so is the topic of this chapter.

41

The Moral Career of the Hollywood Alcoholic Hero

Hollywood's treatment of the moral career of the alcoholic hero moves through three filmic phases (prohibition, pre-classic, and classic), corresponding to the above explanatory formulations and historical moments. In each phase a different set of characteristics is brought to this figure, including the accounts for his alcoholism, what happens to him because of his drinking, and his effects on those close to him.

In each film period the alcoholic hero's moral career is typically presented as falling into three phases that correspond to the classic morality tale in Western Civilization (Denzin, 1989c, pp. 18–19): seduction, the fall from grace, and then redemption. Alcohol is the catalyst that moves the alcoholic through these three phases, although nearly all films start with the fall from grace. Entry into recovery typically occurs in a "vital scene of recognition" where the alternative between continued self-destruction and recovery is dramatically clarified. In a moment of insight and bravery the alcoholic hero confronts the truth about himself. This turning point experience and the struggles that surround and follow it mark his heroism. Like the classic "western" hero, this alcoholic hero is often a loner, as well as a person who is reverenced and idealized by others (Wright, 1975). Unlike his "western" counterpart he is self-indulgent, to the point of self-destruction. In the end the hero (or heroine) may not restore law and order, or ride away from civilization, but their recovery, or death is often coded in courageous, altruistic terms, including sacrifice (Lyman, 1990, p. 2).

By 1930 Hollywood had yet to fashion a modern version of this heroic figure, a man, that is, who would confront his alcoholism as a moral and personal problem, who would be caught between his drinking and higher intentions and values, and who would be seen as suffering from a condition that he did not produce, i.e., an illness (see Grant, 1979, p. 33). Such a figure, even though flawed with his alcoholism, would provide a source of identification for others. By his heroic actions he would show those who identify with him how to confront their alcoholism.

Although at least 160 films focusing on a problem drinker had been produced by this time, the 1920s "temperance melodrama" was still the favorite format for the treatment of the alcoholic (Room, 1983b, p. 3), although the comic drunk was also a film staple by this time. In the temperance films alcoholism was subordinated to romance. Males were depicted as being "temporary victims of drinking . . . [their] alcoholism [was] an ambivalent symbol of masculinity . . . [and] it function[ed] as a device to motivate the overall pattern of crisis, separation, and resolution in a romantic dilemma" (Herd, 1986, pp. 228, 225, 219). Problems with alcohol were happily resolved through the love of a good woman (Herd, 1986, p. 218).

The Myth of Alcohol and Creativity

A popular cultural myth holds that creative individuals abuse drugs and alcohol (Denzin, 1987a, p. 30). Hollywood has exploited this myth in its treatment of the alcoholic, returning over and over again to the alcoholic writer or star as the personification of this subject. The *Star Is Born* cycle starts this myth. The Production Code through the 1930s made alcoholism in normal families a near taboo topic (Wood, 1970, p. 88). If problems with alcohol were going to be treated, such problems had to be located in a site far away from normal, everyday life; what better place than Hollywood's own backyard.

By the 1930s Hollywood had established the tradition of portraying "purported upper-class lifestyles, and glamorous occupations such as actor or singer" (Room, 1985, p. 12). The topic of alcoholism was salient within the filmmaking community, for many of its members had experienced personal problems with alcohol (Room, 1985, p. 12) (e.g., D. W. Griffith, Raymond Chandler, F. Scott Fitzgerald, Charles Brackett, the Barrymores, see Zolotow, 1977; Room, 1985, p. 12). How better to make Hollywood appear to be treating a major social problem than by producing films about stars becoming drunks? Throughout the 1950s and 1960s alcoholism "biopics" or filmed autobiographies and biographies became a favorite type of Hollywood film. The alcoholism stories of Lillian Roth, Helen Morgan, Buster Keaton, and F. Scott Fitzgerald would quickly be told. (This biographical thrust of the alcoholism film continues to the present day, e.g., *The Betty Ford Story*, 1987; *Barfly*, 1987; *Bird*, 1989; *Wired*, 1989). By reflexively focusing on its own social structure, as a site of excessive drinking, Hollywood capitalized on its cultural meanings as a place of "sin", wealth, dazzling dreams, wild parties, and excitement (Room, 1985, p. 13). This move allowed studio owners such as David O. Selznick to produce films about Hollywood that self-consciously turned "the movie game into a cultural institution" (Sklar, 1975, p. 192) that created, kindly treated, and then discarded its problem drinkers.

The Emergence of the Hero

With *What Price Hollywood?* (1932), a film that combined comedy and tragedy, the foundations for the modern alcoholic hero are created.[1] He would undergo, as just indicated, three transformations, attached, in part, to three specific film cycles. In his first phase, he would, like the 1920s drunkard, lack will power. However, his occupation changes. Instead of being a railroad engineer (*The Curse of Drink*, 1922; *Tin Gods*,

1926), a war veteran (*Girl of the Port*, 1930), or a social outcast (*His Dog*, 1926), the new, postprohibition alcoholic subject was, as noted in Chapter 1 (and above), a part of the Hollywood star system. A lonely, highly talented male, this figure is seriously flawed by a compulsion to drink that interferes with his ability to work, or form lasting intimate relationships with women. His "alcoholic" story is contained within the "Hollywood glitter" film (Sklar, 1975, p. 192), and subordinated to his romance with a rising star and her career. This version of the hero is contained in the first phase of the *Star Is Born* cycle (1932–1937). It is challenged in 1945 with *Lost Weekend*.

In *Lost Weekend* (phase two) the "drunkard's experiences" (Agee, 1945/1958, p. 183) are presented for the first time in graphic, realistic detail. *Lost Weekend* became, as noted in Chapter 1, the film against which all future alcoholism films were judged (see also Chapter 10). Here the alcoholic is an ordinary man, not a Hollywood star. His creative characteristics (a failed writer) define how he thinks of himself (e.g., sober he is a nonentity, drunk, a Shakespeare). His diseased condition is openly discussed, even though his story is contained within a romantic melodrama. *Lost Weekend*, like other social consciousness, social problem films of the late 1940s and 1950s (Cook, 1981, pp. 442–44), challenged the Hollywood Production Code (in its focus on alcoholic drinking and the presentation of homosexuality); it attempted, however, to be neither pro- nor antiprohibition (Wood, 1970, pp. 87–89). Wilder described the film in these words: "It is the Odyssey of a serious drunk . . . neither a comic nor a disreputable character . . . a dignified man . . . a hopeless alcoholic" (Wood, 1970, p. 89). *Lost Weekend* moves the alcoholic clearly into phase two where his heroic struggles with himself become the film's focus.

In phase three this ordinary character must meet A.A. and its disease theory of alcoholism. This he does (along with his female counterpart, see Chapter 4) in a series of films beginning in 1951 (*Come Fill the Cup*), followed by *Come Back, Little Sheba* (1952), *Something to Live For* (1952), *I'll Cry Tomorrow* (1955), *Voice in the Mirror* (1958), and ending in 1962 with *Days of Wine and Roses*. (By my determination this is the sequence of A.A. films in the classic period, e.g., films with explicit and implicit references to A.A.) This emerging hero is still employed in a so-called creative occupation (e.g., journalism, teaching, commercial artist, advertising), a medical-related field (chiropractor), or the law. However, Hollywood would not let go of its *Star Is Born* entertainment version of this hero. He would appear again in 1954 (and in 1976), untouched by the transformations that had been introduced with the *Lost Weekend* and the A.A. films of the classic period.

The origins of the contemporary alcoholism film are given in the above cycle, or grouping of movies, which also includes *Notorious** (1946), *Humoresque** (1946), *Smash-Up: The Story of a Woman** (1947), *Under Capricorn** (1949), *My Foolish Heart** (1949), *Young Man with a Horn* (1950), *Night into Morning* (1951), *The Country Girl* (1954), *Written on the Wind* (1955), *Hilda Crane** (1956), *Bottom of the Bottle* (1956), *The Joker Is Wild* (1957), *The Helen Morgan Story** (1957), *The Sun Also Rises** (1957), *The Buster Keaton Story* (1957), *Too Much, Too Soon** (1958), *Ten North Frederick* (1958), *Rio Bravo* (1959), *Beloved Infidel* (1959), and *From the Terrace** (1960).[2] These films, many of which were domestic melodramas, "made alcoholism an emblem of middle-class America" (Elsaesser, 1973/1986, p. 303).

In this chapter I examine this alcoholic hero, taking him through the three stages just discussed. In historical sequence, my films are *What Price Hollywood?* (1932), *A Star Is Born* (1937), *Lost Weekend* (1945), *Come Fill the Cup* (1951), and *A Star Is Born* (1954).

The *Star Is Born* Cycle: The Price of Hollywood Is Alcoholism

The *Star Is Born* cycle created an all-American couple, who have gone by three sets of names. In *What Price Hollywood* they would be called Max Carey and Vicki Lester (originally Mary Evans), although they never marry. In *A Star Is Born* (1937) the couple becomes Norman Maine and Esther Blodgett (who is renamed Vicki Lester), names they would hold through the 1954 remake, until in 1976 when Norman becomes John Norman Howard and Esther's last name becomes Hoffman. These are stories of love killed by alcoholism. They are tales of altruistic sacrifice for in each the alcoholic hero gives his life for his wife's career. They are fables of moral commitment. In each the alcoholic's wife takes his name as her own, "thus allowing him to be symbolically restored to the moral community because of his sacrifices" (Lyman, 1990, p. 2). They sustain the temperance melodramatic myth that the love of a good woman can cure alcoholism. The *Star Is Born* alcoholics never embrace the disease conception of their condition even though they do (1937, 1954) enter sanitariums to dry out. (Only in 1976 will this drunk call himself an alcoholic.)

The Stories

The message of the first two versions of the *Star Is Born* series is simple: the price of Hollywood stardom is alcoholism, personal destruction, and death. The storylines of these two films are intertwined. *What Price Hollywood?* (see Rogers St. Johns, 1924) begins with an attractive waitress (in 1937 she is an aspiring actress), in a Hollywood cafe, Mary

Evans (Vicki Lester), meeting a drunken, highly successful director, Max Carey (he becomes a falling star in 1937), who promises to make her into a Hollywood star. This he does, falling in love with her as well, but she marries Lonny Borden, a wealthy young polo player. In 1937 they marry one another, after Norman promises to stop drinking. Max's drinking worsens. So does Norman's, who enters a sanitarium to dry out. Both men's careers falter, after their women win Oscars. They no longer get directing or acting jobs. Arrested and jailed for drunk driving, they are rescued by their respective women (Mary and Esther/Vicki Lester) and taken to their mansions, where each commits suicide.

Here is how Max dies. Mary has just told him, "You are going to be dry from now on." After she leaves the room he takes a bottle from a cabinet, pours and drinks two quick shots, walks to a mirror hanging on the wall, looks first at himself in the mirror, and then at his picture setting on the bureau taken when he was in his prime. Comparing the two reflections of himself, he lights a cigarette. Drinking scenes from his life flash by on the mirror. He turns away, returns with a gun, puts it to his chest and kills himself. Norman's death is similar. After learning that Esther is giving up her career for him, he walks out of their Malibu home into the ocean and drowns himself. As Esther is closing up her mansion, preparing to return to North Dakota (her original home), her grandmother arrives and calls her a coward for quitting. Esther makes a new film. Introduced to an international radio audience as "Vicki Lester, the girl who has won the heart of the world," she says, "Hello, this is Mrs. Norman Maine."

Two Drunken Souls

From their drunken, comic opening scenes, to their respective death scenes, Max and Norman are presented as out of control drinkers. Max starts his days with Bloody Marys, marks his bottles of whiskey, takes his first drink of the day from a bottle hidden in his medicine cabinet, and drinks on the job. Norman does likewise, and is repeatedly told that his work is interfering with his drinking. At the party where Esther first meet him he is shown drinking three full glasses of scotch, one after the other. He, like Max, is warned by friends that alcohol has taken control of his life. "You are going the way of so many others. A man forgetting who he is. Your real friends can't stand to see you start to fall apart. The first signs are always the same. Not being able to remember your lines, the hangovers, all because you have to have a good time." He knows this and so does everyone else in his life. He drunkenly interrupts Vicki's acceptance speech at the Academy Awards and demands three awards for the three worst performances of the past year. His death is directly related to his drinking, his failed career, and his effects on Vicki's career.

Drinking Explanations

The films fail to offer a detailed explanation for either man's drinking. Apparently Max is addicted to the whiskey and has lost his self-respect. Moments before he commits suicide he tells Mary, "I am all dead inside. I don't feel anything. I've lost it. I'm washed up in pictures. I haven't got it anymore. It's all gone in here [pointing to his heart]. From where I am they don't come back." His alcoholic suicide is thus explained. Dead inside, shamed by his decline from power, slipping farther and farther down because of the whiskey, he loses all self-respect. He never attempts to stop drinking. He was intoxicated when the film begins, hungover, and barely sober when it ends.

The film, at one point, suggests that Mary is the cause of Max's decline. A gossip columnist asks "Which famous director is angry over a new star's sudden fame and marriage?" However, Max's drinking was out of control before he met Mary; her winning the Academy Award for best actress merely marked her rise to fame and his accelerating decline into uncontrolled drinking. His decline was independent of her rise to fame. (This same pattern holds for every other film in this series.) But by making Max a half-comic figure (e.g., "What the picture business needs is light wines and beers), the film wavers in its treatment of alcoholism.

Norman's alcoholism is different from Max's. His is more deeply motivated, and is tied to his inability to find an object of true love. By the time he finds Esther his alcoholism has taken control of his life. Still, unlike Max, he attempts to stop drinking, first on his own, and then with help. In this confrontation with his drinking problem, he moves beyond Max's denial. He deals with his alcoholism as a problem that stands in the way of obtaining and holding onto better things in his life.

His unhappiness (anhedonia) is a key to his alcoholism. Standing on a balcony, looking over the Hollywood hills, after the release of their new film, he tells Vicki that "A Star Is Born . . . Happiness is one thing I never had. Lots of times I told myself that I'd found it and I've never stopped looking for it. It has come, but too late. You can't throw away everything in your life the way I have and have anything left that is good enough."

The Critics

What Price Hollywood? was given short shrift by the reviewers. Although Max's excessive drinking was noted by the reviewers, it was not the main theme in their comments. The attention, instead, was given to the film's attempt to be both a comedy and a serious treatment about life in Hollywood. The reviewer for the the *New York Times* (1932) wrote that "there has recently appeared the literate pastime of joking at Hollywood . . . [*What Price Hollywood?*] is partly a serious lecture on what happens to a star once she becomes a star . . . [and] a gentle comedy about how she rises to that . . . height." Noting that its earlier sections are very amusing, the reviewer disputed the film's attempts to become serious. "Then it begins to take itself seriously . . . the director, slipping down into the dregs of his drink commits suicide in the star's home . . . it [the film] might have been worse. All plot and it could have been much worse."

Bakshy (1932, p. 111) focused on the film's title. "If we are to believe the authors and producers of this film, the price of Hollywood is the social downfall and degradation of those unable to resist the temptation of drink, and the perpetual agony and thwarted home life of those who, thanks to their eminence, are constantly exposed to the public gaze . . . we had better not ask what it is that drives the Hollywood geniuses to seek oblivion in drink." McCarten (July 1932, p. 45) wrote of Lowell Sherman's performance, that he took on the "more obnoxious traits of Lionel Barrymore [while being] cast as a brilliant director who goes to the devil through drink." In contrast *A Star Is Born* was accorded the status of an instant classic. Phrases like unforgettable, legendary, the "most affecting movie ever made about Hollywood . . . one of the grandest heartbreak dramas that has drenched the screen in years" (Crowther, 1954a) were, seventeen years later, still being applied to this film, which continues to be a top film rental.

Gendered Heroes

Reading the films as "Hollywood" glitter texts, the critics failed to examine how women were central to the telling of this story. The early *Star Is Born* cycle capitalized on gender. The new alcoholic star required a woman to take care of him. This he got with a female star whose career climbed while his sank into oblivion. Her duties were many. She had to manage her own career, care for him, and manage their household (they never had children). This alcoholic male gave Hollywood and America the new, modern working woman. She upheld the traditional values of family, while she pursued a work career. Her work career, however, was one that was played out in the Hollywood dream factory, itself a totalitarian, racist, sexist social structure (see Powdermaker, 1950, pp. 329–32; Mast, 1976, p. 117).

I turn next to two films (*Lost Weekend*, and *Come Fill The Cup*) that unequivocally establish the filmic presence of an alcoholic hero, while seriously addressing the topic of alcoholism, its causes, and its treatment.

In the Beginning There was *The Lost Weekend*

If a canonical film can be said to exist in the "alcoholism" genre, it is *The Lost Weekend*. Virtually every film in the classic period (1945–1962) that followed this 1945 release (with the exception of the comedies) was unfavorably compared to this text. *Come Fill the Cup* (Crowther, 1951), *Smash-Up* (Crowther, 1947), *I'll Cry Tomorrow* (McCarten, 1956), and *Days of Wine and Roses* (Hartung, 1963; Crowther, 1963) were all called second-rate versions of *The Lost Weekend*. As will be noted in Chapter 9, contemporary films continue to be unfavorably compared to this text. Maslin (1988a,b) praised *Clean and Sober* as the *Lost Weekend* of the 1980s. Canby (1981b, p. 23), unfavorably compared *Only When I Laugh* to *Lost Weekend* and Ringel (1987, p. 9) used *The Lost Weekend* to describe Henry and Wanda's escapades in *Barfly*. In short, the film has maintained its canonical status for nearly fifty years.

Lost Weekend raised one key question (see below) that reviewers since would not let go of: the cause(s) of alcoholism. Although other problems were raised when it was released (its melodramatic resolution, its construction of Don's character as a split personality), it was for its failure to adequately explain the cause of his alcoholism that bothered everyone (see Crowther, 1945; Farber, 1946; Smith, 1945). This criticism would then be brought to bear on subsequent films through the classic period. Crowther (1947, 1951, 1952, 1956) complained that the alcoholics in *Smash-Up, Come Fill the Cup, Come Back, Little Sheba,* and *I'll Cry Tomorrow* were undermotivated. McCarten (1954b) made the same judgment about Frank in *Country Girl,* as did Hartung (1963) about *Days of Wine and Roses.*

A number of firsts are associated with *The Lost Weekend*. There is, for the first time, an attempt to "seriously depict the madness associated with alcoholism" (Flemming and Manvell, 1985, p. 139). This is the first film to use the term "alcoholic" to describe the star's drinking problem. It is the first to use and present the medical model of alcoholism. It is the first film to feel A.A.'s presence. On 3 July 1944 Billy Wilder wrote A.A. asking for literature to assist in the production of the movie (Kurtz, 1979, p. 294). [Paradoxically, in 1944 Jackson's publisher sought A.A.'s help in promoting the book (Kurtz, 1979, p. 294).] Finally, the film, although radically breaking with the *Star Is Born* cycle (and other earlier treatments of the problem drinker), is continuous with this series because it centers on a male alcoholic who struggles with his sobriety. Its departure from earlier films is established by the continual focus on a man caught in the depths of alcoholism who heroically struggles with himself and the bottle.

The Story

Set in New York City, the film is the story of Don Birnam, a frustrated, well-educated, somewhat wealthy, alcoholic writer, who goes on a drinking binge that lasts from Thursday to Tuesday, the time that corresponds to when he is left alone by his brother and fiancée. Over the course of the weekend he is shown in the constant pursuit of alcohol. Left with no money, he resorts to stealing money intended for a cleaning lady, selling his typewriter to buy alcohol, and degrading himself in a nightclub when he steals a woman's purse. He tears his apartment apart as he looks for a lost bottle. He is taken to the alcoholic ward of Bellevue where he experiences the DTs.[3] Escaping he steals a bottle of whiskey from a liquor store, returns home, and again experiences DTs. He sees an imaginary mouse crawl out of the wall. The mouse is slaughtered by an imaginary bat. He steals Helen's coat to buy a gun to kill himself. Helen catches him and tells him he is "weak to the core, just a sponge who only wants to soak up alcohol."

Back at the apartment, he walks to the bathroom, looks into the mirror, the reflection of his face, along with the gun are shown to the viewer who sees the scene through Helen's eyes (as Max's suicide scene from *What Price Hollywood?*). She coaxes him to have a drink, "I'd rather have you drunk, then dead." He tells her that he is already dead, that he "died this weekend of alcohol and moral anemia, fear, shame and DTs." She tells him that "there is no cure except just stopping." Asking her if she expects a miracle, she says yes. Just then Nat brings his typewriter back. She exclaims, "Someone, somewhere, sent this back. Why? Because you are to stay alive! Because he wants you to write!"

Don asks, "What am I gonna write about? About a messed up life, a man and a woman and a bottle, about nightmares, horrors, humiliations." Helen answers, "put it down, to whom it may concern, and it concerns so many people." Don picks up a glass of whiskey, looks at it, drops his lighted cigarette into it, turns to Helen and states "I'm gonna put this whole weekend down, minute by minute, the way I stood in there packing my suitcase, only my mind wasn't . . . on the weekend . . . my mind was hanging outside the window . . . suspended, just about 18 inches below, and out there in that great big concrete jungle I wonder how many others there are like me, poor bedeviled guys on fire with thirst, such colorful figures to the rest of the world as they stagger blindly toward another binge, another bender, another spree." The film closes on the bedroom window, where, at the beginning of the movie, a whiskey bottle was hanging by a string, moving slowly in the breeze.

Alcoholism Markers, Causes, and Consequences

The film quickly establishes its topic, a man obsessed with alcohol, with the opening shot of the bottle hanging out the window, Don pulling it up, attempting to untie the rope that holds it and put it in his suitcase, while telling Wick that he has not touched the stuff for 10 days. As the above story summary reveals, alcoholism markers are everywhere. What is critical is how the film establishes the meanings of alcoholism ("a drink at night, medicine in the morning"), elaborates its causes (Don's failure as a writer), and spells out its consequences (self-degradation). Critical here is the triadic, enabling relationship (Bateson, 1972b; Denzin, 1987a, Chapter 6) between the three principals who are trapped in an alcoholic relationship that is driven by Don's obsessions with alcohol, his binges, his failed attempts at sobriety, and their attempts to control his drinking. (As he is packing for the weekend, Don refers to himself as the invalid and Wick as his nurse. In an early meeting with Helen he calls himself the family drunk, for whom the cure has not taken.)

There is no trust between Helen, Wick, and Don. When Don talks Wick into going to the concert with Helen, and delaying their departure for the country until 6:00 P.M., Helen asks, "You'll be here when we come back?" Don retorts, "I told you I'm not leaving this apartment," and shouts at Wick, "O.K. If you don't believe me, here are my keys, why don't you lock me in like a dog." Helen intervenes, "We've got to trust Don, that's the only way." [This pretense at trust is shattered when Wick looks out the bedroom window and sees Don's bottle hanging over the ledge (on these pretense contexts see Glaser and Strauss, 1967; Denzin, 1987a, pp. 136–39)]. Ignoring this situation, Helen says to Don, "I know you're trying. We're both trying. You're trying not to drink and I'm trying not to love you." Don overhears Helen ask Wick, "What if he goes out and buys another bottle?" Wick, "With what? He hasn't a nickle. There isn't a store or a bar that will give him five cents worth of credit." Helen implores, "Are you sure he hasn't another bottle hidden someplace?" Wick assures her, "Not anymore he hasn't. I went over the apartment with a fine tooth comb." Proving Wick incorrect, Don steals the $10 left for the cleaning lady, goes to a liquor store, buys two bottles of rye, and then enters his favorite bar where he buys a drink. Thus begins his lost weekend. In these lines to Nat, the bartender, he explains his relationship to alcohol: "I may never touch it . . . not a drop. . . . I've got to know its around, that I can have it if I need it. I can't be cut off completely. That's the devil. That's what drives you crazy."

The enabling structure of Wick and Helen's relationship with Don is revealed in the following dialogue. Helen: "If he is left alone anything can happen, and I'm tied up at the office every minute, all Saturday and all Sunday. I can't look out for him." Wick argues: "If it happens it happens. . . . I've had six years of this . . . Who are we fooling? . . . We've reasoned with him, we've babied him, we've watched him like a hawk . . . We scrape him out of a gutter and pump some kind of self-respect into him and then he falls back in everytime." Helen offers sympathy: "He's a sick person. It's as though there were something wrong with his heart or his lungs. You wouldn't walk out on him if he had an attack. He needs our help." Wick argues, "He won't accept our help. Not Don, he hates us. He wants to be alone with that bottle. . . . Why kid ourselves. He's a hopeless alcoholic. . . . Let go of him Helen. Give yourself a chance."

In these lines the film enunciates the classic position that drunks are hopeless alcoholics, and the modern view that they have an illness (see Beauchamp, 1980, Chapter 1). Helen's refusal to let go reveals her commitment to the belief the alcoholic is both sick and in need of love, while Wick's letting go would be called, in contemporary Al-Anon terms, "tough love" (Al-Anon Family Groups, 1986, 1987). The causes for his alcoholism must still be determined.

In Jackson's novel the causes of Don's alcoholism are connected to his latent homosexuality, which is not addressed in the film, except in a brief interaction Don has with an attendant at Bellevue (see Wood, 1970, p. 88, and Dick, 1980, p. 54). The novel [and the film] also explore the myth (Jackson, 1944/1983, p. 221) that creative men are alcoholics, but then dispenses with any solution to the causes of the condition, arguing (p. 222), "To hell with causes—absent father, fraternity shock, too much mother, too much money, or the dozen other reasons you fell back on. . . . They counted for nothing in the face of the one fact: you drank and it was killing you." In this line Jackson espouses the A.A. position that the causes of alcoholism are irrelevant.

The film is not so direct. In an earlier flashback sequence[4] Helen had argued that "if one cure didn't take, there are others. There must be a reason why you drink. The right doctor could find it." He answers, "Look, I'm way ahead of the doctors. I know the reason. The reason is me. What I am, or rather what I'm not. What I wanted to become and didn't. . . . A writer . . . I'm 33 years-old. . . . I've never done anything, . . . I never will do anything, zero, zero, zero." Helen refuses his request to get out of his life, arguing, "Why? Because I've got a rival, because you're in love with this [the bottle]? You don't know me. . . . I'm going to fight and fight." The cause of his alcoholism, then, is the fear of failure, the fear of writing. This fear led to his drinking, and the drinking now controls his life. He is two people; Don the drunk and Don the writer. Don the writer has no self-confidence: Don the drunk has confidence (he wrote one story in college that was published in *Atlantic Monthly* and reprinted in *The Reader's Digest*), but he is always too drunk to write. His declaration to Nat that he is going home to write the novel (*The Bottle*) contains the suggestion that being able to write his own experiences will cure his alcoholism. In fact the film implies that this occurs, for it ends with his resolve to write his story. His lost weekend was not lost afterall, contrary to the novel, which has him preparing for another binge.

The Critics Read *The Lost Weekend*

The critics were (and continue to be) ready to accept Wilder's film as "the odyssey of a drunk" (Wood, 1970, p. 89). It was called one of the best movies of this or any other year (e.g., Hartung, 1945, p. 205; *Life*, 1945, p. 133; McCarten, 1945, p. 112), a cinematic work of art (Hartung, 1945, p. 206), a "shatteringly realistic and morbidly fascinating film [whose] most commendable distinction is that it is a straight objective report, unvarnished with editorial comment or temperance morality" (Crowther, 1945, p. 17).[5] Its ability to translate Jackson's novel into film, with "great fidelity" (Crowther, 1945, p. 17), realism (Hartung, 1945, p. 205), and honesty (Smith, 1945, p. 20), was praised, as was its commitment to seriously treat alcoholism. McCarten (1945, p. 112) wrote, "The problem posed by *The Lost Weekend* is a lot more important than any that Hollywood has tackled in a long, long time, and it is presented in thoroughly adult fashion." The reviewer for *Newsweek* (1945, p. 112) claimed that it was "another milestone in Hollywood coming of age. It took a lot of courage . . . to bring Jackson's terrifying case study of an alcoholic to an escapist-minded movie audience." [In keeping with the language of the day, reviewers used the nineteenth-century term "dipsomaniac" (thirst + mania) to refer to Don's condition.] Flemming and Manvell (1985, p. 137) called it "the first nonmelodramatic feature made by Hollywood on the issue of alcoholism." Herd and Room (1968, p. 32) argue an opposite reading, stating that it "continued the conventions of the 'drunkard's progress' in temperance movies . . . good and long-suffering woman, devoted to her inebriate man, is a familiar figure in 19th century temperance fiction."

Causes and Cures

Reviewers (see Ediger, 1988), faulted the film on its explanation of Birnam's alcoholism, contending that the novel handled this film with much more depth and realism. (This is a typical criticism of film; that is the "art of motion pictures has its limitations . . . it can present accurately and honestly the outward behavior of a man . . . it cannot, as the novelist can, enter his mind, or . . . his soul" (Smith, 1945, p. 20). Smith (1945, p. 20) argued that the film touched the "mystery only lightly, and then its explanation is false and puerile, and is invented for the purposes of simplification, and finally for the happy ending. . . . Birnam drank because he had a split personality . . . two men in one body, a creative writer and an alcoholic." He elaborated this criticism: "Bracket and . . . Wilder must have felt that they were inspired when they thought of this Jekyll and Hyde idea. At the very end . . . they kill off the alcoholic . . . leaving the novelist, suddenly worthy of the love of a good woman." Dick (1980, p. 54) suggested that what was interesting about Birnam was his duplicity, not his alcoholism, since the film gave no convincing answer for its causes. Kahn (1946, p. 141) complained that "it is clinically misleading to say that by his own resolution he could do himself any good at all. It would have been useful to say . . . that alcoholism is suicide . . . and that the Don Birnams of the world need expert help— the doctor, the psychiatrist, *and* the community." Agee (1945/1956, p. 183) wrote that he "saw nothing in it that is new, sharply individual or strongly creative." He facetiously took notice of the liquor industry's concern with the film in the last line of his review, "I understand that liquor ineresh: innerish: intereshtsh are rather worried about this film. Thash tough (p. 184)." Agree even argued that the film did not go far enough, "There is very little appreciation . . . of the many and subtle moods possible in drunkenness" (Agee, 1945/1958, p. 183). Roffman and Purdy (1981, p. 257) similarly found the treatment of the causes of alcoholism to be superficial, noting that the film, like other postwar films, "centers on the hero's identity crisis and its resolution through the efforts of the patient heroine."[6] Hartung (1945, p. 206) disagreed with the critics who objected to the note of hope at the film's end, claiming that "we could not bear to have the film end as the book did with complete hopelessness. . . . The film doesn't say don't drink. It says drunkenness makes man lose his dignity, and continued drunkenness is an illness that must be cured."[7]

Bacon, reviewing the film for the *Quarterly Journal of Studies on Alcoholism* (1948, p. 405), argued that it was competent, but that it did not make clear that Birnam was ill, and it implied that "anyone who drinks will become a Don Birnam, that the situation of the alcoholic is absolutely hopeless, and hospitals and doctors are not only useless for this condition but are . . . heartless, inefficient, and horrendous. From the standpoint of the professional student of the problems of alcohol and alcoholism, faulty, even dangerous, implications are present in *The Lost Weekend*." Brower (1946), in an opinion poll, found no support for Bacon's assertions. A majority of the viewers felt that the film portrayed the alcoholic as "an individual who is ill and who requires specialized treatment" (Flemming and Manvell, 1985, p. 138). Viewers did agree with Bacon on the point that the hospital treatment of alcoholics was "brutal, inefficient, or at best apathetic" (Flemming and Manvell, 1985, p. 138). Significantly only "12 percent thought all alcoholics are . . . like the hero" (Flemming and Manvell, 1985, p. 139). Both Brower and Bacon seemed to feel that films about alcoholism should not present graphic details about the suffering or treatment of alcoholics (Flemming and Manvell, 1985, p. 138). Their articles seemed to reflect the prevailing feeling "that medical and psychiatric problems should remain under the aegis of the medical community, and should not be presented to the public" (Flemming and Manvell, 1985, p. 138).

Brackett and Wilder were praised, except for the criticisms noted above, for the script, the photography, and the direction. Roth (1980, p. 1010), for example, extolled the poetic dialogue and Wilder's use of the cinematic circle "as part of the circle motif in the flashbacks." Crowther (1945, p. 6) wrote that "Wilder and . . . Brackett . . . have achieved . . . an illustration of a drunkard's misery that ranks with the best and most disturbing character studies ever put on the screen." [Frank Faylen's portrayal of the male nurse in Bellevue was praised as an "inspired movie portrait of homosexuality" (Farber, 1946, p. 23).]

Back to the Film: Undoing the Critics?

The criticisms of the film's resolution of Birnam's alcoholism were primarily based on its unfavorable comparisons to the novel. Although virtually all of the critics praised the film's serious treatment of alcoholism as a disease, they regarded the happy ending as unrealistic. Almost everyone doubted Helen's hope that the right doctor would find the answer to Don's dual personality. The film's premise that the love of a faithful woman would aid in the cure for alcoholism was also questioned. Only the social science reviewers challenged the harsh, nightmare view of Bellevue as a form of medical treatment (also Ritson, 1979). None of the reviewers examined or discussed the triadic relationship between Don, Helen, and Wick, which was the interactional basis of Don's alcoholism. They thus perpetuated the film's latent theme that alcoholism is solely an individual disease, independent of the social world that surrounds the alcoholic. In faulting the film for failing to offer an adequate theory of Don's illness the reviewers rejected the disease theory of alcoholism. This rejection allowed them to focus (as they continue to do) on the will power, nondisease theory aspects of alcoholism.

Although the film is ostensibly about Don, Helen's place cannot be diminished. She, like Esther Blodgett, is a working woman. Like Esther she loves an alcoholic. Unlike Esther, she provides her alcoholic lover with the support that apparently puts him on the path of recovery. She provides the interpretations of his writing project and it is she who tells him that he could not have written his story until he knew its conclusion. By keeping a place for the long-suffering girlfriend in its text, the movie sustains the belief, established long before the *Star Is Born* cycle, that the love of a good woman can get a man sober.

But the *Lost Weekend* adds something new and important to this belief. It forces the alcoholic (and the audience) to endure the pains of withdrawal, locating in that experience the death of the drinking self. When Don says that he died of alcohol and moral anemia, fear, shame, and DTs, he references the death of this alcoholic self (see Jellinek, 1962). In short the experience of being an alcoholic contains the seeds of sobriety. The film makes this point by its constant focus on Don and what he endures on his lost weekend. The film argues for Helen's presence at this point, for it is she who nurses the newborn sober self into existence. The *Star Is Born* cycle did not do this. Max and Norman were never shown in the depths of DTs, nor was there ever a mention of the death of the drinking self.

Lost Weekend locates Don's recovery in the moment of recognition that occurs when his DTs are experienced. In this sense the text reproduces the classic formula of tragedy, "where all comes clear and Oedipus or Lear stands face-to-face with the truth about himself. He knows, in a moment of tragic insight, who is he" (Schudson, 1988, p. 237). The alcoholic hero experiences such a moment. For Max and Norman this insight produces suicide, for Don and Lew (below) recovery.

While fashioning its modern version of the alcoholic hero, "where antagonist and protagonist are in the same man, and the conflict is internal" (Kahn, 1946, p. 141), the film also leaves a space for love and commitment, showing that alcoholism is both a relational and an interactional disease of self (see Denzin, 1987a, Chapter 6). It presents alcoholism, not as a moral, or biological problem, but as a medical illness and a psychological disorder centering on an unstable self (see Lewington, 1979, pp. 26–27). It made alcoholism a topic that could be taken seriously, without resorting to comedy. It created a middle-class, respectable version of the alcoholic, free of the glitter of fame. The storyline, which is almost completely controlled by Don's obsessions with alcohol, still contains the seeds of a love story. In these moves the film is forward looking, while it refuses to completely give up the romantic themes of the melodrama. It gave Hollywood a new, commercially promising way of treating alcoholism, as it created what would become the "classic" picture of the alcoholic hero who suffers the horrors and degradations of his disease.

In having Don write his own story, *Lost Weekend* further cemented the foundations of the alcoholic hero. This figure goes beyond altruistic suicide. He devotes his life, not his death, to helping others. In having Don tell his own story Wilder connects recovery to the A.A. position of storytelling. This aligns his modern hero with this self-help group, and with the classic concept of the hero who helps others do what they cannot do for themselves.

After *Lost Weekend*, as noted earlier, at least 28 feature films with a major character marked by alcoholism were made in the classic period (see Room, 1985, p. 20). I turn now to *Come Fill the Cup* (1951), the first Hollywood film to actually use the A.A. model of recovery and alcoholism, including employing "A.A.'s theme of drunks helping other drunks" (Room, 1985, p. 8). This position is so strong, that at one point the main character's employer complains, "the place is beginning to look like a branch of Alcoholics Anonymous."

Come Fill the Cup was adapted by Ivan Goff and Ben Roberts, from a novel of the same name, by Harlan Ware (1952). True to the novel, the film's storyline is part *Lost Weekend* and part *The Front Page*. It turns the alcoholic into a full-fledged, popular culture hero in the mold of the 1930s and 1940s crime novels (e.g., Hammett) and films of urban violence (e.g., *White Heat*). Films like *Come Fill the Cup* offer a "realistic expose of corruption in the big city, presided over by the private eye" (Fiedler, 1966, p. 499). This figure is an outsider to society, a journalist, or ex-cop. He speaks the language of ordinary people. He is "the cowboy adapted to life on the city streets" (Fiedler, 1966, p. 499). Lew Marsh embodies this character. An ex-journalist, he battles not only his alcoholism, but also corruption and crime in Chicago.

Come Fill the Cup (1951)

Lew Marsh is fired from his job of city-editor for chronic drunkenness. On the same day he loses his long-time girl friend Paula, also an editor. He drinks himself down to skid row and an alcoholism ward, where he experiences DTs. Leaving the hospital, he moves in with Charlie, a recovering alcoholic, with six years sobriety, who teaches him one day at a time how not to drink. Five years later he is given back at his old job of city-editor, where he has helped three newspaper men get sober. He is asked to sober up Boyd Copeland, a gifted composer, but a drunken playboy, now married to Paula. Boyd is involved with Maria Diego, Lennie Carr's (a gangster) woman. Lew and Boyd agree to attempt to sober up Boyd. Charlie dies in an accident intended to kill Boyd. Boyd suffers extreme DTs, sobers up with Lew's help, gets his wife back, and Lew write's the "Front Page Story" about bringing down Lennie Carr.

Alcoholism Signifiers

The film, with its two alcoholics extends the "alcoholism" themes of *Lost Weekend* in several distinct ways. It has two characters experience DTs. It shows a loving woman (Paula) abandoning and then standing behind her alcoholic husband (Boyd). The term alcoholic, drunk, lush, and dipso are frequently used to describe Lew and Boyd. Lew states, in answer to the question why he drinks, "A lush can always find a reason if he's thirsty. If he's happy he takes a couple of shots to celebrate his happiness. If he's sad, he needs 'em to drown his sorrow, low to pick him up, excited to calm him down, sick for his health, and healthy it can't hurt him."

Almost immediately the film introduces A.A.'s concept of alcoholism. The morning he is discharged from the hospital, Lew's doctor makes the following speech (also quoted above): "You have an incurable disease, alcoholism. Liquor is as poisonous to you as sugar is to the man with diabetes. The only sure treatment is to quit. You do it alone. You're an alcoholic for the rest of your life."[8] Lew answers "I'd like to try it. Once you hit bottom there's only one way to go, and that's up." The biological elements of the disease theme are further developed when Lew meets Boyd for the first time. Boyd tells Lew that "you could describe the human kidney, and the wet brain, and alcoholic psychosis, and cirrhosis of the liver and DTs."

The film explains how one gets sober in the following speeches. Charlie asks Lew what made him quit." Lew states, "It was a sound I heard. As I was lying in the gutter it kept coming at me like an animal, a whirring sound." Later, when Lew is asked to sober up Boyd, he repeats the "angel feather's" story. John Ives has asked him to find out why Boyd drinks, so that he can help him get sober. Ives, "the boy is running away from something. Find out what makes him drink." Lew, "This sounds like a job for a psychiatrist. Ives: "We tried psychiatrists, the last one used campus terms like aspiration levels, frustrations, getting him away from the negative milieu of the home, that sort of thing." Lew, "There's only one thing that really pulls a drunk up short, the sound of angel feathers, a peek into the void. You quit because you are afraid to die. You run away from life, but you run away from death too. Sometimes its easier to live, and then you quit. Maybe. . . . A lot of guys quit the club when they hear it."

When Boyd is experiencing DTs, Lew tells him, "The wagon's never an easy ride, not for us." Lew sees a gun that Boyd intends to use reflected in a mirror and offers him a drink. Boyd knocks it away. "I quit. I keep seeing Charlie's face bleeding. I saw the bottle and the gun, I'm sick of it, I quit." Lew asks him, "Heard the angel feathers, huh?" Boyd, "I'm sick of fighting. I can't go on." Lew tells him that "There's only one way. With guts, you quit. . . . You just face up to it, alone, and afterward, if the going gets tough and you get that fuzzy taste under the tongue, call me and I'll come runin." The film also uses the device of testing the alcoholic's sobriety. Lew doesn't drink when he reads that his Paula is getting married. Calling himself an alcoholic, he states, "There's never a minute I don't want a drink. I could lie under a Niagara of whiskey and guzzel it dry and tomorrow I'd be back in the gutter." When Charlie is killed he enters a bar and orders a drink but puts it down and walks away.

A.A. appears in the dialogue in critical moments. At one point Charlie asks Lew if Boyd has joined A.A. In the film's climax Lennie Carr asks "What'd I do, walk into one of those A.A. meetins?" Earlier, as noted above, Lew's boss says the office looks like a branch of A.A. As Charlie is about to die, he asks Lew, consistent with A.A.'s concept of working with others, "to bring the kid along like I brought you along."

In developing the "Angel Feather" theory of why an alcoholic decides to try and get sober, the film distinguishes another kind of drunk. Lew is describing Boyd and comparing him to the men in his office who have sobered up. "Give me the reformed lush, the ex-dipso lets himself go. Work takes the place of liquor" . . . "Those ex-lushs on the paper—they're different, they wanted to quit. He's [Boyd] a happy drunk, he'd rather be plastered. You've gotta scare 'em, or knock 'em out, or dig a knife into his conscience." The concept of rehabilitating an alcoholic is also used. Julian states, "Your reputation for rehabilitating drunks has caught up with you." Lew, "I don't know how it's done. . . . You never stop paying for the bottle, you pay and you pay and you pay."

Consistent with the film's implicit (and explicit) A.A. position, the causes of Lew's drinking are never addressed, except in the speech quoted above where he explains when and why lushs drink. Boyd's drinking, however, is connected to his relationship to his mother. Paula, doubting that Boyd will stay sober tells Lew: "I've seen Boyd sober before, until his mother gets back from Europe. . . . Its always the same." John Ives appears to echo this theme when he tells Lew, " "He's made it. I've packed Dolly off on a world cruise."

The Critics Read the Film

Critics were not impressed by the fact that the film represented Hollywood's first attempt to present the A.A. point of view. They did not respond favorably to the mixing of genres, i.e., newspaper story, gangster film, social problems/alcoholism film (Cook and Lewington, 1979, p. 78). It was unfavorably compared with *The Lost Weekend*. McCarten (1951, p. 155) observed, after denigrating the film's premise that "the first drink is the depth charge that eventually flounders the lush," that "these glancing remarks might lead you to think that it is as serious a work as *The Lost Weekend*, which, as you know, really got a good grip on the problems of the alcoholic. Unfortunately . . . its virtues are almost hopelessly marinated in good old Hollywood oil." *Time* (1951, pp. 118–19) suggested that the film had "some of the kick of *The Lost Weekend*. But the rest is watered down with flat melodramatics." Crowther (1951, p. 47) complained that "Strong drink is not the only oppression indicated by *Come Fill the Cup*. He praised Cagney's performance, criticized the film's "tedious . . . romance, simplified psychology and tongue-parching temperance talk," and says that Cagney gives Boyd "the treatment prescribed for the alcoholic tribe." The reviewer for *Newsweek* (1951, p. 103) noted that "The lengthy and difficult pattern of decline and fall and rehabilitation is traced in sketchily but with considerable seriousness and clinical persuasion." The same reviewer, noting Lew's place as "the office A.A.," quipped that he "is the self-destructive victim of the bourbonic plague." This reviewer also referred to Lew's "terrifying confinement in an alcoholic ward," while the reviewer for *The New Yorker* (McCarten, 1951, p. 155) spoke of "the horrors of the alcoholic ward." The concluding sentence in the *Time* (1951, p. 119) review sums up the attitude of the American critics, "The film's crude mixture of social problem and underworld formula is epitomized in the climax: a plug-ugly points a gun at Cagney and orders him to take a slug of bourbon."

The film was somewhat better received by British reviewers. Cook and Lewington (1979, p. 78) quote *The Spectator*: "Not as seriously disillusioned as *Lost Weekend* . . . the film . . . makes a sincere attempt to analyze the tragedy of alcoholism, stressing particularly that it is a disease, and that no emotional appeal or sound argument can reach its bearer. A look into the abyss is the only cure." Room (1985, pp. 607) was more critical, arguing that Lew's alcoholism is left unmotivated, while

Boyd's is explained in psychodynamic terms. As if *Cup* and *Weekend* had not been made, in 1954 Hollywood returned with another version of Norman and Esther.

A Star Is Born (1954)

Beyond the difference in casting, and the focus on music and Garland's singing, the 1954 remake differs only slightly from the 1937 original. The grandmother is missing. Esther has no life prior to Hollywood, and she is a singer, not an actress. Except for these changes, the 1937 and 1954 films are virtually the same. However, the 1954 script focuses more attention on Norman's drinking and its effects on Esther. Esther asks Oliver "what is it that makes him want to destroy himself? You've known him longer than anyone else." Oliver replies, "Don't you think I've tried through the years to help him. I don't know." Esther, crying, says, "Well I've got to find the answer. Do you know what it's like to watch someone you love just crumble away bit by bit, day by day in front of your eyes? Love isn't enough. . . . I'm afraid of what's happening to me because sometimes I hate him. I hate his promises to stop, and then the watching and waiting to see it begin again . . . I hate me because I've failed too." Oliver introduces a sense of fatality into the situation, observing (on the night they bring Norman home from jail), that "Twenty years of steady and quiet drinking does something to a man. Long before it showed in his face it showed in his acting. . . . That's why he slipped. . . . It was him . . . there's nothing left. He's just a shell of what he once was. Its gone for good." When Esther shuts herself off from Hollywood, she is confronted by Danny who gives a variation on her grandmother's speech from the 1937 film: "He was a drunk and he loved you and he took enormous pride in one thing in his life. You. Your success. He didn't want to destroy the one thing he had pride in. Now you are destroying it and if you kick it away it is like he never existed." This rephrasing of the altruistic position, as given in 1937, is sufficiently powerful to return Esther to filmmaking and to lead her to reclaim Norman's name as her own. Norman did not die in vain.

The Critics

Movie reviewers, with few exceptions (McCarten, 1954a, p. 145), praised the 1954 remake (Knight, 1954; Hartung, 1954a, pp. 60–61; *Life*, 1954a; Harvey, 1954; *Newsweek*, 1954a), and compared it favorably to the original 1937 hit. The strategy of reading the film as a comment on

62   A Star Is Born

Hollywood, while giving less attention to the drinking problems of Norman Maine, was maintained in the 1957 reviews. The reviewer for *Newsweek* (1954a, p. 86) was typical: "When Fredric March and Janet Gaynor first acted out this story about a movie star who hits the skids while his wife is en route to stardom, it was a fresh way of viewing Hollywood." Knight (1954, p. 28) praised the film for its success in "reproducing Hollywood [with] a high degree of verisimilitude." While the focus on Maine's drinking was slighted, the personal career of Judy Garland was highlighted. Many reviewers made reference to her four year absence from Hollywood, her mental and physical breakdown, and her suicide attempt (see Harvey, 1954, p. 32). One reviewer (Harvey), retitled the film, calling it, after Garland's successful return to films, *A Star Is Reborn*. Judy Garland was the star, in this double sense. Reading the storyline through her career, reviewers like Hartung (1954a, p. 61) noted that "the picture jerks many a tear. . . . It paints this man as a heel . . . but even for her he cannot straighten himself out. She has cause to be bitter and unhappy . . . [this is a] touching story of two people trying to help each other and failing." The reviewer for *The Catholic World* (1954, p. 222) argued that "the suicide at the end . . . is not likely to appeal to Catholics as the inevitable solution to the problems of the principals."

Reading the *Star Is Born* Cycle

Contrary to Roffman and Purdy (1981, p. 257), this series of films through 1954 only partially takes up alcoholism as a serious theme (see also Chapter 6). The underlying structure of the entire cycle is the original myth (falling star meets rising star) fitted to the format of Hollywood looking at itself. But this is a superficial look. Hollywood never points its finger at itself. The films never locate the blame for the falling star's death in Hollywood's own "unreal," "pretend," "make-believe" social structure. The fading star's "alcoholism" is ultimately explained as an individual failing or a failure of will. His failure is compared to the successes of his wife and other stars that are accomplished without a fall into drugs and alcohol. In these ways the cycle places the blame for the star's problems on the star.

The *Star Is Born* films are "women's films." They belong to that variety of women's films that focus on maternal dramas and working women (see Doane, 1987; Haskell, 1973/1987, pp. 153–55). This cycle mixes genre types in terms of narrative mood (comedy, melodrama), visual style (mainstream Hollywood, musicals, comedies), and plot structure (romantic triangles, the price of success, marriage, divorce, remarriage;

on these points see Doane, 1987). They are melodramatic stories, co-written by women (e.g., D. Parker, J. Didion), centering, in part, on superwomen, weak men, women's sacrifices, strengths, choices, the dangers of excessive love and bonding, the power of work, wealth, and fame. With this female subject Hollywood kept its version of female "stardom" alive in the imaginations of young "beautiful" American women. It made "becoming a star" part of the inner fantasies of many young women. In the process it served to further turn the female body into an eroticized, visual text for American men. Women could play parts in everyday life that were like those enacted by their idols on the Hollywood screen (see Blumer, 1933, pp. 30–73). One of those parts was the beautiful woman who loved an alcoholic. But a bitter moral is embedded in this story. A work career is not the means "by which women can find their fulfillment (Harwin and Otto, 1979, p. 47; Rosen, 1973).

Like a myth this series scarcely changes from remake to remake. It functions as a sacred text that cannot be changed, except in minor ways, to fit its contemporary moment (see Herd and Room, 1982, p. 34). As a result it fails to ever totally take up "alcoholism" as a problem in its own right. Yet because real-life "alcoholic" stars, or stars with problems with drugs and alcohol (L. Sherman, J. Garland), were constantly cast in lead roles, the series kept (and keeps) "alcoholism," in its star-like versions, before the public.

The *Star Is Born* cycle is, then, not about a new alcoholic hero called Max Carey or Norman Maine. It is about Esther Blodgett, the strong woman who goes out and gets what she wants in the world of work. But of equal importance, the cycle is about the alcoholic marriage, its place in American society, and the impoverished, but sacred belief that love will cure alcoholism.

Back to the Films: In Search of a Hero

Return to *Lost Weekend* and *Come Fill the Cup*. Unlike *The Lost Weekend*, which single-mindedly kept its focus on the alcoholic's experiences, *Come Fill the Cup* tries to be several things at the same time. In so doing it clearly led reviewers away from one of its central purposes, which was to add the A.A. message to *Lost Weekend's* picture of the alcoholic hero. But by casting Cagney in the role of the hard hitting, two-fisted ex-drinker, the film created a solidly masculine, recovering alcoholic hero who had none of the feminine, artistic characteristics of Don Birnam or Boyd Copeland. Indeed Boyd is Birnam's counterpart. Like Birnam, he is blocked creatively and has troubled relationships with women. All three men have to experience extreme forms of DTs, and Lew, like Don, spends time in an alcoholism ward. However, the ward that he visits is not nearly as terrifying as the one Birnam escaped from, and while there he confronts a kindly physician who explains his condition to him.

The Phases of the Alcoholic's Career

The male alcoholic in the prohibition, preclassic, and classic periods passes, then, through three filmic stages corresponding to the *Star Is Born* cycle, and the radical interventions of *Lost Weekend* and *Come Fill the Cup*. In each stage he is seen as passing through three phases, although the first is typically only implied. He occupies a place of fame, he falls from grace, and then he recaptures grace, through sobriety or death.

In the texts under consideration a struggle over representation is occurring. The *Star Is Born* cycle keeps the lack of will power, non-A.A. nondisease picture in front of the filmgoer. This series, with its easy explanations of alcoholism, provides a convenient point of reference for the radical texts that attempt to present alternative views of the alcoholic's condition (medicine, psychoanalysis, A.A.).

With *Weekend* and *Cup* a clear alcoholic hero has been established, and he comes in two forms: the artist–musician–writer, and the newspaper man, the cynical man among men who can travel in all worlds. This new hero, unlike Max Carey or Norman Maine, does not commit suicide. He is no longer the tragic hero of the *Star Is Born* cycle. He has looked in the eye and come back. He has had a quasi-religious experiences (angel feathers) and experienced a form of hell and death. He now moves through the world as an ex-drunk who writes and tells his story for others, so that they can come back, like he has. This new hero, though, like Max, Norman, and John, inflicts his pain on the working woman in his life. But his woman, especially Helen, unlike Esther, grasps more deeply the nature of his disease, and stands by him as he attempts his recovery.

In these five films Hollywood gave the American movie-going public multiple images of the alcoholic. All of his alcoholic characteristics have been revealed, including denial, self-pity, self-degradation, guilt, obsessive drinking, suicidal tendencies, the experiencing of DTs, trips to sanitariums, wild dreams, broken promises, and repeated failures to stay sober. Pitted against himself, this film alcoholic was both tragic and heroic, at times comic as well. But one thing was certain. He was caught in the throes of something he could not control, and that thing was alcoholism. Neither he nor others could explain why he was the way he was. This mystery haunted reviewers who read the films in terms of their ability or inability to give a final cause to alcoholism.

The introduction of the disease concept transforms the alcoholic. A.A.'s alcoholic is a hero, a person who has hit bottom and comes back up again. His transformation changes the woman in his life. His struggle challenges her to not abandon him as she rises to new levels of endurance and pain. Yet she is a necessary part of his recovery. By turning her back on him, she opens the door for him to sink ever deeper into his alcoholism. But his move is not without cost, for her love will not ever let her fully leave him. She cannot leave something she has started. She is part of the cycle that both defines his alcoholism and his recovery. Her presence at both ends of this process signals just how important she is. His loss of her is the human cost he must pay for his disease. Despite her importance, it is clear that she finds fullest self-realization through her identification with this male alcoholic figure. Her place in his life is more important than the fulfillment she finds in her work. Just the opposite holds for the male, for his fulfillment comes from work.

But in the Lew Marsh story it is not what she does that sees him through the worst moments of his alcoholism. It is another alcoholic, one who has gone through the experience before. So in creating the new version of the alcoholic hero, *Come Fill the Cup* changes the hero's relationship to the woman he loves. In the process it changes the hero, for in the *Lost Weekend* he had to endure DTs on his own, without the interpretive help of another who had been there before. Birnam had Helen's love, but not an understanding born from the experience. Lew had Charlie and Boyd had Lew. This is the twist *Come Fill the Cup* adds to the alcoholic's filmic situation and it is a twist that is straight out of A.A.

Five movies, then, separated by a space of 22 years, connected by parallel scenes, each focused, in its way, on an alcoholic and his drinking, on violence, guns, and tortured alcoholic faces reflected in mirrors, suicides, deaths, and the participation of family members and friends in the alcoholic drinking act. In this short time span significant changes in Hollywood's version of the male alcoholic can be observed.

By 1951 he has a disease called alcoholism, which is like diabetes. It is a disease that can be cured only through abstinence and the help of persons who are themselves recovering alcoholics. Psychiatrists are of no help. Alcoholics Anonymous is the answer. Twelve years after A.A. appeared on the national scene (A.A., 1939), and 10 years after Jack Alexander's article on A.A. was published in the *Saturday Evening Post*, the movement appears in a major Hollywood film featuring a major star. The alcoholic hero will never be the same again. Causes of his illness are now rendered, at least partially moot, although, as I will show in later chapters, Hollywood (and the critics) will not give up in their search for a cause of alcoholism, or their infatuation with the *Star Is Born* myth. (Norman Maine will not die.) Still, his disease and its cure remain gendered productions for they seemingly require the love and commitments of a good woman. Directly and indirectly she gets him to A.A. and this organization then does the work she could not do.

A.A. changes the temperance melodrama as the format for presenting the alcoholic's story. It inserts all of the above features into a new text, while still retaining the picture of an alcoholic hero as one who struggles against himself to overcome a compulsion that threatens to kill him. But this new text retains its hold on the past by not letting go of the presence of a loving woman who struggles to find her place in his obsession. She is yet to be seen as a sick person suffering from a familied version of his alcoholism. This will come later. An explanation for why this person is perpetually unhappy is now given. Alcoholism is both the cause of and the signifier of anhedonia. This cause and signifier disrupt the alcoholic's Oedipal relations with others.

In the next chapter I take up the problem of the alcoholic woman, and examine how Hollywood attempted to make her a heroine. Whether the female alcoholic finds a male who stands by her, like she stood by him, when he was the alcoholic, is a major question I shall address.

Notes

1.   Roffman and Purdy (1981, p. 257) suggest that "only with Prohibition a major issue in the 1932 elections did the movies take up the issue of alcoholism." They cite *The Struggle* (1931) and *Wet Parade* (1932) but not *What Price Hollywood* (1932) to support their conclusion. Room (1984, 1985) suggests that the "wet generations . . . coming of age during and after the First World War" was another factor that led to the focus on alcoholism movies in this time period.

2.   Films marked with an asterisk focus on a female alcoholic.

3.   The musical sound track is so effective, especially in this scene, that in one alcoholism treatment center I studied (Denzin, 1987b), detoxification counselors would not show the film to residents because the "music makes them so upset."

4.   See Doane (1987, p. 47, and the discussion in the next chapter) on the significance of flashback scenes in psychoanalytically influenced films. It may be argued that Don's cure is at last partially accomplished in this extended flashback sequence for he sees and relives his alcoholic past and sees how his drinking has destroyed his ability to write his great novel.

5.   It quickly became a box office success and was one of the top 20 money-makers in 1945. This success opened the door for other scripts dealing with alcoholism. The reviewer for *Atlantic* (Kahn, 1946, p. 140) reported that "Literary agents with a 'drunk story' are plied with aromatic perfectos . . . one film company has already pinned down the title *Alcoholics Anonymous* from the organization of that name, for the bargain price of $50,000. Twelve years later, a film reviewer for *The New Yorker* (McCarten, 1958, p. 91) would call *Too Much, Too Soon,* and *I'll Cry Tomorrow* "lush films," noting that such movies had become popular since "Wrestling with John Barleycorn . . . became a popular Hollywood sport when the excellent film *The Lost Weekend* proved a box-office dandy."

6. Roffman and Purdy (1981, p. 258) explain the happy ending in terms of studio insistence. "Studio head Buddy Da Silva told . . . Wilder 'if the drunk wasn't an extremely attractive man, who apart from being a drunk could have been a hell of a nice guy and wanted to be saved, the audience wouldn't go for it.' " They note that "Paramount had been reluctant to make the film in the first place, afraid that it wasn't commercial enough and sensitive to pressure from liquor interests and Prohibition groups."

7. As if in response to this interpretation of the film, Seagrams, "the second largest whiskey company in the U.S. . . . bought huge six column advertisements in the country's leading newspapers urging everyone to go see the picture . . . at the bottom of the page, they added. . . . "Some men should not drink" (Wood, 1970, p. 92).

8. This is A.A.'s allergy theory of alcoholism: "action of alcohol on . . . chronic alcoholics is a manifestation of an allergy. . . . These allergic types can never safely use alcohol in any form at all" (A.A., 1939, 1955, 1976, p. xvi). In this move A.A. eschews any solution concerning the cause of alcoholism, it simply argues that certain drinkers have this allergy.

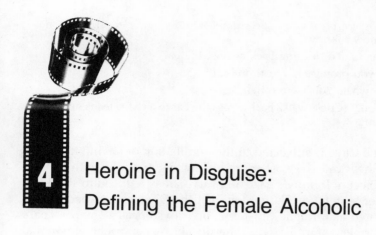

4 Heroine in Disguise: Defining the Female Alcoholic

"It's a story of degradation and shame."

(Ralph Edwards introducing Lillian Roth
to the "This is Your Life" TV audience)

Consider the following dialogue from the 1948 film *Key Largo*. Haskell (1973/1987, p. 206) regards it as "one of the most degrading scenes [for women] in cinema." Gaye walks uneasily down a staircase to the bar of the small hotel where Johnny, Frank, Nora, and James are all seated or standing. She goes to the bar, with shaking hands pours herself a drink, grasping the glass with both hands, she raises the drink to her mouth.

Johnny: "Hey, didn't I tell you no drinkin."

Gaye (to Johnny's reflection in the mirror): "Oh please honey, just one."

Johnny: "One thing I can't stand is a dame that's drunk. I mean they turn my stomach. They're no good to themselves or anyone else. She's got the shakes, see, so she has a drink to get rid of em. That one tastes so good so she has another one. First thing you know she's stinko again."

Gaye (wringing her hands): "You gave me my first drink Johnny."

Johnny: "Everybody has their first drink . . . but everybody ain't a lush . . . why ain't you a singin star instead of a lush? . . . You sing us your song, you can have a drink."

Gaye: "Can I have the drink first?"

Johnny: "No, the song, then the drink."

Gaye (singing): "Moanin low, my sweet man, I love him so, but he's as mean as can be . . . he's the kind of man needs a woman like me. Don't know any reason why he treats me so poorly. What have I gone and

69

done?" . . . voice breaks . . . she stumbles to the bar, pleads: "Give me
that drink now Johnny."
Johnny (arms folded, leaning back against the bar): "No."
Gaye: "But you promised, you promised."
Johnny: "So what. You were rotten."
Gaye: "No, no." (Cries, walks back across the bar to a chair, leans head on
arms, sobbing).

In this scene Gaye is subjected to the humiliation of having to sing to
get a drink. She is called a washed up lush who gets stinko with the first
drink. The object of Johnny's gaze and fury, she is reduced to slave-like
status in order to get a drink that will halt the DTs she is experiencing.
She is presented as a fragile, unstable, quasihysterical woman. A bare
shell of her former self, puffy-faced, hardly able to control her emotions,
she is no longer sexually attractive. Yet she identifies herself through her
man, Johnny, and asks why does "he treat me so poorly"? She has lost
everything to her alcoholism: her looks, her voice, her class, and her
man.

The performance Johnny forces on her only underscores the depth to
which she has fallen. In her halting song, with its poignant, questioning
lines, she emerges as an object of morbid fixation and obsession for the
spectators in the room, especially Johnny, who appears to find great
erotic and sadistic pleasure in witnessing her degradation (see Mulvey,
1977 and Doane, 1987, p. 5 on male spectatorial desires and the gaze).
Her "alcoholism" is used to turn her into a doubly disgraced object:
a woman who is a drunk. Cast in this identity, her inferior status of
woman is further degraded by her disease of alcoholism.

The Moral Career of the Female Alcoholic

The male alcoholic, as noted in the last chapter, underwent three
filmic transformations from the Prohibition through the classic periods.
In each moment his career was divided into three phases: seduction,
fall, redemption. A victim of unresolved Oedipal conflicts, unable to
form bonds with women, perpetually unhappy, this figure sought solace in alcohol. His heroic characteristics (bravery, self-sacrifice, extreme
suffering, death) arose out of struggles with himself. This meant that he
confronted himself in a moment of crisis, heard "angel feathers," and
made a decision to turn his life around. The resolution of this crisis then
opened the door for the hero to reenter society. He did this, either
symbolically, through altruistic suicide, or interactionally, by helping
others overcome their alcoholic condition. In his *Come Fill the Cup* ver-

sion this hero becomes a two-fisted fighter, a classic version of the cowboy set down in the streets of Chicago. By 1951 this hero had also found A.A.

The female alcoholic does not follow this path. She does not become a crime fighter (although Gaye does steal the gun that kills Johnny!). She does not give her life to save others. She does not go through the same filmic phases as her male counterpart. There is not a *Star Is Born* cycle for women, although 4 of the 12 women's alcoholism films made between 1946 and 1962 were biographies of female stars (see titles below) while only 3 of the 16 films during this period dealt with male stars (Bix Beiderbecke, *Young Man With a Horn, The Buster Keaton Story, Beloved Infidel*). Her filmic cycle is shortened. She passes through two interpretive stages, marked first by psychoanalysis and then by A.A. Although the stages of seduction, fall, and redemption are also applied to her moral career, her heroine-like qualities are sexually coded. Her fall is directly related to the violent sexual troubles her alcoholism creates. This connection between sexuality and heroism does not occur for the male alcoholic.

The Feminization of Alcoholism: Can She be a Heroine?

When the figure of a woman enters the "alcoholism film" her femininity exaggerates the pathological dimensions of the disease, for as Foucault (1973, p. 4) and Doane (1987, p. 38) observe, femininity and the pathological are coded together in patriarchal culture. Since the 1940s women alcoholics have been presented in negative terms (Harwin and Otto, 1979; Herd, 1986; Room, 1985). A woman in the male alcoholic's space is inserted into an already contaminated place that is made even worse by the stereotypes her culture has about drunken, sexually loose women (see Gomberg, 1982, pp. 345–46; Ediger, 1989). The male alcoholic in the early modern films simply got drunk. His female counterpart in the 1940s and 1950s gets drunk and sexual. Sexuality and alcoholism were negatively joined in the female alcoholic film.

Within two years of *Lost Weekend*, the female alcoholic would emerge in the Hollywood alcoholism film and take her place alongside the alcoholic hero.[1] She would appear as Angie, in *Smash-Up: The Story of a Woman*, a film called by critics, *"The Lost Weekend of a Lady"* (Crowther, 1947, p. 31). Between the years 1946 and 1962, at least 13 movies centering on a female alcoholic were produced.[2] In all but three of these films she was either a playgirl (*Notorious*) or an actress, singer or entertainer, occupations typically reserved for "tainted" women who had turned their back on their proper place in the family.

These women would all be presented as being unhappy, lonely, restless, dependent on others, in constant need of approval, often from parents. They would perceive their lives as not being their own, feeling that they were misfits in the careers others had created for them. They had professional careers, but experienced conflicts between work and family. While receiving public acclaim for their accomplishments, they would be presented as seeking personal fulfillment in marriage. Alcohol would help in their attempt to resolve this conflict between their public and private lives (see Harwin and Otto, 1979, pp. 38–39). Their alcoholism would be seen as being caused by this conflict between external pressures and internal needs and desires to be married women (see Herd, 1986, p. 242; Harwin and Otto, 1979, p. 38).

These films had the characteristics of "woman's affliction or medical films" (see Haskell, 1973/1987, pp. 163–64; Doane, 1987, Chapter 1). But to the classic woman's affliction film the ingredient of alcoholism was added. They centered on woman, the disease of alcoholism, and the various attempts of friends, lovers, parents, psychiatrists, and doctors to cure the illness. This feminization of alcoholism served to create a subgenre within "woman's films," which would also extend to all alcoholism films; that is, this cycle of films feminized male alcoholism. [They took the culturally created feminine characteristics of passivity, neurosis, weakness, and dependence and applied them to the male alcoholic. The degradation of female alcoholics spread to the degradation of the illness for males. Woman became the cultural metaphor for alcoholic (see Herd, 1986, p. 232).]

The Woman's Cure

This sexualization of alcoholism opened the door for the psychoanalytic treatment of the illness. This corresponded with the period (1940–1950) of Hollywood's most intense involvement with psychoanalysis and the incorporation of psychologists and psychoanalysts into film scripts (see Doane, 1987, p. 45; Schneider, 1977; Kubie, 1947; Fearing, 1947). Women alcoholics would be presented as losing their neurotic preoccupations with appearance (narcissism). Early childhood fixations on mothering and fathering figures would be stressed, as would the need for domination by a strong male (see Doane, 1987, p. 41). The other symptoms of her illness, including emotionalism, masochism, hysteria, and a deterioration in appearance, would deprive her of the status of an attractive, beautiful woman. The trajectory of her illness would leave its traces on her body, which in its decline would be less sexually desirable. Her sexual passions would also be read as markers of her disease, which might be called a disease of "nerves." These symptoms would become the measure of her illness, and symbolize a version of feminine pathology (see Doane, 1987, p. 176). Her illness would amplify all of the undesirable aspects of femininity in a punitive, moralistic way (see Doane, 1987, p. 62).

The cure for her disease would typically be produced only by a male, either a psychologist, a psychiatrist, or a "neutral" male in A.A. Her subjectivity, taken away by her alcoholism, would be given back in the cure that was guided by a man. The physician–psychoanalyst would be given the power of vision that would penetrate the inner psychic life of the female alcoholic. His medical gaze would transform the woman into a new, attractive, erotic object. His talking cure would offer another narrative version of her life story. In these respects psychoanalysis validated the gender stratification system that was already in place when the female alcoholic became a filmic topic (see Doane, 1987, p. 46).

Cinematically, many of these films employed the "flashback" technique as a way of taking the woman back to a past that caused her alcoholism. In the "mise en scene of memory" (Doane, 1987, p. 47), self and scene are matched and the causes of her illness are discovered. In this way the women's alcoholism films give priority to the immediacy of vision. It "is not the speech between psychoanalyst and patient which acts as the medium of recovery. Rather, through *seeing* her past (and presumably reliving it . . .) the patient understands herself" (Doane, 1987, p. 47). (This technique, as argued in the last chapter, was also employed in the *Lost Weekend*, for Don's long flashback sequence enabled him to relive his alcoholic past and his alcoholic relationship to Helen and his writing.) By utilizing this technique these films bring elements of tragic heroism (self confronting self) to the female alcoholic. Unlike the male (who may see these things himself) her moment of recognition must be mediated by an "other."

Two Ways of Being Heroic

Whereas alcoholism, for the male alcoholic, was seen as creating the conditions for a tragic, but heroic figure, it operated in just the opposite way for women. Alcoholism, for the alcoholic hero, appeared to symbolize defeat, but it carried few implications of flawed, or negative sexuality. The alcoholic woman, on the other hand, is represented as promiscuous, and sexually aggressive. She becomes a heroine only through the resolution of her problem drinking and her relocation back in the family. She leaves public life behind, for that world was one of the causes of her alcoholism. The male overcomes the self-indulgence of alcoholism on his way to becoming a hero and doing things in public places, in the service of the larger society. The female must overcome her sexuality and her alcoholism before she can be a heroine. Once sober, she can return home to care for herself and her family.

In this chapter I explore these themes, giving primary attention to two films, *Smash-Up: The Story of a Woman*, and *I'll Cry Tomorrow* (1955). The first of these two films offers a psychoanalytic–medical treatment for alcoholism, while the second presents A.A. as the solution to the alcoholic woman's situation.

Smash-Up: The Story of a Woman

Smash-Up is the second modern (1945–1962 period) alcoholism film, and the second to have A.A. involvement.[3] It repeats the medical view of alcoholism given in *Lost Weekend*, while introducing a psychiatrist who seemingly offers the cure for the illness. The film begins at the end of its story, with a scene set in a hospital room. Angie, face covered with bandages, mumbles to her husband, doctor, and nurse, "I have to call in two minutes. I need a drink, I need a drink." It then flashes back to the beginning of its story, to a bartender in a nightclub ("The Elbow Room") pouring two shots of whiskey in a glass that are taken on a tray to Angie, who drinks them just before she goes on stage. The camera lingers on her face as she tips the glass to her mouth.

Against the advice of her agent, Mike, Angie Evans (Conway), a promising nightclub singer, gives up her career for marriage ("girls do get married"), to Ken Conway, a fledgling singer and song writer. Ken's career as the "singing cowhand" quickly takes off. They buy a country home outside New York City. Angie has a baby (Angelica). She finds that while earlier she needed a double before performing, she now needs several drinks to deal both with the fear of meeting people in social situations and the frustrations and boredom of being a lonely housewife with nothing to do. As her drinking increases, the marriage deteriorates. She believes that Ken is having an affair with his secretary, Martha. On several key occasions she gets drunk at the wrong time, embarrasses Ken, and in one violent scene has a fight with Martha.

After one of her drunken scenes Ken consults with Dr. Lorenz, complaining that he can't keep Angie "off the stuff." Lorenz tells him that "you could have, before she ever got to this stage." He then goes on to observe that men like Ken, "with all the best intentions in the world, make their wives idle and useless" and by giving Angie everything she wants he "has taken all responsibility away from her [and] left her life with no values. . . . She has turned to this" [alcohol]. Then he tells Ken she has a disease: "Your wife is the victim of a disease [alcoholism] and there is only one cure. That is to give up liquor entirely. They are like diabetics who have to reject sugar and take insulin. Alcoholics must give up alcohol, live without it. . . . She may not be ready yet. She will never be ready until she faces her illness and she herself wants to change." Ken files for divorce and custody of their child, claiming that her drinking makes her an incompetent mother.

Following an evening of solitary drinking in bars, where she is nearly picked up, she wakes up naked and hungover in a cheap apartment. While drinking a shot of whiskey, offered her by the wife of the man in the apartment, she sees young children playing outside in a school yard, and resolves to get her daughter. She takes Angelica to the country. Drinking heavily, she passes out, sets the house on fire, and nearly kills the two of them. Rushed to a hospital, she and Angelica are saved. Days later, Dr. Lorenz, who has a classic "middle-European psychoanalytic demeanor" (Room, 1985, p. 8), tells Ken: "Her entire world was built around you. She thought she had lost you . . . to Martha . . . she made it up to justify her drinking . . . in her private world, to which she retreated with the bottle . . . there she could imagine and justify every-thing."

In the closing dialogue of the film, after Dr. Lorenz has left the room, Angie, in classic A.A. (A.A. 1939/1976, p. 315) language, speaks to Ken: "I've gotta tell you something. It had to happen the way it did. I needed to hit rock bottom before I could change. Now I'm not going to be afraid again. We're going to have a wonderful life together darling."

The Markers, Causes, and Consequences of Alcoholism

From its opening to final scene *Smash-Up* is bounded by the markers of alcoholism. There are close-ups of Angie drinking double shots, taking secret drinks from bottles hidden in the cupboard and the closet. She gives speeches about getting high tonight, extols the virtues of "old fashioneds," and explains how drinks give her self-confidence (her favorite, a stone fence, "puts poise in apathetic people, after the second your spine turns to solid platinum"). She is shown having blackouts, drinking before parties, and stumbling as she walks. Her drunken, slurred speech at parties is emphasized. Her growing preoccupation with alcohol and loss of control over drinking serve to define her as a problem drinker in the eyes of others, including her husband, her doctor, or former manager, and her husband's best friend, Steve. This definition of who she is overrides her other identities, including wife and mother.

The consequences of her alcoholism deprive her of these valued identities and nearly kill her, yet these consequences function to create the conditions for her final recognition of her disease. Consistent with Lorenz's theory that she will not change her drinking until she faces her illness and wants to change, the narrative takes her to the slum apartment, and through the fire.

The Scene of Recovery

The cure for Angie's alcoholism is located in the fire and in her drunken dream, which is shattered by Angelica's screams. This dream records the significant moments in Angie's life, in which scenes from her marriage flash through her mind. The events move from the recent present to the past, and include her fight with Ken when he tells her he has had enough, her fight with Martha, her telling Ken, just after Angelica is born, that "it will be like this forever," Ken singing to Angelica in the nursey, and her telling Ken that she is pregnant. This dream erupts into the present, with Angie pulling Angelica out of bed, running through the fire and out of the house, with the house going up in flames in the background. The next sequence takes the viewer to the flashback that opened the movie, with Angie lying in the hospital bed, crying "My baby, My baby."

In these moments of degradation and near death she faces the bottom she has fallen to. In her final flashback a merger of her alcoholic self and her destiny is revealed. From this scene emerges the last lines she speaks in the film. Her disease led her to hit rock bottom. Angie's cure was given in the fire.

Causes

The causes of her illness–disease are threefold. The first is occupational and relational. The film says that husbands who give their wives everything deprive them of responsibility and create the conditions for boredom and low self-worth (e.g., when told that he must give Angie more responsibility Ken allows her to have a cocktail party). At one point Angie states, "Did you ever sit day after day, night after night staring at your hands? I have. So you take a little drink . . . there's something creative about pouring a drink." After Ken files for divorce[4] and locks Angie out of the apartment she attempts a comeback as a nightclub singer, taking back her maiden name. Yet she is unable to remain sober, even as she struggles to prove that she is a worthy mother. Indeed, her only periods of continuous sobriety occur when her place in the family is unthreatened, and when she is able to perform maternal duties associated with either helping Ken in his career or caring for Angelica. The clear implication is that Ken and the institution of marriage caused Angie's alcoholism. The film entices the viewer into believing that had she not left her career she would have not become alcoholic. But this interpretation is incomplete because Angie was drinking alcoholically before she married Ken.

The second cause of her alcoholism is never explained. Angie lacks self-confidence and is afraid of people. When asked by her housekeeper (Mary) why she is taking a drink before meeting Ken at a party she replies, "You know when I used to sing in nightclubs, I was so blamed scared I had to have two drinks even before I would go on." (Mary: "What were you scared of?"). "I don't know, just people I guess."

The film employs the dream sequence as a method of revealing Angie's inner fears. The following dialogue occurs in the first such sequence. Angie has gotten drunk at a cocktail party. She is asleep in her bed. Angie: "If I have another drink I won't be frightened or shy." A female voice intrudes into the dream "Oh she's a nice little thing, really. But you know radio. Full of big stars like Ken, and the women they happen to marry before they were successful." Angie: "Would you like to see my baby?" Mike's voice is next heard: "Do you think you can hold him just because you have a baby?" Angie: "Oh, I'm trying so hard. If I could just get some self-confidence. Yes another drink, just one more." Mike challenges her: "Insidious, isn't it?" Angie: "You know maybe I could work with him." Then Ken's voice is heard: "I want my wife to have every good thing that there is." Angie counters: "That's the thing darling. Of course there's no sense in it when you can give me everything, but I'm, afraid Ken, I'm afraid. Ken. Help me. Help me. Please help me. KEN." (She rises up out of bed, screaming.)

Ken wakes up: "Angie, what's a matter darling? You just had a bad dream. I'm right here with you. Maybe if you had a few less when you drink. I'd have nightmares too if I drank as much as you do." Angie: "I don't know what happened to me. I begin to feel so inadequate somehow and I need courage and it gives it to me." Ken: "But that's so foolish." Angie: "Oh darling, if I could feel it was still us. You and me together. That you need me, the way you did when you were first starting. If we could go away for a little while. A weekend even." Ken: "We will darling. Any weekend you say." Angie: "This Friday then, just you and me and the baby. Just anywhere, I don't care." Ken: "This Friday I've got that benefit. Martha' got a million things lined up for me to do." Angie: "Then how about next week?" Ken: "Next week. We will darling, just as soon as possible."

This dream and its subsequent spillover into the waking world illustrate Angie's belief that alcohol fuels her self-confidence. Her diminished status as the wife of a radio entertainer, and her attempt to define who she is through her baby are also revealed. Mike's remark hints at the insidious nature of her "drinking disease," while Ken's inability to schedule a free weekend reveals how his job has taken precedence over their marriage. His comment about Martha also suggests, contrary to Lorenz's position, that Martha is not a figment of Angie's imagination.

Still, the lack of self-confidence explanation of her alcoholism leaves the original source of her fear unaddressed. It offers situational–relational interpretations of her current situation, indicating that she has no place in the marriage. Nor does this position account for the fear's absence at the end of the film.

The third cause of her illness is given in Dr. Lorenz's disease interpretation of her condition. He tells Ken that she has passed the stage where she can control her drinking. As suggested above, she was barely in this phase when the film began. What moved her to the loss of control stage is never directly addressed,[5] although the film's narrative offers the housewife-boredom theory, coupled with her fear of people as its partial explanations of this change in her drinking career.

The following exchange occurs when Angie is told by Dr. Lorenz that she is an alcoholic. *Dr.*: "There are people who even drink in the morning. . . . Your husband is extremely disturbed about you." *Angie*: "So I take a drink once in a while. What of it? Does that make me a lush or something?" *Dr.*: "There are a lot of people who drink to excess. They are not a [alcoholic], they are just sick." *Angie*: "He [Ken] had no right to tell you." *Dr.*: "He had every right. Because he loves you. But only you can help yourself in the final analysis Mrs. Conway. By facing what's happened, and resolving to conquer it." *Angie*: "You're just as sanctimonious as he is. It's my business what I do. I don't hurt anybody but myself." *Dr.*: "How about your husband and your child?" *Angie*: "And I thought you were my friend. If you don't mind Dr. Lorenz, will you please excuse me?" She exits to her bedroom and gets a hidden bottle of whiskey.

Alcoholism as It

The "it" that must be faced and conquered is left ambiguous by the doctor, although it is clear by the doctor's demeanor that he knows what the "it" is, even if she is unwilling to confront it. He gives her no leads concerning how this conquering might occur. However, by flagging morning drinking as an indicator of the illness, a symptom Angie will later exhibit, he gives her an out concerning whether or not she has this illness. In the same breath she can flaunt the negative label of "lush" and claim that she is neither a lush nor an alcoholic. But Lorenz will not let up. He insists on calling attention to the damage she is doing to her husband and child. At this point she exits the room and has a quick drink from a hidden bottle, confirming the accuracy of Lorenz's observations for the viewer. In this way the film aligns the viewer with the medical–psychiatric position exemplified by the doctor.

The Critics

All critics compared the film to *Lost Weekend*, usually unfavorably. Crowther (1947) stated that *The Lost Weekend* was a "hard and plausible binge, while the current booze drama . . . is soggy and full of . . . corn. It has much more resemblance to *The Drunkard* [1909] of ancient memory than to the best film of 1945. . . . All it lacks to make it an outright melodrama is a pair of swinging doors . . . it studiously appeals to the sympathies of ladies" (1947, p. 31). Crowther also compared the film to a radio daytime serial. He lamented its inability to tell another version of *The Star Is Born* story, for here the woman's star falls while the males rises. The reviewer for *Newsweek* (1947, p. 95) called it the distaff version of "Lost Weekend" and "a psychological phony . . . nevertheless [it] reveals a glimmer of understanding about its serious theme [which is] hidden under a bushel of corn." McCarten (1947, p. 44) wrote that "the lady drunk in 'Smash-Up' is absolutely intolerable." *Variety* (1947, p. 12) suggested that it was a "highly interesting and capable job" and "Susan Hayward gets her biggest break to date." O'Hara (1947, p. 39) called it a *"Lost Weekend* with . . . very good schmaltz . . . it might have been a great piece . . . if they hadn't tried to reach every kind of audience." Then he observes, "It succeeds in presenting, often in a very moving way, a problem still considered daring in the movies." But at this point he turns facetious, arguing that "Dipsomania is an issue that touches the lives of more people today than the problems, say, of homicidal mania, or white slavery, or conquering the wasteland."

Busch (1947, p. 79) noted Jellinek's part in the film, and suggested that it "realistically portrays the problems of a shattered marriage and should scare the daylights out of an estimated half-million serious women drinkers in the U.S." He then went on to write a short column called "Lady Tipplers: Suggestions Are Offered for Improving Their Behavior," where he suggested that "drinking in the home [for the lady] . . . poses problems, but at least it does not constitute a public menace." The same reviewer offered a brief discussion of the theories of women and work (they could have been written by Talcott Parsons whose 1950 essays on the American family located women in the home), noting that psychiatrists agree that modern women . . . are emotionally upset." He compares the one school that "says that women are miserable because they . . . have not achieved economic, intellectual and emotional parity with men," to the other school of thought that "says that women . . .

have been advancing in the wrong direction . . . their efforts to achieve parity . . . have merely got them more mixed up than they were in the first place, and they should now go back to cooking, sweeping and attending to their children . . . whatever may the cause of women's difficulties, the cure will be long delayed . . . in the meantime, the milder cases can . . . make themselves less of a burden to the rest of the population" (Busch, 1947, p. 81). The same reviewer then offers a series of sexist tips for the female tippler: "when entering the bar the lady should do so without fanfare, taking a table near the door. While drinking, her articles of personal apparel or adornment should not fall into disarray. If accosted by a gentleman, she should reply graciously. She should not grab other people's fruit, olives or pretzels, and refain from patting dogs. She should leave after half an hour and go home." (Critics felt no need to write such articles about male drinkers in the 1940s.)

The negative reactions to the film seemed to reflect three processes: The film's inability to match up with *Lost Weekend*, its melodramatic plot structure, and its topic, the female alcoholic. Hollywood and A.A. may have been ready for a female alcoholic, but it is not clear if the movie critics were. Reviewers faulted the movie's explanation of Angie's alcoholism. Crowther (1947, p. 4) was representative: "the reason for the lady's dipsomania seems completely arbitrary and contrived." In this gesture reviewers were able to discount the film's message, and relegate it to the category of a tear-jerker woman's film. Roffman and Purdy (1981, p. 259), for example, argue that "The film's feminist viewpoint is lost in the soap opera plot. . . . Ultimately the film is about Susan Hayward wallowing in softly lit, sumptuously designed luxury far removed from Wilder's hard-edged realism."

The fact that reviewers faulted *The Lost Weekend* for its treatment of alcoholism's causes seemed to go unnoticed in the receptions *Smash-Up* received. Only the reviewer for *Commonweal* (Hartung, 1947, p. 38) viewed the film in entirely positive terms: "If Hollywood is to continue making films about alcoholics, let us hope that these pictures continue to show the kind of understanding that prevails in *The Lost Weekend* and the newest addition to the series. . . . *Smash-Up* . . . Susan Hayward succeeds in making us understand what this woman is going through as she resorts to drink to drown her feelings of insecurity and inadequacy."

Reviewers ignored the medical model of alcoholism presented in the film. Few took seriously the film's attempt to address the place of women in postwar American society. (By comparing its text to Wilder's immediate classic, they ensured their own unfavorable interpretation of the film.) This move then supported the refusal to read the movie as a thoroughgoing "feminist" treatment of alcoholism. Reviewers could hide their sexism behind film aesthetics. And that is what they did.

Back to the Film

Despite the reviewer's refusal to take seriously *Smash-Up's* version of the alcoholic heroine, it must be read as a woman's film that was attempting to do for woman alcoholics what *Lost Weekend* did for men. The participation of A.A. advocates in the film's production suggests that its broader aim was to educate American society about the disease of alcoholism. In this respect its choice of a woman alcoholic was doubly strategic. But by creating a woman's story, the film (in the reviewer's eyes) went in too many directions at the same time. It was part alcoholism film, part woman's film, and part melodramatic commentary on marriage, work, and unhappy housewives.

The film's treatment of alcoholism and the female alcoholic heroine go unnoticed in such readings. The very terms that define melodrama, romantic love, music and singing, conflict between men and women, near tragedies, and happy endings, led reviewers to write negative evaluations of the film. But how could a story about a female alcoholic not involve these elements? Female alcoholism, like male alcoholism, is a gendered production. It requires the presence of an "other" who will define the effects of the alcoholic's conduct on the relationship that joins the two persons together. Given the necessary presence of such a relationship, a film's narrative will be trapped within the confines of a love story that goes wrong because of alcoholism. It is impossible for Hollywood not to tell some version of a love story when it takes up the topic of alcoholism.

Smash-Up adds several important ingredients to this story-line. It feminizes alcoholism. It presents an "other" (Ken) who refuses to stand by his alcoholic wife (unlike Helen, Paula, or Esther or Vicki who stood by their alcoholic men). It shows, in line with the *Star Is Born* cycle, that unemployment and being at home are unacceptable alternatives for persons who have once worked. Max and Norman's alcoholism took on deadly overtones when they left the world of stardom and work. The same thing happened to Angie. Reviewers refused to note how this reversal in the work relationship is intimately connected to both male and female alcoholism.

Smash-Up continues the theme of connecting the alcoholic's recovery to the experiencing of tragedy and deep pain. Although Angie never goes through DTs, she is nearly killed by the fire that was produced by her drunkenness. This theme, which is elaborated through the speeches of Dr. Lorenz, argues that recovery begins with discovery. That is the alcoholic will not quit drinking until he or she sees what a mess his or her life has become. *Smash-Up* goes beyond *The Lost Weekend* in the way it medicalizes this position. Like Wilder's film, it leaves the causes of the alcoholism unanalyzed, while also leaving the viewer with the implausible conclusion that this alcoholic, having made this self-discovery, will never drink again.

The film, in a twist on the classic woman's film, has the psychiatrist confront the husband, not the woman. Ken, not Angie, gets the full brunt of the physician's lectures on alcoholism. The film hesitates on this point. Lorenz could have been shown confronting Angie more directly about her alcoholism, but it did not. This apparent hesitation is consistent, however, with the film's commitment to the domination of Angie by males. The film leads the viewer to see Angie's condition through a double male vision: first Ken's and then the doctor's. The text diminishes Angie's struggle and leads to the focus on the problems her condition causes for Ken as father and husband. It remasculinizes her alcoholism and makes it a male, not a woman's problem.

By having Angie fail in her attempt to go back to work, the film states that there is only one place for her and that is at home as mother and wife. On this note the film is quite firm, and it makes Angie pay a high price for her sobriety and her place. Ken's costs are kept to a minimum. And here the film apparently turns back on its feminist principles and makes the woman pay for the male's inability to see that he created the conditions for her problem. But it adds a twist, for it forces Ken to tell the doctor that "I didn't understand when she called for help. I failed her." With this admission the film passes its weak judgment on husbands who give their wives everything and leave them with no responsibilities. Men are still in control.

The film draws back from its feminist principles at the very moment when it could have criticized postwar American society's movement of woman out of the workplace and back to the home (see Doane, 1987, p. 4). It placed the blame on women who could not make the adjustment back to being just housewives.

I'll Cry Tomorrow (1955)

Based on Lillian Roth's[6] best selling autobiography (1954), by the same name, *I'll Cry Tomorrow* is a "true" fictionalized story, a version of which had been earlier told by Ms. Roth on the television show "This Is Your

Life."[7] It is the fourth Hollywood film (preceded by *Come Fill the Cup*, 1951, *Come Back Little Sheba*, 1952, *Something to Live For*, 1952) that directly involves A.A. It is the first woman's alcoholism movie to show actual A.A.'s presence, and the first to show a woman recovering through the efforts of this organization.

The film begins with Lillian as an eight year old, traces her rise as a child and then adult Broadway and movie star, follows the decline of her career, takes her through three marriages, which correspond to her out of control drinking, details her recovery in A.A., and concludes with her appearance on "This Is Your Life." It opens with these lines on the screen, "My life was never my own—It was charted before I was born."

Lillian's Alcoholic Career

Lillian is immediately recognized as a child star. She gets lead roles on Broadway and then enters films. She falls in love with David, an old childhood playmate, who has become an attorney. Soon after their marriage he dies of a mysterious illness. Insecure, restless, mourning David's death, and unable to sleep, Lillian is given a glass of whiskey by her nurse. Alcohol gives her self-confidence and she begins to drink more and more. She meets, and during a drunken weekend, marries her second husband, Wally, a soldier. They spend huge amounts of money, while her income begins to decline. Unwilling to be known as Mr. Lillian Roth, Wally and Lillian divorce. She meets her third husband Tony, a violent, alcoholic con man at a party. He tells her he can control his drinking and proposes that they go on the wagon together. They marry. He goes off the wagon and she follows. He begins beating her and calling her a drunk and a lush. She leaves him in California, returns to New York City, and quickly sinks to skidrow, where she is shown drinking in lower class bars. She and her mother are now living in a cheap apartment. Lillian's mother attempts to control the amount she drinks. Beginning to experience DTs, she takes money from her mother, checks into a cheap apartment, walks to a window, and contemplates jumping. Suddenly a light hits her face, she falls back from the window ledge, passes out on the floor, wakes up, leaves the apartment, and walks to an A.A. office. There she meets Jerry, Selma, and Burt. She tells them her story. They sit with her as she experiences DTs. Burt becomes her sponsor and they fall in love.[8] She becomes involved with the A.A. entertainment committee. The film ends with Burt, Lillian, and her mother walking down the aisle to appear on Ralph Edwards' national television show. Edwards's voice is heard, "It's a story of degradation and shame. . . . This is your life Lillian Roth."

Mother and Daughter

The center of the story is the mother–daughter relationship, a classic double-bind relationship (Bateson, 1972a, pp. 271–278) in which the mother criticizes her child while proclaiming her love for her. The following scene, from the film's opening sequence, displays this relationship. Lillian and Kati have gone to an audition. Lillian did not get the part. Her mother had told her to go introduce herself to the director. After she does this Kati comes up to the director and says, "I can't imagine why she's doing this." The director remarks, out of their presence, "Those stage mothers are all alike." Lillian asks: "Are you a stage mother?" Kati pulls her by the arm, shoves her to the ground, "Don't you ever let me hear you say that again, do you understand. I love you. I didn't mean it. Did I hurt you? Don't cry anymore. You can cry tomorrow."

The mother deprives her daughter of any autonomy, and attempts to make all decisions for her. The better her daughter does, the more the mother criticizes her. Lillian rebels. Before David dies, she tells Kati, "I want to be David's wife. . . . I want to be a real wife, not one who's away on tour. I want to be there when he comes home. If I want to sing, I can do it for my husband and friends. I just want to settle down with David." To this Katie replies, "All this time we've struggled for this [stardom]. You don't turn back. You're a star." When she breaks from her mother, after David's death, this center of control in her life disappears, and is replaced by alcohol, and the next two marriages where she seeks, but does not find, love and acceptance. Having made a claim to be a wife and not a star, she finds that her career continues, in spite of her desires.

The double-bind relationship between mother and daughter finally comes to a climax, just before Lillian finds A.A. Lillian has just come home from skid row. Kati speaks: "Alright it's my fault. I made you become an actress. I've been a bad mother. You had to support me. . . . You don't know at all what I tried to save you from. The kind of freedom I never had. I tried to give to you by making you Lillian Roth."

To this Lillian angrily replies, "So, you admit it. You invented Lillian Roth. So look at me. I'm the looking glass you created to see yourself in (points to self). Alright see yourself now in me. Look at this ugly picture." In this mother–daughter verbal battle the underlying double-bind structure of the relationship is fully revealed and challenged. However, Lillian still remains under her mother's control. Although Kati admits that every word she has spoken is true, Lillian insists on apologizing: "Momma, it's not true. You know how I get when I need a drink. I go out of my mind. Momma, don't cry. It kills me when you cry . . . remember what you used to tell me. Cry tomorrow."

Enter A.A.

The sickness of the mother–daughter relationship exposed, the film must now bring Lillian to A.A. She stumbles into the offices of A.A. There is even the implication that she is divinely directed to their office, for just before she climbs up on the window sill she shouts, "Oh dear God help me." Once inside her life is reinterpreted within the A.A. framework. Burt's talk provides the conditions for Lillian's cure.

The following exchanges between Lillian, Jerry, Selma, and Burt reveal how this occurs. Lillian, with her back to the A.A. door, states, "I, I've gotta talk to someone." Selma: "That's what we're here for. . . . Tell us about it." Lillian, crying, "You see, she started drinking when she was 18 and she never really stopped. I can't stay" (she gets up). Selma: "Oh, stay and talk." Burt: "Want to try to begin, uh?" Lillian: "My story isn't funny. I can't live and I can't die." Burt: "If you wanted to die, you never would have walked through that door." Lillian: "The first drink I can remember. I can't. I can't talk. Nobody'd understand" (gets up out of chair and turns toward doorway). Burt: "We've all been through this ourselves. We understand. It isn't so hard to understand." The interaction shifts to the room where Lillian tried to kill herself. Burt, Selma, and Lillian are present. Lillian begins (sobbing), "Well it looks to everyone like I didn't care. That I was shameless and I didn't care what I did (hands shaking badly). I cared the most when I was the most disgusting. I was trying the hardest. . . . With all my heart I tried."

The next day, sun streaming into the room, Lillian tells Burt, "I tried to kill myself in this room, right at that window, and I couldn't do it. It wasn't fear and that's strange because I've been frightened all my life. But it wasn't fear." Burt: "The will to live." Lillian: "Then why did I come to this? Why." Burt: "Our quarrel with fate. Some of us, mine, all of us, it leads to self-pity, and self-hate, and self-destruction." Lillian: "I don't understand. What do you mean, quarrel with fate?" Burt: "Sure, all alcoholics have one. When I was a kid . . . this polio paid me a visit. After that I hated everybody and everything. I started to drink. Day in year out. Finally you hit the bottom. You die or you fight. You live. I did both in a way. I was lucky enough then to meet these friends who'd been all through it themselves. . . . They help me . . . and I hope we help you the same way" (Lillian wipes tears from her eyes).

Burt's words create a space for Lillian's story. He tells her that she has been no worse than anyone else. He explains her will to live and tells her that A.A. has a place for her. In his talk he functions as a quasipsychiatrist offering a cure for Lillian's illness.[9] He masculinizes A.A.'s message and carries that message, in masculine form, to her. It remains for the film to have a woman tell a story that is like Lillian's. This occurs in the following sequence.

The film moves next to an A.A. meeting where the A.A. message is directed to Lillian, Kati, and Ellen. Burt chairs the meeting. Behind the podium, on the wall, hangs the "Serenity Prayer" ("God grant me the serenity to accept the things I cannot change, the courage to change the things I can, and the wisdom to know the difference"). The large room is filled with men and women in suits, ties, formal dresses, and hats. The American flag is to the side of the podium. Burt: "Good evening. I'm Burt McGuire [audience (Hi Burt)] and I'm an alcoholic. Well tonight's an open meeting. Everybody's welcome. . . . All our members are anonymous. We try to place principles above personalities. Also, some of our members are kind of funny. They didn't use to mind being seen in the best places so drunk they couldn't stand up, but they're still a little bit sensitive about being seen here cold sober [camera cuts to Lillian, her mother, and Ellen]. Each of us once walked through that door for the first time [camera lingers on Lillian's face]. Now those of you who are alcoholics please raise your hand. [Lillian raises her hand]. Thank you."

A man and then a woman speak. The woman wears a dark dress and a dark hat. "I'm Marge Bellney, and I'm [hesitates, looks down at Burt, holds out her hand to him], I still can't say it." Turns to wall, crying. Burt: "Now take it easy. There's no hurry." Marge steps down, stops, "I'm an alcoholic" (applause), smiles. "I started drinking at the age of 14. By the time I was 18 everyone was saying I was a drunk (camera focuses on Lillian, who is looking intently at Marge). What I'm finding out is that without alcohol the world's a beautiful place and I'm seeing it for the first time. I want to thank everyone for helping me" (smiles and sits down to applause).

In these speeches the film takes on the voice of A.A. It informs the viewing audience about A.A.'s principles of anonymity, while presenting middle-class members who have found their own version of skid row. In its gendered presentation of the member's acceptance of alcoholism, the speeches show that A.A. has a place for women as well as men. A.A.'s path to recovery is contrasted to death and insanity (Burt: "We have three choices: A.A., the psycho ward, or the graveyard"). He distinguishes between newcomers and oldtimers, and in his gentle treatment of Marge indicates that it takes time for everybody (especially women?) to admit that they are alcoholic.

By continuing to play off Lillian's face, the camera defines her place as a newcomer, and shows that this kind of talk applies directly to her life story. In aligning the viewer with her, the film moves the audience to accept A.A. just as she does. Having seen her story, the viewer knows that Burt's, Richard's, and Marge's words are true. The film is structured to make the viewer a believer in A.A. It is an A.A. film with a happy ending.

The Critics

The film received mixed reviews. Crowther (1956, p. 18) faulted the film for its failure to explain Roth's alcoholism. He argued that "alcoholism isn't glamorous. It it is ugly and splotched. And to be convincing to the viewer it must be clearly and ruthlessly explained. The one weakness of this picture is its failure to make it seem compulsory that the heroine should take to belting the bottle." The reviewer for *Time* (1956, p. 92) contended that "A drunk . . . is a drunk, and 117 minutes is a very long time to have one around . . . if there is anything more tedious than a lush, it is apt to be a reformed lush." Hatch (1956, p. 78) echoed this complaint, "Drunks are not amusing; they are terrible bores, and Miss Roth was no exception . . . the movie has no suspense and little conflict." The same reviewer faulted the treatment of A.A., complaining about the film's connection between Miss Roth crying out for God's help and her walking into A.A. in the next scene. He wrote, "How much religion the directors of this valuable agency introduce into their therapy is their business, but I am made uncomfortable by this assumption of divine sponsorship."

McCarten (1956, pp. 110–11) contended that the film had more "bathos than pathos." Calling it a study of a *"lost-weekend* lady" he faulted the script because it "never makes her motivations entirely clear . . . [but] when she finally hits bottom, she becomes a truly sympathetic figure." The film critic for *Newsweek* (1956, p. 117) also dwelled on the film's interpretation of Roth's alcoholism, "[it] pokes around, a little too patly, with the sources of her trouble. . . . Summing Up: Ladies section of *The Lost Weekend.*"

Life (1956, pp. 117–18) connected the film to Roth's real-life story, "The story of a comeback, good news anywhere, is a particular favorite in the shaky world of show business and no comeback in recent years has been so spectacular, or so widely publicized, as that of Singer Lillian Roth . . . [it is] the latest and best of Hollywood's recent spate of deglamorized biographies." This theme of the real-life story was also discussed by the critic writing for *America* (1956, p. 487): "The fact that it [the story] is true serves in large measure to suspend audience disbelief and gives it almost automatically an added dimension." The fact that it took two people (Mike Connolly and Gerold Frank) to help Ms. Roth write her true life story goes unnoticed in these comments. This same reviewer (p. 488), building on the true story theme, suggests that the film's strong drama "lies in its ability to increase our understanding of, and compassion for, our less fortunate fellow human beings." [The reviewer for *Library Journal* (1956, p. 360) made a similar case for the film's realism, honesty, and ability to create understanding "of the problems and treatment of alcoholics."] Under this logic if the story had not been true, understanding would presumably not have been built.

In contrast to the above critics who felt that the film left Lillian's alcoholism unmotivated, Hartung (1956, p. 403) argued that "In telling the Lillian Roth story, *I'll Cry Tomorrow* has one great advantage over most movies dealing with people who become victims of drink or dope . . . it makes clear how Lillian got that way." He then goes on to discuss the mother–daughter relationship, her early feelings of being unloved, her insecurities, her sorrow after David's death, and the powerful effect of her mother's injunction to put off the crying until tomorrow. "By the time we see the grown-up Lillian . . . we know that she is ready for the big cry that will follow the first major crisis." Hartung also positively evaluated A.A.'s place in Lillian's recovery, while criticizing the film for not going into greater detail on "the religious themes in Miss Roth's real story."

Barbara Goldsmith (*Woman's Home Companion* 1956, pp. 14–15) was effusive, calling it a "dramatic new movie . . . that will bring new understanding and new hope to women everywhere." Goldsmith used the film as an occasion for writing an essay on female alcoholism. She observed that Lillian,

> was not merely an alcoholic, she was a woman alcoholic. While the ratio of women alcoholics to men is only one in six, recovery for women is both physically and psychologically more difficult . . . our society provides in the home many easy ways to conceal liquor and a place away from the world to recover from the aftereffects . . . the stigma of alcoholism is greater for women than men, giving them stronger feelings of guilt, greater inhibitions in appealing for help. It is hard to find the emotional problems that create women alcoholics. Their reasons do not fall into easily recognizable categories, which makes analysis extremely difficult. Still, Lillian Roth did come back.

This observer fails to note that Lillian Roth was not a housewife.

Harwin and Otto (1979, pp. 39, 41, 42) take Lillian's "My life was never my own" line as evidence to support their general position that women in alcoholism films are presented as not being "autonomous either in their choice of career or continuation of it. Rather they are cast into parts to fulfill the ambitions of others." They suggest that "although outwardly in control [these women] of talent and independence, inwardly remain insecure children motivated by desire to gain parental approval . . . the relationship that Lillian form[s] with [her mother] is . . . pathological" (pp. 39, 41). Roffman and Purdy (1981, p. 259) connect this film, and *Smash-Up* with other alcoholism movies in the 1950s (i.e., *Come Fill the Cup* which "continued to examine dipsomania in terms of personal melodrama."

It remains to consider Ms. Roth's relationship to the film. Reacting to this doubling experience of seeing her life story on the screen, and reliving her relationship to her mother, she vowed "I'm never going to see that picture again. It takes too much out of me" (Roth, 1958, pp. 121–23).

Back to the Film Through the Critics

I'll Cry Tomorrow was tied for fourth as the highest money-making film in 1956. Any interpretation of the movie, including the reactions of the critics, must confront its autobiographical foundations, and the enormous popularity of the book from which it drew. Lillian Roth was a national figure in American popular culture when the film was released. If reviewers had criticized the film's story, they would have been perceived as writing negatively about this cultural figure. No one was completely willing to do this, hence the uniform high praise for Susan Hayward's performance. By reading the film as a biographical account of a real star's life, critics could then place it within a genre called the "deglamorized Hollywood biography" thereby avoiding the hostile, melodramatic reading given *Smash-Up*. Roth's life story was taken more seriously because she was a real person, a real star, a product of Hollywood's glamor world.

By grounding their positive readings in the film's "realistic text" reviewers undercut their earlier aesthetic judgments of *Lost Weekend*, which was only partially biographical. With *I'll Cry Tomorrow* a film's success is judged in terms of its ability to faithfully represent the life of a real person. In this move film ceases to be an art form that reproduces, but departs from the everyday world. But the bringing of realist criteria to the text allowed the reviewers to write favorable (if mixed) accounts of the film's alcoholism content. The film brought the woman alcoholic in through the front door. *Smash-Up* did not do this. The figure of Angie Evans was not strong enough to carry the story of a female alcoholic in postwar American society; Lillian's was.

The realism of the critics kept them attached to the question of what causes alcoholism. As noted above, only two reviewers felt that the film adequately explained why Lillian became an alcoholic. This insistence that a film explain alcoholism (something science has yet to do) gave the reviewer a platform for criticism, and this was the wedge they used when they critically evaluated the movie. This allowed them to avoid its obvious "woman's film" overtones, while praising the star and chastising the director for offering an undermotivated account of her alcoholism. They had it both ways.

Only Hartung (1956, p. 403), who keyed on the film's title, saw adequate causal explanations of Lillian's alcoholism in the movie. Her mother's lesson, that you cry tomorrow, not today, created an invention; a facade-like woman, who could not feel, or show emotion, except on stage. Taught to always smile and keep her emotions inside, Lillian became an emotionally divided self with two lives. Her public life could never measure up to her mother's standards. Deprived of a private life, except for her short-lived love with David, she yearned for a space where she could feel, be felt, and be loved as a person who was not a performer. But she was not permitted to have a private life. Her marriages, after David's death, were all public affairs, lived out in expensive restaurants and night clubs. There was no inner Lillian.

Alcohol fueled her inner life, joined the two parts of her emotionally divided self, and allowed her to mask her inner insecurities. But lacking a person with whom a private life could be lived, she turned more and more to drinking. She became trapped in an addictive cycle of denial and secret drinking. Leaving Tony, no place to go but home, she returns to confront her mother in a penultimate scene where the false foundations of their relationship are brutally exposed. But even in this moment of truth she backs off, for her mother's hold on her is too strong. It even reaches out and touches her from the movie screen when she sees her mother.

Her mother is the only permanent figure in her life. To destroy her would be to destroy herself. But the confrontation with her mother precipitates the final breakdown and turn to A.A. and recovery. This move, however, is mediated by her image of God, who intervenes and takes her to Burt and the A.A. program where she finds unqualified love and acceptance, things her mother had never been able to give her.

The constant "other" in her life, Kati defines Lillian's alcoholism for her. It is she who tells her that she is becoming a drunkard, in the confrontation in the apartment, the day she later experiences DTs in the small cafe. This is the turning point in her relationship to alcohol. Although Wally would complain about her drinking, he did not call her a drunk. By the time she gets to Tony she has internalized the "hopeless drunk" image of herself. He tells her only what she already knows. Her alcoholism thus becomes a symbol of her failure to live up to what her mother wanted for her.

Her trip down the Bowery, in and out of low class bars, merely signifies how far down she has fallen. The self she presents to the men who ask her to sing in the bar is the self of a child, in the ravaged body of a woman in the late stages of alcoholism. The bottom she hits on the Bowery takes her back to the film's opening scene in which she was publicly humiliated by her mother. Her mother created the conditions for her alcoholism. Her drinking became a symbol of her rebellion against Kati, for through drinking she exerted self-control over her life. But the double-bind that Kati had laid could never be escaped. Once the first drink was taken, her daughter was doomed to become an insecure, despondent, guilt-ridden alcoholic.

Although critics were generally kind to the film's treatment of A.A. they ignored the film's final patriarchal solution to Lillian's problem. When she is asked to appear on "This Is Your Life" she goes to Burt and asks him what she should do. She tells him "they want me to come out to California and get up before 40 million people and tell the shameful, disgusting story of my life, and my comeback before I started. . . . I couldn't tell the story of my life. I'd be too ashamed." Burt invokes A.A. in his answer: "Well, if you were sure you'd never slip back again, this might do an awful lot of good. If you ever did slip back, it might do a great deal of harm." [By invoking an altruistic end, do this for the good of A.A., Burt places her in a double-bind. If she refuses she refuses the organization that gave her back her life. If she accepts and slips (drinks) she also lets the organization down. She has no choice.] Lillian presses Burt for advice, and he tells her "This is graduation day. This is your life. Not mine. Not Katis."

She tells her story for A.A. That was Burt's answer, and A.A. gave her the story to tell. In asking for Burt's advice she relinquishes control over her own story. But he had given it to her, so it was his to give. She merely told it. Her words ring true. Her life never was her own, not even in its final telling.[10]

Creating the Alcoholic Heroine

Two films, separated by a span of eight years, *Smash-Up* and *I'll Cry Tomorrow*, create the figure of the female alcoholic in powerful, enduring ways. All of the signifiers that are brought to bear on the characters of Angie and Lillian, including sexual and self-degradation, violence, insecurities and guilt, mother and father fixations, conflicts between professional careers and family, broken marriages, loss of a life story, and cures supplied by males, will be repeated, over and over again, in all future films about the female alcoholic.

These and the other female alcoholism films of this time period brought women out of the closet and gave them a man's disease. They made alcoholism an all-American illness. But the feminization of the affliction carried a double message. Cast inside the format of the "women's movie," these films attempted to bring women back into the home, while they publicized the fact that women got this thing too. The space of the home was shown to be unstable, even while it was controlled by male patriarchy. Angie's story argues that without responsibilities and duties, women will become alcoholics.

But these two stories go even deeper. They suggest that there is no place for the figure of woman in postwar society. If she pursues a professional career at the expense of family she risks alcoholism. If she gives up career for family, she is also in danger. Hence the alcoholic heroine in the modern period is truly tragic. She has no place to go.

This, however, is not the story these films intended to tell. Their intentions, as argued above, were to carry the story that anyone, but especially women, could become an alcoholic and recover with dignity. In telling their recovery stories, these two films repeated the dramatic devices that had worked in the earlier films about male alcoholics. Hence the emphasis on DTs and hitting bottom. What distinguishes the female from the male alcoholism film in this period is the bottom that has to be hit. Women must go farther down than men, before they recover. They must experience fires, and the Bowery, and lose everything, including sexual self-respect.

To get back to the safe place called home women must confront a male who will perform the cure for them, and this cure will masculinize their life story. In this turn, these films keep women under the control of men. They contain the powerful message that drinking is a man's game, and if women attempt to play, they will fail in ways that are far more painful and degrading than those that a man experiences. The female alcoholic heroine is defined, then, solely in male terms. Her heroism arises out of the fact that she has lost and then regained her dignity and her beauty. These are male terms. The patriarchal culture defines the boundaries of female alcoholism. This is the story these films tell. That they give these tales of degradation happy endings attests to the power of myth as it works in Hollywood's dream factory. Women, after all, are here to be protected. When they falter and fall from grace, they will be cared for, and for this they have men to thank.

Notes

1. Actually the 1942 film *The Falcon Takes Over* featured a female alcoholic, and *Notorious* (1946) starred Ingrid Bergman as a problem drinker, although her drinking ceases to be a problem by the film's end. For present purposes I will treat *Smash-Up* as the first modern woman's alcoholism film.
2. She is contained in the film grouping listed on pp. 44–45 of Chapter 3. Herd (1986, p. 231) notes that in the 1920s only 7% of the alcoholic characters were women, by the 1960s 34% were female. Room (1985, p. 9) and Herd (1986) dispute Harwin and Otto's (1979, p. 37) claim "that few films have been made

about women alcoholics." Room observes that of the "32 major characters presented as active alcoholics in . . . films [made between 1945 and 1962] 12 are women. This is . . . an overrepresentation in comparison with the gender distribution of 5½ males to every female alcoholic which was generally accepted for the U.S. at the time."

3. As noted, *Lost Weekend* is the first film to have this involvement. Before production of *Smash-Up* began a "copy of the script was sent to Marty Mann (the first woman to sober up in A.A.) . . . [who] saw this as an excellent opportunity to promote the medical model of drinking . . . [she] went to Hollywood where she spent two weeks coaching Susan Hayward . . . an uncut version of the film was sent to Jellinek at Yale . . . who was enthusiastic about the educational potential of the film and wired his approval" (Johnson, 1973, pp. 282–83). There is some indication that Bill Wilson was also involved in the project (A.A., 1984, pp. 327, 343). As indicated in Chapter 3 *Come Fill the Cup* is the first film to actually mention A.A. while *Come Back, Little Sheba* (1952) will be the first to actually bring A.A., in the form of meetings and sponsors, into its text.

4. Ken is a typical husband in this respect. Eight of ten husbands are likely to divorce their alcoholic wives, while eight of ten wives of alcoholic husbands are likely to stay with their husbands (see Gomberg, 1982, pp. 345–46).

5. This is Jellinek's (1960, 1962, p. 363) third phase of alcoholism. It is preceded by the prodomal phase, which is characterized by blackouts, which Angie also has. The film has located Angie in the crucial phase of alcoholism. No wonder Jellinek was enthusiastic about the film's educational value. It visually represented his theory.

6. Born in 1910, a child star on Broadway at the age of 8, she started drinking at the age of 20 and did not stop until 1946, when, after remembering an article by Marty Mann about how A.A. had saved her life, she stumbled into an A.A. meeting, sobered up, and began a comeback in a second career as a nightclub singer. She had five marriages, was institutionalized several times for her alcoholism, and was also treated by psychiatrists, including the psychoanalyst A.A. Brill. She had earned over one million dollars by the age of 34, but was broke and unemployed when she found A.A. (Roth, 1954, p. 247). The film version of her story omits her conversion to Catholicism. She wrote a second autobiography (1958) that dealt with her life after the film of her life story was made. According to Robertson (1988, p. 81) Roth "became the first of a long line of show business stars to confess her alcoholism and her salvation through A.A." (See Wholey, 1984, for a collection of personal statements by recent Hollywood stars about their alcoholism.)

7. This particular show aired in January of 1953 (Roth, 1954, p. 342). It was so popular it was rebroadcast twice (*Life*, 1956, p. 117). Her book was published in June of 1954, became an immediate bestseller, and was translated into 18 languages, including Braille (Roth, 1958, p. 18). It was pursued by several Hollywood studios. She had given a verbal option to MGM and had requested that Susan Hayward be given the title role. She coached Hayward, who attempted suicide through an overdose of alcohol and sleeping pills during production (Roth, 1958, pp. 118–120). The Hayward–Roth relationship represents a curious case of one performance reproducing another, where the boundaries between theatrical performance and life no longer matter. Hayward became Roth, and Roth became Hayward.

8. A sponsor is a more experienced A.A. member who helps a newcomer get sober in A.A. (see Denzin, 1987a, pp. 181–82). A.A. (A.A. 1976, p. 26) lore

has it that males should not sponsor females. This is because sexuality is seen as possibly interfering with becoming sober. Lillian and Burt break this rule.

9.   Robert Hatch, the reviewer for *The Nation* (1956, p. 78), used the words "revivalist-psychiatrist" to describe Eddie Albert's "brilliant portrayal of the A.A. leader."

10.   Of course there is never a final telling (see Denzin, 1989d, Chapter 4). Lillian recognized this when she published her second autobiography in 1958. In each of her tellings (the original autobiography, Ralph Edward's show, the film, the second autobiography) she is turned into a commodity, a marketable object bought and sold in the commercial marketplaces of American popular culture. Ironically, her stories were the vehicles for her recovery. But in the very moment of telling her life she once more lost control over who she was and who she had become.

Creating the Alcoholic Family

Lola: "Maybe you could take me to a
       movie tonight?"

Doc: "I may be doing some 12-Step
       work tonight."

(Come Back, Little Sheba)

The alcoholic family, that family form defined by the presence of an alcoholic in its midst, is an alcohol-centered social structure (see Denzin, 1987a, pp. 118–19, 1987b, pp. 76–84, 1987c, pp. 11–13; Jackson, 1962; Steinglass and Robertson, 1983). Daily life is organized around the alcoholic's struggles with drinking, drunkenness, and not drinking. Although every alcoholic thus far studied was located in some semblance of a family unit, the effects of his or her alcoholism on the family were not the central topic of the film. Missing in these films was the presence of a domestic life, or a household associated with the alcoholic's family. In keeping with the biases of the biographical, self-control, medical-disease models that organized the scripts of these movies, alcoholism was presented as an individual disease.

Three social realism films made between 1952 and 1962 challenged this myth. *Come Back, Little Sheba* (1952), *The Country Girl* (1954), and *Days of Wine and Roses* (1962) focus solely on the alcoholic family, and conceptualize alcoholism as a family illness. They implicated alcoholics and their spouses in a complex interactional world where double-binds, denial, repressed and negative emotionality, imaginary others, bad faith, and resentment dominate daily, domestic life (see Denzin, 1987a, Chapter 5; Basic, 1989). These films created the modern version of the alcoholic family.

95

Making Alcoholism a Family Problem

The vehicle for bringing the family into the alcoholism film involved a partial shift away from the biography of a blocked writer or musician, or a Hollywood director, or a Hollywood star, to the marriage of an ordinary man to an ordinary woman. By letting go of a star's life story, a space was created for stories about the ordinary mid-century family and its problems. The family became the site where alcoholism's most destructive effects were played out.

In the 1950s the cultural, economic, and social structures of capitalism were creating massive changes in the organization of American work and family life (see Cherlin, 1983, pp. 58–60). The myth of a happy, small town existence was being challenged (see Sinclair, 1964; Bell, 1960; Gusfield, 1963). Women were moving in and out of the labor force in ever greater numbers, although the employed husband and the housewife at home was still the typical pattern. Large-scale, multinational corporations were becoming the work site for men and women (see Mills, 1959).

Psychoanalysis, as noted in the last chapter, was the dominant psychology of the time. Alcoholism was increasingly medicalized and feminized during this period. Freudian themes of neurosis, narcissism, incest, infantile fixations, unresolved Oedipal complexes, and distorted male–female sexual relations are woven into the narratives of these family alcoholism films (see Herd, 1986, pp. 229–31).[1] In them impotent, weak males are married to strong dominant women, or nagging wives henpeck their silent husbands. Heavy, alcoholic drinking reflects the male's defeat (Herd, 1986, pp. 230–31). These marriages are traps (Herd, 1986, p. 231). The only way out is to walk away. These dramas were interior, and claustrophobic, focusing on the alcoholic husband and his wife and their inner struggles (see Herd, 1986, p. 230). Emotionality and sexuality were repressed. Gender, sexuality, alcoholism, and family were thus fused in ways that had not been present in earlier films that focused only on the male or female alcoholic.

The Career of the Alcoholic Family

The alcoholic families that are presented in these films move, or have moved through the stages of denial, adjustment, disorganization, reorganization, and recovery that Jackson (1962, p. 487) has identified (see also Ablon, Ames, and Cunningham, 1984). In none of them is alcoholism completely denied. The members have adjusted to its presence, experienced disorganization because of it, reorganized themselves in the face of it, and attempted some form of recovery. These are recovering alcoholic families (Denzin, 1987c, pp. 12–13) where at least one member is in a recovery group (A.A.), or struggling to get and remain sober. Yet each family is suffering from alcoholism's effects.[2]

The intimate relations that stand at the center of these marriages are shaped by the four structures of experience outlined in Chapter 1: the alcoholic drinking act, the negative effects of sobriety on intimacy, forms of sexuality connected to alcoholic drinking, and the negative emotions connected to the past.

These four structures turn or have turned the marriage into a battle-ground. Love and desire are destroyed, or severely tainted, often replaced by masochism, sadism, indifference, hate, bad faith, and spurious emotionality (on these forms of relating to another see Sartre, 1943/1956, pp. 361–413, and Denzin, 1987a, pp. 118–23). Complex double-binding communication structures emerge (Bateson, 1972a). Schismogenesis, or collective interactional destruction is set in motion (Bateson, 1972b). The partners struggle to control one another's moods and feelings. The members hide behind self-imposed emotional shields that belie an inner fear that they and the relationship are about to explode. Pleasure from the relationship, such as it is, lies in those labile zones of interaction in which no explosion, battle, argument, or fight has occurred.

The temporal structures of the relationship are located in the past. The alcoholic and his or her other struggle with the effects of drinking and being sober are located in the present. This struggle diverts the alcoholic's attention away from the marriage, leaving the other (and the alcoholic) to either dwell in the dreams of the alcoholic past or to seek intimacy elsewhere. The inner life of the relationship turns on external events and experiences, and not on shared experiences the partners have with one another (see Simmel 1950, pp. 126–127, 324). Violence, fear, betrayal, and guilt replace the positive emotions of love and affection. Alcoholic eroticism and sexual desire produce indiscretions, guilt, remorse, and anger. Barriers come up, communication becomes spurious, and sexual intimacy disappears, becomes voyeuristic, or, when it occurs, it does so when the partners are under the influence of alcohol. Sexuality, drinking, and intimacy destructively intertwine. The alcoholic's relapse from sobriety is presented as being caused by the intimate emotions associated with eroticism and sexuality. The marriage, as a consequence, becomes an interactional structure based on madness, indifference, ingratitude, betrayal, indiscretion, masochism, and sadism. This cycle of negative experience may eventually destroy the marriage, or drastically alter it.

Melodrama and Social Realism

The postwar family melodrama became the model for the family alcoholism films of this period (Herd, 1986, p. 229). The traditional love and romance cycle that structured the happy family, fantasy melodramas of the 1940s is now challenged (on these see Haskell, 1987, Chapters 5 and 6; Higham and Greenberg, 1968, Chapters 3 and 4). Social realism has taken over (Ray, 1985, pp. 129–153). Hollywood discovered that there was a market for such films, even though their outlooks were bleak and depressing (Ray, 1985, p. 138). [Hollywood also turned more and more to presold pictures, movies "based on an already successful novel, story [or] Broadway play" (Ray, 1985, p. 131). *Come Back, Little Sheba* and *Country Girl* were successful Broadway plays, and *Days of Wine and Roses* was a highly successful made-for-television production.] There are no happy reunions of lost family members as in a Frank Capra film like *It's a Wonderful Life*. Under this new format a happy ending was drastically redefined. In this respect they have some of the characteristics of "film noir" (see Gifford, 1988; Silver and Ward, 1979; Higham and Greenberg, 1968, pp. 1–5). They have no triumphant heroes or heroines who rise from the ashes of their alcoholic fall to write and tell their life story for others. There are no pictures of collective family units holding hands and marching merrily off into the future. These families are happy if they have just survived. The American dream is not working. Alcoholism and the times have done them in.

Come Back, Little Sheba (1952)

Sheba is a dog, Lola's pet, and she has been gone for a long time. Lola dreams of her return, hence the title of the film. Doc is a married middle-aged recovering alcoholic who attends A.A. meetings every night and does frequent 12-Step work with Ed, his A.A. sponsor. He is coming up on his one year A.A. anniversary. He is a chiropractor. He and his wife (Lola) have a routinized, 20-year-old marriage. They get up in the morning, he fixes his own coffee, they minimally talk, he leaves for work. Lola keeps asking if Sheba will come back, while Doc keeps telling her that dreams are "funny," and that they have to let go of the past. Lola repeatedly appears in a dressing gown, and often sleeps until noon. Her house is seldom tidy.

On the day the story begins Lola rents a room to a young, sexually attractive college art student (Marie), who dates an aggressive young male (Turk), while she is in the process of becoming engaged to a solidly middle-class, respectable young college graduate (Bruce). Marie would have been the age of Doc and Lola's own child who died at birth (leaving

Lola unable to have other children). Both Doc and Lola are sexually intrigued by the young girl and her aggressive boyfriend who models for Marie's drawings. They each spy on the the young couple as they neck and kiss on the living room sofa. Marie arouses Doc sexually, yet he turns away from her.

Marie's presence in the home awakens a semisexual, intimate dancing relationship between Doc and Lola. Prior to this intimate interlude, Lola has led Doc back into their past, talking about their first date, the night they layed together in the grass, and asks him if they did wrong. Doc replies that you "can't deny God or convention." Lola asks him if he is sorry he had to marry her. He tells her that they agreed never to talk about the past. Lola replies that "if the baby had lived everyone would have known" and then states that "you had to give up your studies and support a wife, you would have been a real doctor today." Doc tells her that "what's done is done. We have to forget the past and live in the present . . . besides, when my family died and left me all that money I coulda gone back. We coulda had a nice house, we coulda adopted, since you couldn't have another baby."

Following this interaction, as they are dancing, Lola and Doc are interrupted by Turk and Marie. Doc leaves for an A.A. meeting while Lola goes to bed. Lola reminds Doc that the next night she is having a special dinner for Marie and Bruce. Doc comes home, sees the light on in Lola's room, goes to bed, can't sleep, comes back downstairs, looks at the whiskey bottle in the cupboard, where it has sat for a year, grabs it, slams the cupboard door shut, goes back to bed. Marie and Turk who have stolen back into the house passionately embrace and audibly struggle. The next morning Doc takes the bottle of whiskey out of the kitchen cupboard. He misses the elaborate dinner Lola has planned for Marie and Bruce.

Planning to serve drinks to the young couple, Lola looks for Doc's bottle and finds it missing. She calls Ed and tells him the bottle is gone. Early the next morning Doc comes home drunk. He puts a new bottle back in the cupboard, but is seen by Lola as he tries to sneak upstairs. He asks her for the morning paper. She tells him there is no morning paper. He says, "I must be drunk then." He attacks her with a knife, threatens to kill her, calls her a slut, and tells her she's good for nothing. He asks her where Marie is. "You and Marie are just a couple of sluts. Bruce will probably have to marry her, just like I had to marry you. What are you good for?" He lunges at Lola, throws his mother's china against the wall, and tells Lola to get him a drink. He takes another drink. Lola escapes his grip, calls A.A., and Ed and another A.A. member take him to a hospital where he keeps mumbling "My pretty Lola." On returning home, Lola calls her mother and says "Doc's sick again. Momma, ask

Daddy if I can come home for awhile." Her father refuses to let her come home.

Doc returns home a week later, sober. He embraces Lola, tells her he loves her, asks her forgiveness, and asks that she never leave him. Lola affirms her love for him, fixes him breakfast for the first time in years, and serves him juice. She relates a dream in which Sheba dies. In the dream Marie and Lola are at a football stadium, as big as the Olympics, where Turk is on the field throwing a javelin. But Turk keeps changing and so the manager of the field, Lola's father, throws him out. Doc takes his place and throws the javelin so high it never comes back. She and Doc then take a walk and they pass little Sheba who is dead. Lola tells Doc that "Little Sheba is never coming back, and I'm not gonna call for her anymore." Doc tells her dreams are funny, and that it's good to be home. He smiles serenely at Lola and she at him. Thus ends the film.

Locating Alcoholism

As noted in the last chapter, this is the first film to actually bring A.A. interactions and signifiers into its text. It does this by showing an actual A.A. meeting, where A.A. slogans, prayers (The Serenity Prayer), and birthdays (years of sobriety) are celebrated (Chair: "Good evening folks, I'm an alcoholic, welcome to A.A. Tonight we have four birthday babies"). Around the kitchen table Doc and Lola have discussions about A.A. sponsors and going on 12-Step calls, that is visiting alcoholics who ask for help (Doc: "You help yourself by helping other alcoholics, who are mostly disappointed men, sometimes they are on skidrow"). A.A.'s allergy theory of alcoholism is presented (Lola to the mailman: "Alcoholics can't drink like normal people. They're allergic to it."), as is its principle of anonymity, which is broken by Lola (Lola to mailman: "You know my husband's Alcoholics Anonymous."). The history of alcoholic drinking in Doc and Lola's marriage is presented almost immediately (Lola to Doc: "When I think of how you were, always drinkin and gettin into fights. I was so scared." Lola to mailman: "You should have seen Doc before he gave it up. He was awful. He lost all his patients. . . . You wouldn't believe it now, he's got all his patients back."). When he becomes drunk, his violence is connected, in part, to his drinking, which produces a trip to the locked ward of hospital to dry out. *Come Back, Little Sheba* is an A.A. film, from beginning to end.

The Critics

The film was read through three lenses: Inge's case study of Doc and Lola, the original Broadway production, and Shirley Booth's performance. Kalb (1952, pp. 26–27) stated that Inge shows, "almost as a case history, the heartbreak of little people, the frustration of their wholly conventional lives . . . [the play] has been translated to the screen with fine fidelity." The same reviewer argued that Booth's performance succeeded in conveying the emptiness of her life, "her pathetic dependence on her husband, her romantic visions of the past . . . and the reminders of her slovenliness—the broken bedroom slippers, the formless housedress, the hairbrush on the kitchen table." Doc, the same reviewer noted, is not just a drunk. "Behind the bottle stands a promising medical career blasted when he left medical school."

Time (1952b, p. 66) labeled it "a minor, but moving tragedy on a major theme: the lives of quiet desperation that men lead . . . Inge's play . . . has carefully and faithfully been transferred to the screen." *Newsweek* (1952, p. 64) judged it to be "one of Hollywood's few outstanding movies of the year" and called Booth's performance "Hollywood's best of the year." Crowther (1952, p. 24) called the screen version of Inge's play "as poignant and haunting a drama as was brought forth upon the stage. For this we may . . . be grateful to Burt Lancaster and Shirley Booth, who contribute two sterling performances." Crowther, like other reviewers, focused on the story of "the commonplace, middle-class home of the middle-aged couple . . . [and their] two pathetically cramped and wasted lives. McCarten (1952, pp. 59–60) praised Booth's performance, saying "Her portrait of a loving, not too bright lady driving a sensitive man to drink looks so authentic it is unsettling."

Farber (1952, p. 434) was negative. He argued that the producer failed to make Inge's somewhat "touching and funny play into a movie," while complaining that it had a "crawling pace, crowded with plaintive touches, . . . the only cinematic trait lies in its concentration on trivia." He suggested that its "realism . . . tends to reiterate the twisted sentimentality of left-wing writing that tries to be very sympathetic toward little people while breaking its back to show them as hopelessly vulgar, shallow, and unhappy."

Slight notice was given to A.A.'s or alcoholism's place in the film. (Perhaps such an emphasis would have been box-office poison, for A.A. was still a young organization and had yet to be fully accepted by the American public.) *Newsweek* merely noted that "Doc has managed, however precariously, to stay on the wagon for a year with the help of Alcoholics Anonymous." *Time* avoided all mention of A.A., and merely noted that Doc "is a chiropractor and a reformed drunk." Kalb (1952, p. 27) observed that "a number of important sequences have been added [to the movie]—notably an A.A. meeting." Crowther said that "Philip Ober . . . does a first-rate job as a pillar of Alcoholics Anonymous who is the steady and reliable friend in need. One of the few excursions of the camera away from the home to look in on an A.A. meeting is one of the nicer bits of Americana in the film." McCarten (1952, pp. 59–60) was negative. "There is a representation in the picture of what purports to be a typical meeting of A.A.'s and I must say it struck me more as a tribute to the gregariousness of the human race than as a venture into therapy, the proceedings have a depressing resemblance to a get together in some mission off Mott Street."

By diminishing A.A.'s and alcoholism's presence in the film, critics could avoid their usual questions concerning alcoholism's causes. In turn, this permitted them to treat the A.A. addition to the text as a nice excursion into Americana. But in avoiding Doc's obvious daily struggles with sobriety, they failed to see that this struggle created the underlying currents of discontent and malaise that defined the marriage for the two partners. Doc's alcoholism, like Lola's "Sheba," are symbols of the failure that is stitched into the center of this shared life that is pulling the two of them down into madness and destruction. Indeed Lola's slovenly appearance, and Doc's quiet, emotionless reserve activate these two symbolic structures of meaning and tell the viewer, almost from the opening scene of the film, that this marriage is dead and something out of the past has killed it. That thing is alcoholism and the broken dreams these two will never realize.

No reviewer focused on the film's implicit thesis that alcoholism is a family disease, for their attention was drawn to the performances of the two stars. Yet they all made note of the marriage itself, and how it had become a desolate, lonely place inhabited by two frail, broken human beings. Their readings treated the film as being about something else, that something else being Inge's picture of broken dreams in middle-class family life in small town America. In this reading they missed Inge's other major point, namely, that when dreams are broken for the middle class, alcoholism is not far behind.

The most extended treatment of the film's presentation of alcoholism is given by Herd in 1986 (pp. 231, 234, 236, 243–44), who offers an interpretation that locates the film within the genre of postwar Freudian family alcoholism melodramas. Such films, she argues, as noted above, present pessimism, failure, claustrophobic family life, weak, impotent husbands, and strong wives. She reads Doc as a "momma's boy," unable "to handle his sexuality and drinking in a constructive manner" (p. 234). She also suggests that his alcoholic recovery is identified with impotence and sexual abstinence and that Doc is doomed to a life of drab security and submissiveness to his wive's control. She connects this reading to Elsaesser's (1973/1986) argument that the postwar family melodrama was based on the Freudian family myth that early personality defects lock an individual in a cycle of tragedy and destruction. Under this Freudian reading alcoholism signifies impotency, failed masculinity, and libidinal blockage.

I challenge this Freudian interpretation. The film is about freedom, control, and sexuality in the alcoholic marriage. More specifically, the film is about the four structures of experience that stand at the center of the alcoholic marriage. A strict Freudian reading suppresses an interactional interpretation of the film. It focuses on the alcoholic personality, and not on the relationship the alcoholic has with his (or her) spouse. Furthermore, it fails to take into account the shared biographical history that connects Doc and Lola, including the fact that they had to get married, that he dropped out of medical school, and that he, for years, was an active alcoholic "always fighting and throwing things."

By focusing only on the alcoholic, Herd's reading diminishes Lola's place in the film. She is the other who defines Doc's alcoholism. She is the mirror to one side of his alcoholic self; the legacy of his violent alcoholism that destroyed her youthful beauty. The film's negative feminization of Lola (her slovenly appearance, etc.) carries forward the loss of femininity theme in the female alcoholism films examined in the last chapter. She takes on the visual characteristics of a female alcoholic, even though she never drinks.

In a sense the movie is about her and her acceptance of her husband's alcoholism. More deeply, it is about her acceptance of her lost child, her lost relationship with her father, and Doc's lost medical degree. Little Sheba represents her past and a past that she will not let go of. It is necessary, then, to read the film, not as a study of an alcoholic personality, but as a study of an alcoholic marriage, and of lost intimacy in the marriage. The film is about the past and how the past shapes and destroys the present.

Back to the Text

The viewer is led to believe that Doc's drinking career spans the length of the marriage, and coincides with the forced marriage, the loss of the child, and the medical degree. His sobriety, measured by his one year A.A. birthday, has brought a degree of stability to the marriage and his work, for clients lost during his alcoholism are reported as coming back. Still, they need money, which is why Lola rents the room to Marie.

To remain sober Doc becomes heavily involved in A.A. This involvement introduces an external element into the relationship that detracts from what they would share exclusively with one another. Doc enters into an intimate sponsor relationship with Ed while Lola holds onto her dream of Little Sheba. Sobriety brings two negative elements into the marriage: the past, and Doc's A.A. involvement, especially his 12-Step work. Hence, the empty interactions that are revealed between Doc and Lola at the beginning of the film can be interpreted, in part, as being due to his sobriety. More is at issue. In A.A. folklore (Denzin, 1987b, Chapter 5) the first year of sobriety is the hardest. Doc has made it through the first year. In A.A. this is a major accomplishment. Doc and Lola both recognize this, for she goes with him to receive his one-year birthday cake.

But the apparent intimate emptiness of the marriage is not just due to Doc's sobriety and A.A. involvement. Lola is part of the picture. She lives in the past, dreams of Little Sheba, lays around the house, sleeps until noon, and does not fix Doc breakfast. Forced into marriage at an early age, shunned by her father and mother, and married to an active alcoholic, she retreated into the past in order to find a safe place for herself. In the past, in her sleep, and in her dreams she escaped the harsh realities that life had forced on her. Doc became alcoholic; she fled to late adolescent dreams. They both escaped the present; each was a casualty of an American dream that did not come true. They cohabited in the same space, but lived separate, intimate realities, where each hides from one another.

Marie brings three new elements into the marriage and into the Delaney house: youth, her vibrant sexuality, and her relationships with Turk and Bruce. These three elements breath new life into Doc and Lola's relationship, and then, because they awaken the buried past, they place strains on Doc's sobriety. Doc relapses in those key moments in the film when sexuality and the past combine to draw him to the sacred bottle in the kitchen cupboard. The narrative confirms the argument that alcohol and sexuality are joined in the alcoholism film.

Turk represents wild, uncontained sexuality. Bruce represents conventional, respectable sexuality and marriage. Marie, like a double, is drawn to Turk's wild, erotic demeanor, and flirtatiously leads him on, only to turn him down on the night before Doc's relapse. Lola, like Marie, has two sexual selves. One self rocks and rolls and gyrates to the music from the noon radio show called "Taboo," and dances seductively with Doc. The other sexual self dresses slovenly, and has dreams about Sheba. Doc's sexual, intimate self comes alive in the dance with Lola, which is called to an embarrassing halt by Turk and Marie: the film's representatives of wild, unconstrained sexuality. Doc, unable to join these two selves, relapses and in the relapse throws the past at Lola.

The past haunts the film. Doc's sobriety is continually defined in terms of his drinking and fighting days. Its very title speaks to the past. Sheba, the little dog who wiggled her cute little bottom when she was given baths, symbolizes the tabooed sexuality that brought Doc and Lola into marriage. Sheba's departure signals the demise of sexuality and intimacy in their marriage. But Lola's refusal, until the end, to let go of

Sheba symbolizes her desire to hold onto the sexual dreams that swept her out of late adolescence and into adulthood. Lola, the dreamer, wants that past, in some form, back in the marriage. And she succeeds. By bringing Marie into the house she unwittingly creates the situation that makes Doc deal with the past that they agreed to never talk about. Granted, he has to have a relapse to talk about it, but talk about it he does. Afterward he affirms a love for and an intimate bond to Lola that she had not known since marriage. By going back to the past, the film brings Lola and Doc into the present. In the present, after the relapse, they confront the bad faith, the denial, the emotional power struggles, and the dead dreams they had constructed and lived over the years of alcoholic married life.

Earlier I argued that alcoholism films speak to the problems of controlling and regulating emotionality, sexuality, and desire in everyday life. *Come Back, Little Sheba* conforms to this reading although its treatment of the issue is complex.

Lola and Doc are forced into marriage by a postwar society that refuses to allow an unmarried woman to carry her own child. Although society accepts her marriage, her father does not. Never allowed to enter her father's house again, she lives her adulthood with this father absence as a scar on her inner self. Rejected by the original father figure in her life (Lacan, 1949/1977), she turns to Doc, calls him Daddy, and lives out her torturing indiscretion inside the alcoholic marriage they built together. The film suggests that Doc's alcoholism is also a result of the original tabooed sexual act, for it brought his promising medical career to an end.

The marriage that Doc and Lola are forced into cannot tolerate any hint of the wild sexuality that originally drew them together. This is why Doc relapses. The film even hints at the position that alcoholism is an acceptable solution (up to a point) to the strains of a forced marriage. But the film will not settle for this solution. It goes farther. It demands that a cathartic experience be undergone. This requires a reliving of the past. Only after the past has been openly addressed can Lola and Doc have a free, open, cleansed intimate relationship based on mutual love and respect.

Society requires that both Doc and Lola pay their debt for going against God and convention. She was forced to live with the dreams of a dead dog. He became an alcoholic. This is the final message. The alcoholic family bears the guilt of sexual transgressions. Everyone pays, nobody wins. If sexuality and desire are to be regulated in postwar society, a price has to be paid. *Come Back, Little Sheba* suggests that the price is high.

The Country Girl (1954)[3]

Like *Come Back, Little Sheba, The Country Girl* is a study of an alcoholic marriage, in this case a 10-year-old one, between an alcoholic, has-been Broadway actor–singer, Frank Elgin, and Georgie, his wife from the country, who married him because she never had a father.[4] The story involves three persons, Frank, Georgie, and Bernie, the young director who takes a chance on Frank ("If you drink you're out") and casts him in the lead part of a new Broadway play. In this triangle Frank and Bernie love Georgie, while Georgie and Bernie both try to help Frank stay sober for his Broadway comeback. Frank, in turn, seeks Bernie's approval, while he fears and loves Georgie, and mourns the death of their young son, whose death he feels he caused. Georgie is presented as a domineering wife who attempts to control her weak, alcoholic husband. This control extends to her attempts to manipulate Bernie in Frank's best interest. Bernie takes Frank's side in the drama, and accepts his definition of the marriage, of Georgie's alcoholism (a lie), which started Frank's drinking (a lie), and her suicide attempts (a lie), after the death of their son. Frank gets the part, falls off the wagon in Boston, gets sober again, and gives a stunning first night performance in New York City. Bernie falls in love with Georgie and asks her to leave Frank. She refuses and stays with Frank. At the end of the film all of the lies, deceptions, and misperceptions that have been built up between the three characters have been exposed.

An Alcoholic Interactional System

The subtleties of the story lie in its handling of the deceptive communication system that exists between Frank, Bernie, and Georgie. The key to unraveling this system is knowing that the three parties are caught in an interactional relationship based on bad faith, misinformation, lies, paradox, double-binds, and contradictory choices (see Basic, 1989 on these terms and their relationship to this film).

Georgie is the maligned party. Frank is the window to her, and he is the person who has to lie about her in order to maintain his standing in Bernie's eyes. Frank has a choice not to lie, but when he tells the truth, he must contradict what he has already told Bernie, and by telling the truth he confirms what Georgie already knows about him, that he is a weak person afraid of responsibility. Georgie, on the other hand, never lies, but her actions are seen (incorrectly) by Bernie as being the cause of Frank's problems, when, in fact, without her, there would be no Frank.

Frank tells stories to Bernie about Georgie that Bernie believes because he defines all women (like his first wife) as being domineering and cruel. (Bernie to Frank: "My wife was so twisted, she once said to me, 'I hope your next play's a flop, so the whole world can see how much I love you even though you're a failure.'") Frank tells stories to Georgie about how Bernie is controlling him ("He doesn't understand me"), which Georgie believes because she thinks Bernie is trying to manipulate Frank. Georgie tells stories to Bernie ("He's heading for a bender"), and calls Frank a "cunning drunkard" and herself a "drunkard's wife." These statements are not believed by Bernie because he thinks she is controlling Frank ("Why is it that women think they understand men? You make him tense and uneasy."). For Frank to get and keep his part he must act strong in front of Bernie. When he acts strong (or weak) he confirms Bernie's belief that Georgie is pushing him. When he acts strong Georgie knows he is lying (for he is weak), but Bernie thinks he is telling the truth, that is, he has been made weak by Georgie. If Georgie were to tell Bernie how weak Frank really is she would undermine Frank's credibility in the part. When she first attempts to be truthful, Bernie of course does not believe her. The viewer sees the story through Bernie's eyes, and thus comes to believe that Georgie is the domineering woman Bernie thinks she is.

Frank's Lie

Frank's lie is the key to the story. He tells Bernie that Georgie has not always been domineering. "When I first met her, she was as fine a person as you've ever seen. . . . Then our son died. I came home . . . one night. . . . There she is stretched out across the bed dead drunk. With her wrists cut and bleeding. . . . Inside a year she was a hopeless drunkard. So, in an effort to give her some purpose in life, I made her feel that I needed her in my work. . . . She started taking over everything then. She became very possessive . . . had to be with me all the time. . . . She had fits of depression, and one time she set fire to a hotel suite. That's when I started hittin' the bottle pretty hard." Bernie asks: "Does she still drink?" Frank: "No she stopped when I began." Bernie: "That figures. You are the weak one now. That's what she wanted."

With this story Frank then explains that he had to give Georgie power over him: "I had her convince me that it was her idea, not mine." In this exchange Frank succeeds in casting Georgie in a negative light, while offering an account of his own problems with alcohol. Bernie accepts this definition, for it confirms his own double-binding experiences with women. The next day over lunch Georgie will reveal how she is trapped by Frank, although Bernie does not believe her. She states: "Being an actor's wife is not the easiest of jobs. If I tell him he's magnificent, he says I'm not being honest. If I tell him he's not magnificent he says I don't love him." This is a classic double-bind situation, for as Georgie knows both statements cannot be true at the same time.

Bernie reveals the situation the next day. Georgie tells him, "Whether you like it or not, Frank's weak. He's a leaner. And I happen to be the one he leans on." Bernie replies, "Did it ever occur to you that your strength might be the very reason he *is* weak? I don't like strong women Mrs. Elgin."

Unmasking Frank

Frank must get drunk in order for the two orders of truth that structure the story to be revealed: Bernie has fallen in love with Georgie and Frank has been lying all along about Georgie's alcoholism. Frank enters a bar, starts drinking, and experiences again the flashback scene associated with his son's death. He throws a glass into the mirror behind the bar and passes out. The next morning Georgie reveals to Bernie, in front of Frank, that Frank's stories about her suicide attempts, slashed wrists, being a hopeless drunk, and her fits of depression were just lines from "His big speech in one of the plays you admired him in when you were a hat check boy."

The revelation of Frank's duplicity forces Bernie to apologize to Georgie: "I don't know where to begin to apologize Mrs. Elgin." Georgie will not accept the apology: "All I want is my own name and a modest job to buy sugar for my coffee!. . . . You can't believe that a woman is crazy out of her mind to want to live alone, in one room by herself!"

Looking into Georgie's eyes as she makes the speech, Bernie moves toward her, takes her in his arms, and kisses her. She pulls away: "How could you be so angry at someone you didn't even know?" Bernie: "Maybe I really wasn't. Maybe I screamed at you to keep myself an angry distance." Georgie: "No one has looked at me as a woman for years and years." Bernie: "I never knew there was such a woman. Loyal and steadfast."

In the next scene Frank confesses all to Bernie. He admits that he used the accident as an excuse to drink, for drinking was his way of dealing with fear. Frank: "Oh, I'd blame it on the accident. After I'd milked every tear out of it, I cut my wrists . . . just enough to bleed myself back to the center of attention. So everybody felt sorry for me again. . . . That's the way I wanted it. To keep it that way I lied. Oh God, how I lied! I even lied about Georgie!"

Frank's Alcoholism

Frank's alcoholism is now explained. His slips, hidden bottles, use of cough syrup, and excuses for drinking are now out in the open. He is the weak man Georgie said he was. The film must now elaborate its stand on drinking, drunkards, and their cure. Bernie to Frank: "There are as many reasons for drinking as there are drinkers. But there are only two reasons why a drinker stops. He dies, or he decides to quit. All by himself." Frank: "I'm not sure I have. I faced the crisis in Boston and I got away with it. Just about anybody can face a crisis. It's that everyday living that's rough. I'm not sure I can lick it, but I think I gotta chance. The point is, Georgie, what about us?" She replies, "Frank I married you for happiness. Yours and mine. If necessary I'll leave you for the same reason." She then blames herself for trying to control him in Boston. Frank counters her apology, stating that he has put her through ten years of Hell. On this note the film comes to its conclusion. Georgie refuses Bernie's offer of love, and rejoins Frank.

The Critics Read the Film

Hartung's review (1954b, p. 312) was typical: "By no means a pleasant picture, but it is certainly one of the year's most engrossing. And its honesty when . . . it agrees that there is no easy cure for alcoholism is commendable . . . [it] is full of compassion and understanding for all alcoholics, and for those who live with them." The film was uniformly praised for its casting of Crosby, Kelly, and Holden in the key parts (see McCarten, 1954b, p. 61; *Time*, 1954b, p. 96; *Newsweek*, 1954b, p. 107). Crowther (1954b, p. 3) called Crosby's performance the key to the film's power, and saw in Odet's story a "searching and pitiless thing [that] cuts to the hearts of three people without mercy or concern for their deep shame." He noted that the heroic figure is Georgie, but observed that her credibility depends on Crosby's interpretation of Frank. *Look* (1954, p. 164) and *Life* (1954b, p. 106) commented on Crosby's playing an alcoholic. The reviewer for *Life* warned Bing's fans that they "will be shocked at their idol's slouched shoulders and drawn face." (He had been warned not to do the film, but decided that it was not a story about an alcoholic, but a story of regeneration, *Life*, 1954b, p. 106.) Schwartz (1955, p. 21) complained that it was symptomatic of too many recent films that offer "a tragedy with a happy ending."[5] The reviewer for *Newsweek* (1954b, p. 107), repeating a critic's familiar argument concerning how any given film explains the causes of alcoholism, suggested that "A bit of sticky padding . . . tries to explain Elgin's compulsive drinking by attributing it to his feelings that he was responsible for his son's death. . . . There may be a point in trying to soften a revealing case study of an alcoholic, but the dramatic gain is negligible." Shuman (1962, p. 127) noted that Frank's "lies about his past became so real for him that they cease to be lies at all [and that] . . . his drinking has tended to shut the world out of his life . . . the chances of his personality undergoing any real transformation would be very slight. . . . He represents, as much as any Arthur Miller or Tennessee Williams protagonist, the prototype of the failure of modern American man."

Unraveling the Text

Herd (1986, pp. 235–36) interprets the film, as she did with *Come Back, Little Sheba*, through the Freudian family melodrama model. She writes, "Elgin . . . is immature, dependent, completely lacking in confidence . . . . His wife is a determined, strong-willed woman. . . . The conflict . . . centers around whether she is overly ambitious and dominating, thus emasculating him. The dilemma resolves when we learn that [her] ambitions are not misplaced and that [he] has masked his own weakness and vulnerability through a thickly woven net of lies."[6] Missing in this reading is the interactional system that joins the three characters, and the fact that Georgie bears the mark of Frank's alcoholism.

Contrary to the critics, the film is not about Frank, or Georgie, or Bernie. It about an alcoholic marriage and an interactional situation that has been built on misperceptions, lies, and deceit. Bernie illuminates the underlying dynamics of the marriage; dynamics that were there before he appeared on the scene. Georgie and Frank are trapped in a set of double-binds. If she praises him he thinks she is lying. If she does not praise him, he thinks she does not love him. If she helps him he thinks this means she thinks he cannot stand on his own two feet. When he takes on a new role and slips, she takes the slip to be a measure of how she has failed him. If he loses a part it is her fault.

They love and respect one another, but Frank's downward turn after their son's death has inserted into the marriage a sense of failure, defeat, loss, and humiliation that has been worsened by his alcoholism. He has lost both career and self-respect. Georgie, as a country girl, persists in clinging to a set of values that has nothing to do with the theater, a world that is still a mystery to her. To keep Frank going, she has resorted to becoming a mother, rather than a wife, and has aged considerably beyond her 30 years in the process (Shuman, 1962, p. 133). As a mother, she attempts to get her child–husband back on his feet, knowing that his defense against failure is to drink, lie, and return to the guilt-ridden past where he is haunted by their son's death.

Frank's weaknesses defined her strengths, and were what, in part, drew her to him. She tells Bernie, near the end of the film, about what it was like before their son was killed. "He drank a little, wasn't too dependable, but it was only a pathetic hint of frailty in a wonderful, glowing man. That appeals to a lot of us. It did to me. I was so young, his weaknesses, they seemed touching and sweet. They made me love him more." In Frank she found the father she never had. Together they had a successful marriage, she became a "poised" country girl, and he had a successful career, until the death.

While she, on the surface, is the strong member of the marriage, in fact it is Frank who controls the relationship. His weaknesses controlled her, even in the early days of the marriage. Now his lies to Bernie manipulate her into embarrassing situations. His turning Bernie against her further diminishes her power, as his rises. His slips weaken her already fragile control over herself and his part in the play. His lies to her about Bernie serve to undermine the positive contributions she wants to make to his performance.

But it is not his performance that concerns her. It is his self-respect; without that she wants out. For his self-respect becomes hers, and together theirs. With it, she will stay, and stay she does. However, her decision to stay would not have been made if he had not experienced his crisis in Boston. By twice reliving the death of their son, and twice slipping, and going back on stage and giving a strong performance, Frank proved to himself, and to Georgie, that he could stand on his own feet again. Before he could do this, he had to expose himself to the fear of punishment that came from unraveling the lies he had told Bernie. In this move he freed himself from the double-binds he had created for the three of them. He found, too, that he had freed them to find a love he had not been able to show to Georgie. In these moves he found the respect he had lost. That's why she stays.

Frank walks out of her life, but not before thanking the two of them for helping him get sober, expressing admiration for the love that obviously exists between she and Bernie, and also expressing regrets for the 10 years of Hell he has put her through. In staying Georgie affirms the validity of her own country girl identity, poised, sophisticated, self-confident, and solidly committed to the marriage she entered into 10 years ago as a young girl. In the end she has found her father and a husband.

This alcoholic marriage, like that of Lola and Doc, was the victim of an alcoholic past that continually controlled the present. This was the set of facts Odets began with. He allowed them to unfold within the play that overlapped with the play that the three characters were playing on stage. He showed how the alcoholic marriage both ravels and unravels itself when the double-binds on which it is based are finally torn apart. This tearing apart, he suggests, can occur only when a crisis erupts within the interactional system that otherwise threatens to destroy itself and its members. For such a transformation to occur a third party must be inserted into the relationship. This party, as the character of Bernie demonstrates, and Simmel (1950) argued, shifts and alters the existing power structure in the destructive dyad. This member exposes the underlying paradoxical, contradictory double-binding social structure on which it rests.

Thus Bernie, like Marie, saves an alcoholic marriage. He and Marie are the outsiders who destroy the destructive patterns of interaction the husband and wife had, until their arrival, been doomed to live out.

Days of Wine and Roses[7]

Joe, a bachelor, works for a San Francisco advertising agency, promoting products and procuring women as dates for rich clients. Early in the film he states, "I want to be a PR man, not a pimp." He is a heavy drinker. He meets and marries Kirstie, who works as a secretary in the same office building. She does not drink, but he teaches her to drink Brandy Alexanders. She quits work and they have a child named Debbie. Joe loses his job because of his drinking and gets another one in Houston. While there Kirstie, who is now drinking more heavily, falls asleep, drunk, and nearly burns down the apartment. Joe loses the Houston job. He returns to San Francisco. One day, looking at his reflection in the window of a Union Square bar, he has a self-revelation, returns home, and tells Kirstie, "We've gotta talk about somethin. Look at me. I'm a bum. Look at us (pulls her over in front of a mirror), a couple of bums. . . . You know why I've been fired from five jobs in four years . . . its booze. Kirstie: "A couple of drinks." Joe: "We stay drunk most of the time. I'm a drunk and I don't do my job and I get fired. . . . We've turned into a couple of bums. We've gotta do something. We're gonna get sober and stay sober and that means not a drop. Are you with me." Kirstie: "I'm always with you."

They leave the city and go to Kirstie's father's, a gardener who lives south of the city. They remain sober one month. To celebrate, Joe buys three pints of whiskey and hides one bottle in the father's greenhouse. He and Kirstie begin drinking and get drunk. Joe goes to the greenhouse to find the hidden bottle. In the process he destroys the greenhouse. Kirstie enters her father's bedroom and attempts to seduce him. He drags her to the shower.

Joe is next shown experiencing DTs in a padded room. (He is screaming and moaning like a caged animal. He attempts to bite his black male nurse.) An A.A. member visits and introduces himself, "I'm Jim Hungerford, I'm an alcoholic. They say you want help." In the next scene Joe is showing Kirstie A.A. literature and telling her about A.A. meetings.

She says, "No." Joe pleads with her, "Jim says they're wonderful. Just a bunch of alcoholics trying to keep each other sober and it works." Kirstie: "No. I don't even know why you let them give it to you. They must think you're a bum or something." Joe: "I asked for it. I must have needed help. I was in the hospital." Kirstie: "Well you didn't belong there." Joe: "I was there. Nobody belongs there. I passed out in the middle of Mission Street." Kirstie: "All right, you had too much to drink. That doesn't mean you're an alcoholic." Joe: "We're just goin' to a meeting. Now what could we lose?" Kirstie: "You can go. . . . I'm not gonna go. I'm not an alcoholic and I refuse to say I am. I refuse to ask for help for something that's just a matter of self-respect and will power. I refuse to get up in front of a bunch of people and degrade myself. I know I can't drink because it gets the best of me. I will just use my will power and not drink and that's the end of it."

The film moves next to an A.A. meeting. It is four months later. Joe has been sober since his first visit with Jim and has attended many A.A. meetings. Outside the meeting, which is held in a church, Joe debates with Jim over how he does not want to say he is an alcoholic in front of this bunch of people. He argues that "Kirs has been sober four months, just like me and she has never said she is an alcoholic. She claims she can do it on will power alone." Jim: "Can you?" Jim opens the meeting: "My name is Jim Hungerford. I'm your chairman for tonight. Now all I have to do to qualify myself is to say that I drank too much, too often over too long a period of time. Welcome to the regular weekly meeting of the Mason Street Group of Alcoholics Anonymous." He then reads A.A.'s preamble, which states the purposes of the organization. The camera moves throughout the smoke-filled room, showing young to middle-aged, middle-class men and women in suits and ties and dresses somberly listening. Joe is introduced as a man who is speaking for the first time in four months. As he moves to the podium A.A. slogans are brought into view.[8] Joe speaks: "My name is [clears throat], My name is Joe Clay [pause]. I'm an alcoholic."

Joe takes a job back in the city, earning little money, but staying sober. Kirstie starts to drink again. Joe returns home from work and finds an empty bottle of vodka left on the bed. He calls Jim. The film's stance on the causes of alcoholism is revealed in the conversation they have. Joe: "I can't see how this could be happening to us." Jim: "You took too many drinks." Joe: "A hell of a lot of people drank as much as Kirs and I ever did and they're not alcoholics." Jim: "Its a lottery Joe and you lost." Joe: "Yeh, no way to find out till it's too late, uh?" Jim: "You remember how you told us about Kirstie's obsession with chocolate candy when you first met. Well a very perceptive psychologist might have told you then that she was a potential alcoholic. But neither of you would have believed him, and besides, he might have been wrong. Joe, how many strawberries does it take to start an allergy and which is the one that gives ya the hives? Alcoholism is an illness. It's pretty hard to diagnose an illness until you've got it. Come on Joe it's your turn of hives."

Kirstie calls Joe from a motel and asks him to come. He goes against Jim's advice. She seduces him; as he takes a drink, she challenges him: "What did they do to you in that A.A. place, anyway? Aren't you a man anymore? Can't you hear a woman calling to you? I don't want any of your mealy-mouthed, holier-than-thou boy scouts with cold feet, who don't have the guts to take a drink?" Joe and Kirstie both pass out in the bed. Joe sobers up again after another bout with the DTs, gaining one year sobriety. Kirstie returns, apologizes for her sexual excursions outside the marriage. She states: "there were lots of detours, but I never looked at them." Joe asks her to come back home. Stating "There's no threesome, you, and me and booze. No booze." Kirstie leaves, Joe looks at her as she walks by a bar, Debbie leaves her bedroom and asks, "Daddy, when is mommy coming home." Joe answers, "Mommy has to get better before she can come home. Mommy's sick, like I was. She can get better, Daddy did." Kirstie walks out of the apartment. Joe is together with Debbie. A neon sign spelling "BAR" flashes off and on in the night light, its reflection caught in the window of the apartment as Joe looks out into the street for Kirstie who has disappeared into the darkness. So ends the film.

The Markers, Causes, and Consequences of Alcoholism

Like *Come Back, Little Sheba, Days of Wine and Roses* is an A.A. film. However, unlike "Sheba," which had A.A. in its opening sequences, *Days* does not become an A.A. story until Jim Hungerford makes his entrance into the text. His appearance ushers in the usual signifiers of A.A.'s presence: 12-Step Calls, sponsors, meetings, slogans, the allergy theory of alcoholism, and the contrasts between this theory and the theory of self-will. *Days* adds the ingredient of a female alcoholic. In a twist on the feminization theme observed in the purely "women's alcoholism films," Kirstie takes what could be interpreted as a strong masculine, self-will position in her refusal to accept A.A.'s theory of alcoholism. Her alcoholism masculinizes her response to the disease, even while she is shown becoming sexually promiscuous, losing her sexual appeal, and abdicating her family responsibilities. Joe is feminized by his alcoholism. He takes on Kirstie's family responsibilities, and willingly accepts A.A.'s position on self-will, surrender, and the need for obtaining the help of others.

Days, like the alcoholism films that preceded it, traces the trajectory of the illness in the subject who is doomed to catch the disease. It repeats the experience of "hitting bottom," giving male and female versions of how this bottom is confronted and defined. Joe's DT's take him straight into A.A. Kirstie never experiences them, and hence her bottom is cushioned, and this perhaps accounts for her unwillingness to let go of the self-will position. It reproduces the harsh images of treatment established by earlier films in the genre (see Ritson, 1979), while continuing the practice of presenting A.A. in a favorable light. The rejection of A.A. by Kirstie is an anomaly, for every A.A. film, to this point, had shown alcoholics accepting A.A.'s view of the disease.

Days is the first picture of the alcoholic marriage in which the husband and wife are both alcoholics (see Harwin and Otto, 1979, p. 48). This picture repeats the themes outlined at the beginning of this chapter, namely the negative effects on alcoholic drinking on the sexual, intimate, and daily domestic forms of interaction in the marriage. As Kirstie and Joe slip farther and farther into alcoholic drinking, domestic violence, household fires, bitter arguments, lost jobs, and degrading sexual experiences take control of their everyday life. Alcoholism has destroyed their marriage. There are no dreams from the past that can be remembered. They have found no common ground on which recovery could be built. The film's unhappy ending echoes the words of Ernest Dowson, whose poem gave the film its title, "They are not long, the days of wine and roses, out of a misty dream our path emerges for a while, then closes within a dream." Joe and Kirstie's dream is over; the wine and the roses killed it.

The Critics

The film met with mixed reactions. It was unfavorably compared to *The Lost Weekend* and to earlier temperance films. The ending was also criticized, while the treatment of A.A. was praised, as were the performances of Lemmon and Remick. Hartung (1963, pp. 493–94) was typical: "In spite of its many realistic scenes, *Wine and Roses* is little more than a shallow movie about shallow people who drink deep . . . one loses interest in them long before the plot gets down to the principal theme: the evils of alcoholism." Hartung wrote favorably of A.A.: "The fine work done by A.A., their prayer (Serenity), and their insistence that an alcoholic admit he's an alcoholic merit unreserved commendation." *Time* (1963, p. 81) complimented the film in these lines: "All drunks are dull, and the rule generally applies to movies about drunks. The last exception was 'The Lost Weekend.' This is another." He then quarelled with its treatment of alcoholism. "Something is seriously missing in this movie, and something seriously wrong. What is missing is a fundamental attempt to understand the social, emotional and spiritual nature of alcoholism. What is wrong is the attempt to be entertaining at all times. . . . It isn't much fun to sit through a 117-minute drinking party without a drink in your hand."

Crowther (1963, p. 7) connected the film to earlier temperance movies,[9] and then compared it to more recent films on the topic: "there is still pretty much of the spirit of the oldtime temperance plays in the dramas we've had upon this subject in recent years—such eloquent items as 'The Lost Weekend' and 'Come Back, Little Sheba' to name two." He then gives faint praise: "A grim, graphic, heartrending account of the agony of two people in the clutch of booze. . . . As a straight, ruthless visualization of an alcoholic's fate, with the bouts of delirium tremors and 'dry-out' and all the rest, it is a commanding picture, and it is extremely well-played by Mr. Lemmon and Miss Remick. . . . But . . . they do not bring the two pitiful characters to complete and overpowering life. The couple in this picture, unlike the sot in *The Lost Weekend*, seem to be horrible examples that we face objectively. We shudderingly watch them suffer, we do not really suffer with them. They are impressive performers in a temperance play." Crowther felt that Klugman gave "a good account of a compassionate member of A.A.," while McCarten (1963, p. 121) argued that the screen play "succeeds far more as a tract for Alcoholics Anonymous than as a work of art." Kauffman (1963, p. 31) faulted the film because "the characters are insufficiently motivated or grounded." He also raised the temperance theme noted by other reviewers: "The tedium is . . . tinged with the ludicrous as an aura of temperance lecture begins to cloak the film, undispelled by sporadic attempts at 'Lost Weekend' psychological candor. It finally reduces to a discourse on the Evils of Drink, too blatant to be affecting. Alcoholism is not funny, but Carry Nation is." *Variety* (1962, p. 6) called it a "Very depressing tale . . . a film of emotional impact but basically limited appeal. . . . It requires maximum involvement and profound compassion from an audience to be appreciated. . . some may find it an almost intolerably depressing 117 minutes . . . the wife's [final] decision is horrible and odd, and sure to baffle most filmgoers. It appears to be a matter of absolutely illogical and inflexible pride." *Newsweek* (1963, p. 88) repeated this criticism. "What makes the film especially regrettable is that until the strategic error at the end, it is an entirely honest effort. . . . But there may have been sweeter roses, and the days of wine have yet to be truthfully filmed."[10] The reviewer elaborated this position: "The ending . . . denatures the alcoholism, turning it from grim reality to dramatic device, and escaping from the battle of the bottle into the more manageable battle of the sexes. A theory of film structured this interpretation. "For the 'problem' film to succeed, it must not be too formal a work of art. (For all its crudities, *'The Connection'*[11] had the courage of not having any ending at all; it simply stared fixedly at the ineluctable fact of narcotics addition.)"

Sociological Readings

Herd (1986, pp. 237, 240, 244), Room (1985, pp. 7–8, 10), and Harwin and Otto (1979, pp. 38–44) offer compatible readings of the film. Once again locating it, like *Sheba*, within the Freudian family melodramas of the 1950s and 1960s, they suggest that it deals, especially in the case of Kirstie, with an immature, female alcoholic, with an addictive personality, locked in an Oedipal relation with her father. Kirstie's feminization of alcoholism turns her disease into promiscuity and "willful" overt sexuality, as a means of achieving self-validation (Harwin and Otto, 1979, p. 38). Harwin and Otto (1979, p. 44) suggest that Kirstie wishes to destroy her father, yet fears losing him, and uses alcohol as a means of achieving gratification and revenge against him. Herd and Room suggest that Joe's alcoholism signifies failed masculinity and impotence. Room argues that the film delineates the two paths to recovery for alcoholism prevalent in the 1950s and 1960s: will-power and A.A., Kirstie's refusal of the A.A. path is explained, he suggests, by her taking on the masculine identity that Joe relinquishes. Joe becomes dependent on A.A.; she opts for male will-power. These readings emphasize the Freudian and A.A. overtones in the film. They do not explicitly locate the film within the larger work and gender order of the early 1960s.

Back to the Film

On their first date, after Joe has introduced Kirstie to Brandy Alexanders, they are on fisherman's wharf. He describes their relationship in the following words: "Man meets girl, a beautiful, sweet, lovely nice girl, a girl too nice for him. He finally manages to get a date, hauls her down to the bay, gets himself loaded, cries like a baby on her shoulder and tells her his story. What a love story." Joe's story is classic: a handsome man falls in love with an attractive, sexually desirable woman. Kirstie's story parallels Joe's. Under the influence of the brandy, which she says "makes me feel good, I feel wonderful," she says of herself, before she moved to the city. "I was a pretty girl. I was wasting my sweetness in the desert air." She later relates a dream to Joe. It involves monsters in the sea. She states: "I dreamed that they murdered me, over there, my father came in and took my body home. He talked a blue-streak. I was dead and couldn't hear him. My father doesn't talk, he used to talk to my mother. . . . Now that she's dead he hardly talks at all. They used to say 'together in heaven'." She goes on. "I come down here just to not go home." Joe finishes a pint of whiskey, drops it into the bay. Kirstie, looking longingly into his face, says, "The days are not long, the days of wine and roses. Out of a mystic dream our paths emerge for awhile, then close within a dream. I guess we should be getting back."

In the above scene Joe has described his job. "I wanted something steady, with class, something where you don't hate yourself, something you don't have to do. I want to advise people. I want to help them to relate to the public. I want to help a good client benefit others. I'm like a garbage man, a eunuch in a harem." Kirstie, in describing her work and being sexually "eyed" by her employer, stated: "sometimes you have to swallow your pride on account of your job."

Love, Desire, Political Economy, and Alcoholism

The above scenes reflect how love, desire, and alcoholism and political economy are heterosexually coded in this man-meets-woman love story. These emotions are shaped by alcohol and drink. Intoxicated, both characters tell partial, intimate life stories that reveal their attempts to find respectable, middle-class life-styles. Under the influence, they fall in love; three scenes later they are married. Alcohol has broken through Kirstie's emotions and opened her to Joe's advances. On marriage, Kirstie stays home and has a child, while Joe continues to work. The couple live the ideologically appropriate 1960s middle-class marriage. Yet Joe's alcoholism destroys his corporate occupational career, while Kirstie's alcoholism nearly destroys their home. Hence alcoholism's effects simultaneously move outward to the social structure and inward to the home. It plays out its influences through the gender stratification system that has been reproduced in their marriage. Joe's alcoholism is due to his inability to handle his job; her alcoholism is attributed to the boredom of being a mother and a housewife. They are both casualties of the 1960s social structure. (In this respect they are unlike Frank and Georgie, whose marriage seemed to stand outside history. Joe and Kirstie have a simple marriage, compared to the complicated interactional structure that trapped Frank and Georgie.)

Faced with alcoholic despair they retreat from the city and return to the country, where Kirstie's father lives. Here, in the pastoral surroundings of the greenhouse, they sober up, aided by the father, nature, and will-power. But more than sobering up is going on. They return to Kirstie's father, the man discussed in the wharfside dream; the man who doesn't speak, the man who rescued Kirstie when she was killed by the monsters. It is significant that after a month of sobriety the father offers Joe a beer, which is immediately followed by his and Kirstie's relapse.

The return of the father is coded in the film as a return to death, which is signaled by the offering of the beer. The relapse that follows has Kirstie entering her father's bed, an incestuous act that is refused. In the act Kirstie turns away from her husband who is drunkenly destroying the greenhouse in search of alcohol. Kirstie is living out her dream; she is also taking her mother's place in her father's life. Rebuked by her father, she will later have numerous affairs during her drunken departures from Joe, claiming that in them she is seeking a love that she does not have. And during this time she will begin living with her father, while Joe works in the city and takes care of their daughter.

The film is about family and sexuality. Alcoholism and wild sexuality are the signifiers of family destruction. The film holds up four versions of family life: Joe's parents, a song and dance team that plays Vegas and appeared on Ed Sullivan; Kirstie's parents, who loved one another, but seldom talked; Joe and Kirstie's family destroyed by alcoholism, with Joe caring for Debbie; and Kirstie having sordid affairs, while living at home with her father. The first two versions of family conform to middle-class ideology, but they are not brought up after the opening scenes. The viewer is left with the last two pictures of family life. Kirstie is excluded from her family with Joe and Debbie. Her alcoholism and sexuality make her unacceptable to Joe. Her refusal to accept A.A. signifies her refusal to conform to the middle-class family norm. She is cast out of the family.

The film has no other choice but to leave her with her father. Her association with him signifies the end of "days of wine and roses," for both she and Joe. She returns to her dream, which was enunciated in the early scene of the film. She deals with the ugliness of the world by drinking.[12] Her father carries her home, and she cannot hear him because she is dead. The promise of "days of wine and roses" has been killed by wine and wild sexuality.

By returning Kirstie to the patriarchal father, who blames Joe for Kirstie's alcoholism, the film keeps alive the incest theme that was present in Kirstie's life before she met Joe. From her father's home Kirstie ventures out into the night seeking the love she never received from her parents. It takes the position that he, not Joe, should be her caretaker. In this movie, the film recontains Kirstie in middle-class family life, even if it is in a cold, potentially incestuous relation with her father. Thus the narrative resolves its own problems. Being about family, it must find a place for both Joe and Kirstie. At the end sexuality and family are joined under the households of two males: Joe and Kirstie's father. The film ultimately makes the father responsible for Kirstie's alcoholism and for her wild sexuality, for it is he who failed to give her the original love she required. And faced with this absence of love in her early life, she retreated into the dream of wine and roses that gives the film its title. (For her these two terms signify love and beauty in life.) Joe is freed from guilt; after all he offered his wife a place in *his* family, and she refused to take it. Accordingly, the film's two alcoholic endings are merged in the above resolution. Kirstie is not really excluded from society and family. She has her father.

Emotionality and the Family's Burden

Earlier I argued that by locating alcoholism in the family the alcoholism film reproduces the cultural ideology that makes each family responsible for its own problems. *Days of Wine and Roses* suggests just how far these films will go to contain sexuality and alcoholism. To keep Kirstie in a family, it will send her back to a silent father to whom she is sexually attracted. More is at issue, and this is hidden, while it is contained within the earlier Freudian reading of Herd. Freud was right, but for the wrong reasons. The emotions do find their natural home in the family, and sexuality and desire do find their initial formulations in the mother–father–child triadic social structure. Freud's error, and those of his followers, lies in positing an original (and primordial) incestuous bond between child and parent; for what is bonded is not sexuality, but love and emotional desire. Kirstie never found, nor was she given that love by her parents. This desire, which seeks its own fulfillment, in the body and self of another, is coded by the culture's gender stratification system, which is shaped by the political economy of the social structure. Hence the culture-making institutions of a society mold and create a politics of desire, feeling, and emotional bonding that is specific to each historical moment. This is what a strict Freudian reading misses.

Three Alcoholic Families

Doc and Lola Delaney, Frank and Georgie Elgin, and Joe and Kirstie Clay are larger-than-life, cinematic and cultural representations of individuals and families touched by the disease of alcoholism. Victims of the immediate postwar American dream (Riesman, Glazer, and Denny, 1953; Wiley, 1967) they sought love, intimacy, and sexuality in alcohol and marriage. These three couples were trapped in worlds of gender, family, and work that they only partially made. They used dreams and alcohol to either kill the pain of past sexual, and moral transgressions

(Lola and Doc), or to find a love and intimacy that they had not received from their parents (Kirstie and Joe and Georgie). All three husbands experienced job failures, and the films explain these downward mobility patterns in terms of alcoholism, and failed marital relationships.

The three women provide contrasting, but parallel images of the early postmodern gender stratification system. Lola never worked outside the home. She was judged by her neighbors, father, mother, and husband to be a failure as a homemaker, a daughter, and a wife. Always moving from one apartment to another, Georgie and Frank never had a home. Frank's work was hers. Her identity was defined through him, and together they had failed to hold a job. Kirstie entered the labor market to find a husband, which she did. Her move to the city, to find a job and a man, signals the first break from a closed middle-class family that World War II created. She, like her female counterparts, found herself mid-way between family and work, a condition created by the postwar years. Yet she, like other woman of her generation, went to work to find a husband, and finding a husband they returned home to raise the all-American family. But in the workplace they learned how to drink, how to be sexual, and how to form new emotional bonds with men who also found themselves in new work and family situations. As she became an alcoholic she failed as a homemaker and a mother. Like their husbands, but confined to home and not work, all three women failed to find what they thought they would in family and men.

Absent and present patriarchal father figures dominate in each film. Lola is rejected by her father and can never go home. Georgie never had a father she knew. Kirstie is accepted by her father and returns to him. Each of the films takes the position that women find their subjectivity in and through their relations with men, in particular their fathers. Lola, Georgie, and Kirstie struggle to find the meaning of love, intimacy, and desire in men who have replaced their fathers. Lola calls Doc "Daddy," and Kirstie seeks love in nameless men, while she lives with her father. The "paternal metaphor" (Lacan, 1957–8, p. 8) and the law of patriarchy thus turn each of these films into "women's stories" and into accounts of how feminine subjectivity can be given only through the male–father relationship. Each woman is punished by her father for having broken the law of patriarchy (Weber, 1978, Vol. 2, p. 1007). But more is going on. Each woman experiences a form of insanity or despair (dream delusions for Lola, a crazy desire to live alone for Georgie, and alcoholism for Kirstie) because she has broken the law of the father (see Mitchell, 1982, p. 23).

Doc and Lola and Georgie and Frank represent the first wave of postwar marriages, while Kirstie and Joe symbolize the second wave of postmodern Americans. Their respective moral tales speak to the problems that these two generations, and the others that have followed them, would confront. Balancing marriage, work, love, sexuality, and the emotions inspired by alcohol, these human beings found and find themselves trapped within a social structure that promises more than it can deliver. They are victims of the myth of "wine and roses." Their unresolved Oedipal conflicts have produced shared states of anhedonia; neither the men nor the women can make one another happy.

In Conclusion: Ending the Classic Period

If the "women's alcoholism film" feminized alcoholism, the early family alcoholism movies make the disease a thoroughly interactional, production. Dramatists such as Odets, Inge, Miller, Williams, and O'Neill[13] opened up the topic of alcoholism, and took it away from biographical stories about Hollywood stars. They centered their attention on the family, and showed how alcoholism creates all the emotional experiences that any intimate relationship could ever hope to contain: sexuality, eroticism, tabooed acts, bad faith, double-binds, violence, divided selves, twisted love, old dreams, absent father figures, dead children, alcoholic spouses, sick husbands, and sick wives.

Days of Wine and Roses ends the modern period of alcoholism films. Recall the reviews. Thirty years after *What Price Hollywood?* (1932) and at least 200 films later (see Table 1, Chapter 1) film reviewers are still complaining about the temperance treatment of alcoholism. They are still searching for final causes of the illness. They remain committed to a perspective that is simultaneously prodrinking and antialcoholism. They are opposed to temperance–melodrama treatments of alcoholism, perhaps because these films evoke moralistic memories of this historical period. They still seek and value "realistic" treatments of the disease, which do not use alcoholism as a dramatic device for telling a melodramatic love story with a happy ending. Yet they seem unaware of the fact that Hollywood really tells only one story, over and over again, the story of temptation, the fall from grace, and final redemption, a story that inevitably involves love and the failures of the male–female relationship. They are unsure about female alcoholics and what to do with them. They are not even sure what to call them; not drunkards, but maybe lushes, for they are uneasy with the term "alcoholic."

A.A. remains a mystery whose presence is accepted more in 1962 than it was in 1947 with *Come Fill the Cup*. Reviewers act "as if" they know how sponsors in A.A. act, and they "act as if" they know what A.A. meetings feel and look like. They are also certain that this thing called alcoholism is a disease, and now it has spiritual, moral, and psychological dimensions. The critics have let go of the "self-will" theory that *Days* insisted on attaching to its version of the female alcoholic.

But they have failed to make the move to the familied versions of the disease that the three films treated in this chapter have developed. This is apparently the case for three reasons. Critics read films through the performances that are given by stars. Stars give individual performances. If a performance is strong, the star is good and the movie is good. If the star's performance is weak, the film is weak. And so on. Hence it is difficult to see through a performance to the underlying story which, for the family films, is always interactional. Failing to make this move, the critics persisted in seeing alcoholism as an individual disease, not a family illness.

The films in this cycle also presented alcoholism as an individual illness. Jim's lines to Joe, about Kirstie being doomed to become an alcoholic, are indicative of this position. By the early 1960s A.A.'s allergy theory of alcoholism had yet to show how this allergy could affect entire families. (The A.A. model of recovery, as presented in these films, did not involve families with the disease.) It involved men who left their families and went off to meetings. Hence the thing being treated was the alcoholic, not the family. No wonder, then, that film critics read alcoholism as an individual disease.

The legacies of the modern period (1932–1962) are multiple, and include the following. Filmmakers such as George Cukor, Billy Wilder, Gordon Douglas, John Huston, Stuart Heisler, Daniel Mann, George Seaton, Blake Edwards, and producers such as Hal Wallis succeeded in making alcoholism a profitable topic for Hollywood. At the same time, A.A. established a firm presence in these films, and Hollywood was clearly influenced by the medical and A.A. models in their presentation of the illness. By 1962 A.A.'s framework had become a basic feature of the alcoholism film. After 1945 a serious alcoholism film, it seems, could not be produced without A.A.'s direct or indirect presence in the film's text. This meant that A.A.'s concept of the "bottom" became part of any film's story. Hence the presence of DTs, self-degradation, self-abuse, violence, and the destruction of marriages and families. With the concept of "hitting bottom" came the notion of redemption and recovery, which involved the presence of some or all of the following: a psychiatrist–physician, A.A., a loved-one, a spiritual experience, or self-will. If A.A. medicalized the illness, it also feminized it, and it did this with the "female alcoholism" films discussed in Chapter 4. Paradoxically the medicalization of the illness painted a harsh image of the medical treatment of alcoholics. *The Lost Weekend* set the tone for this negative representation, which was continued through *Days of Wine and Roses*. As Ritson (1979) notes, alcoholics seeing these films would be loath to seek medical treatment for their infirmity. As A.A. and Hollywood worked together, it was natural that Hollywood film stars, themselves victims of the illness, would become topics of these films. Hence the biographical legacy of the modern period.

Cinematically, the flashback, the dream sequence, and the voiceover became standard filmic techniques for presenting the alcoholic's subjective, inner, psychological experiences. These techniques were often combined with the apparatuses of "film noir," including darkened rooms, low-key lighting, lighted faces, and shadowy images. However, the fatalistic plot structure of "film noir" movies was often blended, or modified to fit the storyline of a love story, melodrama with a happy ending. The grimmer, deadlier side of alcoholism was infrequently shown. Hence the importance of the *Star Is Born* cycle, which continues to altruistically sacrifice its version of the alcoholic hero to his disease and his woman.

The Lost Weekend established the viability of a Hollywood star playing an ordinary alcoholic. This precedent opened the door for other male and female stars to play alcoholics. Actors and actresses such as Fredric March and Janet Gaynor, Ray Milland and Jane Wyman, James Mason and Judy Garland, Claire Trevor and E. G. Robinson, Susan Hayward and Eddie Albert, Burt Lancaster and Shirley Booth, Bing Crosby and Grace Kelly, Jack Lemmon and Lee Remick, were inserted into these films, and paired in alcoholic-lover/wife relationships. Such pairings made alcoholism a gendered production, and typically cast the woman in the part of defining alcoholism's effects on the marriage. The star's presence further established the credibility of the alcoholic character as a screen role for prominent Hollywood actors. At the same time it ensured that this character would take on "heroic" and "heroine" like dimensions. Tough guys like Lancaster, idols like Crosby, comedians like Lemmon, and solid stars like March and Mason could play alcoholics and not suffer in popularity at the box office. Female stars like Hayward and Remick could also play alcoholics. Indeed their presence in these roles often added to a film's financial success. The star's legacy, established by the modern period, increased the likelihood that prominent Hollywood celebrities would continue to play such roles.

Stars having DTs, alcoholics committing suicide, divorces, fires, A.A. sponsors, lectures on alcoholism as a disease, recitations of A.A.'s Serenity Prayer, shame, sexual promiscuity, violence, incest, terrified children, angry fathers, lost jobs, biographies of Hollywood alcoholics, love stories, and melodrama were among the legacies of the classic–modern period. Still, the disease was an individual production, something caught by the person. It was not a family illness. It remains for the decade of the 1980s to make this key point. But before that, I turn to what happened to the alcoholic in the 1962–1980 time period.

Notes

1. It is not clear that the authors of the original dramas that formed the basis of the films (Inge, Odets, Miller) had psychoanalytic intentions in mind when they wrote their stories. See Voss (1989) and Shuman (1989) on Inge, Odets (1952) and Shuman (1962) on Odets, and Miller (1988) on Miller.

2. There are three types of alcoholic families: active, where drinking is still occurring; partially recovering, where one, but not all members are in some recovery program (i.e., A.A.); and recovering, where all members are in a recovery program (see Denzin, 1987c, pp. 11–12). In two of the films (*Sheba* and *Days*) at least one family member is in A.A.

3. This Odets play was brought back to the stage in 1982, with Faye Dunaway in the role of Georgie and Dick Van Dyke as Frank. This version was televised in 1987.

4. Georgie's father was in vaudeville and always on the road. At one point she tells Frank, "I might not have married you if I'd had a father." She describes herself in these words, "I'm just a girl from the country. The theatre and the people in it have always been a complete mystery to me." The country girl line is contradicted by the fact that in the simply furnished room she and Frank live in there are books by Balzac, Montaigne, and Dreisser that she reads.

5. Odets was proud of the last scene. "[It] is the best technical job I ever did. It could only be on opening night in New York. What woman would leave her husband then but a real positive horror gal" (Odets, in Aulicino, 1952, p. 57).

6. See Basic (1989) for a powerful refutation of this interpretation. Basic argues that Georgie has no desire for Frank making a comeback as an actor. Her goal is his comeback as a human being.

7. A.A. collaborated on both the television and film versions (Robertson, 1988, p. 91; Miller, 1988).

8. "Easy Does It," "Live and Let Live," "First Things First," "Think, Think, Think." Above the slogans hangs A.A.'s Serenity Prayer.

9. "Today the foes of strong waters are more subtle in how they attack this sometime accessory of social evil, and 'alcoholic' is now the word that describes the problem drinker, rather than 'drunkard.' "

10. The *Newsweek* reviewer also made reference to *The Lost Weekend*. "It is a mark of the maturity of the movies that the mere appearance of a credible drunk on the screen is no longer shocking enough to mask a film's defects. Ray Milland's booze-and-bats bout with delirium tremens was so daring in 1945 that one forgave *The Lost Weekend* for its fortuitously happy ending."

11. A 1961 release, based on Jack Gelber's stage play, about addicts awaiting the arrival of their heroin connection.

12. Harwin and Otto (1979, pp. 43–44) suggest that Kirstie's inability to come home at the end of the film can be read as a failure (her immaturity and inability to cope with "the role of wife and mother) or a triumph (her seeing something about life that Joe doesn't). The antithesis within these two interpretations represents the duality of the film . . . [which] is built on a series of contrasts: the

rural simplicity of her childhood . . . the massive complexity of city life . . . the brightness of the city; the greyness of everyday life . . . the world of alcohol and the world of sobriety. Kirstie . . . embodies this duality; is she a 'dead soul' or is the world around her dead?"

13.   O'Neill's *Long Day's Journey Into Night* was released as a film in 1962. This was a study of a multiply addicted family: the mother to morphine and codeine and the father and one of the sons to alcohol; the other son is dying of TB. Because it is a picture of a family in the 1910s I have not included it in my analysis. It is a superior play and film, equal in force to Albee's study of an alcoholic marriage with an imaginary child, *Who's Afraid of Virginia Woolf?* (1966).

PART III:

1962–1980: THE LOST ALCOHOLIC?

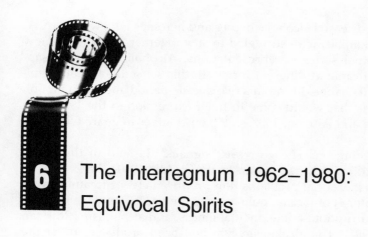

6

The Interregnum 1962–1980:
Equivocal Spirits

"Help me make it through the night."
(Kris Kristofferson)
Interregnum: "The time between reigns.
Any breach in continuity of order."

The following argument organizes this chapter.[1] The years between 1962 and 1980 are commonly understood as a period when, with few notable exceptions, the alcoholic stood out in the cold (i.e., Maslin, 1988b). Observers have assumed that the recreational drug culture of the 1960s, and the aftermath of the Vietnam war pushed to the side any consistent preoccupation with alcoholism as a social problem (see Corliss, 1988, p. 76; Ray, 1985, pp. 153, 254–55).[2] (Table 2 reveals that this is not the case.)[3] As argued in Chapter 1, although the interregnum corresponds to the fall in popularity of the social realist film, the alcohol (and now drug) film did not disappear. If *The Lost Weekend* (1945) started the classic period, then, so the argument goes, *Days of Wine and Roses* (1962) ended it. This was the heyday of "social realism" in Hollywood (Mast, 1976, pp. 315–18). It would not be until 1988, with the release of *Clean and Sober*, that film critics would see a continuation in the treatment of the alcoholic that these earlier films had established (see Benson, 1988a,b; Corliss, 1988; Maslin, 1988b; and the discussion in Chapters 9 and 10).

In this respect the decades of the 1960s and 1970s can be regarded as an interregnum, or a time between filmic reigns when a rupture in Hollywood's treatment of drinking and the alcoholic occurred. Alcohol (and drugs, always equivocal spirits; Gilmore, 1987) became even more so during this time period. Excessive drinking was not automatically connected to the problems that appeared in drinker's lives. Having earlier created diseased alcoholic heroes and heroines who went to A.A. and alcoholic families who struggled to stay together, Hollywood now turned to another series of representations. Alcoholics did not disappear, they just came in different forms. In this sense the "alcoholism" film underwent change during this two decade period and set in motion transformations that would come to fuller expression in the 1980s (see Chapters 7–10, and Altman, 1987, p. 97, on changes in genre films over time).

More was going on. The year 1962 signaled the end of the era of "social realism," which had begun in the middle 1940s (Ray, 1985, p. 273). The realistic, social problems film produced classic treatments (as noted in Chapter 1) of racism, delinquency, unemployment, the returning veteran, corruption, crime, mental illness, and alcoholism (Roffman and Purdy, 1981). The alcoholism film had been produced under the umbrella of the social realist film (Roffman and Purdy, 1981, pp. 9–11). In the 1960s the "auteur policy" (Sarris, 1968; Bazin, 1967, 1971) displaced social realism as the dominant ideology in the production and interpretation of films. Auteurism argued "that one person, usually the director, has the artistic responsibility for a film. This means that films can be studied like novels or paintings—as clearly individual productions" (Monaco, 1981, p. 422; see also Carringer, 1985, p. ix). Sarris constructed a rating system of directors, with 11 categories in descending order. At the top (the "Pantheon" directors) were the comics (Chaplin, Keaton), the genre directors (Ford, Hawks, Hitchcock), and the poet–artists (Lubitsch, von Sternberg, Welles). Category five, "Less than meets the eye," contained the social realist directors such as Huston, Kazan, and Wilder. This list had the effect of removing from prominence the social realist directors of the 1950s (see Schatz, 1981, pp. 8–9). Social realism, and social problems films about alcoholics were challenged by auteurism.[4] Hence many of the films about alcoholics in this time period were made against the backdrop of the "auteurist" influence.[5] However, as Hollywood fell on the agenda of "auteurist" practices, and backed away from the social problems film, television turned to the topic, adapting the "social realist" agenda to the "made-for-TV movie" format" [see Gabbard and Gabbard, 1987, pp. 112–14, and TV films such as *A Sensitive, Passionate Man* (1977), and those analyzed in Chapters 7 and 8].[6]

Table 2 reveals that at least 45 award-winning, top money-making movies, with a focus on excessive drinking and/or drug use and abuse, were released in this time period. Alcoholics, alcoholic marriages, and alcoholic families persisted as topics of attention, but they were treated in ways that significantly differed from their representations in the "classic–modern period." In their search for scripts Hollywood studios,

Table 2.   *Alcohol and Drug Films: 1960–1980*

Year	Representative Films	Year	Representative Films
1960	*Butterfield 8*	1973	*The Last Detail*
1961	*The Hustler*	1974	*The Morning After* (MTV)
1962	*Long Day's Journey into Night*		*The Longest Yard*
	Tender Is the Night		*Woman Under the Influence*
	Sweet Bird of Youth	1975	*Lenny*
1963	*The Prize*		*The Man with the Golden Arm*
	Hud		*Shampoo*
1964	*The Night of the Iguana*	1976	*A Star Is Born*
1965	*Cat Ballou*		*W.C. Fields and Me*
	A Patch of Blue		*Network*
1966	*Who's Afraid of Virginia*	1977	*The Squeeze*
	Woolf?		*The Goodbye Girl*
	Harper	1978	*National Lampoon's Animal*
1967	*Blow-up*		*House*
1968	*The Graduate*		*Coming Home*
1969	*Easy Rider*		*The Deer Hunter*
1970	*M*A*S*H**	1979	*Cocaine Cowboys*
	Woodstock		*The Rose*
	Diary of a Mad Housewife		*The Cracker Factory*
1971	*Little Big Man*		*Apocalypse Now*
	The French Connection		*California Suite*
	The Last Picture Show	1980	*Coal Miner's Daughter*
1972	*Fat City*		
	Lady Sings the Blues		

as they always had (e.g., the use of Inge and Odets in the 1950s; Ray, 1985, p. 131; Mast, 1976, pp. 327–28), continued to turn to classic and contemporary American fiction and drama and there, in the works of Eugene O'Neill, Tennessee Williams, William Faulkner, F. Scott Fitzgerald, and Edward Albee, they found starkly drawn alcoholics who would be played by leading actors and actresses. Although A.A. and treatment centers are gone, alcoholics, and the problems they created, were everywhere present, from comedies, to family melodramas, westerns, and filmed biographies; often presented as "hopeless" cases, like their counterparts in the 1950s, these figures were present in *The Hustler* with Piper Laurie's unstable drinking female figure; Tennessee Williams' *Sweet Bird of Youth*, where Geraldine Page played a fading alcoholic movie queen; Richard Burton's performance of an alcoholic former clergyman in John Huston's *Night of the Iguana* (also from T. Williams); Lee Marvin's performance of a drunken gunman in *Cat Ballou*; *Lady Sings the Blues*, *W. C. Fields and Me*, and *The Rose*, the biographical treatments of drug-addicted Billie Holiday, alcoholic W. C. Fields, and alcoholic/

addict Janis Joplin; *Fat City*, and *The Squeeze*, where Stacy Keach plays first an alcoholic boxer and ex-cop; the remake of *The Star Is Born* with Kristofferson playing an alcoholic-cocaine addict; *The Man with the Golden Arm*, where Frank Sinatra plays a heroin addict; and *The Cracker Factory*, in which Natalie Wood enters treatment for depression, is diagnosed an alcoholic, and ends up in A.A.

The Alcoholic in the Interregnum: Phases in Representation

Further inspection of Table 2 reveals that this interregnum breaks into three phases.[7] From 1960 to 1966 the alcoholic is a problem drinker, and the label alcoholic may be employed, but his or her problem is not alcoholism,[8] it is something else: a bad marriage, a guilty act from the past, the death of a child, a betrayal, an affair, or a flawed self (*Long Day's Journey into Night, Tender Is the Night, Sweet Bird of Youth, Who's Afraid of Virginia Woolf?*). From approximately 1966 to 1976 drinking and drug-using are presented (with exceptions, *Fat City, Lady Sings the Blues*) as unproblematic, carefree activities, which carry few, if any negative consequences for the drinker/user and his or her associates (i.e., *Blow-Up, Easy Rider, M*A*S*H*, Woodstock, The Last Detail, Shampoo*). This is the decade that celebrated the values of America's drug counterculture (see Ray, 1985, pp. 254–55). From 1976 to 1980 the pendulum begins to turn back to the "classic" model.[9] In rapid succession *A Star Is Born, W. C. Fields and Me, Network, The Squeeze, The Deer Hunter, Apocalypse Now*, and *The Rose*, show people having serious problems with drinking and drug use. Ironically, the decade ends both with a critique of the "rock-and-roll" counterculture (*The Rose*, Flemming and Manvell, 1985, pp. 139–145),[10] the Vietnam War (*Apocalypse Now*), and the woman's movement (*Kramer vs. Kramer*). By the end of the 1970s Hollywood had reestablished its connection to the "classic" period in which A.A. and the alcoholic were united in a family melodrama.

In this chapter I will analyze five films that reproduce components of the "classic" image of the alcoholic: *Fat City* (1972), *Lady Sings the Blues* (1973), *A Woman Under the Influence* (1974), *W. C. Fields and Me* (1976), and *A Star Is Born* (1976).

Fat City (1972)

Alternatively praised as Huston's best film in 25 years (Canby, 1972, p. 6; Gilliatt, 1972, p. 53; Knight, 1972, p. 61), and damned for both its refusal to stay close to the original novel (Samuels, 1972, p. 148), and its slow pace and muttering dialogue (Schickel, 1972, p. 20), *Fat City*, on the surface a boxing film, reminiscent of *The Set-Up* (1949), immediately takes the viewer into a place and a time that are outside mainstream America. The time is 1970. The place is Stockton, California, skid row, and the Rescue Mission. Mexican and black American winos are on the street corner. This is the story of Billy Tully and his friends: Oma, an alcoholic barfly who takes up with him while she is waiting for her black lover Earl who is serving time for assault, Ernie, a young, up-and-coming boxer, and Ruben, Billy's former manager. The story, a simple tale of survival, takes place in the world of the down-and-out, where big dreams, failed comebacks, and barroom brawls are daily occurrences. Here days and nights start and end in drunken states. Billy is a broken down, alcoholic boxer. He lives in cheap hotel rooms, gets drunk everyday, and works as a farmhand picking California fruit and vegetables to make ends meet. Deserted 18 months ago by his wife, after losing a crucial boxing match in Central America, Billy is just now ready to attempt a comeback.

As the film begins, Billy, out of shape and overweight from too much drinking and smoking, drifts into the local gymnasium and meets Ernie Munger, a young boxer, whom he introduces to Ruben who signs him up. Ernie is knocked out in his first professional fight. Billy wavers in his decision to resume boxing, and continues his job picking fruit. One evening, drunk at a local bar, he meets and picks up Oma, who is also drunk. The two move in together, drinking and constantly fighting. Billy leaves Oma to return to the ring. Ernie has lost his second match, and subsequently married his highschool girlfriend Faye. Ernie and Billy meet in the fields, where they are both picking fruit. Ernie encourages Billy to get back in shape. Ruben arranges a match for Billy with an aging, sick Mexican. Billy wins, but receives only a small percentage of the winnings. Outraged, he gives up boxing. Returning to Oma's apartment he finds that Earl has returned. Handed his clothes in a box (Earl, "what's a man's is his"), and told never to come back ("Don't come around here no more"), he leaves. Some time later Ernie, who has returned to fighting, encounters Billy, drunk and dirty, outside a skid-row cafe. Billy invites him to have a drink, and Ernie says he does not drink anymore. Billy persists: "Come on. You won't even have a drink with your old buddy. Mind if I say somethin' personal. You remember that first time we met? I said to myself, 'now there's a guy who is soft in the center.' Forget it. . . . You got everythin goin' for you. Can I buy you a cup of coffee?" Sitting in silence in the not so well lighted cafe, served coffee by a Chinese cook, Billy speaks philosophically about life: "Before you can get rollin' your life makes a beeline to the drain." He then pleads with Ernie to "stick around, talk awhile." It is clear that they have nothing to say to one another. The film ends with the words from

Kristofferson's song, "Help Me Make It Through the Night" playing over the credits.

Alcoholism has the best of Billy. This is clear from the film's opening shot of Billy alone in his hotel room with empty bottles on the dresser, moving to his early morning bouts in the bar, to his drinking from a pint in the onion fields. At least, however, he is able to function in the outside world. Oma is not. Shown in only two contexts, the bar and the hotel room, she is perpetually drunk. Her red hair is always in disarray. Her dresses are unzipped, or she appears robeless in a slip. Always foul mouthed, with a glass of sherry near by, she looks only for a reason to fight with someone. Locked in an imaginary struggle with her two ex-husbands and her lover Earl, she takes up with Billy as a convenience, for she dumps him when Earl gets out of jail.

On the night that Billy leaves her they engage in the following drunken interaction, which is typical of their exchanges. Billy is fixing dinner. Oma is sprawled on the bed. She asks Billy for a robe as he throws newspapers and magazines off the table, in preparation for eating. Carrying a bottle to the table, he sees that Earl's box is gone. Billy: "Why didn't you tell me?" Oma: "Cause I just woke up. I guess I forgot. You don't trust me do you?" Billy: "I'm tryin to cook supper. If I didn't cook I wouldn't eat. You drink yours! I want you to eat. You need your protein." Oma: "I don't take orders from anybody. I'm not gonna eat with somebody who talks to me like you do." Billy: "Just forget it! Just go on. Starve to death. See if I care." Oma: "I'll have a little." Billy: "I don't want you to" (he grabs her plate and food falls on the floor). She sits down and drops her cigarette in a glass of sherry. Billy: "How do you like it?" Oma: "Fine!," slamming her fork on the plate. Billy: "I give up! All I've been tryin to do is get you to eat your supper. I'm gonna take a walk." He walks to the door, she tries to stop him, but he leaves. The next time she sees him, when he comes to get his box of clothes from Earl, she screams, "Christ! Mary and Joseph. Look who's here!" Thus ends their relationship.

If Oma lives to drink and fight with men, Billy lives to fight and be a man. Trapped in bitter memories about the fight he lost in Panama, unable to forget his ex-wife, his life circles around the hope that he can get everything back, if he just gets in shape and has one or two good fights. Winning his comeback fight, he cannot accept Ruben's terms for remaining on the payroll. He angrily goes off into the night to start anew a life of cheap hotel rooms, days under the sun in the California fields, booze in pints, and lonely nights in bars, looking for someone to help him make it through the night to the next day, when the cycle starts all over again.

Alongside this cycle stands Oma, caught in her own battle with herself; at least she has Earl back. Billy has nobody. But Ruben will always be there, as he was 18 months ago. And even though Billy is nearing 30, he is not too old to make one more comeback. So life goes on in Stockton.

Huston's film praises this way of life, finding dignity in each of his characters; the alcoholism theme merely becomes one more signifier of what it is like to survive on the periphery, where you have only your body, your soul, and your dreams to live on.

Lady Sings the Blues (1972)

Lady Sings the Blues is the only one of several proposed film biographies of the late jazz singer Billie Holiday (Eleanora Fagin) to make it to the screen.[11] It belongs to that "musical biography subgenre in which a famous star of another era is not so much imitated as evoked by a current star" (Sarris, 1972, in *FilmFacts*, 1972b, p. 394).[12] Dead at the age of forty-four in 1959, Billie Holiday led a life of alcohol abuse and drug addiction. Before she died she wrote her autobiography (1956). The film is a loose adaptation of this book.[13] It is not a happy story. Billie Holiday gave her life for the success she achieved in the white and black worlds of jazz and blues.

Like other films in the biographical "genre" the narrative unfolds in a linear manner, pinpointing the key positive and negative events in her life. It covers the years 1936–1959 in her life. It moves from the rape scene in childhood, to prostitution in adolescence, fame on the road, drug addiction, the fall from grace, imprisonment, the rise again to fame, and the final fall.

While starting in 1936, with an opening sequence of black and white photographs, dated New York City, 1936, the film immediately turns into an extended flashback treatment of her life, detailing the significant moments just outlined: her childhood rape, being turned out as a prostitute in a brothel in Harlem, an early obsession with listening to old blues singers, taking a chance and auditioning as a dancer and singer at a Harlem night club (shades of *Cotton Club*), being discovered by Piano Man, developing her own unique vocal style (called Lady Day), becoming the mistress of Louis McKay, going on a road tour of the south with two white musicians (Reg Henry and Harry), encountering racism with the Klan, developing a dependency on alcohol ("Give me a shot of that bourbon in my bag, will you?"), learning how to shoot-up on morphine and coke, denying her addiction to McKay ("I've only taken a few shots, only when I've need it. I'm not hooked." Louis: "What do you think coke is. It's shit. What are you provin' with that needle?"), being kept off a New York City radio station because of her race, becoming more dependent on drugs and alcohol after her mother's death, threatening to kill McKay when he takes her drugs, checking herself into a sanitarium to get clean (she is given less and less of the drug, no treatment is ever shown), being arrested and imprisoned for violations of the Federal Narcotics Act, getting clean in prison, losing her cabaret license, going back on the road and becoming a star again, relapsing in Los Angeles with Piano Man ("Why don't you get some stuff. I'm really depressed. I'm down."), and returning triumphant to Carnegie Hall. The film ends with Ross on stage at Carnegie Hall singing "God Bless the Child." A spilt screen shows newspaper headlines informing the viewer that her appeal for her cabaret license is denied, that she is rearrested on drug charges, and that she dies at the age of forty-four. The music from this song plays over the film's credits.

This film is a landmark in black motion picture history (Gelmis, in *Filmfacts*, 1972b, p. 390).[14] It makes the claim that the life of a black female musician is as important as the life story of a white female (e.g., Lillian Roth). The film continues the tradition of treating alcoholism and drug addiction in a biographical manner, using a star's life as the vehicle for the telling of this story. Like Roth's movie, the film offers a simplistic theory of her addiction and her relapses. West (1972, in *Filmfacts*, 1972b, p. 392) complains that "The chief problem with this movie is that it fails to explain . . . why her life was filled with tragedy. . . . It is pop culture—Hollywood romance about a talented girl singer and her knight in shining armor lover—smothering all the toughness and gritty realism of black culture and specifically the world of jazz." West also suggests that there is reverse racism in the film, for the white man who gets Holiday hooked stays "uncannily clean."

A Woman Under the Influence (1974)

While read as an account of madness and insanity in the family, shaped by the interactional, double-bind theories of Bateson (Flemming and Manvell, 1985, p. 40), *A Woman Under the Influence* elaborates the twisted relationships that exist in the kinds of disturbed (and alcoholic) families discussed in the last chapter, especially *The Country Girl* and *Come Back, Little Sheba*.[15] In a play on the colloquial phrase "under the influence," Cassavetes's film is set in motion by the events that happen after the night that Mabel gets drunk and comes home with a strange man. Although drinking does not figure centrally in the events that follow this spree, Mabel's madness reflects another influence she is under, namely the double-bind structures of communication that exist in her marriage with Nick.

The sequence of events in the film is straightforward, although how they are told is not so simple. The story takes place over a six-month period, divided into two basic segments, the thirty-six hours that precede Mabel's confinement, the six-month period in the mental hospital, which occurs off screen, and the twelve hours after her return. Here are the events. Husband breaks date with wife. Wife leaves house, gets drunk, picks up man in bar. Husband comes home. Husband and wife fight. Wife begins to go crazy. Wife goes crazy and is hospitalized for six months in a sanitarium where she receives shock treatment. Wife comes home to a family reunion and she and husband go to bed.

The actual telling is more confusing. Nick and Mabel are planning a night out on the town. Mabel spends the day getting ready for the evening, lisening to the opera on the radio, laying out clothes, cleaning the house, and taking care of the children. Nick, a blue-collar worker, calls and says he will be late. Mabel gets dressed, goes out, gets drunk, and brings a man home. At this point Cassavets's editing quickly begins to violate "the reality of events" (Westerbeck, 1975, p. 360) in order to reveal the inner psychological worlds of Mabel and Nick. Things appear to happen out of order. While Mabel is beating off the advances of the man she has brought home, the films cuts to the next morning where we see her waking up alone. This creates the impression that she in fact did not spend the night with him. However, the man emerges from the bathroom a few minutes later. Whether or not he spent the night seems irrelevant to Cassavets's psychological point that emotionally Mabel became involved with him. The action next cuts to Nick's belated return. He brings his buddies home from work for a spaghetti breakfast. Mabel is dazed and afraid. The viewer is still not sure if the man spent the night and waits for Nick to fly into a rage, which he does when he discovers Mabel innocently closeted with the man whose children had come over to play. Mabel comes on to a black member of Nick's work crew. Nick screams, "Mabel, you've had your fun, that's enough! Get your ass down!" From this point the film moves into her insanity. Soon she is on the street in crazy-lady clothes (miniskirt and pink socks), asking strangers for the time of day and flagging down her children's school bus. Her anxiety intensifies. Friends and relatives recoil and freeze in her presence. She withdraws into herself. Nick attempts to shout her out of her state, "I LOVE YOU" he screams. Nothing works and soon the family doctor arrives and she is sent off to the "loony bin." On her return, family and friends gather, at Nick's urging, for a dinner. Still in bad shape, Mabel escapes into a private world in her head. She makes a feeble attempt at slashing her wrists. As suddenly as it has erupted, the scene returns to quiet. Parents and children reassure one another of their love. Mabel and Nick go off to bed. "No final solutions . . . just an episode of tranquility in a rough crossing" (Kopland, 1975, p. 60).

Mabel is a mid-1970s housewife; not a part of women's liberation per se, her battles are against herself, her husband, and her family. No where to go but inside her head, the taking of the drink symbolizes the futility of her situation, yet her desire to escape and to be free. But free she cannot be for she is under the influence of a family and class structure that will not let her go. Her madness is everyone's.

W. C. Fields and Me (1976)

This film is still another attempt by Hollywood to turn the biography of a famous alcoholic entertainer into a commodity. Perhaps the most famous drunk in America, W. C. Fields (1897–1946) brought to the screen a series of classic comedies (*Million Dollar Legs, Wiggs of the Cabbage Patch, Tillie and Gus, My Little Chickadee, The Bank Dick, You Can't Cheat an Honest Man, Never Give A Sucker An Even Break, International House*), which rank next to those of Chaplin and Keaton. Fields was known as an "incurable" insomniac, and a man who drank up to two quarts of gin a day for thirty years. He gave us the character Egbert "So-use," spiked child performer's orange juice with gin, complained about babies who suffer from "milk breath," and apparently hated women, dogs, children, and swans. First a star on Broadway in the 1925 *Follies*, he made the transition to Hollywood in the early 1930s, became friends with a group of fellow alcoholics and heavy drinkers, including John Barrymore, Gene Fowler, Dave Chasen, and theatrical agent Dockstedter, wrote and sold scripts, and by the early 1930s was an established Hollywood star.

During the wrap-up party at the completion of a new film, Fields and his drinking buddies met an aspiring actress named Carlotta Monti. The next day Fields invited her to become his live-in secretary. She remained with him from that time (1932) until his death on Christmas day, 1946. Carlotta Monti wrote a book about her time with Fields and the film is roughly based on this account, although it takes factual liberties with dates, sequences, and information about Fields' life that he shared with Monti (i.e., his marriage).

Critics generally faulted the film for its historical inaccuracies (including when and how Fields got to Hollywood, see Arnold, 1976; Crist, 1976; Knight, 1976, all in *Filmfacts*, 1976, p. 63; Canby, 1976a, p. 28), although some praised Steiger's performance of Fields (Thomas, 1976; Kroll, 1976; Sarris, 1976, all in *Filmfacts*, 1976, p. 63, but see Canby 1976a, p. 28). Despite these disclaimers, the film succeeds in presenting the life of a lonely, bitter, aging alcoholic, who confronted the world with an acerbic, hilarious wit. The night of Field's death, when he asks Carlotta to turn the hose on the roof over his room to create the sound of rain, lingers in the viewer's memory.[16]

A Star Is Born (1976)

Predictably, the *Star Is Born* reappears in the mid 1970s. The 1976 treatment of this by-now familiar story is altered only somewhat from the 1954 version. Now both stars are musicians. John Norman Howard (the new name for Norman Maine) is a fading rock star hooked on drugs (pot, cocaine, downers) and alcohol (Schlitz beer, Jack Daniels and Smirnoff vodka). Esther Hoffman is a rising popular singer, divorced, working with a group called the "Oreos," when she is discovered by John Norman. Like his predecessors, John Norman appears drunk at concerts, misses recording dates, disrupts performances, makes his wife into a star, predicts that he will be trouble for her, and that fame brings problems, takes phone calls for her, embarrasses her when she receives her Grammy Award, quits drinking for a period of time, and then goes back to drinking, has his work contract canceled, and finally commits suicide, this time in a single car accident when he was driving over 160 MPH.

He does not go into a sanitarium to get sober, although he is called an alcoholic by Esther and admits to being one. It is clear that he is a lonely man with no friends, who is afraid to answer the telephone, and uses drugs and alcohol as a way of dealing with his pain and fear of performing (he opens his concerts with these lines, "Are you a figment of my imagination, or am I one of yours?"). Unlike her earlier counterparts, Esther does not make plans to leave her profession, yet in her final concert she is also introduced with her husband's name, as Mrs. Esther Hoffman Howard. The critics were generally unkind to the film (e.g., Canby, 1976c, p. 27, called it a "transistorized remake [and]. . . . the drama it contains is as bogus as the star's performance when she pretends to be Esther Hoffman, unknown singer.").

These two people, Esther and Norman, or John Norman, are cultural heroes, who, like their film counterparts, especially Judy Garland and Kris Kristofferson, symbolize how American society, for 50 years, has continued to look for alibis for alcoholism. Esther and [John] Norman point to an alcoholic marriage that will not go away. *The Star Is Born* story refuses to die for these reasons. It keeps alive three obdurate features of American life: alcoholic marriages, the fantasies of fame and success for women who work, and a love story of sacrifice and loss that appears eternal and universal in its appeal. It remains for the 1990s to produce its version of this fairy tale.

Reading the Interregnum

These five films barely capture the variety of ways alcoholics, alcoholism, and drunkenness were treated in the 1960–1980 period. However, they do reveal how variants on the preclassic and "classic" paradigm prevailed, in particular the use of the musical and film biography of a famous alcoholic or addict in American popular culture. *W. C. Fields and Me*, *Lady Sings the Blues*, and *A Star Is Born* sustain this biographical tradition. *A Woman Under the Influence* and *Fat City* return to the lives of ordinary people, showing how excessive drink can trap a person in a kind of dream-like Hell.

This interregnum, with its three phases, bracketed by *The Hustler* and *Butterfield 8* at one end, with *The Rose* and *Coal Miner's Daughter* at the other, with *M*A*S*H* and *Easy Rider* in the middle, can be read as a period when Hollywood experimented with different variations on the alcoholic and alcoholic–social problems genre. The industry kept this figure alive during an era in American life when all past understandings seemed to be falling apart.[17] This experimentation can be read as setting the scene for further developments in the alcoholic's character in the 1980s where alcoholism would become attached to figures who sought help for their condition while they pursued other activities (i.e., ex-cops in A.A., see Chapters 8, 9, and 10). Hence, while a rupture occurred in the 1960–1980 time period, Hollywood maintained its infatuation with this figure, part evil, part good, part lost soul, who seemingly represents an American "folk-hero-heroine" type who will not go away. I turn next to the 1980 period and the creation of the "new diseased alcoholic family."

Notes

1. For reasons of space, this will be a brief chapter. The film period under discussion deserves several books (see, for example Wood, 1986; Auster and Quart, 1988).

2. Ray (1985, p. 147) argues that although the social problems (and social realism) film was a stable genre throughout the 1950s and early 1960s, starting in the late 1950s (1985, p. 153) Hollywood backed away from the genre (which had also been influenced by the rise of Italian Neorealism in 1945) because it exposed the ideological deficiencies of the American social structure.

also been influenced by the rise of Italian Neorealism in 1945) because it exposed the ideological deficiencies of the American social structure.

3. *The American Film Institute Catalog of Motion Pictures: Feature Films, 1961– 1970* (Krafsur, 1976), as noted in Chapter 1, lists 158 alcoholism films for the 1961–1970 period, and 220 films with drunkenness as a prominent theme. It also lists 78 films dealing with drug addiction, 58 involving drug deals, 39 involving drugs, and 29 representing drug overdose. There is very little overlap between categories for the drunkenness and alcoholism films, but more for the drug films. Hence there were nearly 400 alcoholism/drunkenness/drug films in the decade of the 1960s.

4. I am grateful to Robert Carringer for providing this interpretation.

5. This led to the presentation of antiheroes (*Bonnie and Clyde*), a glorification of "outsiders" and deviants (*Easy Rider*), the playful representation of drinking and drugging (*M*A*S*H**), the redoing of the classic western (*Little Big Man*), and the tendency to exploit previously excluded, or prohibited topics, i.e., profanity (*Who's Afraid of Virginia Woolf?*).

6. A.A. would enter prime time television in the early and middle 1980s in "Hill Street Blues," "Cagney and Lacy," and made-for-television weekly movies, and in the late 1980s, as will be noted in Chapter 8, in "Murphy Brown" (see Heilbronn, 1988 for an analysis of how alcohol and drinking work in 77 prime time, mid-1980s continuing series, including "Dynasty," "Dallas," "Mike Hammer," and "Magnum, P.I."; also see Chapter 7).

7. I am grateful to Katherine Ryan-Denzin for clarifying many of the following points about this list of films.

8. For example, Mrs. Robinson in *The Graduate* calls herself an alcoholic, but this condition is never directly connected to the break-up of her marriage, her affair with Benjamin, or her separation from her daughter.

9. See Lewis, 1982, pp. 385–86 for a history of the federal legislation pertaining to alcohol abuse during the 1960s and 1970s, which included national hearings on the problem (1969–1970), and a National Treatment Act signed in 1970.

10. The 1980s would end with a similiar critique. Although mid-decade *Sid and Nancy* (1986) offers a brutally realistic blackest of comedy account of the late 1970s punk movement "as embodied in the violent and stormy romance of Sex Pistol Sid Vicious and his heroin-addicted groupie girlfriend, Nancy Spungen" (Fenner, 1987, p. 402).

11. In 1968 David Susskind and Charles Martin proposed rival versions of the story, which were subsequently abandoned. Another version was proposed in 1971 by Ossie Davis, and an off-Broadway show, *Lady Day: A Musical Tragedy*, was staged at Brooklyn's Chelsea Theater Center in 1972, just as the film was released. This film presents the first case of a black alcoholic in a mainstream Hollywood film. In 1979 and 1983 Richard Pryor would star in three productions that take up his personal problems with drugs and alcohol [*Richard Pryor—Live in Concert* (1979), *Richard Pryor Is Back Live in Concert* (1979), and *Richard Pryor Here and Now* (1983)]. In 1986 Jenny Gago would play an alcoholism family counselor and recovering addict (*Shattered Spirits*). Adolph Caesar plays the near-alcoholic sergeant in *A Soldier's Story* (1984) and in 1988 Morgan Freeman will star as a recovering alcoholic counselor in *Clean and Sober*.

12. Previous instances of this form includes Susan Hayward as Lillian Roth in *I'll Cry Tomorrow*, Ann Blyth as Helen Morgan, Barbra Streisand as Fannie Brice in *Funny Girl*, Doris Day as Ruth Etting in *Love Me or Leave Me*, and Julie Andrews as Gertrude Lawrence in *Star!*

13.   It was severely criticized for its factual inaccuracies (see *Filmfacts*, 1972b, p. 390–91) and its creation of the "myth" that "without the support of one good, strong man, she would have had an even untimelier end." In her book Holiday said, "I was as strong, if not stronger than any of them. And when it's that way, you can't blame anybody but yourself." In response to these charges producer Jay Weston argued that "the original script was so authentic that it was tantamount to a documentary and was therefore unsaleable" (*Filmfacts*, 1972b, p. 391).

14.   Gelmis argued, however, that "The glossy, dream-machine treatment is an experience heretofore limited to movies about whites. For better or worse, black America is being absorbed into the mainstream of movie kitsch that nurtured us all." Spike Lee reverses this trend in *Do The Right Thing* (1989) and *Mo Better Blues* (1990).

15.   Pauline Kael (1974, p. 172) connects the film to R. D. Laing's theory of schizophrenia, suggesting that this is "the work of a disciple; it's a didactic illustration of Laing's vision of insanity." The film was praised by psychiatrists (see Flemming and Manvell, 1985, pp. 41–44), damned by some film critics (Kael, 1974; Kauffman, 1974), and called by others a major statement worthy of serious discussion (Sayre, 1974, Koplind, 1975). In discussing the New Woman in American film, Koplind (1975, p. 56) calls Mabel's role vanguard and preheroic.

16.   This was "the only panacea for his insomnia" (*Filmfacts*, 1976, p. 62).

17.   The decade of the 1960s in America was defined and polarized by the Bay of Pig's Crisis, the Vietnam War, the Birmingham race riots, the assassinations of John and Robert Kennedy and Martin Luther King, student and counterculture dissent peaking in 1968, the Altamont rock festival deaths of 1969, the Cambodian invasion of 1970, and the right wing reaction to protest (see Ray, 1985, p. 250). By 1960 the postwar had established many of its effects (TV, the cold war, the suburbs, the baby boom), and the "New Frontier" had been in place 10 years before Kennedy announced its arrival. As the 1960s came to an end, marginalized voices (minorities, gays, the elderly, women) began to be heard. As the counterculture pronounced the death of America, they proclaimed the dawn of a new metaphorical frontier, "an image of new possibilities derived from drugs, sexual freedom, and a vague spirituality" (Ray, 1985, p. 255). The new rock-and-roll (The Buffalo Springfield) inspired images of a "new west" to be explored through the use of drugs (*Easy Rider* again). Traditional mythology was alive in this "new" version of the frontier, which was part parody and part pastiche. The decade of the 1970s saw the fall of Nixon and Carter, the ERA movement, and a worldwide recession. Ironically, it would take another decade, the 1980s, before the members of the recreational drug culture of the 1960s would begin to have problems with their drug use. Much like the middle-classes in the 1940s and 1950s who flocked to A.A. with their alcohol problems, a new generation (in the 1980s) is not finding A.A. (and N.A.), and they are products of the two decades where Hollywood's treatment of the alcoholic by and large ignored the traditional A.A.–medical view of alcoholism so prominent in the 1950s.

(1) Daniel Mann, *I'll Cry Tomorrow* (1955).
Lillian Roth, drunk.

143

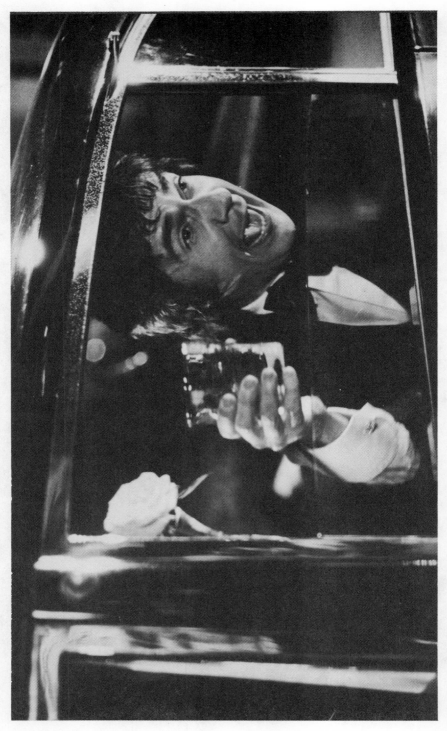

(2) Steve Gordon, *Arthur* (1981). Arthur in limousine.

(3) Billy Wilder, *The Lost Weekend* (1945). Don Birnam at favorite bar.

(4) George Seaton, *The Country Girl* (1954). Frank (Bing Crosby) relapses.

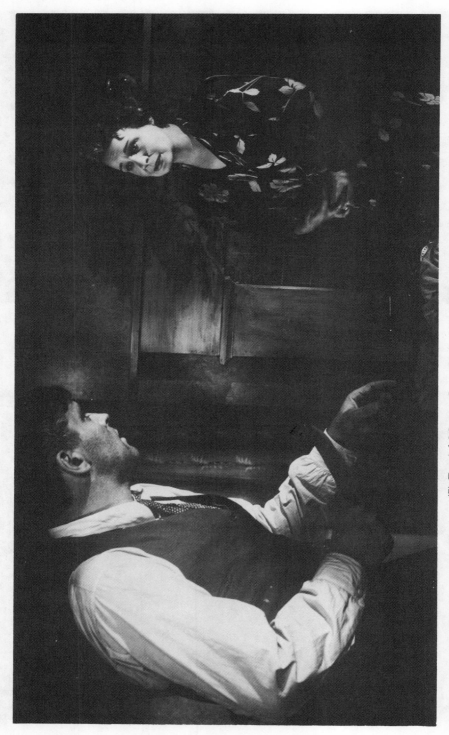

(5) Daniel Mann, *Come Back, Little Sheba* (1952). Doc (Burt Lancaster), drunk, attacks Lola (Shirley Booth).

(6) Steve Gordon, *Arthur* (1981). Playful Arthur in bathtub.

(7) Blake Edwards, *Days of Wine and Roses* (1962). Kirsten (Lee Remick) seduces Joe (Jack Lemmon).

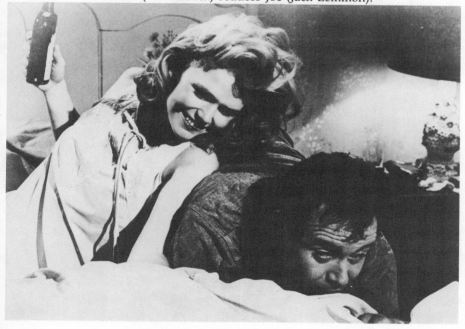

(8) David Anspaugh,
Hoosiers (1986).
Drunken Shooter
on basketball court.

(9) Sidney Lumet,
The Verdict (1982).
Frank consoled
by Mickey.

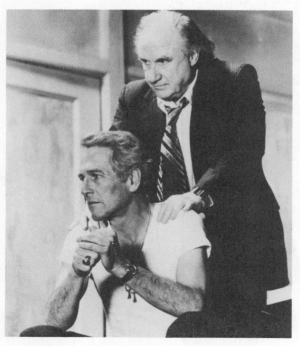

(10) Daniel Mann, *Come Back, Little Sheba* (1952).
Doc at an Alcoholics Anonymous Meeting.

(11) Glenn Gordon Caron, *Clean and Sober* (1988).
Daryl at an Alcoholics Anonymous Meeting.

(12) Glenn Gordon Caron, *Clean and Sober* (1988). Daryl and Charlie in therapy group.

PART IV:

THE 1980s: ALCOHOLISM, THE FAMILY DISEASE

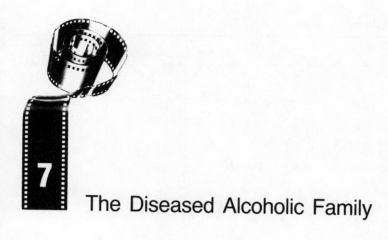

The Diseased Alcoholic Family

> "Mr. Mollencamp, according to the report you have quite a history of substance abuse. . . . In addition to remaining out of the home, I am ordering you to attend weekly A.A. meetings and I am also ordering your family to begin counseling immediately."
>
> (Judge to Lyle in *Shattered Spirits*)

The alcoholic family in the 1980s is now everybody's business. It is no longer (as it was in the classic period) a troubled site that can just be managed by the alcoholic, a spouse, a friendly doctor, God, an A.A. sponsor, and the A.A. group. Alcoholism is now a state issue; a problem to be managed by the courts, medicine, social workers, and family counselors. Hence the judge in *Shattered Spirits* (1986) (quoted above) can, in typical 1980s fashion, order an alcoholic to attend A.A. meetings, send his family into counseling, and issue a court order denying him access to his own home.

The family alcoholism films of the 1980s (see Table 3) are symbolic of radical transformations in the American family structure. These transformations turn on several factors: the expansion of the court system into the family (Donzelot, 1979; Foucault, 1980b; Lewis, 1982), the increased medicalization of alcoholism (Denzin, 1987a, Chapter 1), and, of great importance, the unwillingness of children in the alcoholic family to any longer accept an alcoholic parent for who they are (Rudy, 1989). This unwillingness is justified because of the disease conception of alcoholism, for if the alcoholic has caught this disease he (or she) has an

Table 3.   Alcoholism Films in the 1980s[a]

Year	Male	Female	Male/Female	Family
1981	Arthur	Only When I Laugh Mommie Dearest**		
1982	The Verdict My Favorite Year	Life of the Party* (MTV) Francis		
1983	Educating Rita Rueben, Rueben Tender Mercies The Dresser	Between Friends		
1984	Mass Appeal			Paris, Texas Under the Volcano
1985				Shattered Spirits* (MTV) Sweet Dreams
1986	Round Midnight** Hoosiers Blue Velvet**		8 Million Ways to Die* Hannah and Her Sisters*	Under the Influence (MTV) Vital Signs** (MTV)
1987		Story* (MTV)	Barfly The Betty Ford Story	Ironweed The Morning After The Dead
1988	Arthur 2* Clean and Sober* Bright Lights, Big City**			
1989	My Name Is Bill W.* (MTV) Wired**			
N	15	6	5	8 (34)

[a]This table reclassifies the films presented in Table 1, Chapter 1. An asterisk indicates the presence (or mention) of A.A. A double asterisk indicates a drug/alcohol combination. MTV means made for television. Two films released in 1979 (The Rose and The Cracker Factory) could be added to this list. Both deal with female alcoholics; the first is the story of Janis Joplin and the second is the A.A. story of Joyce Rebeta-Burditt, who also wrote the television script for Under the Influence. This film also deals with the effects of the author's alcoholism on her family. Magill (1986, pp. 215, 217) lists 22 alcoholism and 44 drugs and drug abuse films for the 1982–1986 time period.

obligation to do something about it. A failure to do so signals an abdication of traditionally held (and given) parental authority.

The courts (Lewis, 1982), social science (Denzin, 1987a, Chapter 8), medicine (Straus, 1982), the alcoholism treatment industry (Mulford, 1986; Denzin, 1987b, Chapter 1), the ACOA (Adult Children of Alcoholics) movement and its literature (see Black, 1981; Woitiz, 1983; Wegscheider-Cruse, 1989; Denzin, 1990a; Rudy, 1989), and the made for television films of the present decade (Gabbard and Gabbard, 1987) have turned alcoholism into a disease that bears little likeness to its feminized, familied 1950s' counterpart.

The filmic alcoholic family in the 1980s will no longer sit still and let an alcoholic ruin his (or her) life and theirs. Nor will the courts. They will now go to any length (it appears) to make the pathogenic, alcoholic middle-class family normal. The signifiers of family illness (violence, delinquency, etc.) are now read as indications of a sick structure. This structure will be found to have an alcoholic parent in the background.

From 1980 to 1989 Hollywood made at least 34 alcoholism films.[1] Table 3 presents a classification of these movies in terms of gender, and family, or relationship focus. Of these 34 films, nearly one-half deal with the alcoholic family, or with a domestic situation in which a male and female alcoholic live together (12 of 34). Further inspection makes this number even larger. All of the films classified under the female category could also be placed in the family, or male/female alcoholic column, raising the number to 17. If *Arthur 2*, *Hoosiers*, and *My Name Is Bill W.* are reconsidered as family alcoholism films, which they are, in part, then the total comes to 20.[2]

These numbers elaborate the above arguments. The family alcoholism film came of age in the decade of the 1980s.[3] Like their counterparts in the 1952–1962 period, the films in the contemporary period center on alcoholism's destructive influences on the entire family. However, although children were not an integral part of these early films,[4] they are in the 1980s. Their presence is used as one measure of the effects of alcoholism on the total family, which is now conceptualized as having a disease, called family alcoholism.

Three films are critical to this transformation. The first, *Tender Mercies* (1983), brings an adult child of an alcoholic into the drama; that is an adult raised in an alcoholic home as a child. The second, *Shattered Spirits* (1986), focuses on the effects of alcoholism on young children, while the third, *Under the Influence* (1986), depicts four adult children in an alcoholic home where the father is the alcoholic and the mother is dependent on prescription drugs.

Family alcoholism films of the 1980s speak, in part, to the generation of children whose parents either entered A.A. in the postwar years, or remain in "active alcoholism." These children are now adults who had alcoholic childhoods. These films, like the A.A. films of the 1952–1962 period, are a generational phenomenon.[5] As such, they reflect an underlying text of anger and resentment that is directed to the alcoholic, because of his (or her) neglect of them when they were children.

Influenced by the A.A. ideology concerning alcoholism as a disease, these films further medicalize and feminize the disease. They turn the entire family unit into a diseased entity that must be treated. This move requires that each family member be given a set of traits or characteristics that reflects the different ways alcoholism can affect a child and an adult. Children, as was the case for women when they entered the alcoholism film, must be shown to be negative bearers of this disease. This means they will be given an array of antisocial, maladaptive behaviors that range from the "neurotic," to the rebellious, and the prealcoholic.

A social role theory, often labeled the ACOA (Adult Child of an Alcoholic) theory, is frequently fitted to the social structure of these families, with a three-part role system enacted in the film's story. This typically involves an alcoholic, a codependent (the nonalcoholic spouse), and three to four children who play out the roles of "family hero," "scapegoat," "lost child," and "mascot" (see Wegscheider, 1981; Seixas and Youcha, 1985, pp. 48–49).[6] These role-identities are then fitted to the behaviors of the actual family members represented in the film. These movies also bring to the family unit the double-binds, the lies, the deceptions, and the paradoxical communication structures that were in evidence in *The Country Girl* and *Come Back, Little Sheba*. This is the case because the family disease theory also holds that alcoholism is a disease of distorted communication (see Hobe, 1990; Nardi, 1985; Denzin, 1987b, pp. 77–84).

The family disease theory scripts (or can be read as working its effects on) *Tender Mercies, Shattered Spirits*, and *Under the Influence* [see Kray (1988) on *Under The Influence*]. At the same time that these films celebrate "family," they turn alcoholism into an enemy, or a foe who threatens collective family life. They make the family unit, in all its fragmented forms, a "heroic" social structure that has won major and minor victories in its battles against alcoholism. How this works is the topic of this chapter.

Tender Mercies (1983)

Mac Sledge is much like Frank Elgin, only his songs and his performances differ. He is a broken-down, alcoholic country-western singer, who has lost family (he has not seen his daughter in years) and career to his alcoholism. The film is a story of his recovery as it impinges on two families: his ex-wife Dixie (a country western singer) and adult daughter Sue Ann, and his new family, Rosa Lee Wadsworth (her husband was killed in Vietnam) and her son Sonny.

The signifiers of alcoholism, including Mac's out of control drinking, empty liquor bottles, and the morning after hangover, are present from the outset. The film opens with the sounds of men fighting. The phrase "Give me the bottle," is repeated several times, followed by shouts of profanity, grunts, and the exchange of body blows. Their silhouette is given through a shaded window as the camera cuts to a young woman (Rosa Lee), standing with her hand on the shoulder of a young boy (Sonny), looking toward the sounds in the motel room. The camera cuts back to the room. A final blow is heard, a man falls to the floor and passes out. In the next scene sun is streaming into the room as a man, Mac Sledge, wakes up on the floor. A floor-level camera shot reveals the room through his eyes: empty beer cans, scattered cookies, littered cigarettes, an empty whiskey bottle, and dirt. The sound track begins to play the lyrics of a song, "it hurts so much to face reality." The man walks to a mirror, looks at his bearded face, picks up his hat, which is near a beer can and a vodka bottle, and steps outside the motel room and walks across the driveway. The woman tells him "Your friend said to tell you he had to move on." He asks, "How long have I been here?" She answers, "Two days." He asks, "Fella I was with, did he pay for the room?" She replies, "No." Going back to his room, Mac picks up his jacket, uncovers a whiskey bottle, takes a long drink, throws the bottle back on the bed, and goes back outside: "Lady, I'm broke. I'd be glad to work out what I owe you." She answers, "Alright, but there's no drinking while you're working here." In the next scene Mac is picking up trash along the roadside, and she is cleaning up the litter in the motel room. Mac Sledge has hit bottom.

Within fifteen minutes Mac announces to Rosa Lee, as they are working in a small garden, that it has been two months since he had a drink. He follows this statement with a proposal for marriage, which she accepts (in a schoolyard scene Sonny is asked if his stepfather is still a drunk). A music journalist arrives on the scene, tells Mac that his ex-wife is performing in Austin, and that she told him that alcohol is what "licked" you. He asks Mac, "Do you still drink?" In the next scene Mac tells Sonny that he lost his money through "too much applejack." Mac travels to Austin to see Dixie in concert. They fight. She states: "What the Hell you a doin' here Mac?" He states, "I was hopin' to say hello to Sue Ann." She says: "You stay away from her you hear me, or I'll have the law. All she remembers about you is a mean drunk a-tryin to beat up on her momma. You're dead as far as she's concerned. She never thinks about you. She's happy." The next day Rosa Lee tells him how hard it must be for him not being able to see his daughter. She says that "Every night I thank the Lord for his tender mercies, for you and Sonny." In anger (a song he has written has just been rejected by Harry, his ex-manager), Mac drives off, and in the next set of scenes is seen racing down the highway, forcing cars off the road, stopping at a truck stop, sitting at the bar, arguing with the bartender, and leaving the bar with a bottle, which he does not drink. Sledge writes a new song for his new wife (a young country band records the song), which contains the lines "never felt so right, hard old road behind me, you're what love means to me."

Sledge's 18-year-old daughter, Sue Ann, is next introduced. She asks Mac: "Do you recognize me? How did you recognize me?" Mac: "I just did." Sue Ann: "You've changed. You don't look like your pictures anymore." Mac: "I did try to get in touch with you. I wrote you a few letters. Did you ever get them?" "No." "Well your momma didn't have to give them to you." "I told Momma I was comin. I'm 19. She told me she'd have me arrested. She says you tried to kill her once." Mac: "I did." "Why?" "I got mad. I was drunk. I don't know." Sue Ann: "Someone told momma you were the best country singer they ever heard. Momma threw a glass of whiskey in their face. Do you think you'll ever sing again?" Mac: "It would make things a little easier." Sue Ann: "I don't need no money. Momma set up a trust fund. Everything I got is from your music. I have plenty." Mac: "You have some supper with us?" Sue Ann: "No, I got a date. He's in a band. We have to sneak around. Momma doesn't like him. . . . You know you haven't spoken my name once since I been here. You know my name?" Mac: "I used to call you little sister. I didn't know if that'd mean anything to you or not." She asks him if he remembers the lines of a song he sang her when she was little, "On the Wings of a Snow White Dove." He says he cannot remember it. As she drives off, he sings the song to himself.

The next day Sue Ann returns, and gets money from Rosa Lee because her mother has stopped her trust fund. She asks Rosa Lee if she is a singer; Rosa Lee answers that she sings in the church choir. Sue Ann states, "I thought about being a singer. I don't think I have any voice. I just don't know about the singin' her voice fades off. My daddy's quit drinkin: How'd he quit? did you ask him to?" "I told him he couldn't drink while he worked. Sometimes he went off and got loaded. He just gradually quit."

Sue Ann elopes. The country band returns; Mac and Rosa agree to go hear the new record of his song that has been recorded. The phone rings as they are leaving the house. Sue Ann has been killed in an automobile accident. As Mac goes to the funeral the lines of the song, "It's hard to face reality" are heard again. He goes to Dixie's mansion. She is intoxicated, crying hysterically, yet speaks to Mac: "Hi Mac. Why has God done this to me? . . . I gave her everything in the world she ever wanted. I had nothin' when I was her age. You remember? Gave her everything money could buy. . . . Let me have my little girl." She screams and is restrained by her manager. Mac leaves, returns home. He and Rosa are again working in the garden. Mac: "Why did she die and I live? I don't know why I wandered out to this part of Texas, drunk and you took me in. Straightened me out and married me. Why? Is there some reason?. . . . My daughter killed. . . . Why? I don't trust happenins', I never did. Never will." Sonny comes home from school. Mac gives him a new football. He sings the lines of Sue Ann's song "On the Wings of a Snow White Dove." The film ends with he and Sonny playing catch with the football. Rosa Lee looks on from the porch. His new love song plays over the film credits: "with tender hands you gathered up the pieces of my life. . . . You're the best that ever could be. You are what love means to me." The film's ending is open-ended. Giving Sonny a football suggests Mac is turning away from the musical life, yet the new song playing on the radio and soundtrack suggests he is returning to this world. The audience can have it either way, a "classic alternative to outright ideological suppression" (Carringer, 1989, p. 2).

Off-Screen Drinking

The significance of the multiple alcoholism markers in this film lies in the fact that their presence, with the exception of the opening scenes, is all off-screen. Mac's alcoholism is defined by its effects in the past, which are reenacted in the present through the scenes with Rosa Lee, Sonny, Dixie, and Sue Ann. He is never actually shown drinking; it's the effects of his drinking that the film deals with. Hence its backward looking temporal orientation. On the surface, *Tender Mercies* is an inspirational film (Desser, 1985) that holds out hope for the male alcoholic who has lost work, family, and career to alcoholism. It states that one can find new love, if one lets go of the past. It establishes a form of recovery that occurs under the auspices of will-power, God's "tender mercies," the care and love of a new wife and son, and a return to song writing. The key moments in the film when Sledge is tested and does not drink establish the power of these forces of recovery. Indeed he is able to put the pieces of his life back together, after seven years of drunkenness, because of the power of a new family, which is squarely located within religion, God, and the church.

In these respects the film takes its place in a continuous line of dramas that started with the *Star Is Born* series. It utilizes will-power, and the love of a good woman as its vehicles for establishing alcoholism's cure. To this earlier series it adds God and religion. It repeats the "hitting bottom" theme of the classic period (*Lost Weekend*), and elaborates the important ingredient of the alcoholic confronting the past, which had been suggested in *I'll Cry Tomorrow, Come Back, Little Sheba*, and *The Country Girl*. Finally the film adds a new family to the alcoholic's story. In all previous treatments of the alcoholic's situation, an existing family structure contained and defined the recovery process.

The Critics Read the Film

Reviewers were divided over the film's quality. Corliss (1983, p. 62) said that Duvall makes it "the best American movie of the new year." Crist (1983, p. 53) termed it "a small film that is truly powerful . . . brought to life by . . . Beresford." Simon (1983, p. 508) described it as a "small-scale but splendid triumph for Bruce Beresford." Denby (1983, p. 56) complained that Duvall's performance and the film "is paralyzed by integrity," while Pauline Kael (1983, p. 121) argued that "*Tender Mercies* is proof that a movie doesn't have to be long to be ponderous." The review for *Macleans* (1983, p. 52) described the writing and some of the performances as "comatose," while Canby (1983, p. 21) called it an unexpected hit, a modernist film that both disturbs and soothes the viewer, "full of surprises, the major one being that a film that so unembarrassedly and unashamedly endorses the so-called old-fashioned values could be both moving and provocative." Nearly every reviewer referenced Sledge's alcoholism (see *Film Review Annual*, 1984, pp. 1192–1202), but with the exception of Canby (1983, p. 21), the implausibility of Mac's cure went unnoticed. Rex Reed (1983, p. 41) used the phrase "drunk as a Skid Row derelict" to describe Mac's appearance at the beginning of the film. Kissel (1983, p. 20) called the film a "quiet story about an ex-alcoholic." Reviewers read the film as a small-scale love story, with Rosa Lee at its center; only Kauffman (1983, p. 25) commented on the film's attempt to take a stand on larger issues like morality, and male–female relationships in small Texas communities.

Rereading *Tender Mercies*

The film is about the three women in Mac's life: Rosa Lee, Dixie, and Sue Ann (see also Denzin, 1989e). It is not about him. It is about family, what alcoholism does to families, and women's places in family.[7] Rosa Lee is pictured as being one with nature and the Texas land. She has not been corrupted by the city, and the evils of country music and its lifestyle. Rosa Lee signifies purity, and it is her purity that rehabilitates Mac. The film is also about voices, and speaking, and the loss of voice. It is also about time. The underlying ideological forces are patriarchy, God, religion, and a stereotyped depiction of two different types of women.

The three women in the film are positioned within two categories, which may be variously termed good and evil, sacred and profane, respectable and not respectable, at the center of society, or on its fringes. They are each given a different visual style. Rosa Lee is "constantly seen in close or medium close shots, in slight to full profile. Dixie is seldom shot in medium close range. Sue Ann is always seen in claustrophobic surroundings, and is seldom shown closer than 15 feet from her father. Mac is shot in medium shots, man against the landscape, the archetypical icon of American partiarchal mythology, and tending his little plot of land as his young son looks on. Dixie is not shown out of doors, nor is Sue Ann, except for one five second shot" (Carringer, 1989, p. 1). Rosa Lee is the good woman. She sings in the church choir. She believes in God. Her voice is raised to God's glory. She lost her first husband to the foreign enemy in a war her country had to fight. The core values in her life are God, family, prayer, and love. She is respectable. She embodies the values of middle-class family life.

Dixie and Sue Ann live on the margins of society. They buy their gaudy respectability, such that it is, through Mac's royalties, Mac's songs, and Dixie's performances. Dixie sells herself to the public. As a performer Dixie not only sells herself to the public, but she also represents the unstable position of a free woman without a man. Mac's alcoholism and her own hatred of him have destroyed her. She uses drugs and alcohol to excess and lives in the past. She buys happiness through material possessions. She does not know love, caring, or forgiveness. She attempts to control her daughter and attempts to keep her daughter away from her father. She is antifamily, while Rosa Lee is profamily. Dixie's values are not the values of the film.[8] Hence she must be presented hysterically, as being out of control, as being unable to find happiness through the values she has pursued.[9] Furthermore she must be shown as losing what she values most, her daughter.

Sue Ann is presented as being both good and bad. She wishes to draw near her father whom she still loves, even though she has not see him in seven years. She has been contaminated by her mother who has forbidden her from seeing him and by telling her how evil and violent he was in the past. Drawn to a man who is like her father used to be, a heavy drinking, over 30-year-old country musician, who has been married three times, she is the adult child of an alcoholic, a product of a violent alcoholic marriage, doomed to repeat the errors of her mother (see Black, 1981).

Sue Ann has no "voice." Of the three women in the film she is the only one who does not sing, even though, as she revealed to Rosa Lee, she once thought about being a singer. Her words, "I don't think I have any voice," are significant. The film gives women one of two voices: singing in a choir or singing country music. Country music signifies destruction, when it comes from Dixie's mouth. Church music signifies God's "tender mercies," love, and strength, when it comes from Rosa Lee's mouth. Mac's destruction and subsequent recovery turn on his beginning to sing a different kind of song, the love songs to Rosa Lee. Dixie is trapped in the destructive music Mac wrote and sang during his days of active alcoholism. The movie gives Dixie the singer the voice and words of despair. It gives Rosa Lee the voice and words of God's strength. By depriving Sue Ann of a voice and words, the film leaves her no option but to be destroyed through her own willful rebellion against her mother and her past. As she flees into the future with her drunken husband she is doomed to death. She has not experienced God's "tender mercies."

The film is firm on this point. If Mac is to recover, his alcoholic past must be destroyed. He must be removed from the old triadic family structure involving himself, Dixie, and Sue Ann and placed in a new structure with Rosa Lee and Sonny. If Sue Ann was allowed to live, the film would have to deal with yet another violent, alcoholic marriage. The movie's dominant message is that the past cannot be corrected. It can only be let go of, or annihilated through its own seeds of destruction. Sue Ann is the tragic figure in the film. She has a character defect that is not of her own making. She is destroyed by forces outside her control; that is, by her father's alcoholism and the alcoholic past she inherited from him.

By siding with Sue Ann and against Dixie the film neglects to establish the point that Dixie too is a product of alcoholism and violence. Mac did try to kill her, even though his admission of this point was downplayed in his statements, "I got mad, I was drunk." In fact the film creates the impression that Dixie caused Mac's alcoholism through her attempts to control him, and because she broke her promise to get out of the business after five years. Despite Mac's departure, she carried on, as a divorced woman, raising her daughter in the materialistic, individualistic values of country music. A successful woman, she was trapped in the past, trying to do the best she could. This strategy worked until Mac reappeared. His appearance created the opening for Sue Ann to go back into the past, which her mother had attempted to keep closed. He took Sue Ann from her. By opening up the past, a necessary move, perhaps, for his own recovery, Mac destroyed the two women from his past. The film sacrifices two lives for one. More importantly the film states that family, conceived under God, is the only proper place for woman. Hence in order to establish its truth claims on the world the film must displace both Sue Ann and Dixie.

Rosa Lee moves the film, not Mac. She reflects the film's dominant values. She is not trapped in the past. She is not filled with hatred. She does not express materialistic, individualistic values. She values love, and she lives freely in the present, unafraid of the future. Her life is based on order and harmony. Her text captures Sledge and excludes Sue Ann and Dixie.

And thus, this is a woman's film, but a film about a woman comfortably at home in the house that patriarchy builds. Alcoholism is the vehicle for this movement, but the film is not about an alcoholic, it is about family. By making this choice the film offers us a fictional, not realistic, picture of alcoholism, violence, and the alcoholic family.[10] To establish its dominant message it must be violent and destructive. But it suppresses this violence through its signifying practices that place the two women from Sledge's past life outside the valued structures of family, God, and love. At this level the film tells us that alcoholic families are destructive, and perhaps have to be destroyed in order for healthy families to be created. (Under this interpretation adult children have no place in the new families of recovering alcoholics.) I turn now to *Shattered Spirits*, where a "healthy" family emerges out of the destructions brought by alcoholism.

Shattered Spirits (1986)[11]

This is a TV drama about three months in the life of the Mollencamps, a middle-class family, headed by alcoholic father Lyle, his wife Joyce, and their three children, teenagers Kenny and Lesley and nine-year-old Brian. After a violent binge at home, Lyle is seperated by a court order from his family. Forced to live in a motel, out of work, he joins A.A., while the other family members go to family counseling and Alateen, where they learn that Lyle is an alcoholic, and that they did not cause his alcoholism. Three months sober, back at his old job, Lyle returns home at the film's end to a tearful family reunion.

True to its origins in the "social conscience" made-for-television film tradition, *Shattered Spirits* quickly gets to its family alcoholism theme. Indeed the movie is a textbook application of the social role theory of the alcoholic family outlined above. All is not right in the Mollencamp house. Welcome to a dysfunctional family. Meet Brian (his imaginary name is Throckmorton P. Gildersleeves), the lost child who hides under a table, which he calls the barn, where he plays with two imaginary horses named Scotch and Soda. Lesley, the family star and over-achiever, has taken on her mother's household duties. She feels rejected and misunderstood by everyone, takes her father's side, and does not think he is an alcoholic. Kenny is the family scapegoat. He is failing classes at high school, and is constantly fighting with his father. Mother Joyce, who comes from an alcoholic family, is overwhelmed by every-thing. She is dependent on Lyle's alcoholism, enables his drinking, makes excuses for it, and denies that he is an alcoholic. Doting, alcoholic father Lyle is emotionally and physically violent when he drinks, yet devoted to his family.

The story is organized in two parts, which correspond to life before Lyle is separated from his family, and life after the separation, through to the reunion at the end of the film. These two parts are meant to represent the active alcoholism and recovery lives of an alcoholic family. The first hour of the movie establishes Lyle's out of control drinking and the dysfunctional "role" relationships that have been built up between the five family members.

The second hour takes the family through court, has Lyle called a substance abuser by the judge, introduces him to A.A.,[12] has him enroll in a computer graphics class, gets his job back, learns that his boss is in A.A., shows family meetings at a bowling alley, and at home at a picnic. Three family counseling sessions and two Alateen meetings are pre-sented. The family is depicted in a "normal" happy state as it reorga-nizes itself in Lyle's absence; in the process Lesley is moved out of her prior position of control in the kitchen and the household.

Confronting the Court

The film's decisive stance on the relationship between the court and the alcoholic family is given in the following exchange between Lyle and the judge. The judge, a woman, has just spoken the lines quoted above concerning Lyle having a history of substance abuse. He argues with her, "Excuse me your honor, I'll be the first to admit we've had some problems. There's no question about that, but substance abuse is not one of them." The judge holds firm: "Well your wife and your son Kenny don't agree. Kenny wants to remain out of the home until you stop drinking." Lyle: "That's what I hear your honor. But that's not a problem. I haven't had a drink since these kids were taken away from me. Have I hon? [turns to Joyce]." Judge: "Until we can look into this a little further, I'm going to honor your son's request. . . . The last thing in the world I want to do is break up your family. But the only way I'm willing to send these children home is if you are willing to move out." Lyle: "I beg your pardon. . . . I don't think you understand this family. I sat out in the hall all morning and I saw a lotta of the kinds of people maybe you are used to dealing with." Judge: "You may see your family outside the home. You may not return home, even to visit without the approval of Dr. Mavis Foreman."

Kicked out of the house because of the stand his son has taken, Lyle spends the next 87 days in a motel. Finally he receives Mavis' permission to come home.

The Reunion

The family has picked Lyle up at this motel and helped pack his bags. As they leave Brian finds a bottle of whiskey in a paper bag in the closet. He closes it up and says nothing. The van pulls into the driveway at home. A "Welcome Home" banner hangs from the front porch. Brian gets out, and the bottle breaks on the driveway. Lyle turns and asks: "Hey, where'd that come from?" Kenny answers, without emotion, "From your stuff." Lyle: "Come on, it's not what you think. That dumb thing's been sittin' around so long I forgot it was there. Hey, come on. I didn't even open it. [Joyce is putting the broken bottle in the paper sack.] Don't let this spoil the whole day." Kenny answers: "The bottle was already open." Lyle gives an account: "All right. I had one little drink the night I moved in. But that's it. For the past 3 months I haven't touched a drop [looks at Joyce]. You don't believe me, do you?" Lesley: "I believe you." Lyle: "Thank you." Joyce: "Lyle, the bottle was almost empty." Lyle, in anger: "Alright [raises voice]. So I had a bottle [waves finger in air]. One bottle. What difference does it make? I've been livin' alone in a stinkin' motel for the last three months. I don't think one bottle is doin too badly, do you?" (Joyce is holding Brian against her body, Lesley and Kenny have pulled off to the side, looking on.) Joyce interprets the situation: "Yes I do." Lyle: "You don't have any idea what I've been goin through, have you?" Joyce: "I know what we've all been going through and I don't want to go through it anymore." Lyle asks: "What's that supposed to mean?" Joyce: "It just means you're not ready yet." Lyle: "After all I've been through, I'm not ready yet [waves hands in the air, stomps off, kicks over garbage can]. Well thank you, I'm not ready yet." Lesley runs after him and then cries, "What if it's the truth? What if he hasn't been drinking. How do you think he feels being called a liar after all he's been through?" Kenny: "He was lying!"

In the next scene Brian tells Joyce "I'm sorry I dropped the bottle." She tells him "I'm not. I'm glad you dropped it. Now we know the truth." Brian then attempts to speak the word alcoholism: "How did he catch alca, alcoholism?" Joyce answers, "I don't know." Brian seeks to blame himself: "Do you think it was my fault?" Joyce reassures him,

"No, I know it wasn't your fault. I know he loves you very much."[13]

The film ends with the following sequence. Brian wakes up to the sound of the doorbell. Kenny puts on his shoes, as he climbs out of bed. Lesley puts on her robe. Soft organ church music begins to play. The camera cuts to Lyle at the front door. The entire family starts downstairs. Kenny asks, "Does he have a key?" Joyce: "I gave him one." Lesley, ever worrying about her father, "Maybe he lost it." Brian follows with one of his stuffed animals. Joyce opens the door. A shot, from the inside of the house to the outside, reveals Lyle, who is leaning against the side of the garage. The family is lined up behind Joyce looking out at him. Lyle speaks: "Good morning." Joyce answers: "Good morning." Lyle explains himself: "I ah, made about 7 trips to the liquor store. I called Mavis in the middle of the night and [Joyce walks toward him, hands crossed in front of her] she said maybe the best way I could say I'm sorry is if I gave you these [hands Joyce a shopping bag full of whiskey bottles]. I didn't open any of 'em. I've never asked the kids to skip school before but Mavis wanted to know if we could all come down there and see her in about an hour." Joyce agrees: "O.K. [puts her hand on his head]. You come on inside and we'll get dressed." Lyle (crying): "I'm not ready." Joyce: "O.K. We'll be right out." Lyle: "I'll be here." Joyce goes back in the house. Lyle sits down, Kenny slowly comes out and touches Lyle's shoulder, as Lyle cries. The film ends with this lingering shot of a father and son reunited. Quiet organ music plays in the background. Then the screen fills with the following information.

For More Information Write To: THE NATIONAL ASSOCIATION OF CHILDREN OF ALCOHOLICS, NACOA, 31706 COAST HIGHWAY, SOUTH LAGUNA, CALIFORNIA 92677, 877-8613.

Reading *Shattered Spirits*

The advance billing for this television movie (*TV Guide*, 1986a, pp. 5, 19, 67) gave no notice of its relationship to The National Association of Children of Alcoholics. Indeed it was described as the "story of a family headed by an alcoholic father" (Crist, 1986a, p. 5), as an "incisive drama about alcoholism, with focus on the problem drinker and his family . . . it avoids the slickeries of 'social conscience' TV drama" (Christ, 1986a, pp. 5, 19; Maltins, 1988a). But the viewer seeing the above lines directing his or her attention to an address and telephone number of NACOA suddenly reinterprets the movie from within the ACOA framework. Then the lines written by Crist (1986a, p. 19), "there is a textbook tone and case-history aura to the detailing of the effects of the father's drinking on his three children" take on new meaning. *Shattered Spirits*, as noted above, is a textbook exposition of the ACOA theory of the alcoholic family and its effects on children.

But it is more than this. It is an account of how alcoholism has become a problem of the "state" in the 1980s (see Denzin, 1987a, Chapters 1–2). Domestic violence laws now give the state the power to intervene in a family setting and separate children from their parents, and spouses from violent spouses (see Ferraro, 1989). Courts can mandate family counseling and A.A. attendance and make sobriety a condition of parenthood. Courts can define families as dysfunctional and parents as alcoholics, or substance abusers. In these moves the state implements a version of the ACOA theory, for it takes sides against parents, in favor of children. Lyle perceived himself as being punished by the court, and was finally able to accept that punishment as the condition for being reunited with his family. The punishment translated into Lyle's giving up alcohol and becoming sober. A.A. and counseling were the mechanisms for that transformation and he unwillingly accepted them. It is significant that he is never shown speaking at an A.A. meeting, and he never once calls himself an alcoholic. He merely states that he "knew for a long time that I'd have to quit and finally I did." Every other member of the family calls him alcoholic, but he refuses the label. Hence the importance of the broken whiskey bottle in the driveway and the bag full of bottles at the end of the film. The broken bottle signified Lyle's refusal to accept the court's injunction; the full bag signified his compliance with Joyce and the will of the court.

By making Lyle comply the film does not want to say that he loses his dignity, for it stakes its moral position on the behalf that a sober father deserves to get his job and his family back. And Lyle does. The alternative, being drunk, unemployed, and without family, are unacceptable to him. It is clear, however, that the family is doing quite well without him. Their treatment made them autonomous; his treatment further increased his dependence on them. In this way the ACOA theory that organizes the text sacrifices alcoholics in the name of a higher good, family.

The family alcoholism films of the 1980s make children a felt presence in the alcoholic's situation. Whereas the "other" who defined alcoholism's effects in the modern period was primarily the female, in the 1980s it is the child. This is the theme of *Shattered Spirits*. The judge will not allow Lyle to go home because Brian, Lesley, and Kenny do not want to be around him when he is drinking and violent. Nor, of course, does Joyce, but she attempts to make excuses for him. The children are afraid to go home. By shifting attention to the child in the family and to the effects of emotional and physical violence on the child (and the spouse), films like *Shattered Spirits* spread alcoholism's effects into one of society's most scared symbols: the child. But it is not enough to point a finger at how children are affected. They must be beaten, abused, and turned into emotional cripples. These damaging effects must then be shown as working their damage on the entire structure of relationships that make up the family. Working outward from the child to the family, *Shattered Spirits* heaps all of the negative features of a feminized alcoholism onto the collective family unit.[14]

But there is another story within this larger story and that is the story of Lyle and Kenny. At this level the movie is a father–son drama, a story of a son working his way back to his father and a father working his way back to his son. It is a story of a son coming of age, standing up to his father, refusing to lie for him. By submitting to Kenny's will, Lyle renounces his patriarchal power. His fate is dictated by his son, a condition he would have never accepted in the film's first hour. So even as it tells a story of a father and son reunion, the text has the child telling the father what to do.

This goes beyond the working of a cultural myth about the "wisdom" of children (see Fiedler, 1966, p. 271). It is the implementation of a myth about children, sons in particular, having the power to tell their parents (fathers) what they can do. And so, as the story brings the family back together at the end, it does so on very particular ideological grounds. The moral: alcoholism strips parents of the right to tell their children how to live their lives.

In these respects *Shattered Spirits* is a decisive film. It maps fictional alcoholic experience onto the "real" world of the police, the courts, substance abusers, alcoholism counselors, judges, family violence, enforced sobriety, and ACOA theories of the disease. These points are even more clearly established in *Under the Influence*.

Under the Influence (1986)[15]

Shattered Spirits articulated the ACOA role theory in a family of young adolescents. *Under the Influence* moves this theory one level up. Now the key players are four young adults attempting to leave behind the alcoholic household in which they have been raised. This is a story of five days in the life of the Talbots; a middle-class family from Chagrin Hills, Ohio. Father Noah is an alcoholic. He owns a hardware store. His wife Helen is a homemaker addicted to prescription drugs. The oldest son Steve is a comedian, and family mascot, trying to make it in Los Angeles. The younger son Eddie works for his father and is also an alcoholic. Eddie is the family scapegoat. The oldest daughter Ann is married, and involved in a promising business career. She is the family star, or hero, and an overachiever who is also addicted to prescription drugs. The youngest daughter Terry is a senior in high school, and an art student with a scholarship to college. She is the lost child who pours Noah's bourbon.

The story, like *Shattered Spirits*, is given in two parts. The first hour details Noah's alcoholic drinking and its effects on Eddie, Steve, Terry, Ann, and Helen; it establishes their respective identities as the family scapegoat, comic, lost child, hero, and codependent. The second hour deals with Noah's hospitalization for alcoholism, and the consequences that follow. The family, collectively and individually, is confronted by a physician who tells them Noah is an alcoholic and they are an alcoholic family. They reject this label. Noah is told that he cannot drink again. Ann separates from her husband and enters treatment for her own addiction. Noah leaves the hospital, drinks again, and dies. Eddie accepts the fact that he is just like his father. Helen begins to address her codependency and Steve tells a story about boogie men (presumably alcoholics) who can get you at night.

Significant Alcoholic Moments

The film turns on a series of crises that are produced by Noah's alcoholism, including his being drunk at the police station and having to be picked up by Ann and her husband, his early morning drinking, instead of being at work, a fight with Eddie about his carousing behavior, and his drunken embarrassment of Terry at a school open house. Alongside these episodes, which are defined by Noah's drunkenness, are a series of scenes that are intended to establish that this is an alcoholic family and this condition has produced maladaptive behaviors that are a part of every member. These scenes all have Noah as the focal point, even when he is not present. His negative presence has created a network of sick selves who barely speak to one another, yet share the same family name.

Consider the following interactions. Helen first. When she receives the phone call from the police, telling her Noah has been picked up for drunken driving, she immediately reaches for a bottle of prescription pills. Daughter Ann follows the same pattern. When experiencing a crisis or a problem she takes a pill. After making a presentation at work, which went very well, she runs off to a bathroom and takes a handful of pills. Eddie drinks all of the time. He carries a shotgun in his pickup truck. The morning that Noah is next door drinking at a tavern, instead of being at work, Eddie is shown drinking a can of beer as he waits on a customer. Arriving home before her father, Terry goes to his liquor bottle and pours out several ounces. Then she pours in vegetable coloring and adds water to the previous whiskey level in the bottle. Comedian Steve tells jokes about real families and how they ignore all the important things, like "Junior and his high-powered rifle."

Noah's negative effects are also felt in specific interactions with each of his children. When Ann tells him she received a raise at work he tells her "That's not enough!" He makes Steve tell him a joke and then states, "Well, you're sure no David Letterman." When Eddie proposes that they add a video section at the store he tells him that he is "Stupid and dumb and no damned good!" When Terry tells him about her scholarship to college he denounces her plans and questions why she even wants to go away to college.

Each child has developed a mode of adjustment to Noah's alcoholic hostility. This pattern is shown to be dysfunctional and symptomatic of a denial of the family's alcoholism. Interactions with the physician are critical on this point. The family reacts in disgust when told that "If your dad ever drinks again he will die." Ann even seeks the name of another physician who will give the family another opinion. The doctor also confronts Steve with the fact that he "sees a very sick family" and that "Alcoholics Anonymous could help your father." Steve refuses to hear him, and provides a description of how the family will respond, if told this: "Mother will collapse. Terry will blame herself. Eddie will get drunk and Dad will sit on it." In a later scene the physician tells Helen, "Mrs. Talbot, Noah may be the drinker, but the disease has affected all of you." Helen asks if she can see Ann who is recovering from an overdose of pills. She fails to address the physician's comments.

Having established its picture of a sick, alcoholic family, the film moves to a series of conclusions, all of which occur because of Noah's death. Helen gives hints of going to a therapist. Ann, as noted above, goes into therapy, although for what is never made clear. Terry accepts the scholarship for college. After firing his gun three times near Noah's grave, Eddie screams, "I'm just like him!" and Steve tells him that he has taken the first step (presumably A.A.'s first step).

Reflections on *Under the Influence*

Judith Crist (1986b, p. 5) called this a "social-problem drama that is marked by intelligence and laced with wit." Leonard Maltin (1988b, p. 1132) praised the film: "Writer and recovered alcoholic Joyce Rebeta-Burditt's incisive script delivers a powerful statement." *TV Guide* (27 September 1986b, p. 58) offered this gloss on the story's second-part: "His [Noah's] disease also makes them [the family] come to terms with the denials, guilts and hostilities they have been harboring for years."

These are generous readings. It is not clear that the family has come to terms with its' guilts, denials, and hostilities, for in no scene is there a collective family discussion of what it means for them to be members of an alcoholic family. What is clear is that the story sacrificed an alcoholic for his family. And this sacrifice was accomplished before Noah was able to accept his alcoholism or make amends to his family. Indeed the film argues that he was unwilling to make either of these gestures. If Lyle Mollencamp was forced to his knees by his disease, Noah took the other path, which was death. He would rather drink than accept his alcoholism. His drinking represented for his family his final rejection of them.

Under the Influence is an angry film. It says that many alcoholics never make up to their children. Their children go into early and middle adulthood bearing the scars of an unrepentant alcoholic parent. This burden is unforgivable, for there is help for the alcoholic and he (or she) has a responsibility to get better. Noah symbolizes a generation of untreated alcoholics. His four children are products of that generation. They are adult children of an alcoholic. They are mad at him. They are afraid of him. They don't understand him and they don't understand themselves. They are, in their own ways, just like him. This is what they find most terrifying. And this is the film's final message. Untreated alcoholics deserve what they get. But their children do not deserve what they got. They are the final, fatal victims of a disease that could have been treated.

Three Pictures of the Alcoholic Family in the 1980s

Four alcoholic families: Mac Sledge's two families, plus the Mollencamps and the Talbots. Two different views of the alcoholic, his disease, and his family. Mac and Lyle recover. Mac has the help of God and the love of a good woman. Lyle has A.A. and Mavis. Noah dies drinking. Medicine, love, and A.A. could not reach him. Mac and Lyle have understanding families who take them in, or back. Noah's family runs from him and he from them. Mac's family has no sense that it is alcoholic; Lyle's does, and Noah's kin have at least been told that they are. The "state" stayed out of Mac's and Noah's families, but not Lyle's. But how could it have entered Noah's, for his children were all adults. This state of affairs serves to underscore *Under the Influence's* position that adult children have no recourse for help; they have only themselves.

The dominant ACOA themes that structured all but *Tender Mercies*, clearly establish different positions on the alcoholic family in the 1980s. The story of the Mollencamp family is happy. Like *Tender Mercies*, everybody is back home, pleasantly contained within the confines of the all-American nuclear family system. The Talbots are a fractured family. There is no longer even a negative center that could draw the members together and then apart. Noah's dead. The members have no collective resources on which to draw. Alcoholism has destroyed their family.

This destruction is perhaps typical. One in ten alcoholics receive treatment for alcoholism (Denzin, 1987b). According to A.A. myth the other nine either die alcoholic deaths or go insane. In these respects *Under the Influence* represents a culturally believed pattern of adaptation to alcoholism. More importantly it brings to the surface a level of emotionality about alcoholism that has been suppressed in earlier periods and earlier films. It positions adult children against their parents and further asserts a child's right to be angry at a parent who does not seek help for alcoholism.

As markers of the times, these films symbolize how far into society the disease called alcoholism can go. Temperance-like in their morals, these texts hold the family and the child up as the most sacred of society's symbols. Society will tear the alcoholic family apart in order to save it. And nobody really complains. This evil alcoholic figure may have to be destroyed, if the family is to be saved. I turn now to the alcoholic heroine in the 1980s.

Notes

1. These films continued the practice established in the classic period of casting leading Hollywood figures in major roles: P. Newman, D. Moore, D. Hopper, F. Dunaway, J. Lange, G. Rowlands, J. Woods, J. Garner, J. Bridges, M. Rourke, J. Nicholson, M. Caine, J. Fonda, R. Duval, H. D. Stanton, M. Sheen, A. Griffith, and A. Finney. Leading directors were also associated with the 1980s films: Huston, Beresford, Schroeder, Wenders, and Lynch. The contemporary series follows the pattern of drawing on biographical material for storylines, although the emphasis on ordinary people who are alcoholics continues. The occupations of alcoholics in the 1980s includes entertainers, priests, lawyers, stock brokers, policemen, small businessmen, and (still) housewives. As noted in Chapter 6 (note 6) TV was also a major force in the treatment of alcoholism (including addicted teenagers) in the 1980s. One of every five alcoholism films in the 1980s has been made for television.

2. This reclassification reflects the slippery nature of my system of categorizing films. But clear-cut boundaries cannot be drawn in the 1980s, contrary to the situation in the classic period.

3. However, it is only the white middle-class family that comes alive in these films; no nonwhite, or gay and lesbian families are represented. Of course this was also the case for the classic period (see Chapter 6, note 11).

4. Only Debbie in *Days of Wine and Roses* could be said to be part of an alcoholic family, and her place in the story is largely marginal. The dead son in *The Country Girl* and the dead baby in *Come Back, Little Sheba* do not count, although their symbolic presence was certainly part of the alcoholic relationship constructed by their "parents."

5.   Robin Room suggested this point.

6.   Other roles that circulate in the literature on the alcoholic family include placaters, adjusters, and enablers (see Nardi, 1985, pp. 207–8). *Shattered Spirits* and *Under the Influence* enact all of these roles. In these ways a version of social science works its way into the representations of the alcoholic family. Persons from "real" alcoholic families then learn to attach these representations to their own experiences.

7.   By focusing on Duvall's performance, Beresford's direction, and Horton Foote's dialogue, reviewers lost sight of the film's second story, which is Mac's resolution of his relationship with Dixie and Sue Ann. They read his "ex-alcoholic" status as an indication of how his past had already been dealt with. In fact, as argued above, his "alcoholism" signifies a past life that must be unraveled and put right in the present.

8.   The review in *Macleans* (1983, p. 45) makes this point. The reviewer, after praising Betty Buckley's powerful performance of Dixie, observes that the movie "lavishes its concentrations on the wrong people"; that is not on Dixie.

9.   On women, hysteria, and the hysteric's voice see Mitchell (1984, pp. 289–90) who contends that "The hysteric's voice . . . is *the woman's masculine language* . . . talking about feminine experience."

10.   There are two key contradictions in the film's text. The first involves Mac's getting sober, and the second involves the answer to Mac's question concerning why he is alive and Sue Ann is dead, and why he wandered out to this part of Texas, and you took me in. His "cure" seems more fragile then the film suggests, and of course he came to Rosa Lee's so as to find a new family. (See Denzin, 1989e, pp. 48–49 for a discussion of these two points.)

11.   The title, of course, is a play on words. The spirits of the family have been shattered by alcoholism, and the spirits in alcohol have done the shattering.

12.   The usual A.A. signifiers are present in sign-form at the second meeting Lyle attends, including the "Serenity Prayer," and the 12 Steps. The well-dressed, middle-class male speaker, in lines like those spoken by Burt in *I'll Cry Tomorrow* and Jim Hungerford in *Days of Wine and Roses*, states, "If you drink long enough or hard enough, you either die, go insane, or you join A.A."

13.   As this interaction is occurring, Lyle is at the "Reliable Liquor Store with a clerk, holding a fifth of whiskey." Lyle, to the clerk: "No, let's make it a pint. Yeh, that's good. No, wait a second, make it a half a pint, no, no, I'll just make it one of these [picks up a minature], no, make it two of these [picks up another miniature]. No, no, just a half pint." Buys it. Recall the representations of an experience like this in *Tender Mercies*.

14.   It is significant, and no accident, that the family is cured by a woman. In this subversion of the usual strategy of having a male offer the cure for alcoholism, the film repeats the theme of the modern period where women brought, or attempted to bring their men back from alcoholism (e.g., Helen St. Clair). Now a woman brings an entire family back to health. Part of Lyle's recovery rested on his acceptance of Mavis's control over the family.

15.   The following discussion draws from Denzin (1987d). I will give a rather abbreviated treatment of this film, because of this earlier, extended analysis.

8

The New Alcoholic Heroine

"I'm a drunk, plain and simple . . . drunkenness is a disease."

(Beatrice in *Life of the Party*).

"I'm funny when I drink."

(Georgia in *Only When I Laugh*)

The female alcoholic heroine in the 1980s inherits several complex structures of meaning. As a third-generation cultural creation,[1] she wears the halo of denigration established by her predecessors in *Smash-Up*, *I'll Cry Tomorrow*, and *The Days of Wine and Roses*. She has low self-esteem, has hit a sexual bottom, found and lost men, and in the process has experienced sexual degradation. Her recovery, when it comes, like the recovery of Angie and Lillian, will be carried by a male (after a turning point experience), even when she confronts A.A. Her heroism will be defined in terms of the return to family and becoming sober. Her unhappiness (anhedonia) will be connected to sexual, career, and family failures. However, unlike her earlier counterparts, she also finds that her alcoholism is now defined as a family disease.

The 1980s give her another meaning structure, and this is institutional treatment for her disease. The first alcoholic in film to go to a treatment center for alcoholism is a woman. The state's intervention into the diseased, alcoholic family situation was explored in the last chapter. However, none of the male alcoholics experienced institutional treatment for their alcoholism. (In the preclassic and classic periods males went into sanitariums or lock-up wards to dry out or recover from DTs; but they are never shown receiving treatment.) This is not the case for the 1980s female alcoholic: her familied, feminized version of alcoholism

175

requires entry into a treatment center. (By the end of the 1980s males will enter treatment, see Chapter 9.)

The female alcoholic comes into her own in the 1980s. Eleven of the 34 alcoholism films listed in Table 3 are about her. Her occupations, as before, involve the family–work dichotomy; she is either a housewife or a performer. Her filmic career alternates between two interpretive (melodramatic) phases (A.A. and temperance): she is either a housewife cured by A.A. and treatment, or a free spirit who recovers through will power and the love of a good man.

In this chapter I examine *Only When I Laugh* (1981), a comedy, *Life of the Party* (1982) and *The Betty Ford Story* (1987) (made for television movies based on the biographies of real-life people), and *The Morning After* (1987), a genre mystery thriller with Hitchcock overtones (Milne, 1987, p. 181).

The female alcoholic heroine in the 1950s became alcoholic, in part, because she had forsaken either family for work, or work for family. Finding that she had no place to go, her drinking became a means of dealing with her loneliness and estrangement from others. She was trapped in a double-bind. The female alcoholic of the 1980s finds once more that family is not everything, and she too learns that a male-given, family-centered identity is not enough. These traditional terms will not make her happy, nor keep her sober. Indeed they contribute to her unhappiness and her alcoholism.

The woman alcoholic of the 1980s seeks and expresses a freedom from traditional boundaries and barriers that was not available to women in the immediate postwar years. This freedom turns against her and undermines her project of self-realization. In the films under consideration it is too much for her; it is presented as a burden that she cannot carry. Accordingly, she must be recontained by the forces of family and society. Her alcoholism, the consequence of her inability to be fully responsible, has created situations that she can no longer manage.

Her entry into treatment is not solely based on family matters. Over one million Americans received some form of institutional treatment for substance abuse in 1985 at a cost of over 15 billion dollars (Denzin, 1987b, Chapter 1). Treatment for alcoholism is now commonplace. What is significant is that films first address the total-institution-like (Goffman, 1961), environment of the substance abuse center through the figure and eyes of women (Denzin, 1987b, Chapter 3). This is not surprising. The family alcoholism films of the 1980s transformed the condition of alcoholism into a disease that required professional help. This familied, feminization of alcoholism presented the alcoholic as a child-like and helpless person. A danger to self and others, the female alcoholic threatened to annihilate not only herself but also her family.

No wonder then that she would be either forced or led into treatment; society's agents of social control must make her be a responsible woman. Her alcoholism thus signifies a basic threat to social order, for the uncontained, wild, rebellious woman cannot be allowed.

At the same time that her alcoholism becomes a "treatable" phenomenon, it is also changed into something else. Films such as *Hannah and Her Sisters* (1986), *Eight Million Ways to Die* (1986), and *The Morning After* (1987) use the alcoholism, or problematic drinking of a female character as just one device that moves the plot of the narrative. Their alcoholism is not the sole focus of the story being told. It is presented as a part of the character's make-up, but the dominant story-line is about something else, i.e., an affair, a murder, or a style of life. In this way the female's alcoholism is subordinated to another problem. She is simply presented as an individual who, while being alcoholic, is central to the story in other, perhaps even more important ways. (For example, in *Hannah and Her Sisters*, a character's absence from a situation is explained by the lines "She is at her A.A. meeting."). This suggests that the increasing feminization of alcoholism is associated with its normalization. These films, in a narrative fashion, make being alcoholic a commonplace occurrence. This serves to destigmatize (Goffman, 1963) the disease. Thus women, the bearers of the most negative meanings of alcoholism, open the way for its destigmatization.

Only When I Laugh (1981)

The following speech is heard as the film's credits play over a blackened screen: "Funny thing is I didn't ever like drinking. . . . I like the people you meet in bars and occasionally I've even liked the people I've gone home with from bars." (A doctor's face appears in the corner of the screen as the speaker continues. A black chair takes shape on the screen, with the speaker's head revealed. To her left is a burning cigarette with smoke curling to the ceiling.)

"I've been here before you know. I don't mean this particular dry-cleaning establishment. . . . Boy I hope we can get it right this time. . . . I want to know I can get through a six months run of a play and not have that falling apart at the seams feeling come over me. I want to spend weekends with my daughter and not have to hide my hands so she won't see them shaking, and I want to walk past a bar at 5:00 in the afternoon and know that I'm strong enough to keep right on walking" (a full shot of the doctor as screen fades to black).

These lines are spoken by 38-year-old Georgia Hines, a divorced, alcoholic, Broadway actress who has lost custody of Polly, her 17-year-old daughter. Her monologue is given to a psychiatrist (continuing the tradition of the male carrying the cure to the female), at the beginning of her 12-week stay in a treatment center for alcoholism on Long Island (actual treatment is not discussed). The lines summarize the film, which is structured by four overlapping storylines: Georgia's alcoholism and her attempts to stay sober after treatment; her reunion with Polly where ACOA issues are addressed; the long-standing friendship between Georgia, Jimmy (a gay actor), and Toby (a socialite); and Georgia's relationship to David (a lover, a director, and playwright), which is reactivated when she agrees to play the part of herself in his new play; that part of her life that involved her last bout with active alcoholism.

Three days after Georgia leaves treatment Polly comes back to live with her. She goes to work in David's play. Twelve weeks after leaving treatment she slips and gets drunk. She embarrasses Polly in front of a boyfriend, goes to a bar, gets picked up, and is nearly raped. The next morning Polly moves out. Later the same day Georgia keeps a luncheon appointment in a Manhattan restaurant with Polly and her ex-husband. Elegantly dressed in black and white, wearing dark sunglasses, she proudly walks to their table, quickly removes the glasses, showing them her battered face. The film ends with the three laughing and apparently sharing in the experiences of the night before.[2]

The Markers of Alcoholism

Georgia's alcoholism is referenced in several self-depreciating ways. While she lost 35 pounds in treatment, she describes her former self as being a big, fat, sloppy, foul-mouthed drunken woman, an overweight, miserable excuse for a human being, an ex-wino. The word alcoholic is attached to her by Jimmy, who in explaining why they cannot get married says "you're an alcoholic and I'm gay." She makes fun of her "low calorie drinks," and refers to her rehabilitation at "Weathering Heights." Her opening monologue references times past when her hands shook and she could not walk past a bar after 5:00 in the afternoon. Her alcoholism is called a sickness by Toby who asks, the night of her binge: "What kind of sickness is it that makes you want to destroy everything beautiful in your life that you have?" In conversations with Polly she reveals that she started drinking early, and that her father had died from his drinking: "I started when I was fourteen and a half, by the time I was sixteen my father was dead and I had developed an un-quenchable thirst [for alcohol]. . . . I never thought I had a problem." (When she was a teenager she wanted to be Susan Hayward. This can be read as a move by Simon to connect Georgia with two of the screen's most famous female alcoholics, Angie and Lillian.)

Her drinking is connected to her sexuality. (In the Broadway version of the story the female lead was an alcoholic nymphomaniac singer.) Her opening monologue with the psychiatrist also reveals that she picks up men in bars. In the play within the play, the character who plays David tells her, "Jesus! All I have to do is look at you and you want to jump into bed."

Her alcoholism has created an adult child of an alcoholic. Georgia, like Polly, harbors a hatred of her alcoholic parent. The night of her relapse Polly makes the following speech. "I'm sorry for anybody whoever tried to do anything for you because you don't give a damn about them or yourself. . . . You're a mother why don't you act like one? . . . Let's talk about all the years I didn't get from you. Where were you, Mother? . . . Well you're around now aren't you and it sure is a disappointment to find out I was better off when you weren't around!!! Drink all you want. I don't give a damn!"

Both hungover, mother and daughter are reunited the morning after the big drunk. Georgia: "I was beaten up by a guy who thought I was trying to pick him up in a bar. Maybe I was. I'm sorry. I'm not ready for you yet." Polly: "When would you like me to leave? . . . I got heavy into martinis last night. I got the general idea of the feeling. If this is what its like not feeling anything about anybody, no wonder mom's so crazy about it." Georgia: "What do you want from me?" Polly: "I don't want you to give me up again. . . . I'm not giving up. I'm going to move back here, even if I'm 83 years old. See you next weekend." Georgia: "Sure." Polly: "When I grow up I want to be just like you" (they hug and cry). Mother forgiven by daughter, the two have apparently found a common ground for a loving relationship, just like the one that binds Georgia, Toby, and Jimmy.

The Critics Read the Film

Canby (1981b, p.23), like most critics, praised the film. "Neil Simon has written what seems to be a new, upbeat, often funny, and, on at least one occasion, harrowing comedy about an alcoholic." He then connects the film to earlier films in the "genre." "Time was, of course, when alcoholics were very big in the award-winning business in Hollywood, especially when Susan Hayward in *I'll Cry Tomorrow*, or Ray Milland in *Lost Weekend*, were allowed to crawl around the floor having D.T.'s, weeping and moaning, and frequently pleading on telephones. There's none of this melodrama here. Though there is the obligatory sequence in which Georgia must fall off the wagon. It would be very difficult to make a movie about an alcoholic without such a sequence— it's built into the situation. Yet *Only When I Laugh* avoids the usual hysteria about alcoholism." Several of the reviewers noted that Georgia had either taken the "cure" for her alcoholism (Malpezzi and Clements, 1982) or had just come home from a "dry-out clinic" (Ansen, 1981b; Keneas, 1981; Denby, 1981b; Coleman, 1982; Brown, 1982). Thomas (1981, p. 2) commented on the film's "convincing depiction of an alcoholic's struggle to stay dry and what it's like to be the child of an alcoholic," while Coleman (1982, p. 24) criticized Simon's comic attempt to deal with the serious problem of alcoholism with only "lots of snappy lines" and "home-truths." Denby (1981b, p. 83) developed this criticism, noting that while "Marsha Mason may *be* an actress, she can't *play* one," and finding in her character a flaw: "Her friends and daughter accuse her of being monstrously self-centered. . . . But what does this have to do with alcoholism of actresses? *Most* actresses . . . are self-centered: but they don't need to drink to be that way. . . . An actress who is also a drunk could be an appalling or terrifyingly funny human being. If Simon and Mason had been able to face what such a woman would be like, the movie might have had some excitement. What's on the screen—the reformation of a gallant, troubled hard-luck gal—is touching but much too conventional. We've seen that story before." Sarris (1981, p. 51) pushes this analysis of an actress playing an actress even farther, arguing that Simon has "tricked up the plot with a Pirandellian twist[3] . . . but Simon seems to lose interest in this rather abruptly." The result, as several critics noted, is a "superior soap opera" (Ansen, 1981b, p. 87), offering "no answers or deep analysis . . . but only the one-liners" (Crist, 1981, p. 49), a "serious comedy [that] is less banal than it might have been" (Keneas, 1981, p. 66), a "rewritten version of [Simon's] demi-flop show, "The Gingerbread Lady" (Schickel, 1981b, p. 88), with "verbal automatons . . . that have been switched on to deliver one-liners and snappy patter" (Keneas, 1981, p. 66). Malpezzi and Clements (1982, p. 270) are more positive and compare the film to earlier treatments of alcoholism: "The subject of alcoholism has been a staple in film melodramas such as *The Lost Weekend* and *Days of Wine and Roses*, but Simon has managed to avoid much of the sentimentality of films such as those by defusing potentially maudlin situations with a wisecrack."

Back to the Film

Reviewers made no reference to the absence of A.A. in Georgia's recovery. This is paradoxical, given the frequent reference to earlier films in the genre when A.A. was presented as an integral element of an alcoholic's rehabilitation. Indeed her relapse is presented as an inevitable consequence of the crises she faced. But the key crisis, the playing of herself in David's play, and the confrontation with David's new girl-friend, received scant attention in the reviews. This neglect is critical for it points, as Sarris (1981) noted, "to an underlying flaw in the film." The Pirandellian twist, which had the potential of forcing Georgia to confront the underlying issues that led her to drink, is simply dropped by Simon. As a result her alcoholism is explained in terms of the rather traditional account that she became one because her father was one. She had a childhood where she never received the love she needed and wanted. She escaped into alcohol, became self-centered, self-pitying, overweight, and vulgar. She abdicated her duties as a mother. She reproduced for her daughter a childhood much like her own.

The film hesitates and backs off at the very moment when it could explore and illuminate Georgia's tortured past with David. Sarris's criticisms stand. But they must be elaborated. The narrowly conceived play-within-the-play falters on its own terms for it focuses only on the David–Georgia relationship. There is no place in it for Georgia's daughter, or her first husband. It treats her alcoholism as if it started in this relationship, when the film tells us that she has been in treatment several times before for alcoholism.

So this is not a reflexive treatment of alcoholism. It is about something else, and that something else, as several reviewers noted (i.e., Malpezzi and Clements, 1982, p. 268), is the love story about the trio of friends, Georgia, Toby, and Jimmy. The reunion of mother and daughter is tangential to this basic storyline. Simon has used Georgia's alcoholism as a vehicle for telling a story about something else: the pain of life and the need for friends. But because Georgia's alcoholism constantly intrudes into the friendship, the film keeps losing track of itself and where it is going. Although it succeeds in bringing to the surface the underlying problems of being the child of an alcoholic, it fails to uncover, in anything but a superficial, comic way, the pains of alcoholic motherhood.

By defusing each of Georgia's problems with comic one-liners, Simon detracts from telling a story about the problems of being a divorced, working female alcoholic mother in the 1980s. Georgia's jokes minimize the pain she feels. Simon leaves the viewer with the idea that a recovering alcoholic can get by with a few dear friends and a good sense of humor. In this move his film aligns itself with *Arthur 2*, where comedy also undermined the seriousness of Arthur's alcoholic situation.

But Georgia is a female alcoholic of the 1980s. She is on her own. Her alcoholism gets her into trouble. She has to go to treatment. She cannot stay sober. Her alcoholism erodes her sexual self-esteem, and she cannot form lasting relationships with men. Family cannot contain her, and she is unable to take on the full responsibilities of being a mother. Nor can she work with any regularity, for her alcoholism keeps pulling her down. These are serious problems. Simon's film suggests that the early 1980s had yet to create a stable place for the recovering female alcoholic. The next two films create that space by reactivating one that males had occupied in the 1950s and 1960s: A.A.

Life of the Party: The Story of Beatrice (1982)[4]

Beatrice O'Reilly joined Alcoholics Anonymous in 1946 in Los Angeles. She belongs to that small company of women who joined A.A. in its early years. A.A. folklore holds her in a prominent position (see Kurtz, 1979, p. 132). In 1951 she started "Friendship House," the first half-way house for recovering female alcoholics in the Los Angeles area. *Life of the Party* is the story of her recovery and her attempts to create this place. Set in its historical moment, the film is told from the point of view of the present, except for the "period" automobiles that appear on the streets and the Harry James, big band music that is frequently heard in the background.

Beatrice (Bea) is a housewife, married to Johnny, a successful businessman. Born in a small Texas town, she still speaks with a southern accent, and uses phrases like "honey," "gal," and "little girl" and was for were. Her favorite coat is a long fur, with the head of the fox at the end. The film opens with Bea and Johnny getting off an elevator after leaving a party. Bea tells Johnny, "I can walk. I spose you're mad at me. How come you never ask where I go, or anything, Johnny? Don't you care? No wonder, the way I look. Hells Bells, I chipped my tooth. Where's my car? Can you forgive your little girl just once? I won't get drunk again. I promise. You know I love you, sugar."

The next three scenes establish Bea's perpetual drunkenness, first at a party, then at family dinner the next day, and later that night in a bar where she picks up a sailor. At the family dinner her sister Abbie tells her "I stopped drinkin a year ago. I found this new organization, Alcoholics Anonymous. You ever hear of them? They have a branch right here in L.A." Returning home, drunk, after rolling the sailor out of her car, in a blackout she wakes up Johnny, holding a knife in her hand. Five days later she is still experiencing DTs in a detox ward. Brought home by Johnny, who immediately leaves on a five day trip, she fires the nurse he has left with her, gets drunk, cuts herself, gets sick in the bathroom, and then calls her sister: "You said they'd welcome me. . . . alcoholic, alcoholic. I want to be welcomed. I need help badly. I'm out of pills, can't eat, can't breathe. I'm scared. Am I gonna die?" Abbie: "No sugar, you're gonna be born." The next day she is visited by two members of A.A., Rita and Tom, who leave her with a *Big Book* and A.A.'s telephone number.

She calls A.A. and goes to a meeting (the usual signifiers are present, e.g., "Keep Coming Back"), where she meets Rita, returns home, and has an argument with Johnny who asks, "Were you saved?" She replies, "I don't understand. All these years I've been comin home at all hours drunk doin' Lord knows what with who and you haven't said a word . . . and now that I'm goin' to a place where I might get well you're mad." Johnny shouts: "Nobody can help you. God knows I tried." Bea: "I know you have. I owe my life to you, but you don't understand. You can't help me. You're not like them."

The next night another argument ensures. Johnny wants Bea to come to a party his boss is giving, where she will be "the life of the party," and she has agreed to speak at an A.A. meeting. Frustrated, hands on her head, staring into her mirror, she has a spiritual experience: "Dear Higher Power I ain't had that spiritual experience A.A.'s all talk about. I gotta speak tonight and I never wanted a drink so bad in my life. If you'll just get me past that damned bar, I swear to you I'll devote the rest of the days I got left here on this earth to helpin' somebody else." At the meeting Bea announces herself as an alcoholic. [As her recovery unfolds from this point forward her appearance moves from "tawdry" (the fox fur over her shoulder disappears), to conservative, tasteful, middle class (tan suits, dark blouses, small hats, pearls), and no orchids in her hair.]

The story moves quickly from this point. She celebrates her first year birthday at an A.A. ceremony. (That night she and Johnny become a sexual couple again. Johnny: "How would you like your old roommate back again?" They then hug and kiss). Four years later, Johnny is dead from cancer (on his deathbed he expressed the fear that A.A. would "take you away from me"). She celebrates her five year birthday, telling Rita that "I'm a bored and useless person." She then asks Rita "How come A.A.'s mostly men?" Rita: "I don't know. Women are more afraid somehow." [The ratio of men to women in A.A. in the late 1940s and early 1950s was 4–1 (Kurtz, 1979, p. 132).] Returning to her vow to devote the rest of her life helping somebody else, she announces that "me and some fellow lady A.A. members are gonna start the first recovery house for women." She and Rita form a nonprofit corporation, rent a mansion for $250 a month, create a set of house rules (admission of alcoholism, 24 hours of sobriety before entering the house, wearing a dress, no dating), and after some struggle fill the house with women alcoholics who have just been released from jail. The film's final sequence of scenes involve Bea in a courtroom pleading the case for her house to a judge and a group of neighbors who have secured an injunction restraining the operation of "Friendship House" in their neighborhood. She wins her case, and is carried victoriously out of the courtroom by her "girls." A voiceover states, "The first recovery house for women in Los Angeles has just celebrated its thirty-first birthday.

Over 10,000 women have passed through its doors. Seventy-six-year-old Bea has helped similar dreams become reality throughout the United States.

Alcoholism Markers

The film is littered with the presence of markers that locate it within the "women's alcoholism" genre. It is the second women's A.A. film (after *I'll Cry Tomorrow*, that is once contact with A.A. is made, the story is contained within the A.A. framework).[5] From Bea's drunken comportment in the early scenes, to her picking up men in bars, her DTs in the detox ward, the hidden bottles she has all over the house, her sister's early reference to A.A., her drunken call to Abbie for help when she speaks the words alcoholic, the 12-Step visit of Rita and Tom, the *Big Book*, her attendance at A.A. meetings, the presence of A.A. signifiers ("Keep Coming Back," the "A.A. birthday" celebrations), her speech to the women in the jail when she states, "Drunkenness is a disease," to her description of addicts to the judge: "a practicin' addict will do anything to get a drink, or a fix, or a pill."

This is an A.A. film with a twist. It shows women carrying the message of recovery to other women. It displaces the male model of recovery given in earlier films in the tradition, and discounts the sexual stigma usually attached to the female alcoholic. It empowers women. It makes them the carriers of the cure for alcoholism. It suggests that the woman's version of alcoholism is one that requires special treatment. That is only a woman can understand another woman's alcoholism, hence Johnny's anger at Rita when she takes over the treatment of Bea, and Bea's statement, "You don't understand. . . . You're not one of them." In this movie, which is classic, the text aligns itself with A.A. ideology (A.A., 1976, p. 180) and asserts that only one alcoholic can understand another (see Denzin, 1987a, p. 74). But it goes farther, and inserts the female alcoholic into the equation, suggesting that the woman's experiences are not like those of the male alcoholic. In this respect the film is subversive, for it suggests that A.A.'s message must be fitted to the specific features of the woman's situation.

It thus creates a special need, arguing that if men, even skid row winos, can have half-way houses, then why can't women. The case for the need is built on the social construction of the skid row male alcoholic, the second most negative alcoholic stereotype in American culture. That is by negating male winos, the text elevates and erases the negative meanings attached to the female drunk in the culture. Women, after all, are not skid row bums who drink wine out of paper bags.

However, for this symbolic gesture to work the film must also address the negative meanings attached to female criminals, for Bea's original women came from the L.A. county jail. This is done by defining the women in the jail as addicts and alcoholics. Bea: "They break the law so they can get a drink." They are criminals because they are alcoholics. She redefines their problem, substituting one label, alcoholic, for another, criminal.

One more step remains. Bea must now show that alcoholic women in recovery are like other women, and hence can pass as normals. She does this in two ways. First she informs the court that she knows what she's talking about when she describes an addict, because "I was one myself." Then she has the women from "Friendship House" stand up in the courtroom. Ten women stand up: two Blacks, a Chicana, an American Indian, and six Whites. When they stand up they appear as "normal" middle-class women: hair neatly done up, appropriate make-up, attractive, yet simple dresses. The house has transformed them from alcoholic criminals, including being prostitutes, into normal, everyday, middle-class women. They look just like Bea and the other, respectable women in the courtroom.

The message is clear. This is a film about women taking control of their own destinies, regaining their dignity, and moving back into mainstream society. "Friendship House," and others like it, have created a double-framed space for alcoholic women; by helping each other, they help themselves overcome their disease and realize a part of the American dream. The film's final scene underscores this interpretation. Bea's girls, laughing and crying, carrying her on their shoulders down the steps of the courthouse, announce to the world that the female alcoholic is no longer a stigmatized, second class citizen. She has arrived.

But how has she arrived? Here the film subverts its own message in two ways. First Bea had to cajole, plead, and beg her case, even demean herself and her "girls" in order to get approval to continue her project. It did not come easily. She had to overcome bigotry and stereotypes. Its success was due to her efforts and perserverence. Here is the first subversive element. "Friendship House" works because of one woman and her vision. The film announces that individuals can change social structures and social attitudes. It reproduces the myth of American individuality. It promotes the attitude that bad things change when good people make it a life mission to do good.

The film erodes it owns project in a second way and this is through the image of woman it puts forth. Bea calls women "girls" and "gals."[6] Her house asks that they wear dresses, even though Bea realizes that they are not comfortable wearing them. When they dress they look like her. When they talk they use A.A. language and talk like her. The text creates two spaces and two identities for women. They can, like Beatrice, devote their lives to helping other women alcoholics, hence work in houses like hers. Or they can go back into society as wives, mothers, and grandmothers, and play the traditional parts in American society that women have always played. In short, they can be contained either by their disease or by their families. Taking A.A.'s side, the movie suggests that it is better to be a sober woman then a drunken female criminal in jail. Who can argue with this?

But there is a final contradiction. Five years sober, having Rita do her nails, Bea exclaims that she is one bored, useless person. Who is to say that her "girls" after five years sobriety will not experience the same boredom? Must they have a spiritual experience that draws them into the volunteer work that filled Bea's life? The film flounders on this point and ends by tying itself in a circle that is potentially self-strangling. What separates Bea from Angie or Lillian or even Kirstie or Cassie? That is what the film struggles with, but fails to satisfactorily find a place for the sober female alcoholic. She is simply back where she started. All that is different is she is sober now, has A.A. meetings to go to, and halfway houses to start and run. I turn to *The Betty Ford Story* where this dilemma is taken to yet another level.

The Betty Ford Story (1987)

In A.A.'s language, Betty Ford (b. 1918–) is a high bottom drunk. Former First Lady of the United States and one of the most admired women in America during her husband's presidency, she did not lose her husband, her home, her job (she had none), or her family's wealth to her alcoholism. What she did lose was the respect of her children and her friends. Confronted with this loss she agreed to enter treatment for her addiction to prescription drugs on April 10, 1978 at the alcoholic rehabilitation center located in the Long Beach, California Regional Navel Medical Center. This film is the story of how she got there. The narrative moves between July 14, 1974 and February 28, 1987 when the show was broadcast on national television. It begins with Mrs. Ford's entry into the treatment center, and then switches backward to July 14, 1974 when Vice-President Ford soon became President Ford with the resignation of Richard Nixon over the Watergate Affair. It then travels forward from July 1974 to May 5, 1978 when Mrs. Ford checked out of treatment. Divided into seven parts, the 100 minute movie closely follows Betty Ford's autobiography (1978) *The Times of My Life*, which contains a hastily written last chapter on her entry into treatment.[7]

The first hour of the story introduces the viewer to Betty's admission into the treatment center, then traces her early experiences as First Lady, presents her treatment and mastectomy for breast cancer, details the two assassination attempts on Jerry's life, and shows her on the Presidential campaign trail in 1976. By the end of the first hour it is clear that Betty is an excessive user of prescription medicine for the pain she experiences from a pinched nerve in her neck and from her arthritis. She is also a heavy drinker. Hour two briefly treats the family's reactions to Ford's loss to Carter, and then moves to Palm Springs, California where the Fords have retired in the Fall of 1987. Betty's pill-taking and drinking begin to have negative effects (e.g., she forgets luncheons!). A family Christmas gathering at Vail, Colorado in December 1987 is presented as an occasion where a family fight occurs over her drinking. The Christmas folly is soon followed by a failed intervention (an organized attempt to get an alcoholic into treatment) attempt by Susan, the youngest daughter. This intervention is followed by a second in which the entire Ford family, along with a physician and a nurse from the Long Beach, Medical Center, confront Betty about her drinking and pill taking and force her entry into treatment. The film then briefly treats her first weeks in treatment, showing her in a treatment group, being confronted by a physician about her alcoholism, writing a press release announcing her alcohol dependency, talking with Jerry about how her life has to change, and then concludes with a clip showing the ground-breaking ceremony for the Betty Ford Treatment Center. The real Betty Ford appears at the end of the film and tells why she and her family agreed to tell their story: "My family and I were involved in this project because it carried a message of hope for those suffering from alcohol and other drug dependencies. For information call the local Alcoholics Anonymous or Al-Anon chapter listed in your phone book, or call the National Council on Alcoholism at 1-800 NCA-CAll." The films ends on this message.

The intervention, which is presented as the dramatic climax of the story, appears, as it does in her book, as an afterthought. The text that precedes the intervention must be read as an autobiographical gloss on the stresses and strains of being a President's wife. In this gloss Betty's drinking and pill-taking are presented as subtexts that symbolize how she is managing the strain of her breast cancer, the campaign trail, and the two attempts on her husband's life. The drinking and pill-taking are not the focus of the story. Indeed the usual signifiers of excessive drink or uncontrolled alcoholism are nowhere present. They all occur off-screen. They are brought to life in the second intervention when each of her children recounts an instance when Betty was drunk, or passed out during a significant family occasion.

The film, then, is really two films. It presents a hidden, private, personal slice of American history as that history was lived from the inside by one woman and her family.[8] It connects alcoholism to families.

188 The New Alcoholic Heroine

At the same time it is an account of one woman's drug dependency. But this is not just any woman. It is Betty Ford, the symbol of the all-American woman, a former dance student of Martha Graham, and a fashion executive, divorced, and now married to an ex-football hero who is President of the United States, mother of four children, a veteran political wife, and now First Lady. *Betty Ford is a woman*, and, at one level, symbolizes the dreams of the women of her generation.

She symbolizes more than a perfect woman, for she became an alcoholic, and this little trick of fate brought her down to the level of all women. Simultaneously every woman, and superwoman, she is now ordinary woman qua alcoholic. The very qualities that allowed her to recover are those that make her like anyone else. But, and this is the film's paradox, for it is more than a story about "a woman caught up in drug and alcohol addiction" (Plott, 1987, p. 1), it is Betty Ford's story. The universal singularity of this story now erases the differences between Betty and every other American woman.

Reading the Film

This is a traditional "women's alcoholism film."[9] Despite the efforts to make it appear to be a forward looking treatment of the alcoholic female, it insists on containing the figure of woman within two structures, one old, the other new: family and alcoholism treatment. Like *Shattered Spirits*, this film shifts authority back to the children and family. The "other" who defines the negative effects of alcoholism is "family." As with Beatrice, Betty's recovery leads her into a new field of work, opening her own treatment center. But this new work was defined and created by her sickness, which was produced by the very constraints that led to her alcoholism in the first place. Happily back in her family, she owes that regained place to her permanent occupancy in the "normalized" spaces running a treatment center gives her.

This is the fate of the all-American woman alcoholic. It's no different from that of any other ordinary, female alcoholic. In 1987 the American social structure still wonders what to do with this person.

Gena Rowlands' portrayal of Betty Ford (like Susan Hayward's Lillian Roth) raises a final issue: the filmic representation of the real life experiences of a public figure who happens to be alcoholic. [This is an age where the "real" is judged against its simulation (Baudrillard, 1983, pp. 145–47).] When the "real" Betty Ford is a media production, whose presence is judged by how she appears on a TV screen, then what is real and what is fiction is no longer clear. The appearance of the "real" Betty, looking better then the "simulated Betty qua Gena" of course quells any doubt about the authenticity of her recovery. [Similarly, the authenticity and sincerity of Ms. Rolands' performance are assured once we learn that she not only consulted with "real" alcoholics as she studied for her role, but was mindful of the fact that "it is rather a responsibility to play a real person" (Mills, 1987, p. 8).]

How does the viewer sort all of this out? Of course it cannot be, and that is the point. With this film television comes of age as the main cultural carrier of messages about alcoholism. It has penetrated the barriers that surround alcoholism in high places, uncovered the dual female addict, taken her into a treatment center, shown how interventions work, and further legitimated a new identity for the female alcoholic. If she has no where else to go or anything else to do, she can carry her message to other women who are like her. The final film to be treated in this chapter subverts this message.

The Morning After[10] **(1987)**

9:00 A.M. Los Angeles. Thanksgiving Morning, November 28, 1986. Alex Sternbergen, an alcoholic actress who no longer gets parts, wakes with a hangover in a strange bed, in a loft apartment, the body of man next to her. "Eye on L.A." is playing on the TV.[11] Bobby Korshack, a photographer known as the king of sleaze is being interviewed. Laying her hand on the chest of the man, Alex feels moisture, and a shock of recognition ("What the fuck?"). It is blood. Crawling out of bed, away from the body, quivering in the corner, fear in her expression, she realizes this is the "real" Bobby Korshack. A knife is sticking out of Bobby's chest ("Hey, what are you trying to pull? Is that one of those tricks?"), and he is dead. Walking out of the bedroom into a stark, devoid of life, white studio, blue and orange shades on the windows, a cat cleaning its paws on a counter, she pours a straight drink, grasps her stomach, and runs to the bathroom. On her knees, hands around the toilet, she vomits, gets up, washes her face, looks in the mirror (only one of several mirror scenes), says "Congratulations," and finishes her drink. Thus begins Alex's morning after.

The story is simple. A murder mystery with a female drunk. Alex has been framed by her husband Jacky (a Mexican hair dresser) and his girlfriend Isabel (the daughter of a judge). Korshack has been blackmailing Isabel, and Jacky has killed him. Running from the crime scene, she wanders through streets shot in "exact pastiche of the Edward Hopper manner, attractive in the solid blocks of colour supplied by the buildings yet desolately grey in the absence of any visible human activity" (Milne, 1987, p. 181). At the L.A. airport she meets Turner Kendall, an ex-cop from Bakersfield, who fixes things like broken toasters. Alex sizes Turner up as a redneck bigot after he cites statistics about the spending habits of "spades." Kendall: "Spades spend money disproportionately on their transportation, also in dressing their young." She snaps, "What are you, the Klan anthropologist?" Turner suspects that Jacky has set-up Alex. In the climax Jacky attempts to kill Alex, who is saved by Turner, who is nearly killed by Jacky. Turner ends up in the hospital. Alex gets sober, and in a long good-bye scene, where Turner reveals that he used to be a drunk, the two decide to stay together.

Alex's Alcoholism

There is no question that Alex is an alcoholic and probably a pill addict. Her alcoholism has gotten her into serious trouble. The signs are everywhere, including her losing jobs, her morning after drinks, the blackouts, waking up next to a strange dead man in a strange place (Alex, "It happens"), the boozy Thanksgiving dinner with Kendall, her wobbly walk, slurred conversations on the telephone with Jacky, morning drinking, her drunken assault on her first husband, Kendall's calling her a blackout drunk and a lush with a record, and her application of the drunk and lush labels to herself.

She has experienced sexual degradation, failures in marriage and work, and loss of self-esteem because of her alcoholism. She is the quintessential female alcoholic of the 1950s in liberated 1980 style. There is no A.A. or treatment, or a friendly physician to carry the message of recovery, only Turner's oblique reference to his own recovery, with the hint that he did it through will power and luck. He stopped drinking and so can she. He will help her; another male to the rescue of the damsel alcoholic in distress.

Her alcoholism is both plot and subplot in the film. If she were not a blackout drunk Jacky could not have pulled his tricks with the perambulating corpse (Milne, 1987, p. 181). Because she is "a terror-stricken alcoholic" (Milne, 1987, p. 181), one of society's broken rejects, Turner is drawn to her. And she is drawn to men who are themselves rejects, or social marginals, the divorced, racist hick Turner, Jacky, the Latino hairdresser, and Frankie, the drag queen. But her alcoholism is also a vehicle for the telling of a modern Hitchcock-like murder mystery, with romantic thriller overtones (Combs, 1987, p. 143), set in "a kind of empty, minimalist L.A." (Wilmington, 1986, p. 1), where "the powerless prey on each other, and both the murderer and the patsy turn out to be victims" (Edelstein, 1986, p. 74).

Her alcoholism does not take her, in the traditional sense, into confrontations concerning sobriety and slips. Indeed her alcoholism is only defined as a problem by Turner. The other members of the world, including Jacky, Frankie, and Red, accept her drinking and style of life. In fact it was something she (and they) joked about (i.e., the morning drink is "the breakfast of champions"). Turner's definitions of her as a lush and blackout drunk are clearly based on his experiences with his own alcoholism. Were it not for him she would not be given these labels; thus one alcoholic (drunk) labels another.

In making his heroine a faded alcoholic actress, Lumet turns a character flaw into a dramatic device. This allows him to make statements about the modern urban landscape, including its emptiness, loneliness, and nightmare qualities where the TV monitors daily life and strangers end up in bed with each other, seeking a single night of comfort in furtive love. The world that Alex, Turner, and Jacky move through is glitter and glare, elegant hair dressing salons, upper class families, darkness and light, clear-blue skylines, pastel countrysides, empty, gray streets, orange painted warehouses, white cats licking their paws in stark white loft studios, baren Quonset hut homes with unpainted drywall ceilings, and used Nancy Drew mysteries lined up on rickety bookcases, bottles of vodka, gallons of Thunderbird wine, aging drag queens, Thanksgivings alone, and rusting, battered, used cars that stall at intersections.

This is Alex's world and it nearly destroys her. Turner thinks he understands it. His streetwise, encyclopaedic collection of racist facts about Jews, "spades," "spics," and "gays" gives him a roadmap through the down and out version of this world that he inhabits. His racism speaks to an unattractive side of the urban scene that Lumet appears to accept, for it is these qualities that eventually endear him to Alex. In the end his recovery from alcoholism simply becomes one more positive character trait that draws Alex closer to him. This, then, is not a film about alcoholism, in its late 1980s feminized versions. It is a melodrama, a story of love and hope, of two human beings fearful of committing to one another, scarred by prior failures in such projects. In this telling Lumet suggests that American society can accept a female alcoholic as the heroine in a murder mystery, love story. Alex inserts herself in a space midway between Ray Milland of *Lost Weekend* and Claire Trevor of *Key Largo*. Turner has transformed her from a stigmatized alcoholic woman into a woman alcoholic who has stopped drinking and fallen in love with a man who has done the same. By inverting the signifiers of alcoholic and woman, Lumet turns Alex into a prototype of the single, modern woman who has lost and now found her way in a hostile, empty world that tends, in the main, to make victims of all of us, but women more so.

The Critics Read the Film

It was read as a *film noir* (Williamson, 1987, p. 23), a taut mystery thriller (Chanko, 1987, p. 231), a Hitchcock thriller (Wilmington, 1986, p. 1; Milne, 1987, p. 181), a thriller with De Palma overtones (Denby, 1987, p. 45), and a comedy–mystery (Canby, 1986, p. 22). Virtually every critic made reference to Alex's alcoholism (e.g., Lida, 1986, p. 10) and Jane Fonda's performance (i.e., Canby, 1986, p. 22), which was compared by Edelstein (1986, p. 74) to Lucille Ball (in the drunk scenes) and Mary Tyler Moore (in the sober scenes). Edelstein went further, and reviewed Fonda's entire acting career, from *Barbarella* to *Klute, Coming Home, The China Syndrome, On Golden Pond*, to her aerobic tapes, and suggested that in *The Morning After* she has simply "come full circle—she's Barbarella with thin thighs" (1986, p. 74). Others did the same, making favorable reference to Fonda's earlier performances as Bree Daniels in "Klute" and Bridges's performance of a treacherous hero in *Jagged Edge* (Williamson, 1987, p. 23), but criticizing their performances in this film. Gelmis (1986, p. 3) suggested that the script "is so glib that [it] barely achieves the dramatic heft of an hour of "Miami Vice—which is to say, it's all glittery surfaces." Several praised the work of Lumet's cinematographer, Andrzej Bartowiak, comparing his landscapes to Hopper paintings (i.e., Canby, 1986, p. 22).

The thread that unites the various readings is its location within the loosely defined *film noir* framework (see Schatz, 1981, Chapter 5). Wilmington (1986, p. 1), for example, defines Fonda's character as a "classic *noir* icon, the seemingly wrongly accused killer on the run—from the cops, the killers, and her own mental blackouts." Williamson (1987, p. 23) elaborates this kind of interpretation, while making the important point that when Hollywood stars move from one film to another they carry meanings with them. Hence no performance is ever viewed in isolation. Jane Fonda cannot just be Alex Sternbergen. She is Bree (the prostitute on the run), and the off-screen star of her own home workout video series. Nor can Jeff Bridges just be Turner Kendall, for many audience members remember his prior performance as Jack Forrester, the killer in *Jagged Edge*, or as Scudder, the burned-out alcoholic cop who sobers up in A.A. in *8 Million Ways to Die* (1986). And of course Sidney Lumet must be remembered by some as the director of alcoholic attorney Frank Galvin (Paul Newman) in *The Verdict* (1982). I quote Williamson at length for she connects the *film noir* interpretation with the issue of what a star brings to a part. "The real drive of the film . . . unlike earlier *films noir* hinges on whether or not a desired *man* is to be trusted . . . there is a relatively new '*homme fatale*' figure in contemporary films

. . . and this is precisely where the 'carried over' [from 'Jagged Edge'] connotations of Jeff Bridges come into play. . . . And it is on this that the film relies . . . for its central frisson: is the man Alex comes to desire the real killer? Unlike the old *films noir* where the plot unraveled through the eyes of the male protagonist, this new type of post-'Coma'[12] thriller takes us through events mainly through the subjectivity of the woman. And just as the old *films noir* offered the hero a choice of good and bad women, here the heroine is offered an ambiguous choice of good and bad men."

Alex and Her Men

Alex is caught between two men. Turner's opposite is suave, debonnaire Jacky (Joaquin Manero), played by Raul Julia (the straight revolutionary in *Kiss of the Spiderwoman*), initially Alex's closest friend and adviser, a man with a sexually ambiguous name, a cultural outsider (an immigrant), both villain and victim. Jacky's opposite, Turner, has a heart of gold, "the raw material of Americanness" (Williamson, 1987, p. 23), but he is a racist and her saviour at the same time, although in the end he stops making his racist jokes.

Alex has two other friends. The aging Frankie ("Honey, I'm a drag queen, not a transvestite!"), and Charlie, the fat, jovial, bartender who gives her money, and does not criticize her drinking. These two characters are placed on the fringes of her world. The audience is asked to play Frankie's open gayness off against Jacky's imputed (by the police and Turner) but not acted out homosexuality. Thus subtext becomes a device for the film's reproduction of cultural stereotypes about homosexuality (closet and out of the closet, queens versus transvestites). At the same time it allows the text to side against the homosexual in favor of the "straight" man (Turner over Jacky), and the "white" racist male over the hispanic "gay." By blending both of these negative cultural characteristics into the same character (Jacky), the text negates Turner's racism, in favor of his down home good will toward Alex.

Alex is left with an ambiguous choice of two flawed men. The narrative resolves this ambiguity by having her take the side of sobriety and the man who saved her from her husband. And this is what this film is all about: the choices women have in the late 1980s. As Williamson observes, the paths are not clearly marked, but they are still framed from within a patriarchal structure that has men defining the choices for women.

On the surface Lumet's film is a melodrama, a story of love and hope, of two human beings fearful of committing to one another. In this telling Lumet is suggesting that American society can accept a female alcoholic as the heroine in a murder mystery love story.

This is the surface, preferred reading of the story. Underneath exists the antigay, racist subtext that is justified in terms of the above happy ending format. But in allowing the preferred readings to stand, the viewer (and the critics) become willing accomplices in support of a conservative feminism that pleads (and hides) its ideological biases in the name of a story that locates a woman in the company of a "good" man who has flaws.

This text's meanings depends on the sexual and racial differences that are enunciated by Turner; these differences create the marginalized spaces Alex occupies. Their presence suggest that women, in order to find their place, have to go to the margins of society where gays and drag queens will give them comfort, warmth, friendship, and support. But these people are not enough, hence the decision to remain with Turner, and the film's return to its comfortable position that asserts that gays and "spics" who, if not evil, are persons about whom jokes can be told.

In making its choices, the film's meanings are contaminated by the acting biographies its three stars bring to the text. This is Williamson's point. We do not just see Jane Fonda as Alex, or Bridges as Turner, or Julia as Jacky. We read their characters through their prior performances, and in these performances each was something different than what they are in this film, except for Bridges who was also an alcoholic ex-cop in a film made just a year earlier. So it is not possible to just see Jane Fonda playing an alcoholic, just as it is not possible to just see Gena Rowlands play Betty Ford as an alcoholic First Lady.

The figure of the female alcoholic has given way to something else. That something else remains elusive, but its recurring presence in the performances like those given by the above actresses serves to erase the original meanings brought to the alcoholic subject. Ponder Canby's closing sentence in his review of the film for the *New York Times*: "In fiction of this sort such men [Bobby Korshack] deserve what they get and alcoholics particularly when played with the kind of intense intelligence Miss Fonda possesses, need never look seriously the worse for wear" (Canby, 1986, p. 22). The illusion has replaced the "real" thing.

As this occurs the traditional alcoholism movie begins to become something else. With *The Morning After* it is called a *film noir* but with a twist, the *"homme fatale."* Now a female alcoholic becomes a variant on the classic noir icon of the flawed woman who was both good and evil, but primarily evil. The power of choice has shifted to her. She is no longer the evil figure who brings down the good man. Now a man has taken on that part. Her strength, even as it is undercut by her alcoholism, allows her to become the stronger figure, and permits her to find her way in a world that is no longer solely defined by family, or her alcoholism. By incorporating the alcoholic heroine into the *film noir* tradition, Lumet finds possibilities for her that could not have been given by remaining within the female alcoholism film as it had been previously established in Hollywood.

The Female Alcoholic in the 1980s

In Chapter 4, I ascribed a number of characteristics to Hollywood's female alcoholic in the 1945–1962 period: hitting a sexual bottom, self-degradation, exposure to violence, neurotic preoccupations with appearance and its loss, insecurities and guilt, fixations on parental figures, broken marriages, loss of a life story, and conflicts between work and family. Her cure was located in a male figure, often a physician or psychiatrist, whose medical gaze would transform her into a new, sexually erotic object. Her recovery, including the return to beauty, would be defined in masculine terms, and she would regain her subjectivity, only it would be from a male point of view.

This process operated for Angie in *Smash-Up*. When A.A. entered the picture, as in the case of Lillian Roth, the medical male figure would be replaced by a man from A.A. Kirsten in *Days of Wine and Roses* rejected both of these models of recovery (medicine and A.A.). She remained locked in a father fixation, insisting that sexuality, not sobriety, was the preferred avenue for the realization of her subjectivity. She would not surrender to A.A.'s version of the medical gaze, as her husband had done. She is the female alcoholic rebel of the modern period.

Angie, Lillian, and Kirsten thus prefigured three responses to the female alcoholic's situation, responses that would be played out again in the 1980s. Angie was cured and returned home, just like Cassie in *The Cracker Factory*. Lillian was cured by A.A. and went on to carry her message of recovery to others, especially women. She set the stage for Beatrice O'Reilly and Betty Ford. Kirsten, the sexual rebel, defined the outer boundaries for Georgia and Alex. Indeed Alex's story can be read, in part, as a continuation of Kirsten's, for one can imagine Kirsten waking one morning in bed with a dead man.

Hollywood and television's alcoholic woman in the 1980s inherits, I submit, all of the above meanings, onto which new ones are added:

1. A struggle with a new-found freedom that has broken down the immediate postwar constraints of family.
2. The institutional treatment for her substance abuse in settings that are far less cold, sterile, and nightmarish than those presented for males in the modern period.
3. The progressive destigmatization of her alcoholism through a process of normalization that subverts the traditional genre treatment of the disease.

Yet, as in the earlier period, the films under consideration persist in making the sobriety of the alcoholic a goal to be attained by the end of the film. In this commitment, they perpetuate the antialcoholism theme that has structured the genre from its beginning. However, as has been repeatedly noted, sobriety for the female typically means the return to family, or to work, which involves carrying the message of recovery to other women. When she pursues these options her story has closure. When she does not it is ambiguous.

Four films, separated by six years: *Only When I Laugh, Life of the Party, The Betty Ford Story, The Morning After*. Two actresses and two housewives. Two versions of the same story. Two open texts, two closed texts. Georgia and Alex leave the viewer to enter an uncertain world. There is ambiguity for Georgia and Alex, as there was for Kirsten. Beatrice and Betty are closed within the tight confines of treatment and family. Their heroine qualities are coded in terms of the courage it takes to overcome the personal pain caused by alcoholism. Alex's heroine qualities are defined in masculine, violent terms.

Alex once more. Her subjectivity is defined by two males: Jacky and Turner. In a pivotal mirror scene, just before he attempts her murder, Jacky transforms Alex from a fearful, unattractive, haggard woman into a confident, beautiful erotic object. In this move Lumet restores Alex's sexuality through the hands of an evil man. However, she does not get sober until Turner is hospitalized for the injuries inflicted by Jacky. Jacky and Turner, her doubles, each gives her something, but neither can give her what the other can. She emerges as a complex figure, a woman who requires two men in order to become whole. Her doubling in the two men, one feminine and the other masculine, suggests a strength and complexity of character that had heretofore been absent in the figure of the alcoholic heroine.

That is, earlier women found all they needed in the medically and sexually neutral physician (or A.A. male), to whom they may have been attracted (i.e., Cassie), and the husband at home. Both male figures signified positive values, and there was no hint of a doubling of the female's character in these two men. Lumet's movie inverts this paradigm, and in so doing thickens the identity of the female alcoholic, making her somehow more sinister and evil than she previously was. He shows that alcoholism does for women what it has always done for men: it draws out the repressed, sexual underside of their being. It worked this way for Kirsten and Lillian, and afterall Don Birnam was sexually attracted to Gloria, and Boyd to Maria Diego. But none of these earlier characters was involved in stories framed within the *film noir* tradition where the flawed male (or female) had quite the power that Jacky wields over Alex.

To repeat, it is apparent that new representations of the alcoholic heroine will tend to occur only when the narrative breaks out of the traditional "women's movie, female alcoholic storyline." Such departures, as in Lumet's movie, create new possibilities of representation, especially when they use a "tainted" heroine as the vehicle for exposing the individual alienation and sexual confusion that now mark the barren postmodern urban landscape. In this world simulated reproductions of real experiences have become the standard against which "real" experiences are measured. But even as this occurs, the female alcoholic in the 1980s, like her counterpart in the modern period, finds herself in a patriarchal world. All that is new is the occasional institutional treatment for her illness. Everything else is as it was 30 years earlier, only more so.

In the next chapter I examine a series of films that take up the subject of the alcoholic male in the 1980s. However, I have not finished with the female alcoholic. She is also present in four of the films I discuss. It remains to be seen if her condition changes when she is paired with a male alcoholic, and, if it does, in what way.

Notes

1. I define a generation by film period. The first generation of women alcoholics references those who appeared in the 1947–1962 time period. The second generation, those who appeared in the 1962–1980 period, and the third generation, those who have appeared since 1980. *The Cracker Factory*, as noted in Chapter 6, is an important bridge film to the 1980s (see also *Francis*, 1982).

2. Polly also got drunk, in an attempt to get even with her mother. The title of the film, *Only When I Laugh*, also the title of David's new play, is taken from an old joke that Georgia tells Polly: "A man has a spear sticking through his chest, and his friend asks, 'does it hurt?' He says, 'only when I laugh.' " Presumably the spear refers to both Georgia's alcoholism and the pain she feels from the life she has led because of her alcoholism.

3. Sarris (1981, p. 51) elaborates: "the ideas of acting out the heroine's disastrous relationship in a play by her ex-lover offers . . . an interesting oppor-

tunity to meditate on the degree to which real-life feelings reinforce a characterization, and the degree to which these feelings begin to compromise the necessary techniques of acting." On the long history of this reflexive tradition within
theatre (and film) see Monaco (1981, p. 446) and Kawin (1978, p. 65).

    4.   This film is routinely shown to women alcoholics in the detoxification
unit of one of the treatment centers I studied (Denzin, 1987b).

    5.   It generated little critical discourse by film reviewers (see Crist, 1982).

    6.   The film's ambiguous relationship to history and temporality partially
explains this image of women. Historically set in the 1950s it reflects a conservative feminism that is made even more ironic because the story is told from the
point of view of the present. Crist (1982, p. 100) perpetuates this problem: "A
fact-based 1982 TV-movie about alcoholism that packs a punch . . . [Beatrice]
wages war against a stingy government bureaucracy—and the lingering public
stigma alcoholics face."

    7.   This last chapter then became the basis of a second autobiography. *Betty:
A Glad Awakening* (1987), released at the same time that her story appeared on
television (on the exploitative elements of this timing see Unger, 1987, p. 23). In
the second book she deals with her treatment and the Betty Ford Clinic, one of
the most famous and expensive treatment centers in the United States, and a
favorite site for Hollywood stars. In the late 1980s the female lead of a new TV
series ("Murphy Brown") will announce that she has just checked out of the
"Betty Ford Clinic."

    8.   The television screen figures centrally in this part of the story. Betty,
Jerry, and the family are repeatedly shown in front of the television set watching
themselves being reported in the news. The reflexive use of the television screen
as a mirror to the subject's place in current events, where the subject looks at
herself, and the viewer looks at the subject looking at herself, is a Pirandellian
twist that only television could make possible; that is the viewer's vicarious
participation in the same events that the subject is watching. Any American
adult in 1987 was likely to have seen (or heard about) Nixon's resignation speech
on television, Ford's announcement for the Presidency, or even the evening
news report from Des Moines, Iowa that Betty watches at one point. Watching
Betty watch herself, the viewer relives, from a different level, a moment of
personal, yet public history; but that history is given a different meaning for its
effects on a single life are now dramatically underscored. At the same time, the
viewer becomes part of one of America's recent, central cultural myths concerning Watergate, Nixon, Ford, and the Ford family's cleansing of the American
conscience during the post-Watergate years. As the 1987 (or 1990) viewer relives
Betty's experiences, he or she is brought into another central issue of the 1970s:
ERA and Betty's support of this amendment (see Thornburn, 1988, p. 57 on how
television reproduces consensus narratives about a culture's central mythologies).

    9.   With few exceptions, this is how the critics read the movie, yet they
found fault in its failure to "penetrate the surface events" (Terry, 1987, p. 1), in
anything but a "formulaic" way (Terry, 1987, p. 1; Rosenberg, 1987, p. 8; Unger,
1987, p. 23; O'Connor, 1987, p. 16; Farber, 1987, p. 26; but see Litwin, 1987).
Several critics saw the appearance of the "real" Betty Ford as an affirmation of
the film's credibility (i.e., Plott, 1987, p. 7).

    10.   The film's title, of course, is a play on the colloquial phrase referring to
how a person who has had too much drink at night feels the morning after. A

drink "taken on waking" is called a morning drink and in some cultures . . . is considered a sign of alcoholism" (Keller and McCormick, 1968, p. 139). Alex is a morning drinker.

11. On the TV screen appear images of women working out, and men pumping iron, obvious references to Jane Fonda's workout tapes.

12. A 1978 mystery thriller.

The New Alcoholic Hero

> "He's as right as any of us."
>
> (Jim, the bartender, describing Henry
> the alcoholic in *Barfly*)
>
> "Hell is my natural habitat."
>
> (Geoffrey, the alcoholic, to his wife in
> *Under the Volcano*)

The male alcoholic in the 1980s is hemmed in from all sides. He bears the weight of more than 50 years of Hollywood filmmaking about his condition. Such modern classics as *A Star Is Born* (1954, 1976), *The Lost Weekend*, *Come Fill the Cup*, *Come Back, Little Sheba*, *The Country Girl*, and *Days of Wine and Roses* have given him heroic properties. He enters the 1980s as a noble, tragic figure who struggles to overcome his obsession to drink. He deals with a life that has been nearly destroyed by his disease, which has been medicalized, feminized, and turned into a family illness. The state has entered the arena, for he can be forced to seek help for his condition, and A.A. is everywhere. He bears the guilt for what he has done, not only to himself, but to his wife and children as well.

Like the female alcoholic, he finds himself located within a postmodern world where he is a wandering outsider, alienated from himself and those he is attached to. He lives in a culture that is on the move, but appears to lack a center. His loneliness and alcoholic drinking symbolize, as they have always done, this failure of the contemporary world to offer a locus and center to existence. His presence, in such diverse, yet same-like urban places as Los Angeles, Houston, Paris, Texas, New York City, Philadelphia, Boston, and Cuernavaca, Mexico speaks to the universality of his condition. He is everyman who feels and thinks deeply about his situation and has found solace in alcohol.

Recall the two Arthurs, Mac Sledge, Lyle Mollencamp, and Noah Talbot. Arthur is the sad, funny drunk, finally forced to sober up to get the family he wants. He is even sent to A.A. He is no longer a funny figure. His alcoholism stretched the limits of comedy. Mac, Lyle, and Noah are beaten down men, failures in their versions of the American dream, and victims of something they did not understand. Their disease was framed within the genre of the 1980s' "family alcoholism" film, where the ACOA theory implicitly and explicitly operated.

In this chapter I discuss nine variations on the alcoholic hero (and heroine), selecting films[1] that do not fall within the traditional family alcoholism, social problems framework.[2] The films are *The Verdict* (1982), *Under the Volcano* (1984), *Paris, Texas*[3] (1984), *Hoosiers* (1986), *8 Million Ways to Die* (1986), *Barfly* (1987), *Ironweed*[4] (1987), *Clean and Sober* (1988), and *My Name is Bill W.* (1989).

Like his female counterpart, the 1980s male alcoholic hero is at a crossroads. Several directions can now be followed. The normalization of his disease makes him an acceptable figure in a film where his alcoholism is a part of another storyline. His alcoholism, however, determines that the story be told against this backdrop, for it adds tension to the narrative (e.g., *The Verdict*, *8 Million Ways to Die*). At the same time he remains a compelling, mythic figure, and a story can be told about his struggles with himself and the bottle (*Under the Volcano*). Normalization keeps alive another possibility, long employed by Hollywood, and this is to accord him (and his disease) a secondary, but pivotal part in another story, as in the classic *To Have and Have Not* (1944) (e.g., *Hoosiers*). Another alternative involves the use of his alcoholism as the necessary ingredient in the telling of a story as he attempts to put his life back together and fails (*Paris, Texas, Ironweed*). In these narratives alcoholism references something that happened in the past. Still another option, more radical, involves the situation in which the alcoholism is valorized and the film tells a story about the joys of this way of life, as in *Fat City* (*Barfly*). A variation on this theme, which builds on the mythic, "alcoholic-as-hero" concept (Spender, 1984, p. ix), pairs a male and female alcoholic as cultural outsiders who have no apparent desire to stop drinking (*Barfly*). Finally there is the traditional path, the one followed by *Clean and Sober* and *My Name is Bill W.*, where the alcoholic is taken through the three-stage cycle of grace, fall from grace, and redemption. These two films complete the preclassic cycle started in 1935 and developed in its fullest forms in the classic period.

The exploration of each of these possibilities, which have been present since the formation of the alcoholism film (it has taken 50 years for them to achieve their present clarity), will reveal the distance the alcoholic hero has traveled since 1932 when Max committed altruistic suicide in *What Price, Hollywood?* and Don Birnam, in 1945, fought off the suicide impulse and decided that telling his story would help those "poor bedeviled guys on fire with thirst."

The Verdict (1982)

Late January in Boston, the present, Frank Galvin, a once-promising lawyer, has turned into a seedy, ambulance chaser. A morning drinker, his hands shake so much he bends over the glass on the bar in order to get the first taste of whiskey into his mouth. Frank is passing the time in his favorite Irish pub, playing pinball, sipping a beer, and looking for funeral announcements in the Boston paper, hoping to find a case. He goes to a funeral home and bribes the undertaker to let him in so he can give the bereaved his business card. He uses mouth freshener to kill the smell of alcohol on his breath. Thrown out and told to never come back, he gets drunk, and in a rage destroys his office, and then passes out. He has lost his pride, his reputation, his wife, and four court cases in the last three years. He gets by on the charity of his old friend, attorney Mickey Morrissey.

Mickey finds Frank in his office, still drunk from the night before, and asks him about the Doneghy case (it goes to trial in ten days), a simple malpractice suit against a leading hospital owned by the Archdiocese of Boston. Sally Doneghy, and her husband, are suing the hospital on behalf of her sister, Debra Anne Kaye, who, lying in a coma, with no chance of recovery, was given an almost lethal dose of anesthesia as she was about to give birth. The Doneghys are seeking conscience money from the hospital, enough to provide "perpetual" care for the victim. The next day the Bishop offers Galvin a settlement of $210,000 (Frank's fee would be one-third this amount), which he immediately rejects ("I can't take it. I'll just be a rich ambulance chaser.").

Frank pulls himself together, confident that he will win, based on the promised testimony of Dr. Gruber. In the preparation of the case he becomes romantically involved with Laura Fischer, the former wife of an attorney. He tells her about the case, "The weak have gotta have somebody to fight for 'em." She offers her legal and clerical services to Frank and Mickey who are going up against one of Boston's largest law firms headed by Ed Concannon ("the Prince of fucking darkness").

On the eve of the trial Frank loses Dr. Gruber. He begins drinking again. He fails to obtain the testimony of a nurse who was in the operating room, but locates another physician, Dr. Thompson (an elderly black), who will testify for a fee. He returns home, disheartened and intoxicated, telling Laura, "We're gonna lose." Laura (angrily, rising her voice): "The damned case doesn't start until tomorrow." Frank goes into the bathroom and closes the door, gasping for breath, "please don't pressure me."

The trial starts the next morning. Dr. Thompson is exposed as a professional witness. Mickey tells Frank, "It's over. There will be other cases." Frank replies, "This is the case." In the next scene Laura is seen receiving a check from Concannon for passing along information concerning Frank's tactics. Frank continues his search for the nurse, Kaitlin Costello Price, who admitted Sally's sister to the hospital. He learns that she lives in New York City. Looking for cigarettes in Laura's purse, Mickey discovers the check from Concannon. Frank calls back to the office, informing them of his intentions to attempt to find her. Laura arranges to meet him in a hotel bar later that afternoon as she has to be in New York to sign divorce papers. Frank meets Kaitlin and she agrees to testify. Informed of Laura's betrayal by Mickey, who has flown down from Boston, Frank, as prearranged, meets her in the cocktail lounge. They exchange a long look, he walks across the room, hits her in the mouth, knocking her to the floor. The next day in court Frank introduces Price as a surprise rebuttal witness. He also produces a photocopy of the admission form that indicates that the patient had eaten a full meal just before entering the hospital. The photocopy provides evidence of medical negligence (the time of the last meal had been changed on the admitting form from one to nine hours), but the Judge refuses to allow its admission into evidence.

Frank gives an emotional summation to the jury. Standing in the center of the courtroom, still wearing his top-coat, a figure almost indistinguishable from the others in the room, facing the jury, he states: "So much of the time we're just lost. So please God tell us what is true. There is no justice. The rich win. The poor are powerless. . . . If we are to have faith in justice, we need only to believe in ourselves and act with justice. I believe there is justice in our hearts."

The jury returns a verdict for the plaintiff, and asks if it can award an amount greater than the original claim ($600,000) the plaintiff requested (Mickey turns his head to heaven and mumbles "Thank you God," Frank appears to be crying). A sequence of shots, moving back and forth between Laura and Frank, end the film. In the first she is shown in a robe, a cloth over her eyes, hair messed up, slightly sprawled out, but propped up on her bed, a plate of food next to her. She takes a drink, reaches over to set the glass on the nightstand, but misses and it falls to the floor. She pulls the telephone onto her stomach and dials. The camera cuts to Frank. The phone rings in his office. His feet on his desk, tie undone, he hesitates, moves toward the phone, and then pulls back. The camera cuts back to Laura in bed; the phone is buzzing as it lies next to her breast. She is staring off into the darkness. The camera cuts back to Frank, phone still buzzing. He reaches for a cup of coffee, takes a sip, and leans back with his eyes closed. The screen fades to blackness. A choir sings a "mass" over the credits.

The Alcoholic in a Morality Tale

This is an old-fashioned melodramatic morality tale that tells two stories at the same time: Frank's recovery from alcoholism, and his victory over the Church and a corrupt legal, political, and medical system that protects malfeasant physicians. The stories are inseparable, for the force and power of Frank's character depend on his ability to first overcome his alcoholism, before he can win his big case. (The Laura–Frank romance and the Mickey–Frank friendship are stitched between these two stories, as is the story of Debra Anne Kaye, and what winning the trial means to her, her sister, and her brother-in-law.)

Frank's drinking is the issue. It is used, especially in the opening scenes, as a marker of his moral decline. He needs a morning drink, not only to shake last night's hangover, but also to get the courage to go to funeral homes looking for cases. If he did not bribe a juror in 1969, today he is not above bribing funeral home directors. His appearance has declined as well, for early in the film he appears unshaven, in rumpled clothes, with shaking hands. It is clear that he has been unable to work since the divorce, and his reputation as a drinker and ambulance chaser is now common knowledge in the Boston legal community. Never far from a drink, he keeps whiskey and beer in his office, and is shown drinking at all times of the day and night. He has pushed his old friend Mickey to the limits.

The first third of the film surrounds Frank with the markers of the classic male alcoholic. This portion of his story could have been easily told in the classic period. However, Frank undergoes two transformations. He decides to turn down the Church's offer, and with Laura's aid he gets his drinking under control. These two steps move his story out of the traditional framework, into a contemporary morality tale. This story, however, also has its origins in the early modern period of Hollywood filmmaking with Frank Capra's characters (Smith, Deeds, Doe) who spoke up for the little people against dishonest politicians and corrupt public institutions (see Sklar, 1983, p. 47). Thus Lumet and Mamet joined two film traditions, the alcoholic's struggle as given in the social problems' film, and the social message, screwball comedies of

206 The New Alcoholic Hero

Capra (on Capra see Schatz, 1981, p. 157; Sklar, 1975, pp. 205–14), into a 1980s version of a 50-year-old Capra social fable (Sklar, 1983, p. 47). Remove the comedy, and replace Paul Newman with an alcoholic Gary Cooper or Jimmy Stewart and you have *The Verdict*.[5]

The critics read Frank Galvin as a "seedy, drunken ambulance chaser" (Hanson, 1984, p. 378; Deutsch, 1983, p. 11), an "alcoholic failure" (Sklar, 1983, p. 47), a "boozing, down-on-his-luck, Boston lawyer" (Magill, 1983, p. 48), a "borderline drunk" (Benson, 1982, p. 1), a "washed-up drunk" (Reed, 1982, p. 72), "a drowned man whose only solace is pinball and the bottle" (Rickey, 1982, p. 90), a "perpetually soused [man] . . . committing suicide at the local bar, shot glass by shot glass" (Gelmis, 1982, p. 63), but a "drunken lawyer determined to redeem his reputation" (Kissel, 1982, p. 8). Denby (1982, p. 62) is more explicit: "Lumet and Mamet have dredged up details of the boozing derelict life—life after the crack-up—that will produce a shock of recognition in anyone who's ever drunk through a weekend."

The "Frank-as-a-drunk" interpretations were filtered through the critics' attempts to make sense of the larger issues the film addresses as a courtroom drama (Maslin, 1982, p. 24), produced in the tradition of social realism[6]: good versus evil, alcoholism, the Catholic Church's place in the trial, medicine, self-serving physicians, cold attorneys, women, the salvation of all people who have fallen or been lied to (Sklar, 1983, p. 47; Asahina, 1982, p. 19).[7]

Back to the Film

Like the film, these readings shift attention away from the necessary recovery story embedded in the narrative. After all, if Frank does not get his drinking under control this will be just another story about a drunk who did not get sober. How, then, does the film accomplish his recovery? Not well. The viewer is given to believe that he sobers up because (1) he is convinced that medical negligence occurred, (2) this is his last chance to turn his life around, and (3) when he was ready to quit Laura bullied him into staying on the case. There is nothing in each of the film's pivotal scenes where the above actions occur to convince the viewer that Frank has in fact made these kinds of momentous decisions. Yet they are presented as events that have occurred in an apparently necessary and sequential order. The film obviously wants the viewer to believe that being thrown out of the funeral home, the drunken violence he directs to his office, and the dressing down he receives from Mickey the next day are the keys to his finally discovering that he has hit bottom. These events then open his eyes to the realization that this is his last case. This leads him to stand up to the Bishop and turn down the offer. He is now committed to the case, so that when he experiences despair, Laura's critical reaction to his "failure" becomes the event that keeps him going. These events, having been experienced, now build on one another in such a way as to keep Frank straight and sober until the film's end. But if Frank is the kind of alcoholic he is presented as being in the opening scenes, then it will surely take more than this case to get and keep him sober. Certainly he has been thrown out of funeral homes before, and this is not the first time Mickey has chastised him.

The narrative, then, stumbles from the very beginning. Its key premise is not supported. As a consequence this particular film fails in its attempt to turn an alcoholic into a modern day Capra hero (Sklar, 1983, p. 47), into a Stallone–"Rocky" figure who, "as an underdog without a prayer of winning suddenly upsets the established order through sheer tenacity" (Hanson, 1984, p. 380). Indeed it is the Capra–Rocky virtues (tenacity, hard work, the love of a good woman, luck and good fortune, honesty, and kindness) that undermine the alcoholism of the Galvin character. In drawing on these values the film paints a thin picture of an alcoholic, a picture that undercuts previous versions of this man who in earlier decades scarcely had time for anything else but his struggle with the bottle. By shifting Frank's battle from the bottle to the courtroom the film turns his drinking into a character defect that would have been cured long ago if the right case (and woman) had just come along.

If *The Verdict* falters in its attempt to use alcoholism as a plot element for another storyline, *Under the Volcano* returns to the theme established in *The Lost Weekend*, that is, the alcoholics' struggles with himself and the bottle.[8]

Under the Volcano (1984)

Nightfall, Cuernavaca, Mexico, 1938: November 1. "The Day of the Dead." The film opens with finely detailed marionettes (black and white skeletons on strings, telegraphing death), with bulging eyes and teeth, dancing in air, to soft musical Mexican strings and horns. Depicting prostitutes, the grim reaper, a crucified Christ, a bride and a groom, Mexican bandits on horses, laughing clowns, and a dead man holding a whiskey bottle, the puppets signify the three main characters whose story is about to be told. They too are puppets on strings. Fate will control their destiny.[9] The camera pans to a view of a mountain top, then to a long shot of a church, and next to the street where, by candle light, peasants dressed in white prepare baskets of flowers for the dead. An obviously drunken figure in black formal attire emerges out of the shadows. Skulls of the dead are reflected in his dark glasses. Meet Geoffrey Firmin, alcoholic, ex-British consul to Cuernavaca. When the sun rises, he will have a reunion with Yvonne, his former wife, an American actress, who a year earlier had an affair with Hugh, his half-brother, a journalist. She has returned, the prodigal wife, hoping for a reconciliation. When day is done Geoffrey and Yvonne will be dead.

The storyline is a "tragedy . . . of a cuckold" (Cross, 1980, p. 27). Unable to pardon Hugh and Yvonne for their conduct, drinking constantly, he leaves them after a bull fight and goes to the Farolito, a brothel, looking for the letters Yvonne wrote him over the past year when she asked for his forgiveness. He orders and drinks mescal, a liquor he had earlier vowed to never touch, "Go thirsty before I'd drink it. Drink for the damned." Reading her letters he mutters, "Not enough. It's not possible. Not in this world." Chasing after him, Hugh and Yvonne discover that he has purchased the services of a prostitute. Leaving the Farolito, abashed, ashamed, and grieving, hearing gun shots, Yvonne turns back, and is killed by a stampeding horse as Geoffrey is murdered by Mexican bandits who think he is a spy. They both die under the volcano called "Popo," a sacred place of Aztec sacrifice.

Told almost entirely from his point of view, filled with his alcoholic, whiskey, and tequila-inspired hallucinations, paranoia, and rambling monologues, this film departs from the novel, yet maintains its allegorical symbolism, including multiple references and representations, at times macabre and comedic, but also tragic, of death, betrayal, forgiveness, and moral and political corruption. The "soft, sad beauty of the [cinematography] of Gabriel Figuero" (Benson, 1984, p. 1) conveys the spirit of Mexico—a sinister, lush landscape, green hills and valleys, fog-shrouded mountain tops, clear blue skies, dark forests, tawdry, beautiful dusty towns, "the passive misery of a culture in which death comes quickly and anonymously" (Denby, 1984, p. 63). It, like the novel, is "perhaps the best account of a 'drunk' in [fiction] and film" (Spender, 1974, p. viii), rivaled only by Charles Jackson's [and Billy Wilder's] treatment of Don Birnam.

I will here deal only with Geoffrey's alcoholism, his final interactions with Yvonne, and their deaths.

An Alcoholic Dies

Geoffrey is a late stage alcoholic, perpetually drinking, always attempting to maintain a balance between drunkenness and sobriety. A highly principled and moral man, he is trapped in a cycle of guilt and rage that is fueled by alcohol. Although the motives for his alcoholic state are never clearly stated, it is evident that he has been deeply wounded by Yvonne's infidelity. Caught in a double-bind, he wants Yvonne back, but he cannot admit this to her, nor to himself, for that would be an admission of love and forgiveness.

The film's penultimate scene occurs over drinks at the bull fights. Yvonne has just pleaded with him to leave Mexico and start a new life with her in Canada. Geoffrey calls for another drink. "Surprise here I'm afraid. Too much moderation [grabs the bottle and takes a drink]. I need a drink desperately to get my balance back" (takes another long drink). He then attacks Hugh and Yvonne: "What an uncommon time they must have had of it, peddling palms [Yvonne turns away], playing bubbies and titties, while I was having bouts with rats and roaches." (Yvonne begins to cry). "I've come crawling back. What more can I do? Let me be your wife." Geoffrey (to self): "When has she ever been a wife to me? Where are the children I might have had? Drowned to the rattling of a thousand douche bags [Yvonne weeping loudly]. Hugh, on the threshold of paradise, puffing over her gilt like a codfish made like a racehorse . . . wallowing in their bliss with my blessing."

The damage done, the double-bind put firmly in place, Geoffrey walks away. All that remains is for him to find her letters.

The film is a story of Geoffrey's search for the lost letters from Yvonne. The letters carry multiple meanings for him. They represent his unwillingness to confront her departure. His refusal to read them reflects his denial of this situation. His inability to answer them ("shaking hands") mirrors his deteriorating alcoholic condition. When she arrives in the flesh he must still find the letters for they represent the "imaginary" and not the "real" Yvonne. If he were to accept the "real" Yvonne, he would have to deal with her sexual betrayal. By constantly fleeing from her, in search of the letters, he runs back to a dream (the last year never happened, she never left). When he finds them of course he cannot accept her written plea for reconciliation. He must betray her, and this he does by buying the services of a prostitute. This done, the symbolic pain inflicted, the only alternative that remains for the two of them is death. He will have sacrificed his life for her, and she for him. An absurd universe, which randomly produces his abject death in a moment of misrecognition has finally acted morally. Geoffrey the existentialist, the worldly philosopher who believes only in private guilt, has died properly.

The moral of the story is clear. The cuckold cannot forgive his wife. His alcoholism, woven through his puritanical moral character, will not allow this. Yet the deaths that follow this decision assume the characteristics of a "horse opera" where Geoffrey's heroics look like a histrionic last stand (drunkly waving a sword at the bandits who hold their guns on him), whose tragic development is banal, comic, absurd, and existential at the same time (see Cross, 1980, pp. 127–28).

The sexual theme that organizes the narrative suggests that the male alcoholic's inner self experiences its greatest wound and betrayal when a wife turns to another man. This turning away signifies a failure of masculinity. Geoffrey's bravado drinking masks his inner failure as a sexual being. To acquit Yvonne of her crime would be to admit this failure, and to confront the fact that alcohol has produced it.

The Critics

Critics read the film through their relationship to the novel, which was usually personally intense (i.e., Merkin, 1984). Many praised the cinematography of Figueroa (Keneas, 1984) and Finney's performance as Geoffrey (Reed, 1984), which captures the Consul's "disintegrating grandeur [and] makes him courtly, generous, ruthlessly honest, [and] physically courageous" (Denby, 1984, p. 63). Others found fault with the script, which omitted so much of Lowry's text (Sterritt, 1984, p. 25), and with Huston's lengthy death scene in the Farolito (Merkin, 1984, p. 19). Reed (1984, p. 23) argued that "the magic in the [Lowry novel] has been trashed, and what is left is just another *Lost Weekend*, with Margaritas" (see also Sprinker, 1985, p. 503). Keneas (1984, p. 55), Pym (1984, p. 226), and Milne (1984, p. 214) unfavorably compared Huston's direction of this film with his earlier works (*Fat City*). It was generally conceded, with Bunuel ["How can you film inside of a man's head?"] (Milne, 1984, p. 214), that the novel cannot be filmed. It is "one of those classics perhaps more saluted than read [or filmed]" (Keneas, 1984, p. 55). Benson (1984, p. 1) contended that Huston failed to create Lowry's double world: "the real Mexico in which the Consul lives, and the hallucinatory one that the Consul . . . sees around him" (but see Maslin, 1984, p. 21). Nor was he able, according to Keneas (1984, p. 55), to capture and combine the novel's fragmented, mix of myth, politics, literature, world history, and religion, with its cinematic flashbacks and jump cuts, most of which are disjointed, symbolic, and largely imaginary. Instead Huston and Gallo produced a "soft-edged romantic triangle" (Keneas, 1984, p. 55; see also Sprinkler, 1985, p. 505), which alternates between Geoffrey acting like King Lear, or his Fool (Merkin, 1984, p. 19), or a "big boiled potato" (Reed, 1984, p. 23), but never like a "truly tragic figure" (Reed, 1984, p. 23), whose "addiction is caused by loneliness" (Sterritt, 1984, p. 25), and whose condition is a manifestation of "the world in these times and the breakdown of values in our century" (Sterritt, 1984, p. 25; also Spender, 1984, p. ix). There is no sense in the film that "The Counsel is a modern hero—or anti-hero—reflecting an extreme external situation within his own extremity" (Spender, 1984, p. ix), or that his alcoholism is caused by "the complete baffling sterility of existence as *sold* to you" (Spender, 1984, p. xx).

The film clearly enters Geoffrey's world and powerfully conveys his addiction to alcohol and the effects of that addiction on him and those who love him. While celebrating, in a negative way, the alcoholic's situation, it fails to enter the deeper world of existence that Lowry intended to reveal; the alcoholic's paranoid, imaginary world of fears, hatreds, dreams, and obsessions. But in attempting to do so Huston keeps alive the myth of the tragic, gifted, intellectual alcoholic who in his struggles with his alcoholism also struggles with himself.

Still, Geoffrey never attempts to quit drinking, and nobody asks him to. His struggles are with himself and with an inner world that he has created. Whether this constitutes tragedy is questionable, for the text is entirely self-centered, and he makes no noble gesture to anyone. However Canby (1984, p. 12) disagrees on this point, arguing that Finney's Consul "emerges as a far more interesting, exuberant, tragic character than any chronic drunk has a right to be, in real life or in fiction . . . the Consul's addiction is, mysteriously, not only a weakness but a conscious choice, and at that an heroic one. This, of course, is the alcoholic Lowry's rationalization."

However, the text illuminates, as argued above, the sexual underside of the alcoholic's being. In this movie it reveals a dimension of male alcoholism that has thus far been given little attention in this tradition; that is the male's sexuality has not figured prominently in earlier treatments of his condition. This stands in stark contrast to the case of the female whose sexuality has repeatedly been shown to be an essential part of her alcoholism.

Compare now Geoffrey and Frank Galvin, two alcoholics who hit different bottoms, two different outcomes. One stops drinking, the other does not. Each confronts a crisis, but reacts differently. Frank's crisis produced a feeling that he had one last chance to change his life. It is not clear, however, that Geoffrey regards the activities of his final day as his last chance to reunite with his wife and make an attempt at starting over. Although Yvonne may have held this position, it is not clear that Geoffrey did. Of course it can be ironically argued that Geoffrey hits bottom. His alcoholism produces his death. Unable, that is, to deal with Yvonne's return, he drank himself into circumstances that produced his death. Thus the similarities between Frank and Geoffrey are only superficial, even though both appear to have last chances to deal with their alcoholism.

I turn now to *Hoosiers*, where the theme of the last chance and its relationship to the alcoholic's situation is again explored, only now the alcoholic becomes a secondary figure in the story being told.

Hoosiers (1986)

It is a small story, a Frank Capra triumph-against-the-odds fable (Harris, 1987, p. 247). In March of 1954 Milan, a tiny rural, southern Indiana high school emerged from a field of 751 teams to win the

Indiana state high school basketball championship. Praised by the critics (Harris, 1987), *Hoosiers* is the fictionalized story of this accomplishment. Milan becomes the town of Hickory. Its basketball team, the Huskers, is coached by Norman Dale, a man banned from coaching ten years earlier because he lost his temper and hit a player. He is given a last chance to get back into basketball by an old friend, Cletus, the high school principal. Shooter, a former star from Hickory, now middle-aged, and the town drunk, volunteers to help Dale. His son Everett plays on the team and has been embarrassed countless times by his father's public drunkenness. Dale takes Shooter on, with the promise that he stay sober. It is the fall of 1951.

The star player from the year before, Jimmy, is in mourning for the previous coach and refuses to play on the team. Jimmy has come under the tutoring of Myra, a high school teacher, who sees a future for Jimmy beyond basketball. She and Dale move from antagonists to friends to lovers. When the team fails to win its early games, the town's Monday-morning coaches rebel. A showdown in the local church hall occurs and the crowd votes to fire Dale. At the last minute Jimmy appears and announces that he is ready to come back on the team, but only if Coach Dale remains. The town reinstates Dale as its coach. Shooter coaches the team to victory in a game that Dale is thrown out of. He relapses when the team reaches the Regional finals, unable to handle the stress, and ends up drying out in the local hospital. The Huskers make their way through a series of close battles to their destiny in Indianapolis. They win the championship game against an all-Black team by using a play designed by Shooter ("the picket fence").

Shot on location, using local residents as extras, the film captures the regional peculiarities and feeling of rural Indiana, including dialect, the passion for basketball (the camera seems to glide up the court with the players), the autumn turn of leaves, the cold winter countryside, the frost-filled earth in early March, black skylines broken by the headlights from a caravan of cars coming home from a basketball game.

The Stories of Norman Dale and Shooter

Two parallel stories, the last chances of Dale and Shooter, thus structure the narrative. Each helps the other to recover and go onto a final victory. Although there is no certainty for Shooter's future, it is clear that Dale will return next year to coach the team, and that he and Myra will continue their romantic relationship.

Shooter appears in only slightly more than a dozen scenes, yet at one level "*Hoosiers*" is the story of his rehabilitation from panhandling town drunk, to successful coach of the team in a crisis, to town embarrassment, to sober-team loyalist, reunited with Everett in a father–son relationship at film's end. (Everett, "How ya doin' Dad?" Shooter, "I feel real empty inside." Everett, "You're gonna get better Dad . . . we're gonna get a house." His appearance is coded to match his drunk–sober states. When drunk he is unshaven, his hair is uncombed, his clothes are in disarray. On three occasions he is shown with a gun, either firing it or holding it. When sober he is clean shaven, hair combed, wearing a suit.) The cause of his alcoholism is left unclear, although he clearly yearns for his days as a high school basketball star.

The alcoholism story, realized through the character of Shooter, appears secondary to the primary story of Hickory winning the State Championship. In fact *Hoosiers* is a story of three victories: Hickory's championship, Dale's successful return to coaching, coupled with his new relationship with Myra, and Shooter's getting sober and being reunited with his son. Without Shooter there would be only the story of Hickory and their new coach. His presence adds another dimension to Dale's character, as it brings a touch of the family alcoholism theme into the story through the alcoholic father–son relationship. Dale and Shooter define one another's personal flaws (alcoholism and violence), and the victories (sobriety and self-control) that have thus far eluded both of them. [Although reviewers (e.g., Harris, 1987; Maslin, 1987) noted Shooter's alcoholism, they did not discuss how it functioned as a reflexive text within the story.] Each man struggles to make good in what is perceived as a last chance to turn a failed life around.

Each man is violent. Shooter's violence is self-directed in the form of destruction through alcoholism, yet also symbolized by his carrying a gun that he fires at strangers. Dale's violence is outward directed, and is symbolized by his repeated ejection from basketball games. The causes of his tendency toward violence (like Shooter's alcoholism) are never addressed. However, Shooter's relapses are caused by his fear of taking on the responsibility of coaching the team when Dale is ejected. Hence Dale's violence fuels Shooter's tendency to drink when afraid, and Shooter's relapses bring out Dale's tendency toward physical violence. (In a pivotal scene with Myra he relives the violent incident that led to his expulsion from the sport. His redemption is hinted at in this scene. She loves him for who he is—"a tough, stubborn willful man." He is healed by the love of a good woman.)

Although each man's story is an account of how the game of basketball carries serious consequences for life, the game is a metaphor for a deeper struggle over self-control, pride, and self-respect. [Religious (and racial—they defeat an all-Black team) themes are also present, for a minister says a prayer before their final game and one of the players insists on praying before and during every game.] By coding alcoholism with violence the film repeats a familiar theme that goes beyond simply stating that the alcoholic is violent. One need not be alcoholic to be violent, although one may be. But in either case, both phenomena erode moral character, and make a man less than he can, or would be. In so doing they make men pariahs, and locate them outside family, home, and work. Significantly, the victories of Dale and Shooter locate both men back inside family, home, work, and community.

Director Anspaugh and screenwriter Pizzo thus produced a moral tale premised on the operation of "compassion and hard work" (Harris, 1987, p. 247), sincerity, honesty, and God in everyday life. To these ingredients, they added will power and self-resolution, arguing that when these terms are joined with love, a man's life can be remade, leading to recovery from such self-destructive characteristics as violence and alcoholism.

But because the film fails to probe the deeper story behind the tale of the two damaged men, only the surface layers of their psychic wounds are revealed (Harris, 1987, p. 247). Perhaps in keeping "with a cinematic reticence—people's private matters stay pretty much their own" (Myra's words), their flaws are swept away in the momentum of the second half of the film, which builds to its victorious climax in Indianapolis (Harris, 1987, p. 247). In these moves the film offers simple solutions to complex problems. But it does so in such a direct and unpretentious way that its moral message seems incontrovertible; somehow Hickory's miracle will become the miracle of Dale and Shooter.

Shooter, like Frank Galvin, expresses a desire to get sober. Like Frank it takes a crisis, will power, and the help of friends to accomplish this end. Shooter's story keeps alcoholism alive in small-town middle-America. The next film brings this condition back to the big city and enlists the aid of A.A. and the ever-present loving woman. Only now, as with Galvin, the main character's alcoholism is part of a larger story. Scudder is prototypical of the alcoholic cop, a social type (like Lew Marsh in Chapter 3) who has been present in mystery fiction and *film noir* since the 1940s.

8 Million Ways to Die (1986)[10]

Generally damned by the critics (Benson, 1986; McGrady, 1986; Hoberman, 1986; but see Denby, 1986) this crime-thriller, "Miami Vice" look-alike story about a gangster war in Los Angeles involving seductive, good–bad hookers (Sunny and Sarah), a rich Columbian drug dealer (Angel), and a swank Black pimp (Chance), requires analysis for two reasons. It keeps alive the myth of the lonely, incorruptible male alcoholic outsider (Frank Galvin, Lew Marsh) who is obsessed with his honor and with seeing justice done in the world. Of equal importance,

A.A.'s presence in the opening, middle, and closing moments make it an A.A. film. Two subplots, divorced Scudder's attempts to maintain a relationship with Laurie, his young daughter, and Sarah's revelation that she is the adult child of an alcoholic father, further elaborate the alcoholism themes that structure the narrative. I will focus primarily on the A.A. elements in the text, drawing attention to how A.A. is put to new uses in this film.

The narrative itself is complex, yet typical of the tough guy, mystery genre. Here the cop is thrown off the force because of his alcoholism. He becomes a suspect in a murder case, pursues the villain who has killed a young, beautiful woman (Sunny), threatens to destroy another (Sarah), and kills him. Disturbed because he was supposed to be protecting Sunny, Scudder, who has just celebrated his sixth month of sobriety at an A.A. meeting, gets drunk and wakes up three days later in pajamas stenciled: "Detox Unit." "How long have I been here?" he asks the nurse, who tells him, "Sorry, that's confidential information . . . you better shake it out a bit more before you go." Appearing animal-like, leaning forward, hair across eyes, face in a painful scowl, shaking, and clutching his stomach, his hospital gown open at the back, he growls at the nurse, "I gotta go." She replies, "One more drink and where ever it is you're going, you're gonna be dead before you get there." Barely able to function, he goes after the Angel, picks up Sarah along the way, who wants to get out of the "life," but is apparently addicted to drugs and alcohol, discovers a huge cocaine distribution operation, blows up the drugs, kills Angel, and appears later with Sarah at a sunrise A.A. meeting on the Los Angeles beach. Good triumphs over evil.

The Uses of Alcoholism and A.A.

The film moves quickly into Scudder's alcoholism. An opening shot shows him and a fellow police officer drinking out of a flask as they approach a house for a raid, where, in the course of battle, he shoots and kills a man. He is next shown drinking heavily, falling off a bar stool in a tavern, and awakening the next morning, shirtless, bottle in hand, on top of a brick wall alongside the family driveway. In the next scene the audience is taken to an A.A. meeting. (The members are dressed in blue jeans, shorts, tennis shoes, and sweatshirts.) Matt speaks: "I'm an alcoholic. So far bein' a drunk has cost me my job, my home, my health. I'm not a cop. I'm not married to Linda anymore" (he leaves the podium passing a poster that reads "Principles before Personalities").

The immediate insertion of A.A. into the text suggests that Matt's struggles, from this point forward, will be defined by his status as an alcoholic who attempts to recover in A.A. The signifiers of lush and blackout are repeatedly applied to him. His friend Joe: "You can't remember anything, you fuckin' lush." Sarah calls him a lush and asks if he is sober enough to know what he is doing. A.A.'s second appearance in the film is indirect and symbolic. Sarah and Matt have spent the night together. They wake up in his bed, he fully clothed, his gun in his right hand, and laying across his stomach is A.A.'s *Big Book* opened to what appears to be Chapter Five, "How it Works." Sarah congratulates him, "At least you stayed sober. You're not a mindless lush after all." Next Scudder describes alcoholism as a disease to Sarah. He has asked her if she was close to her father. Sarah, "No, he's dead. He was an alcoholic." Matt: "That's the worst thing about this disease. You lose that closeness with the people you love the most."

In a symbolic climax, frustrated and in a rage over his failure to kill Angel, Matt goes to a liquor store and buys a bottle of whiskey. Sarah pleads with him, "Please don't do this. Don't do this." He puts the bottle down. They drive to Angel's. He throws the whiskey against the wall, goes in to Angel's house, confronts, and kills him.

The film closes, as it nearly opened, with Matt at an A.A. meeting. He speaks the following lines to a sunrise A.A. group on the beach: "I'm Matt Scudder [close-up shot] I'm an alcoholic, feeling pretty good today. When I first came to this program about a year ago I didn't really believe this stuff. . . . I failed the program three times [the camera cuts to Sarah and Matt walking arm and arm on the beach, his voice-over continues]. But I have been dry a month now, no it's five weeks. This time I may do it for good. . . . When I fall asleep I don't pass out. When that sun comes up, I wake up. I don't come to. I'm in love. What can I say? That's a great feeling man" (the two of them embrace on the beach). An end credit reads, "In Cooperation with Alcoholics Anonymous."[11]

Reading *8 Millions Ways to Die* as an Alcoholism Film

Recall the "A.A." films thus far analyzed (e.g., *Days of Wine and Roses*). Once A.A. enters the narrative, a predictable course of events follows. The drinker hits bottom, experiences DTs, gets into trouble because of drinking, and comes to define their present attempts at recovery as a last chance. The disease concept of alcoholism is introduced, although the causes of the condition will seldom be explained. The alcoholic is taken to A.A. meetings and learns to speak the A.A. language. The member takes on an A.A. sponsor. The person confronts a crisis, a relapse occurs, and other crises are experienced. An A.A. sobriety date is established and a birthday is celebrated. The member is reunited with his or her family and returns to a productive life, either within A.A. and the treatment of other alcoholics, or in a previous occupation. Throughout this ordeal the love of a good man or woman is presented as being central to the alcoholic's recovery.

8 Million Ways to Die is an unconventional A.A. film. It breaks out of, while it retains commitments to the previously established mold. Scudder has no sponsor, is not reunited with his family, loses his old job, and keeps relapsing when he confronts a crisis. Yet he hits bottom at least three times, experiences DTs, gets into trouble during blackouts, does go to A.A. meetings, is tempted to drink and does, learns the disease concept of alcoholism, and is assisted in his recovery by the love of a good woman.

Like *Come Fill the Cup* it is a mixed-genre movie, combining the gangster-mystery film, and the hard drinking alcoholic cop, with an explicit A.A./alcoholism, social problems text. Scudder, like Lew Marsh, enters a world of violence and sexuality where drinking (and now drugs) go together. Unlike Lew, Matt cannot stay sober in this world.

The problem of interpreting this film now becomes clear. It involves a single question, how to explain the above departures from the traditional A.A. movie. There are three answers. The first two are obvious. A.A. is present in Block's novels where Scudder's alcoholism and A.A. are integral parts of the storylines, hence there is no reason for it not to be present in a way that is faithful, at least partially, to the Block text. The second answer is less obvious, but equally plausible. It can be argued that prior filmic representations of A.A. were biased in a direction that emphasized the "ideal" workings of an A.A. based recovery, i.e., the member acquires a sponsor, and so on (see also Denzin, 1987b, Chapter 5). Perhaps the more realistic model is the one followed by Scudder, where the alcoholic wanders in and out of A.A., gets sober, has problems, gets drunk, comes back, gets a chip, gets drunk, hits another bottom, and comes back again. If this is the case, then the film is neither unconventional nor outside the actual workings of the A.A. experience; it is the prior films that are unconventional.[12]

The third answer is more tentative, and connects to the first argument. It is threefold. First, the gangster genre form has repeatedly dealt with drug and alcohol abuse and violence, and hence has always utilized elements of the social problems film, if only as a secondary theme (see Roffman and Purdy, 1981, p. 16). Second, the hero of the hardboiled-detective film in the 1970s, which partially transformed the gangster form of the 1940s (Schatz, 1981, p. 147), has, in the 1980s become a more drug and alcohol aware figure.[13] Part of the tough-guy image is now centered on staying sober in a violent drinking world.

The next move in the transformation of the genre now involves taking a stand against alcohol abuse. Hence A.A.'s presence becomes a signifier of the film's antidrug, antialcoholism stance. This interpretation argues that the invasion of the A.A./disease ideology into Hollywood is now so strong that it is no longer possible to present an alcoholic in the 1980s without addressing, no matter how superficially, the A.A. (or drinking causes problems) point of view (see, for example, the two late 1989 films *Sea of Love* and *The Fabulous Baker Boys*, 1989; but also the discussion of *Barfly* below).

Hence *8 Million Ways to Die* can be read as a post-Reagan film, which says "No" to drugs and alcohol, while it attempts to be a "thriller of rehabilitation . . . that substitutes cops and hookers [for] cowboys and schoolmarms as the generic Adam and Eve in the American garden" (Hoberman, 1986, p. 62). But it does more than this. It opens up new ways for A.A. to operate within a text, while it explores alternative, perhaps more realistic paths to recovery. At the same time it nudges the crime-thriller genre in a new direction, as it reinstates the "tough-guy" image of the macho alcoholic male who fights two battles at the same time: crime and alcoholism. In this fight he seeks to regain a sense of lost honor and self-pride. By winning the sobriety battle, he wins the other battle as well, thereby reclaiming his pride and self-respect. In this sense his alcoholism signifies, as it always has, something more than a disease.

Now *Barfly*, a film that celebrates alcoholism (or at least excessive drinking) and violence in ways that introduce further transformations within the tradition.

Barfly (1987)[14]

Called by critics a "ballad for losers, a song from the underbelly" (Wilmington, 1987, p. 1), a "no-pain version of hit-the-bottom alcoholism" (Carr, 1987, p. 32), a "small, classic, one-of-a-kind comedy" (Canby, 1987, p. 30), the "first great bar movie . . . the most luscious tribute to lushes the cinema has ever produced . . . a . . . human comedy" (Ringel, 1987, p. 1), the "first film to respect drunks as people—not problems" (Strauss, 1988, p. 49), "Barfly" is based on the semi-autobiographical screenplay by Los Angeles poet Charles Bukowski. The story, set on L.A.'s skid row, involves five days and one evening in the life of Henry (he growls like W. C. Fields and walks like Quasimodo), who drinks because there is nothing else to do, and Wanda, his girlfriend, who drinks because it is the only thing to do.

It opens and closes with Henry and Eddie, the macho bartender of The Golden Horn (a friendly bar), in a fight outside the bar in an alley. In between these two brawls, Henry, an unemployed alcoholic who writes poetry and short stories ("Some people never go crazy. What truly horrible lives they must live"), and spends his days and nights as a barfly in the Golden Horn, meets Wanda (a faded beauty, also a barfly), a confirmed alcoholic, who tells Henry, "I can't stand people. I hate them" ("I seem to do better when they're not around,") Henry moves in with her, fights with her, writes poetry, meets Tully the owner of *The Contemporary Review of Art and Literature*, which has published one of his stories, receives a check from her, goes to her home, makes love, turns down her offer to move in ("it's a cage with golden bars"), leaves and returns to Wanda, showering money on her, goes back to the Golden Horn, buys drinks for everyone, referees a fight between Wanda and Tully, and then, as the film ends, exits to the alley for a grudge fight with Eddie.

"Barfly" is a nonjudgmental ("he's as right as any of us"), yet digni-fied street-level view of barfly life in dirty skid row taverns and cheap rundown hotel rooms. Henry's environment has the look and feel of a grotesque, deteriorating, Disneyesque playground filled with bur-lesque, harlequin characters. Neon signs for bars, some with letters missing ("The Sunset," "The Hollyway," "Oasis," "Crabby Joe's") light the street. It is photographed in a grainy, gritty, "giddy neon sheen which captures the drabness of Henry's milieu" (Strauss, 1988, pp. 49–50). The narrative is accompanied by a soundtrack that alternates be-tween the "bump-and-grind" organ, saxophone and drum beat of strip-tease, muted juke box tunes, Mozart piano concertos, soft Coltrane sax solos, and the rise and fall of barfly voices yelling, screaming, swearing, laughing, and cajoling one another.

The film elevates to protagonist status two confirmed alcoholics (drinking and alcohol are present in virtually every scene), who are fearful of falling in love (Wanda: "I don't ever want to fall in love. I don't ever want to do that again." Henry: "Don't worry. Nobody's ever loved me yet"), find in one another a common, existential understanding of life and drinking. Wanda to Henry: "You're the damnedest barfly I've ever seen. You act like some blueblood, like royalty . . . but I've gotta tell you somethin', if a man came by with a fifth of whisky I'm afraid I'd go with him." Henry to Wanda: "Drinking's always my best move. Do you think that's crazy?" Wanda: "What's crazy? I don't know. We're all in some kind of hell. And the madhouses are the only places where people know they are in hell. Who cares, anyway?" Henry: "I don't. I'm just a crazy, beer-drinking wrestler who likes to fart." In this universe drunks and nondrunks are invidiously compared. Henry: "Anybody can be a non-drunk. It takes a special talent to be a drunk. It takes endurance. Endurance is more important than truth."

The film reduces life to the barest essentials. Money for food and drink are all that count, and when they are present it is a cause for celebration. What matters is a solid respect for life as it is lived at this level. Appearance and cleanliness are not especially valued, particularly by Henry who is constantly shown with greasy hair, bloodied knuckles, an unwashed, dirty face marred with stubble, bruises, and caked blood, wearing the same sweat-soaked tee shirt, and pants with dirty underwear. Conferring respect on others is important. Henry asks an old bum for a light: "Hey, buddy! You got a light?" Bum (in an almost cultured English accent): "Well, indeed, I do have that!" Henry: "Thank you, very much." Bum: "The pleasure is more than mine, sir—and my lady."

Violence is ever-present and takes several forms, including blacks attempting to hold up convenience grocery stores, a husband battering his wife, Wanda beating Henry up with her purse, Wanda's alcoholic nightmare when she sees the Angel of Death, Tully and Wanda fighting over Henry, and Henry and Eddie's ritualistic battles in the alley. Yet this violence seamlessly fits itself to the ebb and flow of life along Bukowski's skid row; nobody really takes anything seriously, as Henry remarks when Wanda is trying to peel Tully away from her perfume. "Look girls, be realistic. None of us hardly knows the other. We're basically strangers to each other. We've passed in the night and met again in a bar. Be realistic: there's no reality in any of this. Another round of drinks for everybody!"

Reading the Film

Labeled the most entertaining movie of 1987 (Carr, 1987, p. 32), it was compared to *Lost Weekend* (Canby, 1987; Ringel, 1987), but not *Fat City*, its logical predecessor. [Henry and Wanda may have "made a conscious decision to turn their lives into one long lost weekend" (Ringel, 1987, p. 9), but their lost weekend is comic, not tragic. It is more of a holiday than a hell.] Contrary to the critics, the film is not a "ballad for losers" (Wilmington, 1987, p. 1), or a "no-pain version of hit-the-bottom alcoholism" (Carr, 1987, p. 32), for Wanda and Henry do not see themselves as losers who have hit bottom, and they are not presented this way. In refusing to pass judgment, it can, however, be said to glorify, or pay tribute to the bar life of lushes (Ringel, 1987, p. 1), and to celebrate "the happier side of heavy drinking" (Maslin, 1988a, p. 1).

Dunaway's Wanda is a new kind of female alcoholic. Unlike Susan Tyrrell's Oma (*Fat City*), she is not a whiner, a sloppy, falling down drunk, or a woman who picks violent losers to live with. Nor has her life of alcoholism caused her any apparent problems. She does not wake up next to dead bodies, set fires in her home, embarrass her family at holiday dinners, or experience degradation on skid row. She knows who she is and where she is going. There is nothing wrong with where she is or where she lives (The Royal Palms), or who she lives off of (Wilber).

In these ways this film turns its back on the antialcoholism films that have come before. Its comedy-like features, which turn, in part, on Henry's one-liners, also set it apart from earlier alcoholism comedies (i.e., *Harvey*, *Arthur 2*) where alcoholism was defined as a humorous, but negative character trait. Bukowski's sardonic, laughing, biting, bitter text, and Schroeder's direction, which refuse to take themselves seriously, bring a noble, comedic realism to the ordinariness of life lived in and around the alcoholic edges of skid row.[15] The film shatters Hollywood's long-held tradition of associating skid row life with alcoholism's most destructive effects, including hitting bottom. In this movie it explodes all of the previously held stereotypes about the alcoholic's lifestyle. Alcoholism now becomes something other than a disease to be cured by doctors, A.A., family members or lovers. It is not something to be rid of. In *Barfly* alcoholism and perpetual drunkenness become states of being that are no longer controlled by the medical metaphor. The alcoholic's being is not defined in terms of a struggle to overcome the compulsion to drink. The traditional dimensions of alcoholic heroism are swept away by this film.

In stating that "He's as right as any of us," and in generalizing this statement to all the characters who walk across and through Henry's landscape, the film refuses to pass judgment on the key assumption that has heretofore defined the moral content of society's and Hollywood's view of the alcoholic. In a postmodern fashion it argues that the ancient signifiers surrounding the term alcoholic no longer hold. In this bold movie *Barfly* lays down a challenge to future filmmakers who take up the problem of representing the alcoholic's situation.

Clean and Sober (1988)[16]

This challenge is *not* taken up in *Clean and Sober*, a text that retains a commitment to the traditional realist social problems and the medical position that alcoholism is bad and should be treated. Its release in 1988 signals the beginning of the end of the cycle of alcoholism films started with the *Star Is Born* series and partially completed with *The Betty Ford Story*. A.A. and treatment are finally joined in a single storyline about a dual-addict (alcohol and cocaine, the drug of the 1980s). The film also explores, in ways that previous films did not, all three phases of the moral career of the alcoholic who goes into treatment (prepatient, inpatient, ex-patient, Goffman, 1961). In so doing it extends themes that had been taken over by television in "movie-of-the-week" productions, such as *Shattered Spirits*. (It was directed by Glen Gordon Caron of the popular "Moonlighting" TV series.) Part melodrama, part comedy, the film's two storylines (a love story and a recovery story) compete with one another as the narrative asks two questions: "Can a middle-class yuppie alcoholic–cocaine addict find love with a working class woman, also an addict, who is involved in a violent, battering relationship?" and "Can he stay clean and sober when she dies?" Its answer, not surprisingly, to the first question is no, and to the second yes.

Set in Philadelphia in the present, this is the redemption story (Sterritt, 1988, p. 20) of an alcoholic and cocaine addict named Daryl Poynter, a jaded, cynical, self-centered, yuppie real estate salesman, who drives a silver Mercedes and owns his own condo. A hyper, angry con artist, he has lifted $92,000 from an escrow account, hoping to make a quick stock market killing, only to find that the account has shrunk to $40,000. The film covers the first 30 days of Daryl's recovery experiences, first in a treatment center, then in A.A.

The narrative is divided into three parts corresponding to the three phases of the classic redemption/morality tale. Part one documents Daryl's collapsing life (he wakes up next to a woman who dies a week later from a drug overdose—shades of *The Morning After*, he also runs to the airport!), the day he walks into a treatment center to escape and hide from the world outside. Part two examines his 21-day stay in treatment where he tries to con his counselor Craig and is ordered to leave, does, and then returns, begins to take his treatment seriously, meets and falls in love with Charlie Standers, a slender, 30-year-old, vulnerable, attractive, masochistic (Denby, 1988, p. 134), addict, with a wry sense of humor and an "expressive, slightly ravaged face" (Sawahata, 1989, p. 82), who works in a steel mill and has lived for the last 10 years with an abusive ex-con named Lenny. Part three involves the nine days after he leaves treatment, when he connects with an A.A. sponsor (Richard), loses his job, looks for others, dates Charlie, tries to get her to move in with him, and deals with her death in an auto accident precipitated by her snorting coke. Throughout all of this Daryl stays clean and sober and at the film's conclusion speaks at an A.A. meeting, receiving a 30-day sobriety chip.

Leading the double life of the addict and alcoholic, Daryl approaches every situation in terms of the performance, the moves, and the gestures that will allow him to get what he wants. In keeping with its interpretation of how cocaine addicts (and salesmen) operate, the narrative continually focuses on Daryl's obsession with and frequent use of the telephone, this being his means of contacting his dealer. (Every turning point in the film is preceded by a telephone call.) The gradual dismanteling of this performance-front, and the revelation of the "real" Daryl, is the primary, and most reflective subplot that organizes the film. Consistent with its comedic overtones (including comic references to sexual organs, e.g., the penis is called a coiled snake and a little pecker to be put in park) the text is spliced with one-liners, jokes, and put-downs spoken by Daryl. He uses comedy to manage the tension and strain he is experiencing. (It is also a form of aggression against authority figures, especially Craig.)

The conflict between the middle and lower classes is repeatedly explored in the Daryl–Charlie–Lenny triad. Charlie lives in a lower-class section of town; Daryl in a middle-class suburb. She dresses in jeans and sweaters, he in slacks and dress shirts, Lenny in jeans and leather jacket. She refers to his work in a derogatory way, "I just knew a slick guy like you'd have to do some kind of bogus tap dancing for a living." When she leaves Daryl's house, shortly before she is killed, she tells him, "You don't need me. Look at all you've got. You don't drink out of jelly jars. You wanta say somethin you sit down and figure out how to say it!"

At one level Charlie represents the evils of addiction (she keeps using) while Craig and Richard symbolize recovery and Daryl's return to a clean and sober middle-class way of life. Their values, dress, and speech contrast with Lenny's and Charlie's. The Daryl–Craig–Richard triad prevails at film's end; for Charlie has to be killed. Daryl cannot be united with a using, lower-class woman, even if he does love her. She becomes the film's tragic figure, a victim of her class, its violence, and her addiction, both to cocaine and Lenny.

The film is didactic. Certain obligatory and instructional gestures inform the viewer about the number of lives affected by alcoholism and addiction in America (70 million), take the viewer to A.A. meetings, define A.A. sponsorship ("somebody you can relate to. Somebody's heard all your bullshit before"), A.A.'s Fourth and Fifth Steps ("a searching and fearless moral inventory"), hitting bottom ("when you know your life is no longer manageable"), dry date, A.A.'s concept of powerlessness, and family week in treatment.

Escape to Salvation

Like *8 Million Ways to Die*, this film begins and ends with a speaker at an A.A. meeting. What goes on between these two markers is critical, especially the representations of treatment and Daryl's conversion to recovery. Treatment unravels in three stages: detoxification, confrontations with Craig, and the final submission to the Program. In a rapid succession of scenes he is introduced to the gray, dingy, cold, detox unit, with its highly polished floors, steel beds in the rooms, bright lights in the hallways, and worn-out sofas and chairs in the TV room, where pictures of JFK hang on the walls. He experiences the violence of DTs, including vomiting and a high fever, sees a huge black man blow up the TV ("Gotta get the fuck outta here"), and is told the rules of the Social Rehab center (all therapy sessions are mandatory, urine tests after passes).

His rebellion to the system is immediate. On returning from an A.A. meeting he is given a urine test by Craig who asks: "What the fuck you doin' here? You don't even know you got a problem. Do you know how long you been straight man? Twelve days [both men are at separate stalls, urinating]. Twelve days, three hours and twenty seconds, twenty-four seconds, twenty-six seconds. That's how we do it Daryl. A second at a time, minute at a time. One day at a time. But you gotta know you got a problem." Daryl sets the container full of urine on the top of the stall, "Drink up, will you," and walks out.

Never convinced that Daryl knows that he has a problem, the viewer confronts the last scene of the film with skepticism. Daryl is speaking at an A.A. meeting. "About a month ago . . . I had a few problems and uh, I figured the only way to deal with these problems was to uh . . . disappear . . . I figured what I'd do is check myself into a drug clinic. And uh, the only trick was I had to convince the people in the drug clinic I was an addict. So . . . I figured out all the language and all the gestures and moves so that I could give this really convincing performance. . . . And you fools bought it. Huh. And now, its 30 days later. And, uh . . . I been to a funeral, I been to about 9 million job interviews, I'm $52,000 in debt [grinning, runs hand through hair], and I got this chip [holds up]. I got this startling belief that [sucks air through his mouth], that . . . uh . . . that I am an alcoholic and a drug addict. Huh. [shakes head, runs hand through hair] God knows what we got goin' next month. But if it's anything like this last one. Jesus Christ! [laughter from audience] So here we go. And . . . [holds up chip] thanks for my chip. And thanks for not smoking."

The camera pans the smoke filled room, with close-ups of Donald, Craig, Richard (who holds back tears), and Daryl, who is half-smiling. Van Morrison sings over the credits ("Time for a change. Think I'll go underground and get some heavy rest. Oh, Oh Domino").

Clean and Sober as the End of a Cycle

Reviewers connected Clean and Sober to earlier films in the alcoholism-social problems tradition. Benson (1988a, p. 1) observed, "Roughly every 20 years a film is made that holds the mirror unwaveringly up to the excesses of its day: The Lost Weekend, Days of Wine and Roses and now Clean and Sober." Sawahata (1989, p. 80) made the same observation, calling it "the spiritual descendant of such earlier films as The Lost Weekend and Days of Wine and Roses . . . [because] they share a common thread—ordinary middle-class people's descent into the hell of addiction . . . [with] a 1980's twist: Its protagonist . . . is addicted not only to alcohol but also to cocaine." Maslin (1988a, p. 21) praised its serious treatment of an important problem, and favorably compared it to the more humorous 1988 release *Cocktail*, and the earlier comedy *Animal Farm*. Also drawing connections back to *Days of Wine and Roses, Lost Weekend, Ironweed,* and *The Morning After,* she argued, "there is nothing more reckless than treating [drinking] lightly" (see also Benson, 1988b, p. 29).

The film was faulted for its glossy and commercial "approach to the redemption—or—fall—of the addict" (Sawahata, 1989, p. 82), as well as its "pushy, self-righteous[ness] [that] comes across as the sort of public service penance movie a judge might assign to some Hollywood big shot trying to beat a drug possession rap" (Ringel, 1988, p. 1). Ringel (1988, p. 1) went on, arguing that it "borrows a lot of its slogans and methods from A.A. . . . The difference is A.A. works, this movie doesn't." Carr (1988, p. 67), on the other hand, contended that "The A.A. stuff is harrowingly convincing." The didactic tone of the film, its "offering slides of sick and healthy livers and invoking some of the techniques used by A.A." was also criticized by Maslin (1988b, p. 17). The two stories of addiction and love were seen as being "awkwardly folded together" (Benson, 1988a, p. 6). Ringel (1988, p. 4) suggested that "The film simply isn't dangerous enough. It never gets down-and-dirty about the subtle seduction of addiction." Corliss (1988, p. 76), in contrast, saw the film offering creative solutions to the problems of the American drug culture in the 1980s and 1990s. Ebert (1989, p. 137) suggested that the film is not the story of an ideal recovery . . . because Keaton is not an ideal candidate for recovery. He tells too many lies." He continues, "The subject matter of the film is commonplace . . . for every celebrity who checks into the Betty Ford Center, there are thousands of ordinary people who check in somewhere else, or who pick up the phone and call A.A. Everybody knows somebody like this. But the actual process of surrender and recovery is hardly ever the subject of films, maybe because it seems too depressing."

Critics like Benson (1988a,b), Maslin (1988b), and Corliss (1988) positioned the film in the decade of the 1980s. Benson (1988b, p. 28) argued that *"The Lost Weekend* was the first real rebuttal to [the] prettified view" of drinking as fun. . . . The next mass-audience message was *Days of Wine and Roses* . . . Now we have *Clean and Sober* . . . but until this picture, alcoholism/addiction didn't have its 20-year update for a new film generation. Instead in 1981 we had a detour: *Arthur,* where against all betting odds an alcoholic hero emerged as utterly lovable. . . . But in what seems to have been a decade since *Arthur,* alcoholism has ceased to be even marginally funny." These observations of course ignore the 30 plus alcoholism films that have been produced in the 1980s.

Corliss (1988, p. 76) elaborated Benson's position, calling his review of alcoholism films in the 1980s, "Hollywood Goes on the Wagon." In a comparison of *Arthur 2 on the Rocks, Who Framed Roger Rabbit?, Bird, Wired, Cocktail, Bright Lights, Big City,* he too called *Clean and Sober, The Lost Weekend* and *Days of Wine and Roses's* of the late 1980s. He suggested that a shift in mood has occurred in Hollywood, where "There are more stars at a Rodeo Drive A.A. meeting than there are at the Academy Awards . . . a few moviemakers are taking the pledge to put drug and alcohol addiction on screen." Noting that "traditionally, the big screen and its youthful audience welcomed the happy drunk" he suggests that "for early moviegoers, booze was a truth serum that liberated every endearing character from Charlie Chaplin to Dumbo."

In damning the alcoholism comedies of the 1980s, critics seemed to be taking a stand against the 1960s generation where "the use of recreational drugs was a gesture of political defiance, and movies mimicked it" (Corliss, 1988, p. 76, e.g., *Easy Rider*). Director Caron reinforces this interpretation: "Drugs weren't a by-product of our culture. They were our culture" (Caron, 1988b, p. 76). Thus *Clean and Sober* was read as an overture to the 1990s, "In the overdue national detox program that may be the 1990s, the drug culture could change. On movie screens it already has. . . . Will American moviegoers find the tonic chill of a dramatized A.A. lecture as bracing as the sight of a rabbit who can act like a boozehound? Stay tuned" (Corliss, 1988, p. 76).

Clearly *the* addiction and treatment film of the 1980s (Benson, 1988b, p. 29), *Clean and Sober* is a formula text. Much like *8 Million Ways to Die* and the other A.A. films thus far analyzed, it traces a predictable trajectory for the alcoholic-addict; the one outlined above (pp. 213–214). Daryl hits bottom because of his addiction, experiences DTs, is taught that he has a disease he is powerless over, learns A.A.'s language, goes to meetings, and gets a sponsor.

Unlike the earlier films in this tradition it is the love and concern of a good man (Craig first, then Richard) and not the love of a good woman (Charlie) that is central to Daryl's recovery. However, it is at the level of "conversion" and redemption that the narrative falters. It is never clear that the "real" Daryl has been uncovered, or that Daryl ever really hit bottom.

Clean and Sober is the first film to give audiences an extended view of life in a treatment center. This is where Daryl's transformation and conversion to the A.A. point of view should have occurred, or at least been set in motion. Consider again the moments where this might have happened. As soon as he recovers from DTs he heads for the telephone. Withdrawal from his addiction has not produced surrender. Repeated urine tests produce rebellion, and only surface compliance. The humiliating telephone call to his mother barely penetrates his facade. He experiences the A.A. meeting as a place to put a move on a cute chick.

When he is given a chance to talk in a group he leaves the room and makes a telephone call to his dealer. Although he seems to be shaken by the information from Martin about the death of the woman, he responds in the next scene by telling Craig to drink his urine. He is also shaken by the sight of the flyer on his door calling him a murderer, but he responds by placing a call to his dealer. When he is coerced by Richard into doing an inventory he complies, but cons his way through it and tells Richard "Fuck you" when asked if he is an addict. Thus at no moment during treatment does he appear to be giving anything more than a performance that, while occasionally compliant, denies his alcoholism and addiction. His inner self, if there is one, has not been penetrated.

It is not clear if this facade is broken through in the nine days that follow treatment. He does confess to Charlie that "I'm tryin' to work on my life," but this work primarily involves getting her to come live with him. The loss of his job is not presented as a shattering experience. Only one experience that could have produced the film's presumed change in self remains. This is the death of Charlie. But he is not shown immediately after the death, only days later, just before he speaks at an A.A. meeting, where for the second time in the narrative he calls himself an alcoholic and an addict.

Daryl, unlike Richard, cannot name the time, place, and event that produced his surrender and conversion; nor does the film record this event. All that he can do is relate his con story, and the nature of the performance that got him into the treatment center ("I figured out the language so I could give this really convincing performance"). We must take it on faith that he has "this startling belief that I am an alcoholic and a drug addict." The film offers no evidence or support for this assertion. This is its failure.

But did it fail? On one level, no. The borrowings, with twists, from *The Morning After*, and *8 Million Ways to Die*, coupled with the constant focus on Daryl's desire to get drugs whenever trouble arises, dramatically reveals not only the kinds of problems addicts can get into, but also the depth of their denial. The narrative successfully presents the chaotic life of an alcoholic–addict. Although it appears to stumble in the treatment phase of the recovery experience, it can be argued that Daryl is not alone in conning his way into and out of a drug clinic (see Denzin, 1987a, Chapter 3).

The redemption side of the story remains problematic. It fails to be convincing, for the reasons outlined above. Director Caron wanted to tell a story "about redemption, about an extraordinary period in this guy's life . . . [who's] not an extraordinary guy" (Caron, 1988a, p. 20). Instead he told a story about "a reprehensible, self-involved, self-consumed fellow" (Caron, 1988a, p. 20), who, like many addicts and alcoholics, may have to slip and try again before long-term recovery is accomplished. In its attempts to be something else, including a melodramatic, comedy, love story with a redemption theme, *Clean and Sober* ended up being perhaps more realistic than it intended to be.

Whether it completes the cycle of films begun in 1932 remains to be seen. Whether it signals a massive shift in American popular culture concerning drugs and alcohol also remains to be determined. It is apparent, though, that the original premises of the alcoholism, social problems film (the alcoholic can be saved by desire, medicine, and love), and the modifications of that premise with the entry of A.A. and treatment, have been moved to a new level with the release of *Clean and Sober*. Detox units are still cold places where people have nightmares, and violence occurs. Treatment centers have become places where people are restored to health. Dual addicts are now commonplace and A.A. meetings are not gatherings that need to be elaborately staged, as they were in the 1950s. Ordinary men and women, not stars, can now be alcoholics. Their stories can be told without going into great biographical detail about fathers, mothers, and past family lives. The obsession with the causes of alcoholism has apparently disappeared, for both filmmakers and critics. With *Clean and Sober* alcoholism, (and now drug addiction) become "normal," treatable diseases of living.

My Name Is Bill W. (1989)

As this 1988 film reasserted, as it modernized Hollywood's half-century old treatment of alcoholism, one final piece of the puzzle remained to be examined. This was the story of A.A. It was not until 1989 that this story would be told, and of course by television (ABC). *My Name is Bill W.: The Story of the Founding of Alcoholics Anonymous* is part biography of the co-founder of A.A. and part an explanation of A.A. as an institution. Its appearance is almost after the fact, for A.A. and its understandings of alcoholism are now established presences in American popular culture.

Predictably, the film takes a biographical approach to its subject matter. It offers a narrative that has been common knowledge, in its broad outlines, to A.A. members since the publication of the first edition of *Alcoholics Anonymous* (*The Big Book*) in 1939, with its first chapter, which is titled, "Bill's Story." Appropriately, it is the last film to be analyzed in this book. However, it should have been the first, for it tells the story that every A.A. film since *Come Fill the Cup* (1951) has taken for granted. This interchangeability between the first and last film to be discussed reveals just how pervasive the A.A. story has become in American society. Indeed Wilson's story is told in a way that is shaped by every mainstream Hollywood alcoholism film that has come before it. It contains all of the elements of the classic A.A. movie (i.e., a biographical, melodramatic love story, an alcoholic hitting bottom, having DTs, etc.). Paradoxically it is shaped by the "genre" that presupposed its existence. Its appearance in 1989 is now determined by forces that it created, even though it was never present, except through the existence of the A.A. organization.

This is a version of the story of Bill Wilson (1895–1971), called in A.A. lore, "the bedtime story" (A.A., 1984, p, 8); it is a tale of redemption that he told countless times. Presented in flashback form, it follows the mechanical movie-of-the-week format.[17] The six segments of the narrative span the years 1919 to 1950. They detail Wilson's slide from grace into the world of alcoholism and near poverty, his spiritual experience that begins his path to salvation, the creation of A.A., and his life-time commitment to carry A.A.'s message to other alcoholics.

The first hour of the film covers Wilson's return from World War I, his rise to power and wealth on Wall Street, the start of his problems with alcohol, the crash of 1929, being told by Dr. Silkworth in 1934 about the "allergy theory" of alcoholism (see Chapter 3, pp. 58, 67), his fall into chronic, near skid row alcoholism (1929–1934), his friend Ebby's sobering up in the Oxford Group (on this group and A.A. see Kurtz, 1979, pp. 9, 24–25, 43–44; Pittman, 1988, pp. 151–59; Robertson, 1988, pp.. 50–67), and Ebby's attempts to convince Wilson about how a spiritual experience produced his sobriety. The second hour details Wilson's final fall in December of 1934 and his spiritual experience in Towns Hospital in New York City. (He never drank again.) The narrative then explores his failed attempts over the next six months to sober up alcoholics by "pushing religion down their throats." It next moves to Akron, Ohio and his famous six hour meeting with Dr. Bob (on this meeting see A.A., 1976, p. 180), the formation of the first A.A. group, the spread of A.A. to New York, the publication of *The Big Book* in 1939,[18] the Jack Alexander story about A.A. in the *Saturday Evening Post* in 1941 (after which the membership in A.A. jumped from 2,000 to 8,000 by year's end), and concludes in 1950 with the death of Smith and a trip Wilson and his wife take to California where he struggles to deal with his place in the movement now that Smith is gone.[19]

History as Personal Narrative

The film's narrative entangles and intermixes biography and history in a way that creates the impression that A.A.'s history is really the story of Bill W. (later Smith) and his alcoholism. In this sense, as Derrida

(1985, p. 5) notes, when a biographer or autobiographer (or filmmaker) attempts to describe an account of a life (Wilson's and A.A.'s) a "divisible borderline traverses [the] two 'bodies' " (the work and the life), but this borderline suddenly becomes confused (1985, p. 13). For example, how can A.A. and Wilson be separated? When does Wilson's story begin (or end) and when does A.A.'s story begin (and end)? Is all of Wilson's story relevant to the A.A. story, or does A.A. have a story independent of Wilson?

These issues are further confounded by the film's title, *My Name Is Bill W*. A name carries multiple meanings. It cannot be summed up in a self, or a single life story, for it transcends the life it references (see Derrida 1984, p. 2; 1985, pp. 7–8). The signifier Bill W. refers to more than the man named Bill Wilson who lived from 1895 to 1971. The name signifies, among other things, the name of the man who co-founded A.A. So A.A. defines Bill W., just as the signifier Bill W. defines A.A. The initial W. signifies Wilson's anonymity, the second term in A.A. (For example, the A.A. bumper sticker, "Honk if you know Bill W." carries a double message. The bearer of the sticker is him- or herself undoubtedly an A.A. member and is announcing that to all who know the code that underlies the message on the sticker.) Thus Wilson's name has become a personal, as well as an institutional signifier. [The same problem holds for the analysis of *The Betty Ford Story* for her name now signifies a treatment center, the story of that center, the famous, and not so famous people who have gone there, and her recovery story as well (see for example, Conrad, 1986).]

How the film weaves its way between these two terms (Bill W. and A.A.) is critical to the interpretation of its multiple meanings. The movie begins with a voiceover describing the two men whose photographs fill the screen: "In 1935 Bill Wilson and Dr. Robert Smith created Alcoholics Anonymous. These men had one thing in common. They were drunks. The following dramatization is based on personal interviews and various publications about the life of Bill Wilson and the formation of Alcoholics Anonymous." The narrative must now confront three problematics, namely how to tell three stories: Wilson's, Smith's, and A.A.'s.

It will do this by briefly, but in pivotal ways touching on Smith, for he is the key to the three stories the film attempts to tell. But his introduction into the text again raises the problem of boundaries. Without him Wilson would not have stayed sober on that key night in Akron. Without Wilson's visit (we are led to believe) Smith would not have gotten sober. And, if he and Wilson had not discovered a method of staying sober together, they would not have been able to carry this message to others. Hence without Smith there is no Bill W. and no A.A.

Smith appears only four times. In a flashback at the film's beginning where he is shown on his deathbed, as he and Wilson reminisce about what A.A. has done for them, during the Akron episode, after the publication of the Jack Alexander article in 1941, and finally, in a return flashback, to the death bed scene. In both flashbacks he and Wilson exchange A.A. slogans (e.g., "One Day at a Time").

Once Smith is killed the narrative is free to untangle Wilson from A.A. This it does in the final scenes, when Wilson and Lois walk into a meeting in a church in California. They are welcomed and Wilson introduces himself, "Hi, my name's Bill, Bill W. from New York." Nobody recognizes him. Lois asks Bill, "Are you upset because they didn't recognize you?" Bill: "No, oh, maybe just a little bit." Lois leaves to get coffee and he starts talking to a newcomer (Fred). "My name's Bill. This your first time? You look like you had some doubts. . . . It's like any journey Fred, it begins with the first step." Lois brings coffee. Wilson turns to her, "I may be a while, that O.K.?" Music begins. Wilson starts to tell his story. Fred starts to talk. The camera pulls back, pans the empty room as Fred and Bill continue talking.

The screen dissolves to black: *"Bill Wilson died in 1971. Today, there are more than 75,000 A.A. groups in 115 countries around the world."* Then James Garner appears on the screen: "You can get help for alcoholism by calling Alcoholics Anonymous listed in your local telephone directory or the National Council on Alcoholism." The screen fades to black, with the numbers 1-800-NCA-CALL on the screen.[20]

The California meeting and the closing shot of Wilson and Fred reestablishes the priority of the A.A. story and reduces Wilson to the status of just another A.A. member. But the film will not settle with this. It must again become biographical, and this it does by giving the date of his death. In these moves the film sustains the myth of Wilson and A.A. Wilson's legacy becomes the 75,000 A.A. groups in 115 countries.

My Name Is Bill W. becomes more than a mere biography of an alcoholic who sobered up in A.A. Never far from the official A.A. line, it is a piece of official A.A. ideology that reproduces this organization's version of its place in American society. The film was unable to separate Wilson from A.A. By attempting to tell and unravel the origins of this myth (how A.A. started), the film, like all "origin myths," resorts, in the final analysis to the biographical form that places Wilson and the organization he helped created outside history, politics, and power (on such strategies see Ricoeur, 1988, pp. 19, 180). The interest in Wilson's story, then, is justified because his story is A.A.'s. However, by 1989 his story of recovery, perhaps remarkable in its day, no longer is. Alcoholics have become more than people who help other alcoholics get sober. Wilson's story has been told too many times before (although he is the first male to be entirely located within A.A. at the end of his story). Failing to tell

A.A.'s story, as Smith would have told it, the Bill Wilson story becomes another drunk's life story. It could have been much more. (Perhaps this is why it received mixed reviews.)[21]

The Alcoholic Hero in the 1980s

A detailed reading of seven films, with brief discussions of two others (*Paris, Texas, Ironweed*) has informed this chapter. Nine different versions of the alcoholic hero in the 1980s have been discussed.[22] Although these films stand outside, or alongside the mainstream, traditional family, social problems treatment of the alcoholic, they maintain some allegiance to the traditional Hollywood model of the alcoholic's condition. These several versions, on inspection, reduce to but a handful of variations on a familiar theme.

He is one of two types. In the preferred model he is a mythic figure who embodies good and evil, in the opposite sides of his alcoholic self (Frank Galvin, Geoffrey Firmin, "Shooter," Matt Scudder, Daryl, Bill W.). In the less preferred model he is a mythic hero who stands outside society and joyfully embraces the drinking way of life (Henry and Wanda). He experiences no harm or loss of status because of this choice.[23] In either case, his (or her) drinking and his alcoholism have been narratively normalized. His chronic drunkenness, or alcoholism have become acceptable subplots to another story that is told in the film. However, his alcoholism symbolizes this other story, which will often be about "last chances," and attempts to win a victory over evil in society. In triumphing over alcoholism the character also triumphs over another social ill (a corrupt Church and legal system, cocaine dealers, etc.). (The variation on this theme offered in *Hoosiers* has the alcoholic help another flawed character overcome his tendencies to violence.) On the other hand the alcoholic may struggle against himself and fail. In his loss (Geoffrey) he emerges as a figure whose death stands as an indictment of a corrupt civilization.

If he is a drunk who sobers up, he follows one of two paths. He either stops drinking through will power and the love of a good woman or man (Frank, "Shooter") or he recovers in A.A. In either case he must first hit bottom. This will be symbolized by DTs, degradation, violence directed toward self and others, a sense of being trapped, and perhaps being forced into recovery (Daryl). If the A.A. route is taken the love of a good woman or man will also be required (Matt, Daryl, Bill W.), and a spiritual experience may be necessary (Wilson).

The films of the 1980s continue to present alcoholism as a gendered production. Its effects are always defined by another, a wife, girlfriend, child, friend, the police, or physicians. Like his female counterpart, the alcoholic male in the 1980s also inherits a familied, feminized version of his disease that effects his sexual being. And, like Cassie, Georgia, and Betty Ford, he finds that a treatment center is waiting for him. He too will find that a male carries the cure for his disease. When he is paired with a female alcoholic (Henry and Wanda, Matt and Sarah, Daryl and Charlie, Francis and Helen) his alcohol abuse, or recovery defines her condition. She either mirrors his alcoholic actions (Henry and Wanda, Matt and Sarah), rejects his recovery path (Charlie), or dies a death that could have been his (Helen).

His alcoholism is presented as a state of being that rises, in part, from fundamental instabilities of self. These instabilities, involving fear, self-loathing, and guilt prohibit the alcoholic from either forming, or sustaining intimate relations with others. His alcoholic sexuality turns to impotence (Geoffrey), one-night stands (Daryl, Frank), or celibacy ("Shooter"). Recovery, however, does not always effect sexuality and intimacy in a positive way (Wilson and Lois), although it may (Scudder and Sarah).

Unlike his counterpart in the 1940s and 1950s, the 1980s alcoholic is now free to be more than an alcoholic. Who he is, though, if the film critics are to be believed, is still informed by A.A. and the classic story of his experiences as given in *The Lost Weekend*. Unwilling to let go of this filmic representation of the drunkard, critics persist in comparing his contemporary versions to Wilder's 1945 story. This historical gesture serves to keep today's alcoholic trapped in a prepostmodern world where social problems films with didactic messages are still valued. This movie keeps the focus on the alcoholic's situation, and fails to take notice of the multiple changes he (and American society) have undergone since 1945. Significantly this decade ends with a dual addict (Daryl) and an old-fashioned drunk (Bill W.), suggesting that Hollywood and television producers are looking backward as they grope their way forward into the 1990s. Could it be that the decade of the 1980s exhausted all of the possible ways of representing the alcoholic hero and his experiences?

Notes

1.   These films are drawn from those contained in Table 3, which lists 28 films with a male alcoholic. I am selecting four that pair a male and female, two that overlap with family, and three that focus primarily on a male. A.A. is present in three of the films.

2.   There does not appear to be a solidly traditional, Hollywood social realist, social problems film dealing with the "alcoholic" family in the 1980s. Television has apparently preempted this space. There are no films like *Come Back, Little Sheba*, or *The Country Girl*, in the 1980s.

3.   I will treat this film only in passing, for Travis's problem drinking is taken up in a brief, matter of fact way, almost as an aside, in a pivotal reference to that time in his marriage "when he was drinking a lot and being violent." Like other Sam Shepard plays it deals with a disrupted, violent, "alcoholic" family and the attempt by the male to put the pieces back together again. However, the drinking theme is secondary to the main story, which is about a father–son and then a mother–son reunion.

4.   Space permits only a brief discussion of this film (see below).

5.   Robert Redford had been an early choice to play Galvin. "According to one story, Redford was concerned that the portrayal of Galvin as a down and out drunk might damage his screen image" (Hanson, 1984, p. 378).

6.   Suggested by Robert Carringer.

7.   Read within this larger framework, the opinions were divided. Some faulted the film's resolution of its own conflicts, importantly Frank's situation at the end. Sklar (1983, p. 47) is typical: "he is as isolated, as lacking in a social context, at the end as in the beginning. Is this intended as a comment on our lonely, anomic times?"

8.   Strictly speaking (as Richard Koffler notes) this film is not about an American alcoholic, although it was filmed by an American (John Huston), it starred an English actor (M. Caine), and tells the story of a British alcoholic in Mexico. Malcolm Lowry, the author of the novel from which the film was made, feared that Charles Jackson's *The Lost Weekend*, which appeared before Lowry's work was published, would detract from his treatment of the alcoholic's situation (see Cross, 1980, p. 71; Gilmore, 1987, pp. 18–19; Day, 1973, pp. 309–310).

9.   Katherine Ryan-Denzin suggested this interpretation.

10.   This is the actual title of a Lawrence Block novel that introduces his alcoholic, ex-cop, private investigator, who is separated from his wife and two sons, and lives alone in New York City and struggles to stay sober by attending A.A. In moments of crisis he goes off on painful binges. There are several novels in this series by Block. None of them bears any resemblance to the movie. The title of this film refers, of course, to the fact that in a city of eight million people, there are eight millions ways to die.

11.   This was "a mistake, an inadvertent endorsement, at variance with normal procedures, made by a staff member no longer with the General Services Offices of A.A." (conversation with A.A. General Services Office, 4 January 1990).

12.   I am indebted to Katherine Ryan-Denzin for this interpretation.

13.   See the contemporary crime fiction novels by James Lee Burke, Thomas Cooke, Elmore Leonard, Bill Pronzini, and Michael Allegretto where heroes go to A.A., fret about their drinking, and repeatedly go on the wagon.

14.   *Barfly* (colloquial): "A drinker who spends his [or her] time in bars."

15.   *Ironweed*, also released in 1987, takes up life on skid row, but historicizes its treatment by locating the story in the depression. It, like *Barfly* glorifies skid row life in terms of the honor and dignity that obtains in the lives of the people who live there, but it makes it a place to be escaped from. Bottle-sharing, a traditional skid row alcoholism marker, is common in *Ironweed*, and alcoholic drinking or drunkenness is associated with events from the protagonist's (Francis Phelan) past that haunt him in the present. *Ironweed* makes two negative moves that *Barfly* refuses: the negative representation of skid row and attaching negative biographical consequences to heavy drinking. Like *Barfly* it presents dignified alcoholic men and women. For example, Meryl Streep brings a romantic nostalgia to her character of Helen, and Jack Nicholson plays Francis with a

sense of pathos and guilt that intensifies his tragic life story. He can be read as an "epic hero" (Gilmore, 1987, p. 16). His drinking is used as a dramatic device, "freeing his memory and imagination for long reveries" (Maslin, 1988a, p. 21). The skid row residents in *Ironweed* have no desire to stop drinking, although they periodically do but then start again.

16. The word clean in the title refers, of course, to being free from drugs.

17. *Variety* (1989, pp. 95–96) applied the labels vidbio, telefilm, and vidpic to the film.

18. The work received mixed reviews and early sales ($3.50 per copy) were low (Robertson, 1988, pp. 73–76; Kurtz, 1979, pp. 90–92); however, by 1985, the year of A.A.'s fiftieth anniversary, five million copies had been sold. Wilson received royalties from this and the other A.A. books he wrote. He and his wife received from "$30,000–$40,000 annually by the late 1960s, and by the time of his death . . . almost $56,000. . . . In 1986 Lois received $912,500 from sales" (Robertson, 1988, p. 83).

19. The film also documents the tension between Wilson and Lois over his neglect of her and their marriage for A.A. Wilson, not Lois wrote the chapters called "To Wives," and "The Family Afterward" in *The Big Book*. When she offered to write them he told her "No" (Al-Anon Family Groups, 1987, p. 114). Shortly after this she and Smith's wife started Al-Anon for the wives and family members of alcoholics. Lois gave permission for Wilson's story to be told in this movie form and opened up her files for screenwriter William Borchert (Clark, 1989, p. 2).

20. The credits give "Special Thanks to Stepping Foundation" and the Archives of the General Service Office, A.A.

21. Critics unfavorably compared it to *Lost Weekend* (i.e., *Variety*, 1989, p. 96), complained about the mixing of the Wilson and A.A. storylines (O'Connor, 1989, p. 31; Jarvis, 1989, p. 7; Rosenberg, 1989, pp. 1, 4), while praising the performances of Woods, Garner, Williams, and Sinise (as Ebby). Shales (1989, p. 1) summed up the promise of the film: "We love tales of redemption, of people pulling shattered lives back together, of survivors who crawl out of the ashes and manage to prevail. You might call it phoenix envy." *Variety* (1989, p. 95) expressed the need for it: "It took long enough, but maybe now's the appropriate time to tell the story of Bill Wilson, co-founder of Alcoholics Anonymous and, as a result, Al-Anon and a host of other anonymous programs." Jarvis (1989, p. 7) rendered the critical evaluation that informed all but a few of the reviews, "There's an inspiring and fascinating story to be had in the biography of Bill Wilson. . . . But here, that story is obscured by shallow characterizations, awkward writing and lots of cliches."

22. Consider, also the two *Arthurs*, and the three earlier treatments of alcoholics located in alcoholic families (Chapter 7, Mac, Lyle, Noah). This produces 14 versions of this hero in the 1980s. Note that the comedic version of the figure appears less frequently than the more tragic treatments of his condition.

23. It is in this sense that Henry can be read as a comic figure. When comedy contains the alcoholic, the benevolent side of alcohol as an equivocal spirit is stressed.

10 Hollywood and the American Alcoholic

"They are not long. The days of wine and roses."

Kirsten, in *Days of Wine and Roses*

"How has the alcoholic subject, and his or her family been defined by American feature films during the period 1932–1989?" Throughout this work I have traced the shifting meanings Hollywood has brought to this question, assuming that there is no single agreed on thing called alcoholism, or alcoholic. I am now prepared to offer certain generalizations. I will begin by retracing my steps from 1932 to 1989. This will involve an interpretation of the multiple systems of discourse that have been brought to bear on the alcoholic subject, in particular: (1) issues of gender and genre, (2) the Hollywood studio system and the political economy of film production,[1] (3) discourses on the films by mass media (and scholarly) reviewers, (4) popular culture beliefs about alcoholism, including A.A., and (5) the place of the alcoholic subject in the broader concept of American narrative and dramatic forms. I will also define (or redefine, actually) the alcoholism film in the context of the Hollywood social problem's film. I will conclude with a discussion of the themes of "love and death" (Fiedler, 1966) and "redemption and suffering" (Chase, 1957) in the American alcoholism film.

I have read these movies through the lens of the "alcoholism alibi," arguing that while Americans want to drink, they do not want alcoholics. Films about alcoholics have been organized in terms of the several different forms this alibi has taken. The alcoholic either lacks or has will power. The alcoholic is good or evil. The alcoholic has a disease that is treatable by medicine and A.A. As moral text these films, over

237

time, formed a cycle based on an agreed upon set of representations about the alcoholic's condition and its treatment. These representations drew from taken-for-granted understandings in the popular culture. They were shaped by legacies of the temperance movement, challenges to film Production Codes, A.A., and the National Council on Alcoholism, a change in national concern about alcoholism as a treatable social and personal problem, the emergence of social realist, social consciousness films in Hollywood during the 1944–1962 period, successful box office films about alcoholics, and the shifting moral, legal, and political understandings in American society about men and women, the alcoholic, the drug addict, the alcoholic family, and the children of alcoholics.

Hollywood kept the alcoholism alibi in place by continually returning to this subject and representing his or her experiences in a variety of genres, from comedy to melodrama to tragedy. Hollywood's discourse on the alcoholic cohered in one period (1945–1962), fell apart in another (1962–1980), and came back together in the recent past. It systematically excluded certain classes and types of subjects, especially racial minorities, the elderly, and gays and lesbians. In so doing it reproduced a dominant middle-class ideology about who had this problem and who should be taken care of by society. On inspection, the alcoholism alibi is a stand-in for another set of problems in American popular culture. As a gendered production, alcoholism represents the inability of males and females in this society to form satisfying, long-lasting interpersonal relationships. Alcoholism masks sexuality and desire and the patriarchal relationship between men and women in this culture.

History and Discourse

Dividing my project into five continuous major time periods (Prohibition, preclassic, classic, interregnum, present), I have attempted to show that the systems of cultural discourse brought to the alcoholic's experience by Hollywood have themselves changed over time. In the *preclassic period* (1932–1945) this system wavered between a compassionate treatment of the alcoholic and a view of alcoholism as a failure of will combined with a lingering temperance Prohibition morality. *The Lost Weekend* blended these views in what would become for the critics the "classic" filmic treatment of the alcoholic. *What Price Hollywood?* (1932) and *A Star Is Born* (1937) elaborated the "failure of will" position and created the beginning of one modern mythic, heroic view of the alcoholic; he must die for his self-indulgence and failure of self-control. The altruistic suicides of the *Star Is Born* males reflect this belief.[2] These texts exploited the myth of the creative individual drawn to alcohol as a way of addressing personal and professional problems.

In the *classic period* (1945–1962) these systems of discourse cohered into a model structure of meanings that combined the A.A. and medical models of disease. This model held for the 28 alcoholism films produced between 1945 and 1962. Deploying the seduction, fall, redemption model of the classic morality tale, these films created another modern version of the alcoholic hero (and heroine): a person who overcomes a character flaw at great personal cost. In a critical moment of insight this heroic figure comes to grips with his (her) personal failings and attempts to put his/her life back together again.

The classic model went beyond treating alcoholism as a disease and the insertion of A.A. meetings, sponsors, and 12-Stepping into a film's text. The introduction of the female alcoholic feminized and sexualized the disease. This movie brought to the figure of the female alcoholic all of the negative meanings the culture has about flawed women. The heroine experienced sexual degradation, low bottoms, and near loss of family, as punishment for her failure to keep her place in the home. Unable to cure themselves, they had to find men who could make them better, either psychiatrists or males in A.A. When the alcoholic family was added to the equation, in the three classic films *Come Back, Little Sheba*, *The Country Girl*, and *Days of Wine and Roses*, the diseased female was coupled with a weakened alcoholic male. The combination produced a distorted family communication system, filled with divided selves, double-binds, lies, deceptions, and struggles over sexuality, intimacy, A.A., and drinking. Psychoanalytic themes, however implicit (see Gabbard and Gabbard, 1987, p. 113), informed these key family dramas. Dead mothers and cold, cruel fathers lurked behind crippled women (Lola, Georgie, Kirsten) who looked for husbands who were not there. Unable to be the fathers their wives sought, they turned, in part, to the bottle as a crutch. Alcoholism became a signifier of failed masculinity in these family melodramas.

During an *interregnum* (1962–1980) three competing views of the alcoholic's drinking (problematic, carefree use, and "alcoholic") jostled with one another. In the early 1960s, with the decline of social realism as a film mode, the classic representations of the alcoholic came to an end. Although Hollywood continued to do movies about alcoholics in the "classic biographical mold" (*Lady Sings the Blues*, *W.C. Fields and Me*), films like *Who's Afraid of Virginia Woolf?* and *The Graduate* told stories about how alcoholism destroyed lives but omitted the crucial factor of recuperation through A.A. or medicine. *Fat City* and *A Woman Under the Influence* used drink and alcoholism as signifiers of something else: being trapped in a world of failed dreams, or going crazy.

By the end of the 1970s alcoholics were back in treatment with a disease that A.A. could put in remission. *The Cracker Factory* opened the door to the *present* (or postmodern) period and the emergence of the diseased alcoholic family. This family would now be interpreted by a new theory involving conceptions of dysfunctional families filled with adult children of alcoholic parents. If children were in the background in the family alcoholism films of the 1950s, they were front and center in the 1980s productions. The ACOA theory shaped *Under the Influence* and *Shattered Spirits* and operated as a subtext in *Tender Mercies*.

The family alcoholism films of the 1980s returned to an old theme in American literature, namely the innocence of childhood and the child as the bearer of truths about adulthood (see Fiedler, 1966, p. 271). In these films children set the plot in motion (Sue Ann's return in *Tender Mercies*), takes over adult responsibilities (Lesley fixes dinner in *Shattered Spirits*), and asks embarrassing questions (e.g., Sonny's friend, "Is your step-father still a drunk?"). Their moral position passes judgment on the alcoholic's situation, and in at least one case is used as the basis of the court's decision to order the father out of the house (*Shattered Spirits*). In the working out of this cultural myth about the wisdom of children, these films strip parents of moral authority and open the way for the state to enter the middle class family in ways that had previously been unimagined (but see Donzelot, 1979, pp. 217–234).

The female alcoholic in the 1980s also became a new kind of cultural subject. Those films that gave her children (*Only When I Laugh*, *The Betty Ford Story*) saw fit to place her in treatment because of interventions led by a daughter. Pushed out of the home by a child, defined as derelict in the performance of her duties as a mother, this 1980s alcoholic/woman/mother/wife because a subject whose traditional identities were now erased by the signifiers of alcoholism. She could not be a mother until she admitted her alcoholism, sought treatment, and stayed sober. If she relapsed she risked losing her family/mother identity (Georgia in *Only When I Laugh*). If she was childless like Beatrice, she had to find children, "My girls," and these girls would be alcoholics like their new pseudomother. A.A. invented a new family for her, a fellowship (sisterhood) of women who had also failed in their lives as regular women in American society.

If *Only When I Laugh*, *Life of the Party*, and *The Betty Ford Story* keep the traditional modernist myth of the recovering alcoholic mother reunited with family alive, the postmodern *Morning After* locates its woman in a strange urban family of gays, queens, hairdressers, men who fix toasters, and faded movie stars. No "real" family here, just a shifting mosaic of mutually destructive pieces that work to make Alex's life one thrilling, life-threatening mystery after another. This is the "real" world of alcoholics, another version of the skid row that Lillian Roth fell into. This is the world where nobody is anchored into a comfortable family with a solid middle-class income, a husband at home to pick up the pieces, and children who tell you in one breath they love you and in the next to get out and get help.

Alex is the nomadic, urban alcoholic woman, one level above the streets and she gets bailed out by another nomad, also an urban reject. Racist, lovable Turner lifts Alex up from her sexual degradation, erases the pain she's experienced, exposes her paranoia and neuroses, and turns her (along with Jacky) into a new, sexually attractive erotic object. Waiting until the last possible moment, he reveals that he too is an alcoholic; thus joined by a shared infirmity, the two, in the end, become an alcoholic couple. This will not be a Bert and a Lillian who carry their shared identity and message of recovery to others. Having made their mutual discovery, Alex and Turner will keep the insight to themselves. This film, part *noir*, part traditional woman's melodrama, breaks out of old narrative modes of representation, while it keeps the structures of patriarchy in place.

Women, the Gendered Order and the Gaze

The films about female alcoholics in the preclassic and classic periods reflected the gendered stratification order that prevailed in the 1940s and 1950s. Women were either homemakers and safely ensconced in the feminine household sphere, or they were outside the moral order as entertainers, fallen, single, or kept women. Surprisingly, in the contemporary period (although there is more freedom to enter the occupational world without a man) women are contained by the same categories. In their alcoholism they are represented as fallen individuals who are outside the boundaries of middle-class morality. Trapped within their alcoholism, they are double failures. Taught to drink by men, they now bear the stigma of being female drunks.

In nearly every film women are pictured as victims of male controlled emotionality. Their sexuality and identities have been commodified; they have been turned into sexual slaves, or sexual objects (*I'll Cry Tomorrow*, *Key Largo*, *Days of Wine and Roses*, *The Morning After*). Thus having been transformed, they are now targets for male, sadistic violence (*I'll Cry Tomorrow*). In some cases they are seen as masochistically enjoying this violence (e.g., Wanda in *Barfly*, Oma in *Fat City*).

Their drinking takes them into dangerous places: bars, motels, the beds of strangers. In these strange places they confront violence, death, and degradation (Alex). Women alone take high risks in both the modern and postmodern world. But learning the masculine way, they learn how to drink, to be sexual, and to be violent (Wanda, Kirsten, Oma). In a certain sense these women's films show how American culture produces violent, degraded, vulnerable, abused women. This is the price it pays for encouraging women to drink, be sexual, and be controlled by men. Although these texts present women in an ugly, unfavorable light, underneath, they valorize the feminine, the sexual, and the erotic. Yet they are unable to reconcile these two images: the fallen woman alcoholic, and the cultural idol of erotic woman.

This heroine is placed under a double injunction in the alcoholism film. She is both the bearer of sexuality and the carrier of the stigma of alcoholism. How she handles this weight is often the central problem of the film. She is situated in a way that allows her to hold the male gaze, while she plays to it, often in her decadence (Lillian in the skid row bar). [See Penley, 1989; also Mulvey (1975/1985, 1989a) on the structuring of the male gaze in narrative cinema.] She thus symbolizes tainted alcoholic desire, as she is both spectacle and subject of the film's story. And in this moment, the object of male desire, her alcoholism turns against her and she is held up as a fallen woman, a woman who can neither hold her alcohol nor be sexual. Indeed her alcoholism is used as a vehicle to demystify and ridicule her sexuality; she is turned into a scorned object (e.g., Oma). Her "aura" as woman stripped away, she is made to feel guilt for her stigma—her alcoholism, and for her sexual transgressions. A fetishistic, voyeuristic fascination in her alcoholism is thus produced; for by creating an alcoholic woman, the film has produced all that society wants its women to be. Superficially liberal and forward looking, because they brought the "hidden" female alcoholic out into the open, these 1940s and 1950s films about alcoholic women were really conservative statements about the rightful place of women in American society.

The contemporary (postmodern) female alcoholic heroine, first defined by Kirsten in *Days of Wine and Roses,* and then developed by Alex, Wanda, Oma, and Helen (*Ironweed*), reverses this pattern. She actively engages her alcoholism and her sexuality. Unlike her counterpart in the 1940s and 1950s, she controls the film images that surround her. She makes things happen. She transcends her alcoholism to become the kind of woman society is not sure it wants. She will define her own emotionality, her own sexuality, and she will pick and choose the men with whom she forms relationships. It is not clear that American society is ready for this kind of woman; but these late 1980s films alert us to the fact she is on the landscape.

The many male alcoholism films of the 1980s that did not fall inside the social problem's framework transformed the alcoholic into several things at the same time. Most importantly, being a recovering alcoholic was no longer a full time occupation. Now you could be something else besides a recovering alcoholic: an attorney, a basketball coach, a cop, a real estate broker. You could, of course, still be a full time drunk (Henry) and write poetry, or a full time recovering drunk and carry the message of A.A. to others (Bill W.). Then too, you could slip to skid row (Francis) and be haunted by your past life, or be the proverbial cowboy (Travis) and walk off into the western sunset away from your wife and son. You could also die a drunk, lay your guilt on others, and kill them too (Geoffrey). If you chose to address your alcoholism head-on, so to speak, you got treatment, of sorts ("Shooter"), or the real thing (Daryl, Matt) and find A.A. and a sponsor. Along the way you experienced DTs, hit some kind of bottom, made a decision to do something about your drinking (either stop or continue) and then went on to do other things (win a case, die, fall in love, dream, etc.).

The Alcoholic Couple/Family and Alcoholics Anonymous

Recall the alcoholic couples represented in such films as the *Star Is Born* series, *Come Back, Little Sheba*, *Country Girl*, *Days of Wine and Roses*, *Fat City*, *Life of the Party*, and *Tender Mercies*. With the exception of those dyads surrounded by wealth (i.e., *Star Is Born*, *Betty Ford Story*), or the comfortable signifiers of the middle class (*My Name Is Bill W.*, *Under the Influence*), the couples and families presented in these films live in cheap, small rented rooms (*Country Girl*, *Days of Wine and Roses*, *Fat City*), little working class houses (*Tender Mercies*), or expensive, but look-alike suburban tract homes (*Shattered Spirits*). They live on the edges of respectability. Their cramped quarters symbolize a world that permits little privacy or breathing space, a world controlled by alcoholism where the failures of the past have produced a claustrophobic atmosphere that is always on the verge of erupting into emotional or physical violence.

These couples are knitted together through the negative structures of double-binds that are slowly, sometimes quickly unraveling, threatening at any moment to explode and fall apart (e.g., Doc's drunken attempt to kill Lola). Sexuality has evaporated from the relationship, leaving two lonely persons trapped in the other's presence. Intimacy, when it occurs, happens over a drink. Cut off from others, daily domestic life involves eating, drinking, fighting, sleeping, and working. These couples have shut down and turned their backs to the outside world. In their little rooms they have turned to the serious business of collective self-destruction. Their shared alcoholism symbolizes the failure of an American dream, the happily married couple. These men and women can neither live with nor live without each other. Nowhere to go but inward, they burrow deeper into a daily nightmare of fear and violence, doing only what they know how to do, which is fight and drink.

Wealth, work, and fame cannot buy them happiness, nor can liquor or sexuality. All resources exhausted, these couples either hit bottom and get help, leave one another, kill themselves, or go on, fighting and dreaming that things will get better. These are sad, but perhaps realistic depictions of the American couple. This pair, during any decade, is always at a cross-roads, caught between the dreams and the realities of living or not living with a member of the opposite sex. These men and women reproduce the horrors of their own childhoods, passing along their version of the American tragedy to their offspring. Their family disease, now called alcoholism, has become a signifier of the failure of this larger American dream called family.

Throughout many of the above films A.A. is presented as the saviour of the family, for only by becoming sober can the alcoholic return to the home that alcoholism destroyed. Largely a family of men, the A.A. social structure reproduces its own "sexless" version of family, showing men helping men and women get sober when their families failed. This "new" version of family is present in the explicitly A.A. films (*I'll Cry Tomorrow*, *Come Back, Little Sheba*, *Days of Wine and Roses*, *Life of the Party*, *8 Million Ways to Die*, *Clean and Sober*, *My Name is Bill W.*) where an alcoholic who has hit bottom finds that a new way of life is available if certain things are done. The repetitions of the same A.A. slogans and speeches from film to film show how this new social formation has created its own timeless recipe for recovery. Hollywood appears obliged to repeat these slogans.

A.A. saves and redefines the family, in part by illuminating what the alcoholic initially is not, that is sober and happy. For example, Doc's drunkenness and violence define the tranquil life he and Lola seek and A.A. offers. Life outside A.A. defines the meaning of A.A. in a film. The alcoholic must be shown to be doing things that A.A. recommends against (drinking, not going to meetings), in order to establish how A.A.'s presence is felt when the alcoholic is in the spaces A.A. provides. When Matt decides not to drink the bottle he buys, he follows A.A.'s directives. This move then allows him to speak at the morning meeting at the end of the film, announcing his five weeks of sobriety and the new way of life A.A. has given him. The alcoholic is in the spaces that periodically lead back to A.A. Those spaces are filled by the new sense of family A.A. has given.

The Cracked Mirror and the Alcoholic Self

The split, fractured face of the alcoholic, reflected in a mirror, which is often cracked, is the single, recurring signifier of the alcoholic self in the films I have studied. A doubling of character (the impression of multiple selves) occurs through this use of the mirror to reveal the inner subjectivity, or "mindscreen" of the alcoholic. [Mindscreen: "A visual (and at times aural) field that presents itself as the product of a mind, and that is often associated with systematic reflexivity, or self-consciousness," Kawin, 1978, p. xi; the alcoholic mindscreen is also often filled out with voiceovers, flashbacks, and subjective camera shots.] In every film, from *What Price Hollywood?* to *My Name is Bill W.*, there occurs one or more pivotal scenes when the alcoholic looks into a mirror and sees reflected back a haggard, drawn, defeated face, a mask or persona that has been shattered. In looking into the mirror the alcoholic faces him- or herself and sees what is seen (and felt) in the inner mind, which is often self-loathing (on the history of mirrors in film see Kawin, 1978, pp. 7–8). What is reflected is a labyrinth without a center, only multiple, fractured images, as when Angie and Betty looked into their mirrors and saw only emptiness. This reflection is taken to be a truthful measure of who the alcoholic is; it has an inner reality that cannot be denied. These epiphanic mirror scenes typically occur at a turning point in the alcoholic's life when he or she contemplates choosing between suicide or facing life sober. They often transpire right after a night of drunkenness, or an extended binge.

In this reflected look, which is both barren and devastatingly deep, a specular drama of insanity and destruction is played out. There is "no jubilant assumption of [this] specular image" (Lacan, 1949/1977, p. 2) as there might be for the child who first glimpses sight of herself in a mirror, instead there is revulsion. The alcoholic's life flashes by in the inner mindscreen, which may be reflected in the mirror (Max). What is witnessed is a life of failure, degradation, and shame. Guilt, self-disgust, and paranoia are felt. This mirror-image only confirms what is experienced in the inner self of the alcoholic; an already alienating relationship between the self and reality. This relationship is constantly on the verge of "aggressive disintegration" (Lacan, 1947/1977, p. 4), which will either self-destruct or move forward into a reintegration with the world. In holding the mirror up to the alcoholic's condition, in showing how a character is coming apart at the seams, these films, in their moment of apparent compassion, erode their own moral positions. They make the viewer a double-voyeur; one who gazes on the alcoholic's condition, while scrutinizing and passing judgment on its reflection. The mirror transforms the viewer into a moralist who feels the disgust the alcoholic directs to herself.

Steps retraced, it is now necessary to fit these films into an interpretive scheme.

Genre, Gender, and Discourse

In Chapter 1 (pp. 12–13) I identified several characteristics that define the alcoholism film as a "genre," or a type of film within the social problems film tradition. The initial defining characteristics of such films are present when "the inebriety, alcoholism and excessive drinking of one or more characters is presented as a problem that the character (and others) self-consciously struggle to resolve." I then suggested that the struggle to become sober takes control of the character's life, and is presented in such a way as to make this figure look like a modern hero or heroine who has overcome a great obstacle. The alcoholic character is then placed in a variety of situations, showing drinking, attempts to get sober, relapses, and perhaps final sobriety. In the end the alcoholic is either back in society, or outside the mainstream, leaving family and work behind. Sobriety would be accomplished in one of several ways: the love of a good man or woman, a spiritual turning point, the intervention of A.A., or treatment, or by will power. I argued that this would vary by the gender of the alcoholic. I subsequently suggested (Chapter 3, pp. 42–43) that many of these films would have a biographical focus, and that there would be the presentation of three attitudes toward drinking (abstinence, alcoholism, normal drinking). I also suggested that violence, sexuality, and degradation would be used as plot devices to emphasize the negative consequences of drinking. The family, as argued in Chapters 5 and 7, would be identified as the site of alcoholism's destruction.

I presented these as ideal-typical characteristics (especially in Chapter 1). They have not been present in every film analyzed. The list of negative cases is extensive. Consider the following. Here are the characters (and/or films) who:

1. *Had no negative consequences from their drinking: Arthur, Harvey, Barfly.*
2. *Had no spiritual experience: Arthur,* Geoffrey, Daryl, both Franks, Betty Ford, Alex, Doc, Joe, Matt, Billy, Elwood, Georgia, Lyle, Angie, Norman, Noah, Max, Henry, W. C. Fields.
3. *Did not have the love of a good woman (or man): Harvey, Verdict,* Billy, Georgia.[3]
4. *Were tested and did not slip: Arthur 2,* Lew, Alex, Mac, Matt, Bill W.
5. *Did not experience an A.A. or medical intervention:* Geoffrey, *Arthur, Barfly,* both Franks, *Fat City, Ironweed,* Max, *Star Is Born,*[4] Mac, W. C. Fields.
6. *Did not experience violence and degradation: Arthur, Barfly.*
7. *Did not lose a family or job: Harvey, Arthur,* Noah, Angie.
8. *Were in films with no, or slight biographical focus (e.g., not film biographies: Barfly, Star Is Born,* Max, Lew, Daryl, Matt, Alex, Noah, Frank Galvin, *Fat City.*
9. *Did not value sobriety:* Geoffrey, *Barfly, Fat City, Arthur, Harvey,* W. C. Fields.

10.   *Were not paired with sober, or nonalcoholic characters: Barfly, Iron-weed, Fat City.*

The perfect alcoholism film, the one where all of these characteristics come together, seldom occurs. As argued in the last chapter only as we near the end of this film cycle, with *8 Million Ways to Die* and *My Name Is Bill W.*, do all of these pieces fall into place in a single text. Yet there remains a generic focus to this type of film and it involves the following features, all of which begin with the original premise that this film will be preoccupied with somebody's drinking. The generic alcoholism films look like this.

The "Classic" Alcoholism Film

1.   The alcoholic is an attractive, likable, lovable person.
2.   The alcoholic becomes part of a romantic pair, and is loved and respected by members of a group.
3.   Because of drinking the alcoholic is perceived as a threat to self and to the group.
4.   The alcoholic is told to change or get out.
5.   The alcoholic tries to change, but repeatedly fails.
6.   The alcoholic is rejected by the group, but the lover keeps trying to help.
7.   The alcoholic is offered membership in another group (A.A. or family).
8.   The alcoholic recognizes differences between him–herself and others.
9.   The alcoholic accepts and adheres to the values of this new group.
10.   The alcoholic accepts an invitation to rejoin the old group.
11.   If the old group is no longer there, the alcoholic forms a new group or goes off with the new lover.[5]

This is the story of Bill W. and Matt Scudder. This is the classic A.A. alcoholism film of redemption and salvation. Call it version one of the alcoholism film. With variations, it encompasses the following films: *Come Fill the Cup, Smash-Up, I'll Cry Tomorrow, Come Back, Little Sheba, The Country Girl, Days of Wine and Roses* (except for Kirsten), *Arthur 2, Life of the Party, The Cracker Factory, Only When I Laugh, The Betty Ford Story, The Morning After, Clean and Sober, Hoosiers, The Verdict, Shattered Spirits,* and *Tender Mercies.*

Now consider its variations. Change features 5, 7, 8, and add one more. This yields a situation where the alcoholic makes no effort to change (5), rejects membership in a new group (7), and thinks there is no difference between his (her) drinking and others (8). In the end the alcoholic dies either a real or a symbolic death. This is the tragic story of the drunk who dies a drunk. Call it the "Drunk Dies" version of the alcoholism film. This is *Under the Volcano, Ironweed, Paris, Texas, Under the Influence, W. C. Fields and Me,* and almost *Lady Sings the Blues.* (This is version number two.) It has one important variation (version number three) called the "Drunk Tried But Failed," and it is given in the four versions of the *Star Is Born* cycle. This is the alcoholic who died to save his lover variation on the tragic theme. This drunk was never offered membership in a new group, nor made an effort to find one. He used will power to control his drinking.

Consider next a fourth and a fifth possibility. Take the two clear-cut comedies (*Arthur* and *Harvey*) and the serious comedies, *Arthur 2 on the Rocks, Barfly, Only When I Laugh,* and *Clean and Sober,* and add *Fat City.* This yields two situations: the slapstick comedy about the classic drunk (version four) and the serious comedy about the alcoholic (version five). Arthur and Elwood are seen as threats to their groups, are told to change, and are rejected by their groups, but in the end they are reunited with their loved ones, having made no changes in their behaviors. Arthur 2, Georgia, and Daryl are seen as threats, are told to change, are rejected by their groups, join new groups (of sorts), make changes, and are reunited with their families. Henry, Wanda, Billy, and Oma experience none of these rejections. They are contained with narratives that violate points 4 through 11, just like Elwood and Arthur.

Arthur and *Harvey* constitute, as argued in Chapter 2, a separate type of alcoholism film: the romantic comedy (with variations on the "screwball" genre). *Only When I Laugh* and *Clean and Sober* are romantic, yet serious comedies, which say drink is bad, while *Barfly* may be called the "In Praise of Drink" variant on the serious comedy, and *Fat City* a serious "funny, sad and memorable film about those men and women who are the discards of America" (Champlin in *Filmfacts,* 1972a, p. 362).

This leaves one film, *Lost Weekend.* It does not fit any of the above categories. It is not in the "classic" category, for Don is not offered membership in a new group that changes him. He does not die a symbolic or real death, although he comes close, so the film is not in either of the two variations on the "Drunk Dies" category, and it clearly is not a film that is "in praise of drink." In fact the film constitutes a category by itself, which I call, borrowing a phrase from Agee (1945/1958, p. 183), "The Drunkard's Experiences." No film before or after has presented, in such vivid detail, the actual experiences of an alcoholic fighting with him- or herself and the bottle.[6] Only two come close, *I'll Cry Tomorrow* and *Under the Volcano,* and these two films, as just noted, become something else after they present the drunk's experiences. It is this something else that must now be discussed, for this structural analysis has only scratched the surface of what is going on in all of these "drinking" movies.

Love and the Romantic Couple

What is going on is the presence of love, and all that goes with it, including sex, violence, and a romantic couple. I want to expand this notion by modifying one of the key characteristics that Altman (1987, p. 103) applies to the American film musical as a genre.[7] He contends that without a romantic couple there would be no musical. I want to argue that without a romantic couple there would be no "drinking alcoholism" film. Like the musical, the alcoholism movie involves a romantic couple whose coupling constitutes either a plot or subplot within the narrative. For example, in *The Lost Weekend* Helen loves Don, Don loves Helen, but Don loves booze more than he loves Helen. Another example. Bill Wilson loved Lois but he loved booze more, etc. Alcohol comes between two lovers. Hence a duality of values organizes the couple's orientation; each represents a different cultural value, while each is in agreement on one key value, love. Sober, the alcoholic's values are like the values of the other member of the couple. Drunk, his values contradict hers, or vice versa.

Their values must be joined if the narrative is to reach a happy conclusion. The alcoholic must become sober, or his "other" must agree to join him in drinking. The resolution of the couple's problem becomes synonymous with, and thus "a figure for, a solution to the plot's other enterprises" (Altman, 1987, p. 109). In the alcoholic's case the resolution of his/her drinking becomes a symbol for the resolution of the problems of the relationship. When the relationship is resolved, if the film fits the "classic" A.A. paradigm, the alcoholic's reintegration back into society is accomplished.

If the two lovers are drinkers (Henry and Wanda, Billy and Oma), then conflict on values other than drinking will stand in the way of the plot's resolution, which will turn on the two lovers staying together (i.e., would Henry go with Tully or stay with Wanda?). Billy and Oma could not agree on a shared style of life so they parted ways. Wanda and Henry could, so they stayed together. If one member of the pair values drinking and the other does not, but if both are alcoholic, then there will be no resolution of the conflict over drink, and the pair will have to separate, which is what happens in *Days of Wine and Roses*.

Returning to the "drunkard's experiences," the romantic couple will always be divided over how it will process the drunk's conduct. When Rosa Lee tells Mac Sledge that "there'll be no drinking here" she is saying, "no more drunken fights like I saw in the motel two nights ago."

If the couple drinks together, like Henry and Wanda, and if their drinking causes no problems, then their experiences as drunkards will be normalized. If their drinking causes one or the other of them problems, then the drunkard's negative experiences will occur off-screen or out of the presence of the other lover. In this move the film symbolically disassociates negative drinking from love and romance.[8] Helen, for example, did not see Don's worst drunken acts, nor did Kirsten observe Joe's DTs or Lola Doc's.

Back to Genre and the Happy Ending

As a subtype of social problems film, with the above variations, the "drinking/alcoholism" film now becomes a love story.[9] But it is a particular kind of love story, for in it excessive drinking, and the "drunkard's experiences" become plot devices for moving two lovers toward (Matt and Sarah) or away (Daryl and Charlie) from a happy ending. The happy ending theme, with its variations, of course ties every one of the movies I have analyzed together into a neat package. They are either films of suffering, redemption, and reunion, the story started by *A Star Is Born*, and formed into a classic with *Lost Weekend*, or they are stories of separation and death (more on this below).

There are, then, three generic types of alcoholism films: (1) the classic tale of suffering, redemption, and reunion, (2) the tragic story of death, loss, and separation, with two variations, the "drunk didn't try and died drunk," and the "drunk tried and failed," and (3) the comedies, which have two variants—romantic, and serious romantic—which can either say "drink is bad" or be "in praise of drink."

Standing back, it can be seen that these types divide over whether or not the alcoholic is accepted back into, or is rejected by society, or just walks away. These two generic types (reunion and separation), which are not unique to the alcoholism movie (e.g., the western, Wright, 1975), are then aligned differently in the five key historical moments of the alcoholism film. For each moment the two types of films will be presented, with each of the variations just noted (redemption–salvation, death–separation, romantic–serious comedy). In each case the above 11 steps will be altered to fit the gender of the alcoholic and the ultimate plot resolution adapted by the film. Hence there are male and female alcoholism films of redemption–salvation, death–separation, and comedy that take different forms in each historical period. Knitting all of this together will be Altman's romantic couplet that transforms every drinking/alcoholism film into a melodramatic love story. Now the movie reviews.

Film Critics and the Creation of the Alcoholic Subject

The meanings that critics bring to films reflect and articulate several processes that interact to produce a particular reading of a film. These processes include not only taste and personal bias, but also the ideological stance (right, left, low–middle–high-brow) of the publication where the review appears, the reviewer's "theory" of how a film should work, including judgments on narrative structure, theme, the director, cinematography, production design, soundtrack, the performances of the leading players, the film's place in a genre, and its relationship to prior films of the same type.

The alcoholic in a film review is a double transformation. Once removed from his or her original screen representation, in the hands of the critic the alcoholic becomes a version of who the critic thinks an alcoholic in a film should be. In their construction of the alcoholic subject over this five decade period, critics brought a variety of vocabularies of motive (Mills, 1940) to this subject, including the temperance, anti-, and then pro-A.A. frameworks. These interpretive structures were then fitted to the critic's reading of the way these films should look. Canby (1981b, p. 23), for example, in his review of *Only When I Laugh*, makes reference to the "obligatory sequence in which Georgia . . . must fall off the wagon. It would be very difficult to make a movie about an alcoholic without such a sequence."

During any given time period there are only a handful of critics who write reviews of Hollywood feature films. From 1940 to 1970 the names of Agee, Crowther, Alpert, Miller, Hatch, McCarten, Knight, Farber, Hartung, and O'Hara were associated with such publications as the *New York Times*, *Saturday Review of Literature*, *The New Yorker*, *The Nation*, *New Republic*, and *Commonweal*. (*Time*, *Newsweek*, *Variety*, and *Life* often carried reviews without listing the reviewer's name.) In the 1960s and 1970s a new group of reviewers began to appear, including Haskell, Corliss, Canby, and Crist. By the late 1970s and early 1980s Magill, Benson, Schickel, Kael, Reed, and Maslin (and many others) were regularly writing reviews for the above outlets and a host of new ones, including *Cineaste*, *Films in Review*, *Jump Cut*, *Monthly Film Bulletin*, *New York*, *Newsday*, *Village Voice*, *Sight and Sound*, *Women's Wear Daily*, *New Statesman*. (Film reviewing had become a serious business by the 1980s.)

Each of the 36 films that I have analyzed was reviewed by one or more of the above individuals, and their comments were summarized in my discussion of each movie. (The Filmography lists the number of reviews that were written for each film, as listed in the standard film review sources.) At one level, Baudrillard's (1987/1988, p. 22) reading of history in the postmodern period ("[It] is instantaneous media memory without a past") can be applied to these reviews. Over time there is little continuity in the judgment of a particular film (except for *Lost Weekend*), or in the way a given film is read. Critics have a selective, historical memory that allows them to ignore prior criticisms of any given film. Yet they write as if they have a deep sense of history.

Starting with "Lost Weekend"

As noted in Chapters 1 and 3 *Lost Weekend* is the canonical alcoholism film. Virtually every alcoholism film since has failed to measure up to this text. Its praises were still being sung in the 1980s when, for example, Maslin (1988a,b) called *Clean and Sober* the 1980s version of *Lost Weekend* and *Days of Wine and Roses*.[10] The film was not without its flaws, for critics felt that it failed to adequately explain the causes of Don's alcoholism. They would apply this criticism (Chapter 3) to the other films made in the classic period.

A.A. and Its Causal Theory

By the 1980s critics had forgotten *Lost Weekend's* failure to offer an answer to the cause of alcoholism.[11] But in raising this criticism, critics in the 1940s and 1950s, like Crowther and McCarten, ignored the fact that every film since *Weekend* in fact had an answer for alcoholism's cause: it is a disease.[12] By 1947 this disease was articulated into a version of A.A.'s allergy theory. This theory, in various forms, was repeated in every film in the classic period, from *Come Fill the Cup* to *Days of Wine and Roses*. In claiming that the films failed to account for this condition, the critics were rejecting, although they never addressed it head-on, A.A.'s theory of alcoholism.

This rejection by the critics of the films' narrative solutions to why and how people became alcoholics disguised an unwillingness to relinquish a temperance view of alcoholics and their condition. While A.A. and these films were espousing a disease model of the illness, critics held to a self-control, failure of will position. This can be seen in their descriptions of alcoholics and A.A.

A.A. first. Faintly praised, as if they were afraid of this new organization, critics spoke more negatively than positively. For example, it was called the "alcoholic tribe" (Crowther, 1951), whose gatherings were likened to those that occur "in a mission off Mott Street" (McCarten, 1963, p. 122), with leaders like "revivalist-psychiatrists" (Hatch, 1956, p. 78; also McCarten, 1952). The A.A. meeting in *Sheba* was called by Crowther "one of the nicer bits of Americana in the film." If A.A. was a foreign land, it was filled with men who appeared to be "steady and reliable friends in need" (Crowther, 1952, p. 24), who could be compassionate (Crowther, 1963, p. 7). A.A.'s stress on spiritual experiences, as given in *I'll Cry Tomorrow*, was criticized because it made the critic uncomfortable (Hatch, 1956, p. 78). Although, as noted in earlier chapters, others praised the organization (i.e., Crowther, 1952; *Time*, 1952b, 1963; Hartung, 1956, 1963).

Now the alcoholic. Males were called sots (Crowther, 1963), drunkards (Crowther, 1945; Faber, 1946), reformed drunks (*Time*, 1956), addicts of A.A. (*Time*, 1956), and dipsomaniacs (Crowther, 1945). Females were called tipplers who should not drink in public (*Life*, 1947), lushes[13] (*Time*, 1956), and also dipsomaniacs (O'Hara, 1947). A female alcoholic in the classic period was most frequently called a lush, while males were drunkards, and those in A.A. reformed drunkards. Lady drunks were called intolerable (McCarten, 1947), and a reformed female lush is "more tedious" than one who is not (*Time*, 1956, p. 92). Alcoholics of both genders were also called bores (Hatch, 1956, p. 78). The term *dipsomania* (dipsa = thirst + mania) was often used by critics in place of the popular term drunkard. Apparently they felt they were using a medical term to describe the alcoholic's condition, even though the films used the word alcoholic to describe the problem drinker. In 1963 Crowther would write, "apparently 'alcoholic' is now the word that describes the problem drinker, rather than drunkard." Crowther had been the popularizer of the term dipsomaniac in the previous two decades!

In bringing these negative, everyday terms to bear on the male and female alcoholic, critics perpetuated popular cultural stereotypes about drunkards and lushes. In arguing against the A.A. disease theory they supported the idea that alcoholism is a problem of will power. By supplying more negative signifiers to women alcoholics than to men, they reproduced the gender biases in the popular culture and contributed to the general movement to get women out of public places (jobs) and back in the house after World War II.[14]

By the 1980s reviewers had little trouble using the term alcoholic, and to it they often added the word hero. Ebert (1981) called Arthur an "alcoholic hero" (he was also called a lush and a boozer), while Canby (1984) assigned tragic characteristics to the "chronic drunkard" in *Under the Volcano*. Denby (1986, p. 130) described Matt Scudder with the words, the "hero is alcoholic and a seedy man of honor," while Mac Sledge was called a skidrow derelict (Reed, 1983), and one 1980s reviewer (Benson, 1981) kept the term dipsomaniac alive by using it to describe Arthur.

If there was a major change in the 1980s it was in the description of women. Although they were still called drunks, lushes, "hard-luck gals" (Denby, 1981b), and "terror-stricken alcoholics" (Wilmington,

1986), they also became women who triumphed over adversity. Their drinking in public was no longer an issue; nor was the fact that they worked. A.A. also appeared to be more accepted, both in the generally favorable references to the organization in the reviews of *My Name Is Bill W.*, and in the comments about *Clean and Sober* ("the A.A. stuff is harrowingly convincing," Carr, 1988, p. 67).

Getting It Right

If a film mixed genres (*Come Fill the Cup; 8 Million Ways to Die*) it was criticized. If it was too melodramatic it was criticized (*Days of Wine and Roses; Only When I Laugh*). If its subject was a woman (*Smash-Up; I'll Cry Tomorrow*) it was unfavorably compared to a man's film (*Lost Weekend*). If it was a remake, it was unfavorably compared to its predecessor (later versions of *A Star is Born*). If a "real" life person played an alcoholic in a film (Judy Garland in 1954) then her life spilled over into the text and her life was used as a way of reading not only the alcoholic's character in the film, but her own performance as well. If the film was a biography of a "real" life person (Lillian Roth, Billie Holiday, W. C. Fields,) then its distortion of facts was criticized.

In these criticisms critics held to the general position that too much drunkenness and too much A.A. were boring. This message is clear. The alcoholic subject is of interest to the critic when he or she is something other than an alcoholic. Recall and reconsider these statements: "Hits the bulls eye . . . a cinematic work of art, not a didactic sermon" (Hartung, 1945, pp. 205–6, on *Lost Weekend*); "Wrestling with John Barleycorn, which became a popular Hollywood sport when the excellent film *Lost Weekend* proved a box-office dandy, is the preoccupation of the current Warner Brothers production called *Too Much Too, Too Soon*" (McCarten, 1958); "Glossy melodrama [about] a dipsomaniac" (*Time*, 1947a, p. 97 on *Humoresque*); "Historical romance [about] a moral coward and a tosspot" (*Time*, 1949, p. 99, on *Under Capricorn*); "newspaper office romance, simplified psychology and tongue-parching temperance talk" (Crowther, 1951, p. 47 on *Come Fill the Cup*); "A temperance movie" (Crowther, 1963, on *Days of Wine and Roses*); musical biography (Sarris, 1972, in *Filmfacts*, 1972b on *Lady Sings the Blues*); "1980's version of a 50 year-old Capra social fable" (Sklar, 1983, p. 47, on *The Verdict*); "Another *Lost Weekend* with Margaritas" (Reed, 1984, p. 23 on *Under the Volcano*); "sports drama" (Harris, 1987, p. 247 on *Hoosiers*); "Spiritual descendent of *Lost Weekend* (Maslin 1988a, p. 21 on *Clean and Sober*).

The reviewers read the alcoholism film through three lenses. It is inevitably matched to *Lost Weekend*, then compared to temperance movies, and finally is located within a genre (sports drama, glossy melodrama, musical biography, Capra social fable). However, there is little consideration on the fact that this film as a genre has evolved through and utilized several narrative and genre forms, including the biography, the musical, the woman's and family melodrama, the romantic comedy, and the cop-thriller. The use of such doubly perjorative phrases as "temperance" and "wrestling with John Barleycorn" signals the reviewer's belief that unless this is another *Lost Weekend*, no manner of genre relocation will make it an acceptable movie.

Evidencing a limited and selective historical memory,[15] scornful of the temperance movement and critical of didactic texts, the critics wanted art, not glossy melodramas about dipsomaniacs, or tongue-parching temperance stories. Consequently film reviewers exert subtle and not so subtle pressures on filmmakers (and audiences) to make (and look for) films that either focus entirely on the "drunkard's experiences," or turn this individual into something other than just an alcoholic. In this move the reviewers, perhaps unwittingly, have contributed to the reintegration of the alcoholic into American society.

This process accelerated in the 1980s when film critics seemed to be drawn more and more into the antidrug, antialcohol abuse motifs that circulated through the pre- and post-Reagan popular culture. Indeed, a return to the temperance ethic seems to be on the rise. This ethic is now tempered with the A.A. theory in a way that was seldom present for the critics writing during the "classic" period.*

Loving, Living, and Dying in the Alcoholism Film

In their treatment of melodrama alcoholism films transcend their simple storylines about alcoholics and lovers. Remember Billy Wilder's (1944/1970) caustic comment on Hollywood films cited in Chapter 1: "Hollywood is in a rut. They don't make movies, they remake them." Perhaps Hollywood only tells one story, a love story, over and over again, with slight variations fitted to each genre. If this is the case, then the alcoholic film is a subtype of this universal love story, and this story was being told before movies were made.

Narrative Cinema and American Literature

Narrative cinema is a child of several parents, including the nineteenth and twentieth century realist, melodramatic, gothic, and romance novels (Clough, 1988b; Bazin, 1967, pp. 63, 76–77; Cook, 1981, pp. 13–18, Chapter 3; Roffman and Purdy, 1981, pp. 5–6). Out of the

---

*Throughout this decade, only one critic, Roger Ebert, consistently elaborated the disease theory of alcoholism and the view that Hollywood seems unable to make a realistic movie about the topic.

realist novel comes the myth and the desire for a total cinema (Bazin, 1967, pp. 17–22) that would accurately reflect on screen the actual doings of the social world. From the melodramatic and romance novel come heightened concepts of good and evil (Manichaean themes); happy, but also inconclusive, morally ambiguous endings; a departure from veri-similitude; a desire to probe the human heart and the interior conscious-ness (and unconscious); a fascination with terror, violence, the un-known, and a random, out-of-control universe; the myth of the American frontier, the solitary individual hero (and the anti-hero); the pure, and impure woman, the solitary individual hero (and the anti-hero); women as the carriers of morality; Oedipal themes; the values of love, children, family, God, and democracy; a compassion for the down-trodden, little man (and woman), and the deviant; a fear of women, family, and marriage, coupled with a latent fascination with homoeroti-cism, suicide, death, rape, incest, male bonding, males emasculated by women (mothers); and a preoccupation with masculine pain, suffering, loneliness, separation, reunion, and redemption.[16]

With the advent of narrative cinema (Mast, 1976, p. 37) Hollywood directors and producers needed stories to tell, and as noted in Chapters 1 and 6, the stories they found were already present in the works of the great American and British novelists and playwrights. Hollywood retold the myths (and stories) already present in classic literature. [Twisting a phrase from Fiedler (1966, p. 23), between Hollywood and America there are peculiar and intimate connections. A new artistic form and a new society.] At the level of narrative and story there are few basic differences between the two forms (novel and film); they map and mirror one another.

The alcoholism film is a product of this merger of the American novel with American cinema; throughout its structures can be seen the effects of the realist, melodramatic, romance, and gothic traditions. Still, as argued earlier, the alcoholism film is part of the social realist–social consciousness filmic tradition. In this respect the novel form that pro-vides the foundations of the alcoholism film is to be located in the nineteenth-century temperance novel, which belongs to the tradition of the sentimental novel of social protest (Fiedler, 1966, pp. 262–63). Here is the perfect format for another version of the sentimental melodrama: betrayed, abused wives, and men who are mother's boys and have substituted drink for sex. [Examples of this type of novel include *Miss Ravenel's Conversion*, *Rip Van Winkle*, *Ten Nights in a Bar-Room*, Whit-man's *Franklin Evans or The Inebriate* (Fiedler, 1966, pp. 263–64). *Lost Weekend* is perhaps the most important twentieth century version of this novel form.]

Women

Alcoholism signifies something beyond uncontrolled drinking, this something else being, in part, the loss of self-control, violent emotionality and sexuality, and the containment of these phenomena within that gendered social structure called family. The alcoholic family, in turn, symbolizes not just family, but society at large and the ability of any human group to control its members through law and morality, and willful self-compliance.

Underneath the alcoholic's rebellion lies the fear of love, human bonding, and the commitment to another human being. This is the *other something else* these films are about: love, loneliness, suffering, death, and redemption. It is, then, no accident that alcoholism is a gendered production, for it takes two people to create the bond that alcohol breaks. Nor is it an accident that the woman's recurring presence in these films serves as the emotional and moral barometer of alcoholism's effects on family, love, and self-respect. She is the traditional carrier of moral values in American society (Fiedler, 1966, p.78). If she defines the alcoholic's place in society (and he hers), then their shared experiences, as argued in Chapter 1, must be read as the telling of a single story with Oedipal overtones; how men and women with infirmities work through the universal fear of forming and being contained within a bonded, loving relationship.

The bonded relationships that return alcoholics to society are complex and twofold. On the one hand they involve intertwined hetero- and homoerotic bonding, sexual themes, filtered through a patriarchal social structure that always places males in a dominant position over females. On the other hand these relationships address the problems of pain and suffering; in short, happy versus sad endings.

Sexuality first. Consider Fiedler's depiction of the female as she appears in American literature. "Our great novelists, though experts on . . . loneliness and terror, tend to avoid treating the passionate encounter of a man and woman . . . they rather shy away from . . . the presence of any full-fledged, mature woman, giving us instead monsters of virtue or bitchery" (Fiedler, 1966, p. 24). With very few qualifications this description applies directly to the gallery of women Hollywood has brought forth as the saviours of alcoholics. Esther, Vicki, Helen St. Clair, Lola, Lois Wilson, Linda Moralla, Georgie, and Rosa Lee, to list just a few, are larger-than-life female figures. They serve as the moral overseers of their errant alcoholic lovers, but they do not embody full-fledged erotic sexuality. They are mother figures to their little boy/men/ husbands. In returning to them, in a sober state, these alcoholic males

(Don, Norman, Doc, Bill W., Arthur, Frank, Lyle, Mac) return to the womb and to a woman who is mother, not lover.

The male's emotional intimacies are directed not toward his wife, but to another male. In this he is like Fiedler's (1966, p. 503) American male novelist, who "tends to be defeated in his attempts to deal with [the] love [of a woman]." The alcoholic male, while thinking that he desires the comforts of marriage, appears instead, with few exceptions, to prefer "the sentimental companionship of males" (Fiedler, 1966, p. 370). This male may be a father figure in A.A. (Charlie for Lew Marsh, Lew Marsh for Boyd, Jim Hungerford for Joe, Ed for Doc, Dr. Bob for Bill W., Craig and Richard for Daryl), or a male outside A.A. (i.e., Norman for Shooter, Hobson for Arthur, Mickey for Frank), or a son (Mac and Sonny). Only Matt Scudder turns to an erotically attractive female for support.

The male alcoholic bonds to another male, and in A.A. this bonding is justified in terms of his helping another suffering alcoholic get better. In both *Come Back, Little Sheba*, and *My Name Is Bill W.*, the male is presented as spending nearly all of his free time in the company of fellow-A.A. members. His home life suffers, and his wife may feel, as Lois and Lola did, that they have been sexually rejected. These movies seem to be telling two stories. The husband was driven to drink in part because of an attempt to please his wife. Failing to do this and becoming an alcoholic in the process, his full time allegiance is now to those men who saved him when his wife couldn't. In the more dramatic case, *Days of Wine and Roses*, his wife is presented as the *femme fatale* who leads him back to drink, away from his safe relationship with Jim, the A.A. sponsor. In the end, when Joe tells Kirsten, "no threesome, no booze, you and me, just you and me," he is telling her just you, and me, when he really means, you and me and A.A., but especially me and Jim. The A.A. male has come between Joe and Kirsten. Of course she opts for another male, her father, and her anonymous lovers whom she takes in the darkness of the night.

Drawn to a woman, out of a sense of desire and obligation, yet fearful of her sexuality and unable to meet her demands, the male retreats into the safe company of other males who have been similarly damaged (emasculated) by their wives. Here he finds a new home, a new family. This is a bunch of buddies with whom he can express a "passionless passion" (Fiedler, 1966, p. 368) that neither compromises him to a woman, nor forces him to confront the woman from whom he has for so long run away. These men, like him, have faced death and come back, reborn as recovering alcoholics, saved by a new family of man. Like Oedipus, he has solved his version of the Sphinx's riddle ("Who Am

I?''), learning in the process that if a woman almost killed him, he no longer wants her. He has found mother and she is a man!

Now the woman and their saviours. The films give us not only psychiatrists for Angie, Cassie, Georgia Hines, and Betty, but Burt for Lillian, Ellis for Kirsten (her father), Johnny for Beatrice, and Turner for Alex. These males are another version of the mother/father figure. Their sexuality is put on a shelf as they become caring mothers in the guise of males. In a sense they are also like brothers who take care of their little sisters who have become bad little girls (Johnny and Burt), or they are silent, patriarchal father figures who stand mute in the face of their wives/daughter's failings (i.e., Jerry and Ellis). In each instance (father– mother, husband–brother, father–daughter) they reassert their moral authority over her and return her, like the male, to a complex that now becomes more Electra than Oedipal. Her subjectivity as child/woman/ alcoholic is reestablished. She has found father and he is her husband! (Lola called Doc Daddy, Beatrice called Johnny Poppa, Lillian never knew her father, but found him in Burt, just as Georgia did with Frank in *Country Girl*.)

Death and Rebirth: Toward a Narrative Resolution

Both of these gendered Oedipal journeys are not without pain and suffering, even though they nearly always end happily (but see Mulvey, 1989b, p. 200). In their respective flights from one another, male and female alcoholics experience more than their share of degradation, shame, and pain. When their stories come to an end, happily sober and helping fellow alcoholics, they have undergone a spiritual rebirth. Their alcoholic self has died a death produced by their alcoholism. But when the alcoholics' self dies so too does their sexuality and their attraction to a member of the opposite sex as an erotic object. The evidence is quite strong in this direction. In too many cases erotic love is gone; there is none between Jerry and Betty, Doc and Lola, Mac and Rosa Lee, Frank and Georgie, or Don and Helen.

Hence through their pain and suffering, which produces a spiritual rebirth, these alcoholic men and women journey back to the beginnings of their lives. Here they are reunited with themselves in a primordial family setting (A.A.) where they relive their childhoods with new versions of father and mother. The alcoholism film thus confronts directly the themes of separation and reunion, of chaos and disorder in the social and the psychological worlds. It bridges the two narrative traditions in American literature that Chase and Fiedler have identified, the sad and happy moral tale. It folds these traditions into the figure of a single character, the alcoholic, making this person experience both versions of this narrative. The death, disorder, and separation themes die with the death of the alcoholic self. The reunion and redemption themes merge out of the ashes of this death, in the life of a new self who now finds love with others who have experienced the same spiritual death.

In Conclusion: *The Morning After*

This inquiry has spanned what C. Wright Mills (1959, p. 166; see also Denzin, 1986) would call the modern and postmodern epochs in American life (pre- and post-World War II). It has covered the evolution of American film from the advent of sound to the present. It has presented only a tiny slice of this history, as revealed through the small window that the alcoholism film opens. Using this film as a vehicle for reading transformations in twentieth-century American life, I have repeatedly come back to the themes of gender, family, and the representations of lived experiences in cinematic texts.

As a project in cultural studies (Johnson, 1986/87, p. 72; Cunneen, Findlay, Lynch, Tupper, 1989; Krug, 1990) this work has emphasized the "politics of representation" that work through the languages of popular, filmic culture, so as to create particular images, meanings, and understandings of a particular type of cultural subject, the American alcoholic. I have attempted to show that what "goes-without saying" (Barthes, 1957/1972, p. 11) about the alcoholic is itself the product of the operation and articulation of a set of myths about men, women, love, and drinking in this culture (see Maines, 1989, pp. 867–68).

In this respect Goffman's (1974, p. 562), remarks on everyday life, and the actual doings of flesh-and-blood individuals become relevant: "In many cases what the individual does in serious life, he [she] does in relationship to cultural standards [already] established." It is the status of the "already" established" that has been at issue in this discussion, for there are no longer any originals (see Manning, 1988; Manning and Cullum-Swan, 1990; Eco, 1987). "Flesh-and-blood" individuals are themselves, at one level, copies of already reproduced cultural standards and identities.

A single problem, simultaneously modern and postmodern, persists throughout Hollywood's (and sociology's) perpetual struggle to represent the alcoholic's experiences. This is the problem of the "representation of the real" on the screen. It goes by various titles, including accuracy, realism, verisimilitude, and hyperrealism (see Baudrillard, 1983, p. 146; Clough, 1988b, pp. 93–96). It is repeatedly evidenced in the critics' complaints that a film is either too realistic or not realistic enough when it represents the drunkard's experiences. It is present when a star's life story is incorrectly told on the screen, and a biography or autobiography is compared to the film version of that story. It is present when a film offers an explanation of an alcoholic's alcoholism that fails to satisfy a critic. It is also present when it is claimed that the A.A. methods "ring-true."

I went in search of the alcoholic in the American film. I assumed that one version of the "real" alcoholic would be given in these cinematic texts. Like Baudrillard (1987/1988, p. 5) who went in search of "astral"[17] America, I assumed that the reflections sent from the stars (that is from Hollywood film), would embody a version of the real alcoholic that impinges on, as it draws from and elaborates, the lived experiences of ordinary alcoholics. I found, of course, only other people's pictures of this person. The *astral* was not the real, only a star's or a star-maker's version of the real: Gena Rowlands reproducing Betty Ford, and being more like Betty Ford than the real Betty Ford; Jane Fonda as Alex Sternbergen waking up to the sounds and images of "Eye on L.A." with men and women doing simulated versions of her own workout tape; "real" stars playing "real" stars in the biographical films; Ray Milland having DTs more violent than any alcoholic could ever imagine; Jeff Bridges falling in love with every male alcoholic's dream woman; A.A. slogans (and speeches) taken from A.A. texts repeated in one film after another.

The Morning After, with its multiple meanings, is an apt text for concluding this book. It may be argued that we, like Alex Sternbergen, are in the long durée of an extended morning after. Hungover and still intoxicated from too many images of the real we long for a day where things are "really real," where the old myths really work. However, while representations from the stars may signify astral America, they signify only indirectly the America that is lived at the level of the everyday where an alcoholic wakes up drunk one morning and decides to get help for her condition. The astral signifiers are only reflections of other reflections. They bear only a distant, and at best indirect relationship to the worlds of lived experience that alcoholics confront on a daily basis. Whether American alcoholics have become reflections of the reflections that have been brought to them by the media-oriented postmodern society remains unanswered. Real alcoholics may not be judged against their representations in filmic texts, but some make sense of real alcoholics by viewing films about them.

Of course the alcoholic's story, metaphorically speaking, is universal. It is a gendered, melodramatic, Oedipalized tale that touches everyone. It is always a story of loneliness, guilt, betrayal, self-doubt, false hope, lies, deceptions, broken promises, and semimended dreams. In this tale there is a part of everyone. Hence the never ending attraction of these figures, for his or her story is ours, or could be. To gaze at the two of them is to gaze at ourselves. To watch their story is to watch a story not unlike our own.

Last Call: Wine and Roses

Since the topic has been alcohol, liquor, and drinking, Barthes's (1957/1972, pp. 60–61) observations on wine (and drinking) in French culture are timely: "The mythology of wine can help us to understand the usual ambiguity of our daily life." Change the society and the drink, add roses, and two more points. The mythology of drinking pervades not only daily American life, but it is an integral part of the representations of that life that are given in American film, itself a capitalist system that reproduces the structures of domination that pervade the everyday life world. Four texts—wine and drink, film, capitalism, and the everyday world—intertwine, to recreate, over and over again, the *overarching myth* that through wine and drink the two sexes merge into a heaven-given blissful state that will forever make these two cultural subjects—man and woman—happily joined through the signifiers of wine and roses. Hence the recurrent need for the alcoholism alibi, and the Hollywood film about the alcoholic. Together they prop up this myth when it falters. And shot by shot the myth goes on.

Notes

1. Space restricts treatment of this topic to a mere mention. It is introduced here to mark its place as one of the systems of discourse that impinged on the production of the alcoholic subject. See the earlier discussions in Chapters 1, 3, and 6 (pp. 11–12, 42–43, 130–131).

2. Geoffrey Firmin's death in *Under the Volcano* can also be interpreted in this light. Kirsten's disappearance into the night in *Days of Wine and Roses*, leaving husband and child behind, can be seen as the price she pays for her self-indulgence and belief that she can stop drinking on her own. This is a symbolic, altruistic death.

3. It can be argued that Frank had Mickey's love, Billy had Ruben's, and Georgie had her daughter.

4. The trips to sanitariums to dry out for the two middle Normans (1937, 1954) can be termed medical interventions.

5. The format and model for this list are taken from Wright (1975, pp. 25–27, 48–49). Below I will attempt to expose the limits of this type of structural analysis.

6. Agee faults the film (as noted in Chapter 3) for not going deeper into the inner realm of the alcoholic's experiences (see Agee, 1945/1958, p. 183).

7. Any genre film can draw from other genres, and any film can be read as being in more than one genre. For example, Altman (1987, p. 112) reads *A Star Is Born* and *The Country Girl* as musicals, while I have treated them as alcoholism

films. The musical elements of *The Country Girl*, for example, are secondary to the alcoholic's story that is told.

8. When the two alcoholic lovers drink together, after one has attempted to get sober, and joined A.A. the drinking will be called a relapse, and will become a turning point in the relationship. The last time Joe and Kirsten are sexually intimate occurs during the drinking scene in the motel. The next time they meet they say goodbye.

9. As such they have many of the same characteristics of any genre film, including a dualistic value focus, repetition of themes, cumulative effects across productions, predictability, nostalgia, portability, and symbolism (see Altman, 1987, pp. 330–33).

10. As noted in Chapter 5 this film was uniformly panned by the critics. Maslin's praise of it is an example of what I mean by critics having no sense of history.

11. This is a second instance of film critics having no sense of collective memory. Of course no film appeared to give a suitable answer for the reviewers in the "classic" period.

12. I am not suggesting that the reviewers of the 1980s accepted A.A.'s theory anymore than the reviewers in the earlier decades did. They just stopped asking motivational questions.

13. Lush: a drinker or drunkard; a type of alcoholic on skid row (Keller and McCormick, 1968, p. 129).

14. During the interregnum a new grouping of terms emerged to describe the male and female alcoholic. W. C. Fields was called a lout, a loathsome drunkard, and a terminal alcoholic. Oma was called an alcoholic floozy (Knight, 1972) and a bloated alcoholic (Ebert, 1972).

15. For example, since 1980 alcoholics in Hollywood (and made-for-television) films routinely enter treatment centers for their alcoholism. (A 1990 release, *Postcards from the Edge*, continues this theme.) The treatment–recovery film is now a subtype within this category, but reviewers have not dealt with this variation on the traditional form.

16. This is a summary of Chase (1957) and Fiedler (1966): see also Ray (1985, pp. 56–57) and Andrew (1984, pp. 78–95) for applications of myth theory to American film. On the limits of myth theory see Barthes (1957/1972, 1975, 1977).

17. *Astral*: belonging to the stars. This section draws from Denzin (1990c).

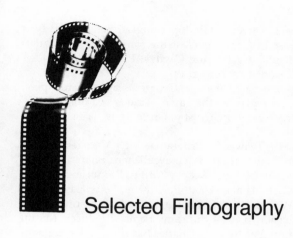

Selected Filmography

The number of reviews for each film, as given in Salem (1971,1982), *Filmfacts*, Magill, *Film Annual Review*, and *Newspaper Abstracts* is given in parentheses after each film. An asterisk after the number in parentheses indicates that the film was nominated for or won one or more awards (e.g., Oscars).

A Woman Under the Influence. 1974. Faces International. Director: John Cassavetes; Screenplay: John Cassavetes; Producer: Sam Shaw. Cast: Peter Falk, Gena Rowlands. (17).

Arthur. 1981. Orion. Director: Steve Gordon; Screenplay: Steve Gordon; Producer: Robert Greenhut. Cast: Dudley Moore, Liza Minnelli, Sir John Gielgud, Geraldine Fitzgerald, Jill Eikenberry. (18).*

Arthur 2 on the Rocks. 1988. Warner. Director: Bud Yorkin; Screenplay: Andy Breckman; Producer: Robert Shapiro. Cast: Dudley Moore, Liza Minnelli, Sir John Gielgud. (7).

Barfly. 1987. Cannon Films. Director: Barbet Schroeder; Screenplay: Charles Bukowski; Producers: Barbet Schroeder, Fred Roos, and Tom Luddy. Cast: Mickey Rourke, Faye Dunaway, Alice Krige. (17).

Betty Ford Story, The. 1987. ABC. Warners Television. A David L. Wolper Production. Director: David Green; Teleplay by Karen Hall based on Betty Ford's autobiography, *The Times of My Life*; Producer: Marsh W. Wolper. Cast: Gena Rowlands, Josef Sommer, Nan Woods. (10).*

Clean and Sober. 1988. Warner. Director: Glenn Gordon Caron; Screenplay: Tod Carroll; Producer: Tony Ganz and Deborah Blums. Cast: Michael Keaton, Kathy Baker, Morgan Freeman, M. Emmet Walsh. (10).

Come Back, Little Sheba. 1952. Paramount. Director: Daniel Mann; Screenplay: Kettl Frings, based on the play of the same name by William Inge; Producer: Hal B. Wallis. Cast: Burt Lancaster, Shirley Booth, Terry Moore, Richard Jaeckel. (18).*

Come Fill the Cup. 1951. Warner. Director: Gordon Douglas, Screenplay: Ivan Goff and Ben Roberts, based on the novel of the same name by Harlan Ware; Producer: Henry Blanke. Cast: James Cagney, Phyllis Thaxter, Raymond Massey, James Gleason, Gig Young. (9).

Country Girl, The. 1954. Paramount. Director: George Seaton; Screenplay: George Seaton, based on the play of the same name by Clifford Odets; Producer: William Perlberg. Cast: Bing Crosby, Grace Kelly, William Holden. (21).*

Cracker Factory, The. 1979. EMI, Television Programs, Inc. A Roger Gimbel Production; Director: Burt Brinckerhoff; Teleplay: Richard Shapirio, based on the novel of the same name by Joyce Rebeta-Burditt; Producers: Richard Shapiro, Paul Cameron. Cast: Natalie Wood, Peter King, Peter Haskell. (0).

Days of Wine and Roses. 1962. Warner. Director: Blake Edwards; Screenplay: J. P. Miller, based on his television play of the same name. Producer: Martin Manulis. Cast: Jack Lemmon, Lee Remick, Charles Bickford, Jack Klugman. (10).*

8 Million Ways to Die. 1986. Tri-Star Pictures. Director: Hal Ashby; Screenplay: Oliver Stone and David Lee Henry based on the books by Lawrence Block; Producer: Steve Roth. Cast: Jeff Bridges, Rosanna Arquette, Alexandra Paul. (6).

Fat City. 1972. Columbia Pictures. Director: John Huston; Screenplay: Leonard Gardner based on his novel; Producer: Ray Stark. Cast: Stacy Keach, Jeff Bridges, Susan Tyrrell. (12).

Harvey. 1950. Universal-International. Director: Harvey Koster. Screenplay: Marcy C. Chase and Oscar Brodney, from Mary Chases's play of the same name; Producer: John Beck. Cast: James Stewart, Josephine Hull, Peggy Dow, Charles Drake, Cecil Kellaway. (16).*

Hoosiers. 1988. Orion Pictures. Director: David Anspaugh; Screeplay: Angelo Pizzo; Producers: Carter De Haven and Angelo Pizzo. Cast: Gene Hackman, Barbara Hershey, Dennis Hopper. (10).*

I'll Cry Tomorrow. 1955. Metro-Goldwyn-Mayer. Director: Daniel Mann; Screenplay: Helen Deutsch and Jay Richard Kennedy based on the book of the same name by Lillian Roth; Producer: Laurence Weingarten. Cast: Susan Hayward, Richard Conte, Eddie Albert, Joyce Van Fleet. (15).*

Ironweed. 1987. Tri-Star Pictures. Director: Hector Babenco; Screenplay: William Kennedy, based on his novel of the same name; Producers: Keith Barish and Marcia Nasatir. Cast: Jack Nicholson, Meryl Streep, Caroll Baker. (10).*

Key Largo. 1948. Warner. Director: John Huston; Screenplay: Richard Brooks and John Huston; Producer: Jerry Wald. Cast: Humphrey Bogart, Edward G. Robinson; Lauren Bacall, Lionel Barrymore, Claire Trevor. (10).*

Lady Sings the Blues. 1972. Paramount. Director: Sidney J. Furie; Screenplay: Terrence McCloy, Chris Clark, and Suzzanne de Passa, based on the book by Billie Holiday and William Duffy; Producers: Berry Gordy, Jay Weston, James S. White. Cast: Diana Ross, Billy Dee Williams, Richard Pryor. (4).

Life of the Party: The Story of Beatrice. 1982. Columbia Pictures Television. Director: Lamont Johnson; Teleplay: Mitzi and Ken Welch; Producers: Ken and Mitzi Welch. Cast: Carol Burnett, Lloyd Bridges. (1).

Lost Weekend, The. 1945. Paramount. Director: Billy Wilder. Screenplay: Billy Wilder and Charles Brackett, based on the novel of the same name by Charles R. Jackson; Producer: Charles Brackett. Cast: Ray Milland, Jane Wyman, Philip Terry. (19).*

Morning After, The. 1987. 20th Century Fox. Director: Sidney Lumet; Screenplay: James Hicks; Producers: Faye Schwab, Bruce Gilbert. Cast: Jane Fonda, Jeff Bridges, Raul Julia. (15).

My Name Is Bill W. 1989. ABC. Garner/Duchow Production. Director: Daniel Petrie. Screenplay: William Borchert; Producer: James Garner, Peter Duchow. Cast: James Woods, James Garner, Jobeth Williams, Gary Sinise. (8).*

Only When I Laugh. 1981. Columbia. Director: Glen Jordan; Screenplay: Neil Simon; Producers: Roger M. Rothstein and Neil Simon. Cast: Marsha Mason, Kristy McNichol, James Coco, Joan Hackett. (17).*

Paris, Texas. 1984. TLC Films. Director: Wim Wenders; Screenplay: Sam Shepard and L. M. Kit Carson (adaptation); Producer: Don Guest. Cast: Harry Dean Stanton, Dean Stockwell, Nastassja Kinski, Hunter Carson. (11).*

Shattered Spirits. 1986. ABC. Director: Robert Greenwald; Teleplay: Gregory Goodell; Producer: Robert Greenwald; Executive Producer: Paul Pompian. Cast: Martin Sheen, Melinda Dillon, Matthew Laborteaux. (1).

Smash-Up: The Story of a Woman. 1947. Universal-International. Director: Stuart Heisler; Screenplay: John Howard Lawson, based on a story by Dorothy Parker; Producer: Walter Wanger. Cast: Susan Hayward, Lee Bowman, Marsha Hunt, Eddie Albert. (10).*

Star Is Born, A. 1937. United Artists. Director: William Wellman; Screenplay by Dorothy Parker, Alan Campbell, and Robert Carson from a story by William Wellman and Robert Carson; Producer: David O. Selznick for Selznick International Pictures. Cast: Fredric March, Janet Gaynor, Adolphe Menjou. (11).*

Star Is Born, A. 1954. Warner. Director: George Cukor; Screenplay: Moss Hart, based on the Dorothy Parker, Alan Campbell, Robert Carson screen play from a story by William Wellman; Producer: Sidney Luft. Cast: Judy Garland, James Mason, Jack Carson, Charles Bickford. (15).

Star Is Born, A. 1976. Warner. Directed by Frank Pierson; Screenplay by John Gregory Dunn, Joan Didion, and Frank Pierson; Producer: Barbra Streisand and Jon Peters. Cast: Barbra Streisand, Kris Kristofferson, Gary Busey. (15).*

Tender Mercies. 1983. Universal Pictures. Director: Bruce Beresford. Screenplay: Horton Foote. Producer: Philip S. Hobel; Co-Producers: Horton Foote, Robert Duvall; Cast: Robert Duvall, Tess Harper, Betty Buckley, Wilford Brimley, Ellen Barkin. (21).*

Under the Influence. 1986. CBS. CBS Entertainment Productions. Director: Thomas Carter; Screenplay: Joyce Rebeta-Burditt; Producer: Vanessa Greene. Cast: Andy Griffith, Joyce Van Patten, Keanu Reeves, Season Hubley, Paul Provenza, Dana Andersen. (1).

Under the Volcano. 1984. Universal. Director: John Huston; Screenplay by Guy Gallo based on the novel of the same name by Malcom Lowry; Producer:

Moritz Borman and Wieland Schulz-Keil. Cast: Albert Finney, Jacqueline Bisset, Anthony Andrews. (21).

Verdict, The. 1982. Twentieth Century-Fox. Director: Sidney Lumet; Screenplay: David Mamet, based on the novel of the same name by Barry Reed; Producers: Richard D. Zanuck and David Brown. Cast: Paul Newman, Charlotte Rampling, Jack Warden, James Mason. (7).*

W. C. Fields and Me. 1976. Universal. Director: Arthur Hiller; Screenplay: Bob Merrill from the book by Carlotta Monti; Producer: Jay Weston. Cast: Rod Steiger, Valarie Perrine, John Marley, Jack Cassidy. (5).

What Price Hollywood?. 1932. RKO Pathe. Director: George Cukor. Screenplay: Jane Murfin and Ben Markson, based on a story by Adela Rogers St. John; Executive Producer: David O. Selznick. Cast: Constance Bennett, Lowell Sherman, Neil Hamilton, Gregory Ratoff, Brooks Benedict. (3).

References

Ablon, Joan, Genevieve Ames, and William Cunningham. 1984. "To All Appearances the Ideal American Family: An Anthropological Case Study." Pp. 199–236 in Edward Kaufman (Ed.), *Power to Change: Family Case Studies of Alcoholism*. New York: Gardner Press.

Agee, James. 1958. *Agee on Film: Reviews and Comments by James Agee*. New York: McDowell, Obolensky, Inc.

———. 1945. "Review of *The Lost Weekend*." *Nation* 161, Dec. 22:697, reprinted in Agee (1958, pp. 182–84).

Alcoholics Anonymous. 1939, 1955, 1976. *Alcoholics Anonymous*. New York: Alcoholics Anonymous World Services.

———. 1967. *As Bill Sees It: The A. A. Way of Life. Selected Writings of A.A.'s Co-Founder*. New York: Alcoholics Anonymous World Services.

———. 1984. *"Pass It On": The Story of Bill Wilson and How the A. A. Message Reached The World*. New York: Alcoholics Anonymous World Services.

Al-Anon Family Groups. 1986. *First Steps: Al-Anon . . . 35 Years of Beginnings*. New York: Al-Anon Family Group Headquarters, Inc.

Al-Anon Family Groups. 1987. *Lois Remembers*. New York: Al-Anon Family Group Headquarters, Inc.

Alexander, Jack. 1941. "Alcoholics Anonymous." *Saturday Evening Post* (March 1):9–14.

Altheide, David. 1985. *Media Power*. Beverly Hills, CA: Sage.

Althusser, Louis. 1971. *Lenin and Philosophy*. New York: Monthly Review Press.

Altman, Rick. 1987. *The American Film Musical*. Bloomington: Indiana University Press.

America. 1956. "Review of *I'll Cry Tomorrow*." 94, Jan. 28:487–88.

Andrew, Dudley. 1984. *Concepts in Film Theory*. New York: Oxford.

Ansen, David. 1981a. "Review of *Arthur*." *Newsweek*, July 27:75.

———. 1981b. "Review of *Only When I Laugh*." *Newsweek*, Sept. 28:87.

Asahina, Robert. 1982. "Review of *The Verdict*." *New Leader*, Dec. 27:19.

Aulicino, Armand. 1952. "How *The Country Girl* Came About: In the Words of the People Involved: Interview with Clifford Odets, Forrest C. Harring, Lee Strasberg, Brooks Atkinson, Borris Aronson." *Theatre Arts* 36, May:55–57.

Auster, Albert and Leonard Quart. 1988. *How the War Was Remembered: Hollywood & Vietnam*. Westport, CT: Praeger.

Auty, Marilyn. 1981. "Review of *Arthur*." *Monthly Film Bulletin*, Nov.:215.

Bacon, S.D. 1948. "Current Notes: A Student of the Problems of Alcoholism Views *The Lost Weekend*." *Quarterly Journal of Studies on Alcoholism* 3, Dec.:402–05.

Bakshy, Alexander. 1932. "Review of *What Price Hollywood?*" *Nation* (August 3):III.

Balsamo, Anne. 1988. "Technologies of the Gendered Body: A Feminist Cultural Study." Doctoral dissertation in process, Institute of Communications, University of Illinois, Urbana.

———. 1989. "Imagining Cyborgs: Postmodernism and Symbolic Interactionism." *Studies in Symbolic Interaction* 10:369–379.

Barthes, Roland. 1957/1972. *Mythologies.* New York: Hill and Wang.

———. 1975. *The Pleasure of the Text.* New York: Hill and Wang.

———. 1977. *Writing Degree Zero.* New York: Hill and Wang.

———. 1981. "Upon Leaving the Movie Theatre," Translated by Bertrand Augst and Susan White. Pp. 1–4 in Theresa Hak Kyung Cha (Ed.), *Apparatus.* New York: Tanam Press.

———. 1985. *The Grain of the Voice: Interviews: 1962–1980.* New York: Hill and Wang.

Basic, Marni. 1989. "Reading the Alcoholic Film: Analysis of *The Country Girl.*" Presented to the 1989 Annual Meetings of the Midwest Sociological Society.

Bateson, Gregory. 1972a. "Double Bind." Pp. 271–78 in G. Bateson, *Steps to an Ecology of Mind.* New York: Ballantine.

———. 1972b. "The Cybernetics of Self: A Theory of Alcoholism." Pp. 309–37 in G. Bateson (Ed.), *Steps to an Ecology of Mind.* New York: Ballantine.

Baudrillard, Jean. 1983. *Simulations.* New York: Semiotext.

———. 1987/1988. *America.* New York. Verso Press.

Bazin, Andre. 1967. *What is Cinema?* Berkeley: University of California Press.

———. 1971. *What Is Cinema? Vol. II.* Berkeley: University of California Press.

Beauchamp, Dan. 1980. *Beyond Alcoholism.* Philadelphia: Temple University Press.

———. 1986. *Doing Things Together.* Evanston, IL.: Northwestern University Press.

Bell, Daniel. 1960. *The End of Ideology: On the Exhaustion of Political Ideas in the Fifties.* New York: Viking.

Benson, Sheila. 1981. "Review of *Arthur.*" *Los Angles Times* (July 17) Calendar:1.

———. 1982. "Review of *The Verdict.*" *Los Angeles Times* (Dec. 16) Calendar:1

———. 1984. "Review of *Under the Volcano.*" *Los Angeles Times* (July 6) Calendar:1

———. 1986. "Review of *8 Million Ways to Die.*" *Los Angeles Times* (April 25) Calendar:6.

———. 1988a. "Review of *Clean and Sober.*" *Los Angeles Times* (Aug. 10) Sec. VI:1,6.

———. 1988b. "Drinking, Sexism and Box-Office Woes." *Los Angeles Times* (Aug. 14) Calendar:28–29.

Black, Claudia. 1981. *It Will Never Happen to Me.* Denver: M.A.C.

Block, Lawrence. 1982. *Eight Million Ways to Die.* New York: Arbor House.

Blumer, Herbert. 1933. *Movies and Conduct.* New York: Macmillan.

———. 1969. *Symbolic Interactionism.* Englewood Cliffs, NJ: Prentice Hall.

Brower, D. 1946. "An Opinion Poll on Reactions to *The Lost Weekend.*" *Quarterly Journal of Studies on Alcohol* 1, March:596–98.

Brown, Geoff. 1982. "Review of *Only When I Laugh*." *Monthly Film Review* (Jan.):7.

Bukowski, Charles. 1987. *The Movie "Barfly," An Original Screenplay by Charles Bukowski for a Film by Barbet Schroeder*. Santa Rosa: Black Sparrow Press.

Busch, Noel F. 1947. "Lady Tipplers: Suggestions Are Offered for Improving Their Behavior." *Life* 22, (April 14):79.

Cahalan, Don. 1987. *Understanding America's Problem Drinker*. SanFrancisco: Jossey-Bass.

Canby, Vincent. 1972. "Review of *Fat City*." *New York Times* (Aug.6) II:1

———. 1976a. "Review of *W. C. Fields and Me*." *New York Times (April 1)*:28.

———. 1976b. "Film View: *W. C. Fields and Me*, 'Anyone Who Hates This Film Can't Be All Bad.' " *New York Times* (April 4) 11:19.

———. 1976c. "Review of *A Star Is Born*." *New York Times Film Reviews: 1975–1976*:298 (Dec. 27:C 16:5.)

———. 1981a. "Review of *Arthur*." *New York Times*. (July 17):10.

———. 1981b. "Review of *Only When I Laugh*." *New York Times* (Sept. 24) C:23.

———. 1983. "Film View: *'Tender Mercies'* Stands Out." *New York Times* (Mar. 13) Sec. II:21

———. 1984. "Huston's 'Volcano' Pays Homage to Novel." *New York Times* (June 22) C:12.

———. 1986. "Review of *The Morning After*." *New York Times* (Dec. 25):22.

———. 1987. "Review of *Barfly*." *New York Times* (Sept. 30) C:18.

———. 1988. "Review of *Arthur 2 on the Rocks*." *New York Times* (July 8):11

Carey, James W. 1989. *Communication as Culture: Essays on Media and Society*. Boston: Unwin Hyman.

Caron, Glenn Gordon. 1988a. "Moonlighting's Caron Talks about His Anti-Drug Film." Interview with David Sterritt. *Christian Science Monitor* 10 August: 20-21.

———. 1988b. "Interview with Richard Corliss in 'Hollywood Goes on the Wagon.' " *Time* (Aug. 22):76

Carr, Jay. 1987. "Review of *Barfly*." *Boston Globe*, Nov. 6:32.

———. 1988. "Review of *Clean and Sober*." *Boston Globe*, Aug.10:61, 67.

Carringer, Robert L. 1985. *The Making of Citizen Kane*. Berkeley: University of California Press.

———. 1989. Personal communication.

Cater Bill. 1989. "Chung Show Using Stars to Re-enact The News." *New York Times*, Sept. 19:15, 17.

Catholic World. 1954. "Review of *A Star Is Born*." Dec. 221–2.

———. 1956. "Review of *I'll Cry Tomorrow*." 182, Jan. 20:137.

Chanko, Kenneth, M. 1987. "Review of *The Morning After*." *Films In Review* (April):231.

Chase, Richard. 1957. *The American Novel and its Tradition*. New York: Doubleday.

Cherlin, Andrew. 1983. "Changing Family and Household: Contemporary Issues from Historical Research." *Annual Review of Sociology* 9:51–66.

Clark, Kenneth R. 1989. "Review of *My Name is Bill W*." *Chicago Tribune* (April 28) Sec. 6:1–2.

Clough, Patricia, T. 1988a. "Feminist Theory and Social Psychology." *Studies In Symbolic Interaction* 8:3–22.

———. 1988b. "The Movies and Social Observation: Reading Blumer's *Movies and Conduct.*" *Symbolic Interaction* II:85–94.

———. 1989. *Writing Technologies of the Subject: Ethnography, Narrativity, and Sociological Discourse.* Unpublished manuscript.

Coleman, John. 1982. "Review of *Only When I Laugh.*" *New Statesman,* Jan. 29:24

Combs, Richard. 1987. "Review of *The Morning After.*" *Sight & Sound,* Spring:143

Conrad, Barnaby. 1986. *Time Is All We Have: Four Weeks at the Betty Ford Center.* New York: Arbor House.

Cook, David A. 1981. *A History of Narrative Film.* New York: W.W. Norton.

Cook, Jim and Mike Lewington (Eds.). 1979. *Images of Alcoholism.* London: British Film Institute and the Educational Advisory Service.

Corliss, Richard. 1983. "Heart of Texas: Review of *Tender Mercies.*" *Time* (March 28):62

———. 1988. "Hollywood Goes on the Wagon." *Time* 132, (Aug. 22):76.

Couch, Carl J. 1986. "Questionnaires, Naturalistic Observations and Recordings." *Studies in Symbolic Interaction, Supplement 2: The Iowa School (Part A):* 45–59.

Crist, Judith. 1981. "Review of *Only When I Laugh.*" *Saturday Review* (Sept.):49.

———. 1982. "This Week's Movie: *Life of the Party.*" *TV Guide* 30 (Sept. 25):A-6, A-100.

———. 1983. "Men Who Need Women: Review of *Tender Mercies,*" *50 Plus* (March):52–3.

———. 1986a. "This Week's Movies: Review of *Shattered Spirits.*" *TV Guide* 34 (Jan. 4):A-5, A-16, A-67.

———. 1986b. "This Week's Movies: Review of *Under The Influence.*" *TV Guide* 34 (Sept. 27):A-5, A-58.

Cross, Richard K. 1980. *Malcolm Lowry: A Preface to His Fiction.* Chicago: University of Chicago Press.

Crowther, Bosley. 1945. "Review of *The Lost Weekend.*" *New York Times Film Reviews Vol. 3: 1939–1948:* 2128 (Dec. 3: 17:2).[1]

———. 1947. "Review of *Smash-Up—The Story of a Woman.*" *New York Times Film Reviews Vol. 3: 1939–1948:* 2175 (April 11:31:2).

———. 1950. "Review of *Harvey.*" *New York Times Film Reviews: Vol. 4: 1949–1958:* 2478 (Dec.22, p. 19:1).

———. 1951. "Review of *Come Fill the Cup.*" *New York Times Film Reviews: Vol. 4:1949–1958:* 2566 (Nov. 22, p. 47:2).

———. 1952. "Review of *Come Back, Little Sheba.*" *New York Times Film Reviews: Vol. 4: 1949–1958:* 3861 (Dec. 24, p. 13:2).

———. 1954a. "Review of *A Star Is Born.*" *New York Times Film Reviews: Vol 4: 1949–1958:* 2818 (Oct. 12, p. 23:1).

———. 1954b. "Review of *The Country Girl.*" *New York Times Film Reviews: Vol 4: 1949–1958:* 2215 (Dec. 16, p. 51:2).

———. 1956. "Review of *I'll Cry Tomorrow.*" *New York Times Film Reviews: Vol. 4: 1949–1958:* 2904 (Jan. 13:18:1).

_____. 1963. "Review of *Days of Wine and Roses.*" *New York Times Film Reviews: Vol. 5: 1959–1968:* (Jan. 18, p. 7:2).

Cunneen, Chris, Mark Findlay, Rob Lynch, and Vernon Tupper. 1989. *Dynamics of Collective Conflict: Riots at the Bathurst' Bike Riots.* Sidney: Law Book Co.

Current Biography. 1945. "Mary Chase." Pp. 98–100.

Damrosch, Leopald, Jr. 1982. "Burns, Blake and the Recovery of Lyric." *Studies in Romanticism* 21:637–60.

Davis, Edward H. 1989. "Viewer's Interpretations of Films About Alcohol," *Studies in Symbolic Interaction* 10:199–212.

Day, Douglas. 1973. *Malcolm Lowry: A Biography.* New York: Oxford.

de Certeau, Michael. 1984. *The Practice of Everyday Life.* Berkeley: University of California Press.

de Lauretis, Teresa. 1984. *Alice Doesn't: Feminism, Semiotics, Cinema.* Bloomington: Indiana University Press.

_____. 1987. *Technologies of Gender: Essays on Theory, Film, and Fiction.* Bloomington: Indiana University Press.

Denby, David. 1981a. "Review of *Arthur.*" *New York* (July 27):50.

_____. 1981b. "Review of *Only When I Laugh.*" *New York* (Oct. 12):83.

_____. 1982. "Review of *The Verdict.*" *New York* (Dec. 20):62.

_____. 1983. "Review of *Tender Mercies.*" *New York* (March 14):56.

_____. 1984. "Review of *Under the Volcano.*" *New York* (June 25):63.

_____. 1986. "Review of *8 Million Ways to Die.*" *New York* (May 12):130.

_____. 1987. "Review of *The Morning After.*" *New York* (Jan. 5):45.

_____. 1988. "Review of *Clean and Sober.*" *New York* 22 (August):132–34.

Denzin, Norman K. 1986. "Postmodern Social Theory." *Sociological Theory* 4:194–204.

_____. 1987a. *The Alcoholic Self.* Newbury Park, CA.: Sage

_____. 1987b. The Recovering Alcoholic. Newbury Park, CA.: Sage.

_____. 1987c. *Treating Alcoholism.* Newbury Park, CA.: Sage.

_____. 1987d. "Under the Influence of Time: Reading the Interactional Text." *Sociological Quarterly* 28:327–41.

_____. 1989b. *Interpretive Interactionism.* Newbury Park, CA.: Sage.

_____. 1989c. *Interpretive Biography.* Newbury Park, CA.: Sage.

_____. 1989d. "Reading/Writing Culture: Interpreting the Postmodern Project." *Cultural Dynamics* II:9–27.

_____. 1989e. "Reading Tender Mercies: Two Interpretations." *Sociological Quarterly* 30:37–58.

_____. 1989f. *"Blue Velvet* Postmodern Contradictions" *Theory, Culture and Society* 5, 2–3:461–74.

_____. 1990a. Presidential Address on "The Sociological Imagination Revisited." *Sociological Quarterly* 31:1–22.

_____. 1990b. "On Understanding Emotion: The Interpretive-Cultural Agenda," Pp. 85–116 in Theodore D. Kemper (Ed.), *Research Agendas in the Sociology of Emotions.* Albany: State University of New York Press.

_____. 1990c. "Postmodernism and Deconstructionism," in David Dickens and Andrea Fontana (Eds.), *Postmodernism and Sociology.* Chicago: University of Chicago Press, in press.

_____. 1990d. "Reading Cultural Texts. *American Journal of Sociology* 8:1577–1580.

_____. 1990e. "Empiricist Cultural Studies in America: A Deconstructive Reading." *Current Perspectives in Social Theory* II, in press.

Derrida, Jacques, 1984. *Signeponge/Signsponge*. New York: Columbia University Press.

_____. 1985. *Otobiographies: The Teaching of Nietzsche and the Politics of the Proper Name*. New York: Schocken.

Desser, David. 1985. "Transcendental Style in *Tender Mercies*." *Religious Communications Today*, 8 September: 21–27.

Dick, Bernard F. 1980. *Billy Wilder*. Boston: Twayne Publishers.

Doane, Mary Ann. 1982. "Film and the Masquerade: Theorizing the Female Spectator." *Screen* 23:74–87.

_____. 1987. *The Desire to Desire*. Bloomington: Indiana University Press.

Donzelot, Jacques. 1979. *The Policing of Families*. New York: Pantheon.

Deutsch, Phyllis. 1983. "Review of *The Verdict*." *Jump Cut* 28, April: 11.

Ebert, Roger. 1972. "Review of *Fat City*." *Chicago Sun-Times* (Sept. 29):18.

_____. 1981. "Review of *Arthur*." *Chicago Sun Times*. (July 20):21.

_____. 1988. *Review of Arthur 2 on the Rocks*." *Chicago Sun Times* (July 8):19.

_____. 1989. "Review of *Clean and Sober*." Pp. 136–37 in *Roger Ebert's Home Movie Companion*. 1990 Edition. New York: Andrews and McMeel.

Eco, Umberto. 1987. "Casablanca: Cult Movies and Intertextual Collage," Pp. 197–211 in U. Eco, *Travels in Hyperreality*. New York: Doubleday.

Edelstein, David. 1986. "Review of *The Morning After*." *Village Voice* (Dec. 30):74.

Ediger, Jeff. 1988. "Reading *The Lost Weekend*." Unpublished manuscript.

_____. 1989. "The Lonely Alcoholic Male." Unpublished manuscript.

Elbaz, Robert. 1987. *The Changing Nature of the Self: A Critical Study of the Autobiographic Discourse*. Iowa City: University of Iowa Press.

Elsaesser, Thomas. 1973/1986. "Tales of Sound and Fury: Observations on the Family Melodrama." Pp. 278–308 in Barry Keith Grant (Ed.), *Film Genre Theory*. Austin: University of Texas Press (originally published in *Monogram*, no. 4, 1973:2–15.

Farber, Manny. 1946. "Review of *The Lost Weekend*." *New Republic* 114, (Jan. 7):23.

_____. 1952. "Review of *Come Back, Little Sheba*." *Nation* 175, (Nov. 8):434.

Farber, Stephen. 1987. "TV Taking a Frank Look at Betty Ford's Drama." *New York Times* (Feb. 25) C:26.

Fearing, Franklin. 1947. "Psychology and the Films." *Hollywood Quarterly* 2:118–21.

Fenner, Jeffrey L. 1987. "Review of *Sid and Nancy*." *Magell's Cinema Annual 1987: A Survey of the Films of 1986*. Englewood Cliffs, NJ: Salem Press.

Ferraro, Kathleen J. "Policing Woman Battering." *Social Problems* 36:61–74.

Fiedler, Leslie A. 1966 (rev. ed.). *Love and Death in the American Novel*. New York: Stein and Day.

Filmfacts. 1972a. "Collected reviews of *Fat City*." 15:361–64.

_____. 1972b. "Collected reviews of *Lady Sings the Blues*." 17:389–394.

_____. 1976. "Collected reviews of *W. C. Fields and Me*." 19:62–65.

Film Review Annual. 1984. "Collected reviews of *Tender Mercies.*" 1192–1202.

Finn, Peter. 1980. "Attitudes toward Drinking Conveyed in Studio Greeting Cards." *American Journal of Public Health,* 70:826–9.

Flaherty, Michael G. 1984. "A Formal Approach to the Study of Amusement in Social Interaction." Pp. 71–82 in N. K. Denzin (Ed.), *Studies in Symbolic Interaction, Vol. 5.* Greenwich, CT.: JAI Press.

Flemming, Michael and Roger Manvell. 1985. *Images of Madness: The Portrayal of Insanity in the Feature Film.* London and Toronto: Associated University Presses.

Ford, Betty with Chris Chase. 1978. *The Times of My Life.* New York: Harper & Row and the Readers Digest Association, Inc.

Ford, Betty with Chris Chase. 1987. *Betty: A Glad Awakening.* New York: Doubleday.

Foucault, Michael. 1973. *The Birth of the Clinic.* New York: Pantheon.

———. 1980a. *Power/Knowledge.* New York: Pantheon.

———. 1980b. *The History of Sexuality: Vol. I: An Introduction.* New York: Vintage.

Freud, Sigmund. 1963. *Jokes and Their Relation to the Unconscious.* New York: W. W. Norton.

Gabbard, Krin and Glen O. Gabbard. 1987. *Psychiatry and the Cinema.* Chicago: University of Chicago Press.

Garfield Messenger. 1950. "Review of *Harvey.*" December: 23.

Gelmis, Joseph. 1981. "Review of *Arthur.*" *Newsday* (July 17) Part II:7.

———. 1982. "Review of *The Verdict.*" *Newsday.* (Dec. 8) Part III:63.

———. 1986. "Review of *The Morning After.*" *Newsday.* (Dec. 26) Part III:3.

Gifford, Barry. 1988. *The Devil Takes a Ride and Other Unforgettable Films.* New York: Grove Press.

Gilliatt, Penelope. 1972. "Review of *Fat City.*" *New Yorker* (July 29):53.

Gilmore, Thomas B. 1987. *Equivocal Spirits: Alcoholism and Drinking in Twentieth-Century Literature.* Chapel Hill: University of North Carolina Press.

Glaser, Barney and Anselm Strauss. 1967. "Awareness Contexts and Social Interaction." *American Sociological Review* 29:669–79.

Gledhill, Christine. 1978 "Klute: Part I: A Contemporary Film Noir and Feminist Criticism." Pp. 6–21 in E. Ann Kaplan (Ed.), *Women in Film Noir.* London: British Film Institute.

———. 1978/1985. "Recent Developments in Feminist Criticism." Pp. 817–845 in Gerald Mast and Marshall Cohen (Eds.), *Film Theory and Criticism,* 3rd ed. New York: Oxford University Press. (Originally published in *Quarterly Review of Film Studies,* 1978.

Goffman, Erving, 1961. *Asylums.* New York: Doubleday.

———. 1963. *Stigma.* Englewood Cliffs, NJ: Prentice-Hall.

———. 1974. *Frame Analysis.* New York: Harper & Row.

Goldsmith, Barbara. 1956. "A Woman Can Come Back." *Woman's Home Companion* 83, Jan. 1956:14–15.

Gomberg, Edith Lisansky. 1982. "Special Populations." Pp. 337–54 in E. L. Gomberg et al. (Eds.), *Alcohol, Science and Society Revisited.* Ann Arbor: University of Michigan Press.

Grant, Barry Keith (Ed.). 1986. *Film Genre Reader.* Austin: University of Texas Press.

Grant, Marcus. 1979. "The Alcoholic as Hero." Pp. 30–36 in J. Cook and M. Lewington (Eds.), *Images of Alcoholism*. London: British Film Institute.

Grossberg, Lawrence. 1986. "History, Politics and Postmodernism: Stuart Hall and Cultural Studies." *Journal of Communication Inquiry* 10:61–77.

Gusfield, Joseph. 1963. *Symbolic Crusade*. Urbana: University of Illinois Press.

Hall, Stuart. 1980. "Encoding/Decoding." Pp. 129–38 in Hall et al. (Eds.), *Culture, Media, Language*. London: Hutchinson.

———. 1986. "On Postmodernism and Articulation: An Interview with Stuart Hall," (edited by Lawrence Grossberg). *Journal of Communication Inquiry* 10:45–60.

Hanson, Stephen L. 1984. "Review of *The Verdict*." Pp. 377–81 in Frank N. Magill (Ed.), *Magill's Cinema Annual, 1984: A Survey of 1983 Films*. Englewood Cliffs, NJ: Salem Press.

Harris, Ann. 1987. "Review of *Hoosiers*." Pp. 245–49 in Frank N. Magill (Ed.), *Magill's Cinema Annual, 1985: A Study of 1984 Films*. Englewood Cliffs, NJ: Salem Press.

Hartung, Philip T. 1945. "Review of *The Lost Weekend*." *Commonweal* 43, (Dec. 7):205–6.

———. 1947. "Review of *Smash-Up—The Story of a Woman*." *Commonweal* 46, (Apr. 25):38.

———. 1950. "Review of *Harvey*." *Commonweal* 53:301–2.

———. 1954a. "Review of *A Star is Born*." *Commonweal* 61, (Oct. 22):60–1.

———. 1954b. "Review of *The Country Girl*." *Commonweal* 61, (Dec. 17):312.

———. 1956. "Review of *I'll Cry Tomorrow*." *Commonweal* 63 (Jan. 20): 403.

———. 1963. "Review of *Days of Wine and Roses*." *Commonweal* 77, (Feb. 1):493–4.

Harvey, Evelyn. 1954. "Review of *A Star Is Born*." *Colliers* 133, (April 30):32–3.

Harwin, J. and S. Otto. 1979. "Women, Alcohol and the Screen." Pp. 37–50 in J. Cook and M. Lewington (Eds.), *Images of Alcoholism*. London: British Film Institute.

Haskell, Molly. 1973/1987 (2nd. ed.). *From Reverence to Rape: The Treatment of Women in the Movies*. Chicago: University of Chicago Press.

Hatch, Robert. 1951. "Review of *Harvey*." *New Republic* (January 15):31.

———. 1956. "Review of *I'll Cry Tomorrow*." *Nation* 182, (Jan. 28):78.

HBO. 1990. *HBO's Guide to Movies on Video-Cassette and Cable TV*. New York: Harper & Row.

Heilbronn, Lisa M. 1988. "What Does Alcohol Mean? Alcohol's Use as a Symbolic Code." *Contemporary Drug Problems*, Summer: 229–48.

Herd, Denise. 1986. "Ideology, Melodrama, and the Changing Role of Alcohol Problems in American Films." *Contemporary Drug Problems*, Summer: 213–247.

Herd, Denise and Robin Room. 1982. "Alcohol Images in American Film: 1909–1960." *Drinking and Drug Practices Survey* 18 (August):24–35.

Higham, Charles and Joel Greenberg. 1968. *Hollywood in the Forties*. New York: A. S. Barnes & Co.

Hitchcock, Alfred. 1984. "Quoted in" Francois Trauffaut (with the collaboration of Helen G. Scott). *Hitchcock/Trauffaut: The Definitive Study of Alfred Hitchcock*, rev. ed. New York: Simon & Schuster.

Hobe, Phyllis. 1990. *Lovebound: Recovering from an Alcoholic Family.* New York: NAL books.

Hoberman, J. 1986. "Review of *8 Million Ways to Die.*" *Village Voice,* May 6:62.

Izod, John. 1988. *Hollywood and the Box Office, 1895–1986.* New York: Columbia University Press.

Jackson, Charles. 1944. *The Lost Weekend.* New York: Carroll & Graf.

Jackson, Joan. 1962. "Alcoholism and the Family." Pp. 472–93 in David J. Pittman and C.R. Snyder (Eds.), *Society, Culture and Drinking Patterns.* New York: John Wiley.

Jarvis, Jeff. 1989. "Review of *My Name Is Bill W.*" *People Weekly* 31, (May 1):7

Jeffre, Leo. 1986. *Mass Media: Processes and Effects.* Prospect Hts. IL: Waveland.

Jellinek, E. M. 1960. *The Disease Concept of Alcoholism.* New Haven, CT: Hillhouse.

———. 1962, "Phases of Alcohol Addiction." Pp. 356–68 in David J. Pittman and Charles Snyder (Eds.), *Society, Culture, and Drinking Patterns.* New York: John Wiley.

Johnson, Bruce Holley. 1973. "The Alcoholism Movement in America: A Study in Cultural Innovation." Doctoral Dissertation, University of Illinois, Urbana-Champaign.

Johnson, Richard. 1986/87. "What Is Cultural Studies Anyway?" *Social Text* (Winter):38–80.

Kael, Pauline. 1974. "Review of *A Woman Under the Influence.*" *New Yorker* 50, (Dec. 4):172–76.

———. 1983. "Review of *Tender Mercies.*" *The New Yorker,* 16 May:119–121.

Kahn, Gordon. 1946. "Review of *The Lost Weekend.*" *Atlantic* 177, (June):140–1.

Kalb, Bernard. 1952. "Review of *Come Back, Little Sheba.*" *Saturday Review* 35, (Dec. 27):26–28.

Kauffmann, Stanley. 1963. "Review of *Days of Wine and Roses.*" *The New Republic* 148, (Feb. 2):31.

———. 1974. "Review of *A Woman Under the Influence,*" *New Republic* 171 (Dec. 28): 20.

———. 1983. "The Quality of Mercies: Review of *Tender Mercies.*" *The New Republic* II, (April):24–25.

Kawin, Bruce F. 1978. *Mindscreen: Bergman, Godard and First-Person Film.* Princeton: Princeton University Press.

Kehr, Dave. 1988. "Review of *Arthur 2 on the Rocks.*" *Chicago Tribune* (July 8):12.

Keller, Mark and Mairi McCormick. 1968. *A Dictionary of Words About Alcohol.*" New Brunswick: Rutgers Center of Alcohol Studies.

Keneas, Alex. 1981. "Review of *Only When I Laugh.*" *Newsday* (Sept. 23) Part II:66

———. 1984. "Review of *Under the Volcano.*" *Newsday* (June 13) Part III:55.

Kissel, Howard. 1981. "Review of *Arthur.*" *Women's Wear Daily* (July 15):36.

———. 1982. "Review of *The Verdict.*" *Women's Wear Daily* (Dec. 7):8.

———. 1983. "Review of *Tender Mercies.*" *Women's Wear Daily* (March 3):20.

Klapp, Orin. 1964. *Symbolic Leaders.* Chicago: Aldine.

———. 1969. *The Hero, The Villain, The Fool.* Chicago: Aldine.

Klein, Dorie. 1982. "*A Star Is Born.*" Review in *PFA Film Notes* 23 (Feb.)

Knight, Arthur. 1954. "Review of *A Star Is Born.*" *Saturday Review* 37, (Oct. 30):28–29.

––––––. 1972. "Review of *Fat City.*" Saturday Review (Sept. 2):61.

Koffler, Richard. 1990. Personal communication.

Kolker, Robert P. 1980. *A Cinema of Loneliness.* New York: Oxford.

Kopland, Andrew. 1975. "Review of *A Woman Under the Influence.*" *Ramparts,* 13, May:56–60.

Krafsur, Richard (Ed.). 1976. *The American Film Institute Film Catalog of Motion Pictures. Vols. 1 and 2. Feature Films 1961–1970.* New York: R. R. Bowker Company.

Kray, Susan. 1988. "The Adult Child Social Movement." Unpublished manuscript.

Krug, Gary. 1990. "The Dawn of Destruction: Nuclear Films in the Age of Innocence." Unpublished manuscript.

Krutch, Joseph Wood. 1944. "Review of 'Harvey' the Play. "*Nation* (Dec.): 624.

Kubie, Lawrence. 1947. "Psychiatry and the Films." *Hollywood Quarterly* 2:113–17.

Kurtz, Ernest. 1979. *And Not-God. A History of Alcoholics Anonymous.* Center City, MN: Hazelden.

Lacan, Jacques. 1949/1977. "The Mirror State as Formative of the Function of the I as Revealed in Psychoanalytic Experience." Pp. 1–7 in *Jacques Lacan: Ecrits: A Selection,* translated by Alan Sheridan. New York: W. W. Norton.

––––––. 1957–8. "Les Formations de L'inconscient." *Bulletin de Psychologie* 9:1–15.

––––––. *Ecrits: A Selection.* New York: W. W. Norton.

Levine, Harry Gene. 1978. "The Discovery of Addiction." *Journal of Studies on Alcohol* 39:143–74.

Lerner, Gerta. 1986. *The Creation of Patriarchy.* New York: Oxford University Press.

Lewington, Mike. 1979. "Alcoholism in the Movies: An Overview." Pp. 22–29 in J. Cook and M. Lewington (Eds.), *Images of Alcoholism.* London: British Film Institute.

Lewis, Jay. 1982. "The Federal Role in Alcoholism Research, Treatment and Prevention." Pp. 402–26 in E. Gomberg, H. White, and J. Carpenter (Eds.), *Alcohol, Science and Society Revisited.* Ann Arbor: University of Michigan Press.

Library Journal. 1956. "Review of *I'll Cry Tomorrow.*" 81, Feb. 1:360.

Lida, David. 1986. "Review of *The Morning After.*" *Women's Wear Daily* (Dec. 23):10.

Life. 1945. "Review of *The Lost Weekend.*" 19, Oct. 15:133–6.

––––––. 1947. "Review of *Smash-Up—The Story of a Woman .*" 22, April 14:79–80.

––––––. 1954a. "Review of *A Star Is Born.*" 37, Sept. 13:163–6.

––––––. 1954b. "Review of *The Country Girl.*" 37, Dec. 6:106.

––––––. 1956. "Review of *I'll Cry Tomorrow.*" 40, Jan. 9:117–18.

Lindlof, Thomas (Ed.). 1987. *Natural Audiences: Qualitative Research of Media Uses and Effects.* Norwood, NJ: Ablex.

Littwin, Susan. 1987. "Why Betty Ford Decided to Share Her Most Painful Moments." *TV Guide* (Feb. 28–March 6):7–11.

Look. 1954. "Review of *The Country Girl*." 18, Dec. 14:164.

Lowry, Malcolm. 1947. *Under the Volcano*. London: Jonathan Cape.

Lyman, Stanford M. 1987. "From Matrimony to Malaise: Men and Women in American Film, 1930–1980." *International Journal of Politics, Culture and Society* 1:73–100 [263–290].

Lyman, Stanford. 1990. "Anhedonia: Gender and the Decline of Emotions in American Film, 1930–1988." *Sociological Inquiry* 60: 1–19.

Lynch, Rob. 1982. "Play, Creativity, and Emotion." *Studies in Symbolic Interaction* 4:45–62.

MacAndrew, Craig and Robert B. Edgerton. 1969. *Drunken Comportment: A Social Explanation*. Chicago: Aldine.

Macleans. 1983. "A Slow Version of a Hurtin' Song: Review of *Tender Mercies*," 16 May:57.

Magill, Frank N. (Ed.). 1986. *Magill's Cinema Annual Cumulative Indexes: 1982–1986*. Englewood Cliffs, NJ: Salem Press.

Magill, Marcia. 1983. "Review of *The Verdict*." *Films in Review*, Jan.:48.

Maines, David R. 1989. "The Alcoholic Self and Its Social Circles." *American Journal of Sociology*, 94:864–73.

———. 1990. (Forthcoming). "On Narrative and Sociologys Phenomena." In B. Gronbeck and M. McGee (Eds.), *Narrative and the Social Sciences*. Madison: University of Wisconsin Press.

Malpezzi, Frances M. and William M. Clements. 1982. "Review of *Only When I Laugh*." Pp. 268–71 in Frank N. Magill (Ed.), *Magill's Cinema Annual, 1982: A Survey of 1981 Films*. Englewood Cliffs, NJ: Salem Press.

Maltin, Leonard. 1988a. "Review of *Shattered Spirits*." P. 946 in *Leonard Maltin's TV Movies and Video Guide: 1989 Edition*. New York: New American Library.

———. 1988b. "Review of *Under the Influence*." P. 1132 in *Leonard Maltin's TV Movies and Video Guide: 1989 Edition*. New York: New American Library.

———. (Ed.). 1989. *Leonard Maltin's TV Movies and Video Guide: 1990 Edition*. New York: New American Library.

Manning, Peter K. 1988. *Symbolic Communication: Signifying Calls*. Cambridge: MIT Press.

Manning, Peter K. and Betsy Cullum-Swan. 1990. "Semiotics and Framing: Examples." Presented to the 1990 Annual Stone-Society for the Study of Symbolic Interaction Symposium, St. Petersburg Beach, Florida: January 28.

Maslin, Janet. 1982. "Review of *The Verdict*." *New York Times* (Dec. 8) C:24.

———. 1983. "Review of *Tender Mercies*." *New York Times* (Mar. 4) Sec. C:8

———. 1984. "Review of *Under the Volcano*." *New York Times* (June 13):C:21.

———. 1988a. "When a Movie Serves a Mickey." *New York Times* (Aug. 14) Sect. 2:1, 21.

———. 1988b. "Review of *Clean and Sober*." *New York Times* (Aug. 10) Sect. C:15.

Mast, Gerald. 1976. *A Short History of the Movies*. Indianapolis: Bobbs-Merrill.

Mayer, Gerald M. 1947. "American Motion Pictures in World Trade." *The Annals of the American Academy of Political and Social Science*, 254:34.

McCarten, John C. 1932. "Review of *What Price Hollywood?*" *New Yorker* (July 23):45.

———. 1945. "Review of *The Lost Weekend*." *New Yorker* 21, (Dec. 1):112.

———. 1947. "Review of *Smash Up—The Story of a Woman*." *New Yorker* 23, (April 19):44.

———. 1951. "Review of *Come Fill the Cup*." *New Yorker* 27, (Dec. 1):155.

———. 1952. "Review of *Come Back, Little Sheba*." *New Yorker* 28, Dec. 27:59–60.

———. 1954a. "Review of *A Star is Born*." *New Yorker* 30, (Oct. 23):145.

———. 1954b. "Review of *The Country Girl*." *New Yorker* 30, (Dec. 25):60–61.

———. 1956. "Review of *I'll Cry Tomorrow*." *New Yorker*. 31, (Jan. 21):110–11.

———. 1958. "Review of *Too Much, Too Soon*." *New Yorker* 34, (Dec. 3):91–92.

———. 1963. "Review of *Days of Wine and Roses*." *New Yorker*. 38, 26 (Jan.):121–2.

McCormack, Thelma. 1986. "The 'wets' and the 'drys': Binary Images of Women and Alcohol in Popular Culture." *Communication* 9:43–64.

McDonald, Gerald D. 1950. "Review of Harvey." *Current Film Features* (November 15):2021.

McGrady, Mike. 1986. "Review of *8 Million Ways to Die*." *Newsday* (April 5) Part III:5.

Merkin, Daphne. 1984. "Review of *Under the Volcano*." *New Leader* (June 11):19.

Merleau-Ponty, Maurice. 1964. "Film and the New Psychology." Pp. 48–59 in M. Merleau-Ponty, *Sense and Non-Sense*. Evanston, IL: Northwestern University Press.

Miller, J. P. 1988. "TV Wouldn't Touch 'Wine' Today, says N. J. Man Who Wrote Script." *Central New Jersey Home News*, Arts/Entertainment 28 August:Fl, F3c.[2]

Miller, Merle. 1950. "Review of *Harvey*." *Saturday Review* (January: 26).

Mills, C. Wright. 1940. "Situated Actions and Vocabularies of Motive." *American Sociological Review*, 5:904–13.

———. 1959. *The Sociological Imagination*. New York: Oxford University Press.

Mills, Nancy. 1987. "Rolands Treasures Betty Ford." *Los Angeles Times*, Feb. 28, Sec. VI:1.

Milne, Tom. 1984. "Review of *Under the Volcano*." *Monthly Film Bulletin*, July:214.

———. 1987. "Review of *The Morning After*." *Monthly Film Review*, June:181

Mitchell, Juliet. 1982. "Introduction—I: Feminine Sexuality." Pp. 1–26 in *Jacques Lacan, Feminine Sexuality*. Jacqueline Rose and Juliet Mitchell (Eds.), New York: Pantheon.

———. 1984. *Women: The Longest Revolution*. New York: Pantheon Books.

Monaco, James. 1981. *How to Read a Film* (rev. ed.). New York: Oxford.

Morin, Edgar. 1984. *Sociologie*. Paris: Fayard.

Mukerji, C. and M. Schudson. 1986. "Popular Culture." Annual Review of Sociology 12:44–66.

Mulford, Harold. 1986. "The Cost of Treating Alcoholics." Unpublished manuscript.

Mulvey, Laura. 1977/1985. "Film and Visual Pleasure." Pp. 803–16 in Gerald Mast and Marshall Cohen (Eds.), *Film Theory and Criticism*, 3rd ed. New York: Oxford University Press. (Originally published in *Screen*, 1977. Also reprinted with afterthoughts in Mulvey 1989.)

———. 1989a. "Afterthoughts on 'Visual Pleasure and Narrative Cinema' inspired by King Vidor's *Duel in the Sun* (1946)." Pp. 29–38 in Laura Mulvey (Ed.), *Visual and Other Pleasures*. Bloomington: Indiana University Press.

———. 1989b. "The Oedipus Myth: Beyond the Riddles of the Sphinx." Pp. 117–201 in Laura Mulvey (Ed.), *Visual and Other Pleasures*. Bloomington: Indiana University Press.

Munden, Kenneth (Ed.). 1971. *The American Film Institute Catalog of Motion Pictures Produced in the United States. Vols. 1 and 2. Feature Films 1921–1930*. New York: R. R. Bowker Company.

Nardi, Peter M. 1985. "Alcohol Abuse and Family Structure." Pp. 205–216 in D. Gutknecht, and E. Butler (Eds.), *Family, Self, and Society*, 2/e. Washington, D.C.: University Press of America.

New York Times. 1932. "Review of *What Price Hollywood?*" July 24:3.

Newsweek. 1944. "Review of 'Harvey,' the play." Nov. 13:82–3.

———. 1945. "Review of *The Lost Weekend*." Dec. 10:112–15.

———. 1947. "Review of *Smash-Up—The Story of a Woman*." 29, Apr. 28:95

———. 1950. "Review of *Harvey*." 36, Dec. 25:64.

———. 1951. "Review of *Come Fill the Cup*." 38, Nov. 19:102–03.

———. 1952. "Review of *Come Back, Little Sheba*." 40, Dec. 29:64.

———. 1954a. "Review of *A Star Is Born*." 44, Nov. 1:86.

———. 1954b. "Review of *The Country Girl*." 44, Dec. 6:107

———. 1956. "Review of *I'll Cry Tomorrow*." 46, Nov. 28:117.

———. 1963. "Review of *Days of Wine and Roses*." 61, Jan. 28:88.

———. 1988. "Review of *Arthur 2 on the Rocks*." July II:68.

O'Connor, John. 1987. "Review of *The Betty Ford Story*." *New York Times* (March 2) Sec. C:16.

———. 1989. "Review of *My Name Is Bill W*." *New York Times*. (April 30) Sec. 2:31.

Odets, Clifford. 1952, "Interview with Aulicino," in Armand Aulicino, " How The Country Girl Came About in the Words of the People Involved." *Theatre Arts* 36:55–57.

O'Hara, Shirley. 1947. "Review of *Smash-Up—The Story of a Woman*." *New Republic* 116, (Feb. 24):39

Penley, Constance. 1989. *Future of an Illusion: Film, Feminism and Psychoanalysis*. Minneapolis: University of Minnesota Press.

Pittman, Bill. 1988. *A.A.: The Way It Began*. Seattle: Glen Abbey Books.

Plott, Monte. 1987. "Review of *The Betty Ford Story*." *Atlanta Constitution* (Mar. 2) Sec. B:1.

Powdermaker, Hortense. 1950. *Hollywood, the Dream Factory*. Boston: Little Brown.

Propp, Vladimir. 1958. *Morphology of the Folktale*. Bloomington: Indiana Research Centre in Anthropology.

Pym, John. 1984. "Review of *Under the Volcano*." *Sight & Sound* (Summer):226.

Radway, Janice. 1984. *Reading the Romance*. Chapel Hill, NC: University of North Carolina Press.

Ray, Robert B. 1985. *A Certain Tendency in Hollywood Cinema: 1930–1980*. Princeton: Princeton University Press.

Reed, Rex. 1982. "Review of *The Verdict.*" *New York Post* (Dec. 8):72.

———. 1983. "Review of *Tender Mercies.*" *New York Post* (Mar. 4):41.

———. 1984. "Review of *Under the Volcano.*" *New York Post* (June 13):23.

Richardson, Laural Walon. 1981. *Dynamics of Sex and Gender*, 2nd ed. Boston: Houghton-Mifflin.

Rickey, Carrie. 1981. "Review of *Arthur.*" *Village Voice* (July 15–21):40.

———. 1982. "Review of *The Verdict.*" *Village Voice* (Dec. 14):90.

———. 1988. *Time and Narrative. Vol 3*. Chicago: University of Chicago Press.

Riesman, David, Nathan Glazer, and R. Denny. 1953. *The Lonely Crowd*. New York: Doubleday.

Ringel, Eleanor. 1987. "Review of *Barfly.*" *The Atlanta Constitution* (Nov. 20) Sect. P:1, 9.

———. 1988. "Review of *Clean and Sober.*" *Atlanta Constitution* (Aug. 12) Sect. B:1, 4.

Ritson, Bruce. 1979. "Images of Treatment." Pp. 51–56 in J. Cook and M. Lewington (Eds.), *Images of Alcoholism*. London: British Film Institute.

Robertson, Nan. 1988. *Getting Better: Inside Alcoholics Anonymous*. New York: William Morrow and Company.

Roffman, P. and J. Purdy. 1981. *The Hollywood Social Problem Film: Madness, Despair, and Politics from the Depression to the Fifties*. Bloomington: Indiana University Press.

Rogers St. Johns, Adela. 1924. "A Hollywood Love-Story." *Good Housekeeping* 77:76–79, 100–105.

Room, Robin. 1983a. "The Movies and the Wettening of America: The Media as Amplifiers of Cultural Change." Presented at a colloquium on "Representations de l'alcool et de l'acoolisme dans le cinema français," 6–7 June 1983, Paris, France.

———. 1983b. "Shifting Perspectives on Drinking: Alcohol Portrayals in American Films." Presented at the colloquim on "Representations de l'alcool et de l'alcoolisme dans le cinema français," 6–7 June 1983, Paris, France.

———. 1984. "A 'Reverence for Strong Drink': The Lost Generation and the Elevation of Alcohol in American Culture." *Journal of Studies on Alcohol* 45:540–46.

———. 1985. "Alcoholism and Alcoholics Anonymous in U.S. Films, 1945–1962: The Party Ends for the 'Wet' Generation." Presented at an International Group for Comparative Alcohol Studies conference on Cultural Studies on Drinking and Drinking Problems, Helsinki, 24–28 September 1985.

Rosen, Marjorie. 1973. *Popcorn Venus: Women, Movies and the American Dream*. New York: Avon.

Rosenberg, Howard. 1987. "Review of *The Betty Ford Story.*" *Los Angeles Times* (March 2) Sec. VI:8.

———. 1989. "Review of *My Name Is Bill W.*" *Los Angeles Times* (April 29) Sec. V:1, 4.

Roth, Dena. 1980. *"The Lost Weekend."* Pp. 1109–11 In Frank N. Magill (Ed.), *Cinema: The Novel into Film*. Englewood Cliffs, NJ: Salem Press.

Roth, Lillian. 1954. (with Mike Connolly and Gerold Frank). *I'll Cry Tomorrow* New York: Frederick Fell, Inc.

――――. 1958. *Beyond My Worth*. New York: Frederick Fell, Inc.

Rudy, David. 1990. "The Adult Children of Alcoholics Movement: A Social Constructionist Perspective." In D. Pittman and H. White (Eds.), *Society, Culture and Drinking Patterns, Revisited*. Rutgers: Center for Alcohol Studies. In press.

Salem, James M. 1971. *A Guide to Critical Reviews: Part IV: Vols. 1 and 2: The Screenplay*. Metuchen, N.J.: The Scarecrow Press, Inc.

Salem. James M. 1982. *A Guide to Critical Reviews: Part IV: The Screenplay Supplement One: 1963–1980*. Metuchen, N.J.: The Scarecrow Press, Inc.

Samuels, Charles Thomas. 1972. "Sightings: How Not to Film a Novel: Review of *Fat City*." *American Scholar*, Winter: 148–54.

Sarris, Andrew. 1968. *The American Cinema: Directors and Directions; 1929–1968*. New York: Dutton.

――――. 1972. "Review of *Lady Sings the Blues*." *Village Voice* (Nov. 23) (In *Filmfacts*, 1972:393–94).

――――. 1981. "Review of *Only When I Laugh*." *Village Voice* (Sept. 23–29):51.

――――. 1983. "Review of *Tender Mercies*." *Village Voice* (March 8): 39.

Sartre, Jean-Paul. 1943/1956. *Being and Nothingness*. New York: Philosophical Library.

Sawahata, Lesa. 1989. "Review of *Clean and Sober*." Pp. 80–83. in Frank N. Magill (Ed.), *Magill's Cinema Annual, 1989: A Survey of the Films of 1988*. Englewood Cliffs, NJ: Salem Press.

Sayre, Nora. 1974. "Review of *A Woman Under the Influence*." *New York Times* (Oct. 14):39.

Schatz, Thomas. 1981. *Hollywood Genres: Formulas, Filmmaking, and the Studio System*. New York: Random House.

Schickel, Richard. 1972. "Review of *Fat City*." *Life* (August 25, 73):20.

――――. 1981a. "Review of *Arthur*." *Time* (August 3):67

――――. 1981b. "Review of *Only When I Laugh*." *Time* (Oct. 5):88.

――――. 1984. "Review of *Under the Volcano*." *Time* (June 25): 68.

Schneider, Irving. 1977. "Images of the Mind: Psychiatry in Commercial Film." *American Journal of Psychiatry* 134:613–17.

Schudson, Michael. 1988. "What Is a Reporter?: The Private Face of Public Journalism." Pp. 228–46 in James W. Carey (Ed.), *Media, Myths, and Narratives: Television and the Press*. Newbury Park: Sage.

Schutz, Alfred and Thomas Luckmann. 1973. *The Structures of the Lifeworld*. Evanston, IL: Northwestern University Press.

Schwartz, Delmore. 1955. "Review of *The Country Girl*." *New Republic* 132, (April 4):21.

Seixas, J. S. and G. Youcha. 1985. *Children of Alcoholism: A Survivor's Manual*. New York: Harper & Row.

Shales, Tom. 1989. "Review of *My Name is Bill W.*" *Washington Post* (April 20) Sec. C:1, 7.

Shuman, R. Baird. 1962. *Clifford Odets*. Boston: Twayne Publishers.

———. 1989. *William Inge*, rev. ed. Boston: Twayne Publishers.

Simmel, Georg. 1950. *The Sociology of Georg Simmel*, Translated and edited, with an introduction by Kurt Wolff. New York: Free Press.

Silver, Alan and Elizabeth Ward. 1979. *Film Noir: An Encyclopedic Reference to the American Style*. Woodstock, NY: The Overlook Press.

Silverman, Joan L. 1979. "I'll Never Touch Another Drop: Images of Alcoholism and Temperance in American Popular Culture, 1874–1919." Doctoral Dissertation, New York University.

Simon, John. 1983. "Merciful Heavens, a Real Film: Review of *Tender Mercies*." *National Review* 29 April:508–509.

Sinclair, Andrew. 1964. *An Era of Excess*. New York: Harper.

Sklar, Robert. 1975. *Movie-Made America: A Social History of American Movies*. New York: Random House.

———. 1983. "Review of *The Verdict*." *Cineaste* 12:47.

Smith, Harrison. 1945. "Review of *The Lost Weekend*." *Saturday Review* 28, (Dec. 29):20.

Spender, Stephen. 1984. "Introduction." Pp. vii–xxiii in Malcolm Lowry, *Under the Volcano*. New York: New American Library (originally published 1947).

Sprinker, Michael. 1985. "Review of *Under the Volcano*." Pp. 499–503 in Frank N. Magill (Ed.), *Magill's Cinema Annual, 1985, a Survey of 1984 Films*. Englewood Cliffs, NJ: Salem Press.

Steinglass, Peter and Anne Robertson. 1983. "The Alcoholic Family." Pp. 243–307 in Benjamin Kissin and Henre Begleiter (Eds.), *The Pathogenesis of Alcoholism, Vol. 6: Psychosocial Factors*. New York: Plenum.

Sterritt, David. 1981. "Review of *Arthur*." *Christian Science Monitor* (August 27):18.

———. 1984. "Review of *Under the Volcano*." *Christian Science Monitor* (July 5):25.

Steudler, R. 1987. "Representations of Drinking and Alcoholism in French Cinema." *International Sociology* 2:45–59.

Straus, Robert. 1982. "The Social Costs of Alcohol in the Perspective of Change: 1945–1980." Pp. 134–48 in E. Gomberg, H. White, and J. Carpenter (Eds.), *Alcohol, Science and Society Revisited*. Ann Arbor: University of Michigan Press.

Strauss, Robert. 1988. "Review of *Barfly*." Pp. 49–52 in Frank N. Magill (Ed.), *Magill's Cinema Annual, 1988: A Survey of Films of 1987*. Englewood Cliffs, NJ: Salem Press.

Terry, Clifford. 1987. "Review of *The Betty Ford Story*." *Chicago Tribune* (March 2) Sec. 5:7.

Thomas, Kevin. 1981. "Review of *Only When I Laugh*." *Los Angeles Times* (Sept. 24) Calender:2.

Thornburn, David. 1988. "Television as an Aesthetic Medium." Pp. 47–66 in James W. Carey (Ed.), *Media, Myths, and Narratives: Television and the Press*. Newbury Park: Sage.

Time. 1947a. "Review of *Humoresque*." 49, Jan. 13:97.

———. 1949. "Review of *Under Capricorn*." 51, Sept. 26:99

———. 1951. "Review of *Come Fill the Cup*." 58, Nov. 5:118–19.

———. 1952a. "Review of *Something to Live For*." 59, March 24:100.

———. 1952b. "Review of *Come Back, Little Sheba*." 60, Dec. 29:66.

———. 1954a. "Review of *A Star Is Born*." 65, Oct. 25:86.

———. 1954b. "Review of *The Country Girl*." 64, Dec. 13:96.

———. 1956. "Review of *I'll Cry Tomorrow*." 67, Jan. 23:92.

———. 1963. "Review of *Days of Wine and Roses*." 73, Feb. 1:81.

Todorov, Tzvetan. 1975. *The Fantastic*. Ithaca: Cornell University Press. *TV Guide*. 1986a. Vol 34, January 4.

———. 1986b. Vol. 34, Sept. 27.

Unger, Arthur. 1987. "Review of *The Betty Ford Story*." *Christian Science Monitor*, Feb. 27:23.

USA Today. 1988. "Review of *Arthur 2 on the Rocks*." July 8:9.

Variety. 1947. "Review of *Smash-Up—The Story of a Woman*." 200, Feb. 5:12.

———. 1962. "Review of *Days of Wine and Roses*." Dec. 5:6.

———. 1988. "Review of *Arthur 2 on the Rocks*." July 6:5.

———. 1989. "Review of *My Name Is Bill W.*" May 10:95–96.

———. 1990. "All-time Film Rental Champs, by Decade." 2 May:114–36.

Voss, Ralph F. 1989. *The Life of William Inge*. Lawrence: University of Kansas Press.

Ware, Harlan. 1952. *Come Fill The Cup*. New York: Random House.

Weber, Max. 1978. *Max Weber: Selections in Translation* (W.G. Runciman, Ed.; E. Matthews, trans.). Cambridge: Cambridge University Press.

Wegscheider, S. 1981. *Another Chance: Hope and Health for the Alcoholic Family*. Palo Alto: Science and Behavior Books.

Wegscheider-Cruse, S. 1989. *The Miracle of Recovery*. Deerfield Beach, FL: Health Communications.

West, Hollie. 1972. "Review of *Lady Sings the Blues*." *Washington Post* (Nov. 2) (in *Filmfacts*, 1972: 392–93).

Westerbeck, Colin L., Jr. 1975. "Review *A Woman Under the Influence*." *Commonweal* 101, (Jan. 31): 360–62.

———. 1983. "Unsung Heroes: Robert Duvall in *Tender Mercies*" *Commonweal* 8 (April):210–11.

Wholey, Dennis. 1984 (Ed.). *The Courage to Change*. Boston: Houghton Mifflin.

Wilder, Billy. 1944/1970. "Interview," Quoted in Tom Wood, *The Bright Side of Billy Wilder, Primarily*. New York: Doubleday.

Wiley, Norbert. 1967. "America's Unique Class Politics: The Interplay of the Labor, Credit and Commodity Markets." *American Sociological Review* 32:531–41.

Williams, Raymond. 1977. *Marxism and Literature*. New York: Oxford.

———.1982. *The Sociology of Culture*. New York: Schocken Books.

Williamson, Judith. 1987. "Review of *The Morning After*." *New Statesman* (June 12):23.

Wilmington, Michael. 1986. "Review of *The Morning After*." *Los Angeles Times* (Dec. 25) Calender:1.

———. 1987. "Review of *Barfly*." *Los Angeles Times* (Nov. 5) Sec. VI:I.

Woitiz, J.G. 1983. *Adult Children of Alcoholics*. Hollywood, FL: Health Communications.

Wood, Robin. 1986. *Hollywood: From Vietnam to Reagan.* New York: Columbia University Press.

Wood, Tom. 1970. *The Bright Side of Billy Wilder, Primarily.* New York Doubleday.

Woodward, Wayne. 1988. "Reading *Harvey* and *Arthur*." Unpublished manuscript.

Wright, Will. 1975. *Six Guns and Society: A Structural Study of the Western.* Berkeley: University of California Press.

Wuthnow, Robert. 1987. *Meaning and Moral Order: Explorations in Cultural Analysis.* Berkeley: University of California Press.

Zolotow, M. 1977. *Billy Wilder and Hollywood.* New York: G.P. Putnam's Sons.

Notes

1.   In 1970 the *New York Times Film Reviews* (1913–1968) was published in a five-volume set. This collection has been continued through 1986. In citing reviews from this source I will list both the page number in the volume (i.e., Vol. 4, p. 2478) and the date and the page number and column of the actual publication of the review (i.e., *New York Times*, Dec. 22, 1950, p. 19:1).

2.   Thanks to Ed Davis for this article.

SUBJECT INDEX

A.A. (Alcoholics Anonymous)
  alcoholic hero version of, 65
  alcoholism concept of, 58–60,
    215–216
  causes of alcoholism theories of,
    252–254
  in *Clean and Sober*, 223–226
  in *Come Fill the Cup*, 57, 59
  in *8 Million Ways to Die*, 215–216,
    217–218
  and family alcoholism, 243–244
  formation of, 4, 5
  in *My Name Is Bill W.*, 228–232
Adult children of alcoholics, 155
Alcoholic couple (*See* Family
    alcoholism)
Alcoholic family (*See* Family
    alcoholism)
Alcoholic hero (*See also* Female
    alcoholic; Male alcoholic)
  A.A.'s version of, 65
  in classic period, 64–66, 239
  in *Come Fill the Cup*, 57–60
  and creativity, myth of, 43
  and critics, 251
  death of, 208–210
  emergence of, 43–45
  in *Fat City*, 132–135
  Hollywood versions of
    and alcoholic subject, place of,
      251–255
    and critics, 251
    definitions of, changing, 4
    explanations of, 41–42
    factors influencing, 4–5
    and family alcoholism, 240,
      243–244
    and female alcoholic, 240–242
    and gender, 241–242, 245–249
    and genre, 250
    in interregnum period, 239–240
    phases of, filmic, 42–43
    in preclassic period, 239
  in interregnum period, 130–132,
    140, 239–240

in *Lady Sings the Blues*, 135–136
in *The Lost Weekend*, 44
moral career of, 42–45
in preclassic period, 64, 238–239
in prohibition period, 64
in *A Star Is Born* (1937), 45–46
in *A Star Is Born* (1954), 61
in *A Star Is Born* (1976), 139–140
in *W.C. Fields and Me*, 138–139
in *What Price Hollywood?*, 43–45,
  48–49
in *A Woman Under The Influence*,
  136–138
and women, 48
Alcoholic interactional system,
  106–107
Alcoholics Anonymous (*See* A.A.)
Alcoholic self, 244–245
Alcoholism (*See also* Alibi of
    alcoholism; Causes of
    alcoholism)
  and A.A., 58–60, 215–216
  in *Arthur*, 31–32
  in *Come Back, Little Sheba*, 100
  in *Come Fill the Cup*, 58–60
  consequences of, 114–115
  in *The Country Girl*, 108–109
  and desire, 118–120
  as family problem, 96–100
  feminization of, 71–74
  in *Harvey*, 25–29
  Hollywood's definitions of, 4
  interactional system of, 106–107
  as "it", 78–79
  in *The Lost Weekend*, 5
  and love, 118–120
  in *The Morning After*, 190–191
  and National Committee for the
    Education on Alcoholism, 5
  and political economy, 118–120
  sexualization of, 72
  in *Smash-Up*, 74, 78–79, 81
  in *A Star Is Born* (1937), 6–7
  .in *A Star Is Born* (1954), 61
  teenage, 7

287